Official Autodesk Training Guide

Learning
Autodesk® Maya® 2008

The Modeling & Animation Handbook

Acknowledgments

Art Direction:
Michiel Schriever

Sr. Graphic Designer:
Luke Pauw

Cover Image:
© 2007 LAIKA, Inc.
All Rights Reserved.

Production Designer:
Diane Erlich

Copy Editor:
James A. Compton

Technical Editor:
Cathy McGinnis

DVD Production:
Roark Andrade, Peter Verboom

Project Manager:
Lenni Rodrigues

Content Marketing Manager:
Carmela Bourassa

Director - Products, Planning and Tools
Michael Stamler

Special thanks go out to:
Mariann Barsolo, Tonya Holder, Mary Ruijs, Katriona Lord-Levins, Robert Lin, Julie Fauteux and
Heather McDiarmid

This book would not have been possible without the generous support of LAIKA Inc. We would like to
extend a special thank you to Nasseem Moradi, Jim Cheek, Skylr Chamberlin and Dan Casey.

Primary Author

Marc-André Guindon, NeoReel

Marc-André Guindon is the founder of NeoReel Inc. (*www.NeoReel.com*), a Montreal based production facility. He is an Autodesk® Maya® Master and an advanced user of Autodesk® MotionBuilder™ software. Marc-André and NeoReel have partnered with Autodesk Inc. on several projects, including *The Art of Maya* and the *Learning Maya* series from version 6.0 to present. NeoReel was also the driving force behind the Maya Techniques™ DVDs, such as *How to Integrate Quadrupeds into a Production Pipeline* and *Maya and Alias MotionBuilder*.

www.NeoReel.com

Marc-André has established complex pipelines and developed numerous plug-ins and tools, such as *Animation Layers* for Maya, for a variety of projects in both the film and game industries. His latest film projects include pre-visualisation on *Journey 3-D* (Walden Media®), as well as Unearthed (Ambush Entertainment), *XXX: State of the Union* (Revolution Studios), *Scooby-Doo 2*™ (Warner Bros. Pictures) and *Dawn of the Dead* (Universal Pictures). He also served in the game industry to integrate motion capture for *Prey* (2K Games) for the Xbox 360™, *Arena Football*™ (EA Sports) and the *Outlaw Game Series: Outlaw Volleyball*™, *Outlaw Golf*™ and *Outlaw Tennis*™ (Hypnotix).

Marc-André continues to seek challenges for himself, NeoReel and his talented crew.

About *Moongirl*

Laika Entertainment

Moongirl follows Leon, a young boy out night fishing with his pet, Earl-the-squirrel. When the moon suddenly goes dark, Leon catches more than he bargained for as a catfish made of stars swallows his lighting bug bait. The fish catapults him up through the sky and straight into the centre of the moon, where he finds a young girl who is responsible for keeping the moon illuminated. Together with the Moongirl, he must ward off the nasty Gargaloons, sinister spirits determined to extinguish moonlight forever.

Moongirl is the first animated short to come out of Laika Entertainment and has already met with critical acclaim. The film has been screened at international festivals and won numerous awards, including Best Short Film at the Animacor International Film Festival in Cordoba, Spain.

Despite its critical success, *Moongirl* actually originated as an experiment—a hybrid between a technology trial run and an art test. Dan Casey, Director of Laika's Digital Design Group, explains that, "We had an opportunity to build a brand new pipeline. Instead of a chrome sphere bouncing on a checkered floor, we wanted to put some kind of concept or focus to it." To generate ideas Laika held an in-house contest, where employees could pitch projects. The most compelling proposal came from Michael Berger, who had an idea for a short film about a girl who lives on the moon, catching stars in a net.

At the same time, the studio was building their director roster for feature projects and they approached Henry Selick, who was already renowned for his groundbreaking work in such films as *The Nightmare Before Christmas*, *James and the Giant Peach* and *The Life Aquatic with Steve Zissou* (underwater visual effects). Casey explains that working with Selick was one of the biggest draws for the team, "It was just an amazing opportunity to work with him."

Selick rewrote *Moongirl* into a darker tale with a twist at the end, where the Moongirl leaves Leon in charge, to be the next in a long line of moon-keepers. Casey describes how the new storyline changed the design, "It went from something cute and fairy-tale to something much more stylized and cutting edge." The company also brought in artist Peter Chan who had worked on *Lemony Snicket's A Series of Unfortunate Events*, *Harry Potter and the Sorcerer's Stone* and colourist Courtney Booker (*The Incredibles*, *Finding Nemo*) to work with Selick to develop the film's aesthetic. Selick, Chan and Booker have since collaborated on a picture book based on the film that has been published by Candlewick Press. They Might Be Giants created the film's whimsical soundtrack.

Part of Selick's vision was for the animation to have some of the feeling of stop motion and not be as smooth as typical CG work. This was a natural fit for the Laika animators since the company's roots are in claymation and stop motion.

Laika was created in 2003, when Nike co-founder Phil Knight acquired the old Will Vinton Studios, a leader in the stop motion animation industry. The company had traditionally done commercial work, animating memorable advertising mascots such as the California Raisins, the Domino's Pizza Noid and most recently the M&M'S Adams family.

Animator Kyle Bell was with the company when it branched into CG in the mid-nineties and explains how the transition wasn't always easy. "We wanted to keyframe every frame because that's how we knew how to operate." Ironically, this is exactly how the animators achieved Selick's vision with *Moongirl*, keyframing a lot of harder poses and not allowing the computer to fill in so much of the in-between.

Some of the most stunning sequences in the film occur in the scene transitions: the opening credits where green fog coalesces into the title, then breaks apart to become lighting bugs; and when the marsh grass sinks into the water as the background shadows rise, becoming trees on a riverbank. Casey explains that these moments presented a challenge on the effects side. "Just getting everything to match up was hard, and not making it look like a cheesy morph."

While dealing with human characters also presented challenges, the biggest obstacle was developing the production process itself. Because the film was designed to work the kinks out and get the team used to a feature film work flow, Casey admits that "A lot of the time, we were building the tracks right in front of the train. If something broke in the pipeline, production people had to stop while we figured it out."

All told, the film took about a year to complete and Autodesk® Maya software was used as the primary animating tool. Laika, and the former Vinton Studios, has been a long time Maya® client, using the software in virtually every aspect of production, including modeling, texturing, effects work and animation.

Casey finds Maya software especially useful in the development department. "The fact that it does everything is helpful. We can quickly do prototype, elaborate on them and turn them into real tools later. I can teach a modeler how to unwrap UVs, do basic texturing and even basic rigging, because it's all right there."

Bell expands on this, explaining that the software's ease of use also makes it attractive. "Somebody can sit in front of Maya with very little background, and you can still make a handful of keyframes and get a general sense of how it works in a short amount of time. It has a fairly simple approach that can get more complex as you go deeper."

Laika is currently in production with *Coraline,* a stop motion feature film based on Neil Gaiman's book of the same title. While the majority of the film uses traditional stop-motion techniques, the company is developing cutting-edge proprietary tools for scene building and rendering using Maya software. Also in production is *Jack & Ben*, a coming of age buddy story that will be the company's first full-length CG project.

This is a very exciting time for CG animation, according to Casey, because audiences are looking for more than just 3D realism. "I think the days of just making a CG film because it looks like CG are probably gone and I think story is going to get better and more stylized looks will be coming our way." Ultimately, this is what makes Laika and *Moongirl* so exciting. "No one else was doing this kind of CG at the time, unless it was a couple people in their basement, so to have the resources of a studio to be able to push something like this was amazing."

Table of Contents

How to use this book

How you use *Learning Autodesk Maya 2008 | The Modeling & Animation Handbook* will depend on your experience with computer graphics and 3D animation. This book moves at a fast pace and is designed to help the intermediate level user improve their modeling and animation skills and understand how they relate to one another in a production pipeline. If this is your first experience with 3D software, we suggest that begin with the *Learning Maya 2008 | The Modeling & Animation Handbook*, as a prerequisite before proceeding through the lessons in this book. If you are already familiar with Autodesk® Maya® software or another 3D package, you can dive in and complete the lessons as written.

Updates to this book

In an effort to ensure your continued success with the lessons in this book, please visit our web site for the latest updates available: *www.autodesk.com/learningtools-updates.*

Windows and Macintosh

This book is written to cover Windows and Macintosh platforms. Graphics and text have been modified where applicable. You may notice that your screen varies slightly from the illustrations, depending on the platform you are using.

Things to watch for:

Window focus may differ. For example, if you are on Windows, you have to click on the panel with your middle mouse button to make it active.

To select multiple attributes in Windows, use the **Ctrl** key. On Macintosh, use the **Command** key. To modify pivot position in Windows, use the **Insert** key. On Macintosh, use the **Home** key.

Autodesk packaging

This book can be used with either **Autodesk® Maya® Complete 2008, Autodesk® Maya® Unlimited 2008**, or the corresponding version of **Autodesk® Maya® Personal Learning Edition** software, as the lessons included here focus on functionality shared among all three software packages.

Learning Autodesk Maya DVD-ROM

The Learning Autodesk Maya DVD-ROM contains several resources to accelerate your learning experience including:

- Learning Support files.
- Autodesk® Maya® reference guides
- Turbo Squid 3D Models

Installing support files

Before beginning the lessons in this book, you will need to install the support files. Copy the project directories found in the *support_files* folder on the DVD disc to the *Maya\ projects* directory on your computer. Launch Maya and set the project by going to **File** → **Project** → **Set...** and selecting the appropriate project.

Windows: C:\Documents and Settings\username\My Documents\maya\projects

Macintosh: Macintosh HD:Users:username:Documents:maya:projects

Project 01

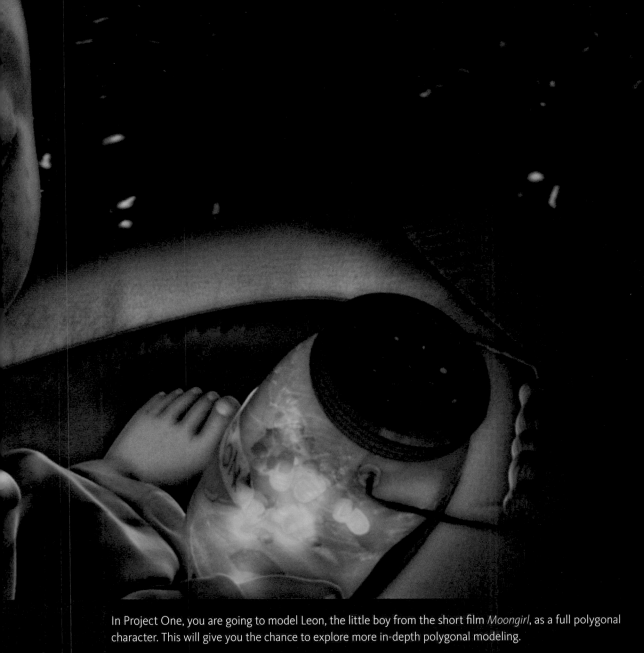

In Project One, you are going to model Leon, the little boy from the short film *Moongirl*, as a full polygonal character. This will give you the chance to explore more in-depth polygonal modeling.

You will start by reviewing the basics of polygon components. Then you will model Leon's body using reference images. Once that is complete, you will model Leon's head and attach it to the body.

These lessons offer you a good look at some of the key concepts and workflows for modeling in polygons.

Once the model is finalized, you will explore polygon texturing.

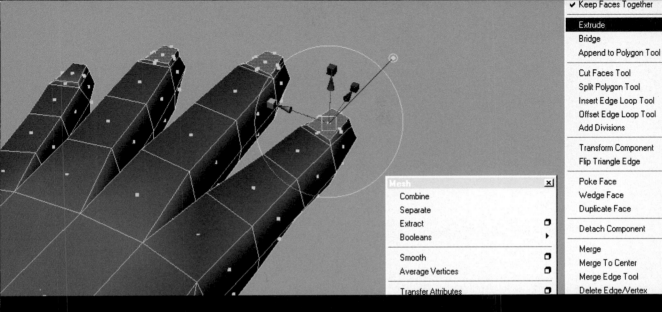

Lesson 01
Polygon Basics

Building polygonal surfaces in Autodesk Maya software is fast and easy. This chapter will cover the fundamental concepts of polygonal geometry and take you through the basic tools and techniques essential to building quality polygonal models.

In this lesson you will learn the follow

- The composition of a polygon;
- How to view polygonal surfaces and components;
- How to edit a simple polygonal model;
- How to diagnose polygon geometry problems.

What is a polygon?

The most basic definition of a polygon is a shape defined by its corners (vertices) and the straight lines between them (edges).

Maya uses polygons to create surfaces by filling in the space defined by the edges with a face. Three sets of edges and vertices form a triangular face, or *tri*. Four sets of edges and vertices form a quadrilateral face, or *quad*. Any number of edges and vertices beyond four forms what is referred to in Maya as an *n-sided* face.

A single polygon face in Maya is sometimes referred to as a *polygon*.

Poly shells vs. poly objects

When several individual polygons are connected together sharing edges and vertices, it is referred to as a *polygon shell*. When connecting faces together there is no limit to the number of faces and their topology; therefore, polygonal meshes can form just about any arbitrary shape desired and are not restricted by the rules that limit NURBS surfaces.

When several polygonal shells are combined together in one shape node residing under one transform node, it is usually referred to as a *polygon object*. The shells may appear to be singular objects but Maya now treats them as one shape, or poly object, or mesh.

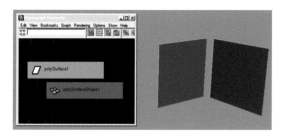

Two polygon shells in one polygon object

Creating a triangle, a quad and combining meshes

You are going to create two simple polygon objects, a triangle and a quad, using the *Create Polygon Tool*. You will then combine the two polygons to form one polygonal object, even though they will still be two separate polygon shells.

1   **Create two simple polygons**

- Switch to the *Polygons* menu set by pressing the **F3** key.

- Select **Mesh → Create Polygon Tool** and in the *top* view place three points; then press the **Enter** key to finish the creation.

You have now created the first polygon.

Repeat *the above step, but this time placing four points to create a quad.*

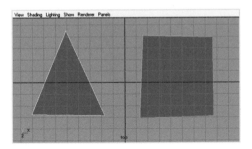

A triangle mesh and a quad mesh

- Select **Window** → **Hypergraph: Hierarchy**.

  You should see two objects: polysurface1 and polysurface2.

- Within the Hypergraph window, display the object's shape nodes by selecting **Options** → **Display** → **Shape Nodes**.

You should now see the two transform nodes and their respective shape nodes listed in the Hypergraph.

2   Combine the triangle and the quad

- Select *polySurface1* and *polySurface2*, and then select **Mesh** → **Combine** in order to create a single polygon object out of the two polygon shells.

  You will notice in the Hypergraph that a third new transform node and shape node has been created, called polySurface3. If you select polySurface3, the two shells will be selected. You may notice that the original two transform/shape nodes still exist. Those nodes are hidden at this time, but they are connected by construction history to the new polygonal object. Maya will commonly leave nodes in the scene until you delete history on an object.

- If you wish to delete these obsolete nodes, select *polySurface3* and then **Edit** → **Delete By Type** → **History**.

Polygon Components

Before you start modeling with polygons, it's a good idea to understand what components make up a polygon and how you can use these components to model in Maya. Some polygon components can be modified in order to directly affect the topology, or shape, of the geometry while other polygon components can be modified to affect how the polygon looks when rendered or shaded.

Vertices

The points that define the corners of a single polygon are called *vertices*, or singularly, a *vertex*. Vertices can be directly manipulated to change the topology of a polygon.

Edges

The lines connecting the vertices of a single polygon are called *edges*. Edges can be directly manipulated to change the topology of a polygon. The outside edges of a polygon shell are referred to as border edges.

Faces

The filled- in area bounded by the vertices and edges of a polygon is called a *face*. Faces can be directly manipulated to change the topology of a polygonal object.

UVs

At the same location as the vertices on a polygon is another component called a *UV*. UVs are used to help apply textures to polygons. Textures exist in a 2D pixel-based space and have a set width and height. In order for Maya to understand how to apply a 2D texture to a 3D polygon, a 2D coordinate system, called *texture space*, is used. The UV at a given vertex is the 2D texture space position, or coordinate, for that vertex. The pixel at that position on the texture map will be located at that vertex. UVs can be selected in the 3D space in Maya but cannot be manipulated in 3D space. In order to directly manipulate UVs, you need to open the *UV Texture Editor*.

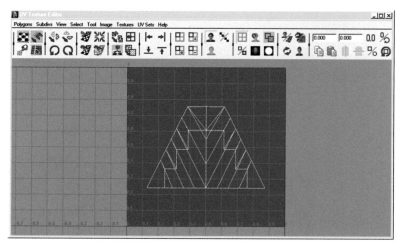

The UV Texture Editor window

Face normals

A polygon face can point in one of two directions. The component used to define the direction is called a *face normal*. Face normals cannot be directly manipulated but they can be reversed if they are pointing in the wrong direction. Maya, by default, draws both sides of a polygon, but in technical terms polygons only have one facing direction represented by the normal direction. When using the Create Polygon Tool, the direction in which the polygon is created will affect the initial face normal direction. When the polygon is created placing vertices in a clockwise direction, the normal will face away from you. When you place vertices in a counter-clockwise direction, the normal will face toward you.

Vertex normals

At each vertex a third component exists, called a *vertex normal*. The vertex normal is used to define how the polygon will look when shaded or rendered. When all vertex normals of shared faces point in the same direction, the transition from one face to another will appear smooth when shaded or rendered. In this state, vertex normals are often referred to as *soft*. Alternatively, when all vertex normals of shared faces point in the same direction as their face normals, a sharp transition will appear between the faces. Vertex normals in this state are commonly referred to as *hard*.

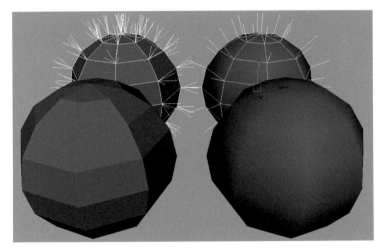

Soft and hard vertex normals

Tip: **RMB** *over a polygon object to easily select polygon components.*

Lesson 01: Polygonal Basics

Assessing and correcting polygon geometry

In this exercise, you will use the *Custom Polygon Display* window to assess different component aspects of a polygon object. You will also use selection constraints to select problematic components based on specific criteria. Once you have assessed the geometry, you will use several polygon editing tools to correct any problems.

1   Set your current project

In order to retrieve the example files easily, it is a good idea to set your current project to *project1* from the *support_files* directory.

- Select **File → Project Set...**
- Choose the *project1* folder from the *support_files* you copied on your drive.

2   Open the stair geometry file

- Select **File → Open** and select the *01-stairs.ma* file.

  You should see a simple scene file with a set of stairs going up and down. This piece of geometry appears to be fine. You will now assess it to identify any hidden problems.

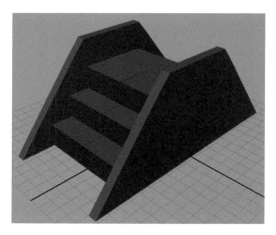

Simple stairs

3   Assess stairs with custom polygon display

Select the stair geometry, select **Display → Polygons,** and then select to display **Face Normals** and **Border Edges.**

  *Most of the items found in the Polygons menu consist of toggles for the various polygonal components. At the bottom of this menu you can find the **Custom Polygon Display** window, which is an excellent tool for assessing polygon geometry all at once.*

The polygon's border edges, which define the border of polygon shells, are now displayed thicker than regular edges, while the face normals appear as a line extending from the center of the face. The border edges show that the stairs are not one shell but two, and half of the face normals can now be seen to be pointing inward.

4   Correct the normals and merge the two shells

- **RMB** over the stair geometry and select **Face** component selection from the marking menu.

- Select the faces on the half of the stairs with the normals pointing inward and select **Normals → Reverse**.

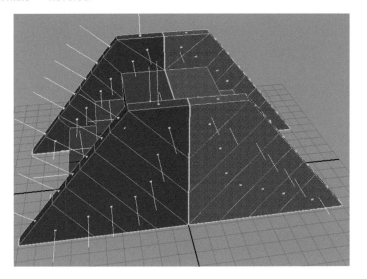

Normals to be reversed

- **RMB** over the stair geometry and select **Vertex** component selection from the marking menu.

- Select the vertices running down the center of the stair geometry and select **Edit Mesh → Merge**.

Tip: *Press 4 to display the geometry in wireframe to ease the selection process.*

You can see that the border edge that was running down the middle of the stairs is now gone, indicating that there is currently only one polygon shell.

5 Floating vertices

When you are modeling with polygons, vertices that are no longer necessary can be left behind accidentally. These floating vertices can present a problem down the road, so it is a good idea to keep an eye out for them and clean them up. While it can be hard to locate these vertices visually, The Maya *Selection Constraint Tool* makes this task easy by allowing you to select polygon objects and components based on different criteria.

- Select the *stairs*, switch to **Vertex** component selection mode and select all the vertices.

- Select **Select → Select Using Constraints** to open the Selection Constraints window with options related to vertex selection.

- In the **Constrain** section, select **All and Next**. Now open the **Geometry** section, and in the **Neighbors** section, set **Activate** to **On** and set the **min value** to **0** and the **max value** to **2**.

- Click the **Close and Reset** button.

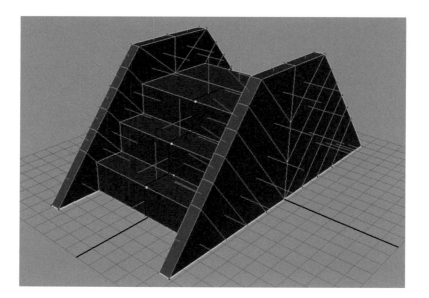

Floating vertices

The floating vertices on the stairs are now selected.

Tip: *By setting the selection constraints to select vertices with a maximum of two neighboring vertices, you ensure that only the floating vertices, which always have only two neighbors, will be selected.*

- With the vertices still selected, press the **Delete** key on your keyboard.

The floating vertices are now deleted, or *cleaned up*, and the stairs are finished.

- Use the **Display** → **Polygon** menu to toggle **Off** the display of the border edges and face normals.

Important polygon considerations

Planar and non-planar polygons

If all vertices of a polygon face reside on the same plane in world space, that face is considered *planar*. Because triangles always form a plane, triangular faces are always planar. If a face has four or more sides, and one or more of its vertices do not reside on the same plane, that face is considered *non-planar*. Whether a face is planar or not is important. A non-planar face may render improperly under certain circumstances and may not export correctly to a game engine.

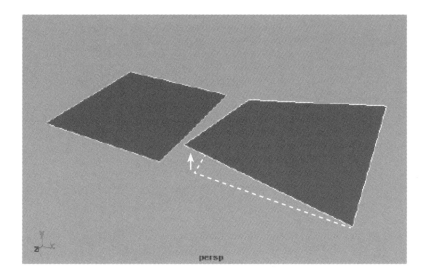

Planar and Non-planar faces

Manifold and non-manifold geometry

While the arbitrary nature of polygonal surfaces provides tremendous freedom and flexibility when it comes to creating surface topology, it can also lead to invalid or *non-manifold* geometry.

Manifold polygon geometry is standard polygon geometry that can be cut and unfolded. Non-manifold geometry is geometry that, because of the way the faces are connected, cannot be unfolded. The three types of non-manifold geometry are:

- *T-shaped* geometry, formed when three faces share a common edge.
- *Bowtie* geometry, formed when two faces share a vertex but not an edge.
- *Reversed normals* geometry, formed when two faces sharing an edge have opposing face normals.

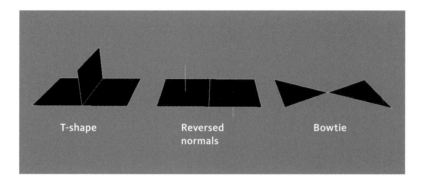

Types of non-manifold geometry

Non-manifold geometry is considered invalid geometry because several modeling operations will not work with this type of geometry. Therefore, it is a good idea to avoid such geometry or clean up polygons that have non-manifold geometry.

Lamina faces

Lamina faces are two faces that share all vertices and edges. The two faces are essentially laminated together and are also considered incorrect geometry.

Polygon cleanup

Mesh → Cleanup... is an excellent tool for dealing with non-planar faces, non-manifold geometry, and lamina faces, as well as other unwanted polygon conditions. It is a good idea to perform a cleanup operation on your models when you are finished modeling to ensure the geometry is good.

Conclusion

Understanding the anatomy of polygons before you start creating polygonal geometry can greatly assist diagnosis of your models. Knowing what you can do with polygon components can help you assess the best way to approach certain situations. Awareness of some of the problem conditions that can arise with polygons will help you quickly correct them. With this base knowledge, you are now ready to begin creating your own polygon objects.

In the next lesson, you will model Leon's body.

Modeling Leon's Body

In this lesson, you will apply Maya polygonal tools and techniques to model a little boy called Leon. You will start by modeling his torso, arms and legs. You'll model the head of the character separately in the next lesson.

In this lesson you will learn the following:

- How to model starting from a cube primitive;
- How to set up reference images with image planes;

Character modeling and topology

It is important to plan before you begin modeling a character. This character will be broken down into three major areas:

Torso

The torso will be built from a primitive cube and extruded to add initial form.

Leg

One leg will be extruded out from the torso and split to add detail. It will later be mirrored.

Arm

One arm will be extruded from the torso in the same manner as the leg, and then mirrored.

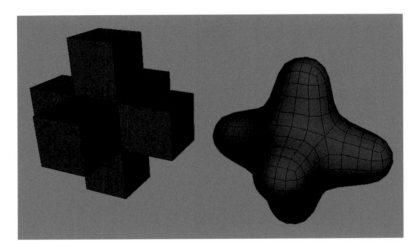

A smoothed object

> **Note:** *When modeling characters, the two most important considerations in designing the flow of topology are (1) matching the shape of the character exactly and (2) designing the topology so it will deform properly when animated. Typically, horizontal and vertical lines of topology will run through your entire character to define the overall shape, and loops of edges will be used to define areas of deformation, such as muscle mass. When creating characters with polygons, you want to define the shape with the least amount of detail possible. If you end up with a mesh that has an unnecessarily large amount of detail, it can become very difficult to manage. Because polygons are linear, you can use a polygon smooth operation toward the end of the procedure to smooth the mesh for a more organic shape.*

Setting up Maya

You should copy the *Learning Maya* support files to your Maya *projects* directory. Support files are found in the *support_files* directory on the DVD-ROM included with this book.

The typical location of the Maya *projects* directory on your machine is:

Windows: *Drive:\Documents and Settings\username\My Documents\maya\projects*
Mac OS X: *Users/username/Library/Preferences/Alias/maya/projects*

> **Note:** *To avoid the Cannot Save Workspace error, ensure that the support files are not read-only after you copy them from the DVD-ROM.*

1   Set your new project

In order to follow this lesson, set your current project as *project1*.

- Go to the **File** menu and select **Project → Set...**
- Click on the folder named *project1* to select it.
- Click on the **OK** button.

   This ensures that Maya is looking into the proper subdirectories when it opens up scene files or searches for images.

Image planes

To help create the character, you will use image planes for reference. Image planes are a great way to develop your model based on display images in the modeling windows.

1   Start a new scene

- **File → New Scene**.

Do not manipulate any of the cameras.

2   Create an image plane for the front camera

- Open the Hypershade window with **Window → Rendering Editors → Hypershade**.
- Select **Tabs → Show Top and Bottom Tabs**.

   The Work Area changes to display both tabs.

- Click on the **Cameras** tab to display all the cameras in the scene in the top panel.
- **MMB+drag** the *frontShape* camera down to the Work Area panel.
- Scroll down to the **Image Planes** category located in the **Create** tab on the left of the Hypershade.

- **MMB+drag** an *imagePlane* onto the camera *frontShape* in the Work Area.

  A connection menu will be displayed.

- Select the **Default** connection from the pop-up menu.

  The new imagePlane is now connected to the camera.

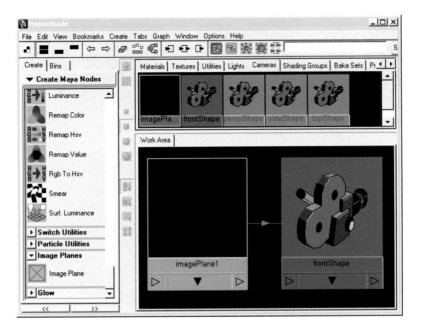

An image plane in the Hypershade

 Tip: *You can click on the Rearrange Graph button to organize the nodes and their connections side by side in the Work Area.*

3   Add an image to the image plane

- **Double-click** on the *imagePlane1* node to open the Attribute Editor.

- Click on the folder beside the **Image Name** attribute and import the image called *leonBodyFront.tif* from the *sourceImages* folder.

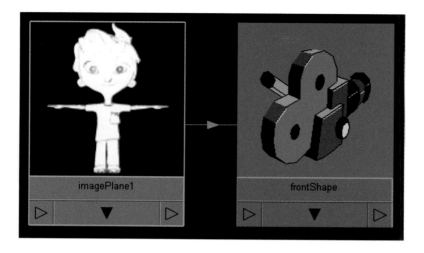

The loaded reference image

> **Note:** *If the cameras were not moved before creating the image planes, the images should be properly aligned. If the image planes do not line up properly, they can be adjusted under* **Placement Extras** *in the Attribute Editor. Use the* **Center X, Y, and Z** *attributes to transform the image plane.* **Width** *and* **Height** *can be used to adjust the size. These attributes are also available in the Channel Box.*

4 **Create an image for the side and top cameras**

- **Repeat** steps **2** and **3** to bring in the image *leonBodySide.tif* for the side camera and the image *leonBodyTop.tif* for the top camera.

5 **Move the image planes**

- Under **Placement Extras**, set the *imagePlane1* **Center Z** attribute to **-20** and **Center Y** to **15**.

- Set the *imagePlane2* **Center X** attribute to **-20** and **Center Y** to **15**.

  Doing so will move the image planes off center and give you a clear view of your geometry in the Perspective panel. It will also let you model the character with his feet flat on the world grid.

- **Close** the Hypershade.

Image planes in Perspective view

Note: *Since the reference images used for the image planes included an Alpha channel, the region outside the character is transparent. This can be useful when using multiple cut views of a model.*

Tip: *You can set the image plane's Alpha Gain to have a lower value so the image is semi-transparent in the viewport*

6 Save your work

- **Save** your scene as *02-leon body 01.ma*.

Model the torso

Now that image planes have been created in the scene for reference, the model building can start. The torso will be modeled from a polygon cube. Initially, the torso shape will be blocked in and used to represent the overall general shape.

1   Create a polygon cube

- Make the front view active.

- Turn **Off** the **Create** → **Polygon primitives** → **Interactive Creation** option.

  When enabled, this option let's you drag in the viewport to create a piece of geometry. It will not be used in this case.

- Select **Create** → **Polygon primitives** → **Cube** → ▢, and set the following:

  Width divisions to **4**;

  Height divisions to **1**;

  Depth divisions to **3**.

- Click the **Create** button.

- **Move** and **scale** the cube so it is placed at the base of the torso at the waist position, and is approximately the width and thickness of the torso.

Tip: *Do not translate the cube on its X-axis. You want to keep the central line of your character at zero on the X-axis so you can model symmetrically.*

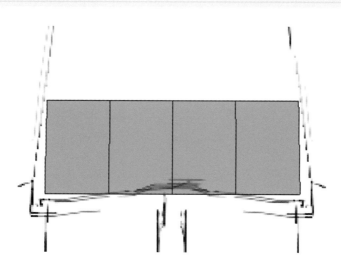

The initial cube

Note: *In your viewports, under* **Shading** → **Shade Options**, *you should set* **Wireframe on Shaded** *and* **X-ray** *modes to* **On**. *This setup will allow you to modify your geometry and see the image plane reference. It will also allow you to assess the flow of the polygon topology.*

- With the cube still selected, press the **F8** hotkey to display the cube's vertices.
- **Move** and **scale** the vertices of the cube to better represent the waist and pelvic regions of the character. Try to follow the shape of the character's shirt.

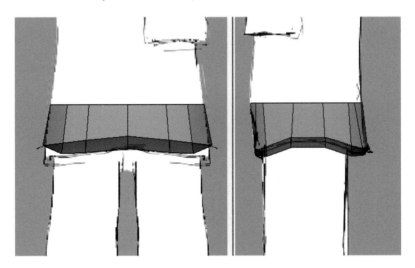

The waist area

> **Tip:** *Remember to make your adjustment in the front and side views. A quick way to switch between the different views is to use the* **View Cube**, *located in the top-right corner of the perspective view.*

- Press **F8** again to go back to Object mode.
- **Rename** the cube to *body*.

2 Extruding the torso

The next step is to create the initial overall shape for the rest of the torso. **Extrude Face** will be used for this step. Multiple extrusions will be used to define the shape at key points moving up the torso.

- Press **F3** to display the **Polygons** menu set.
- Enable the **Edit Mesh → Keep Faces Together** option before extruding.
- With *body* selected, press **F11** and select the faces at the top of the torso.

- Select **Edit Mesh** → **Extrude**.
- **Move** up the extruded faces all the way to the base of the neck.
- In the Channel Box, set **Division** to **6** for the *polyExtrudeFace1* node.

  Doing so defines horizontal lines at important places such as the belly, the pocket, the arms, the base of the neck and the leg emplacement.

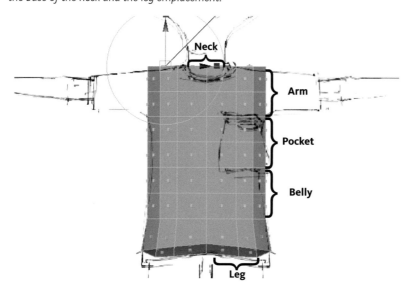

Extrude up the torso

3 Symmetrical editing

A character is typically symmetrical across the center line of the torso. When modeling a symmetrical object, you will want to edit both sides of the object at the same time. In order to simplify this task, the Move, Rotate and Scale tools have the option to reflect any component edits across the origin.

- **Double-click** on the **Move Tool** in the toolbox.
- In the **Move Reflection Settings** section of the **Tool Settings** window, turn **On** the **Reflection** option and set the **Reflection axis** to **X**.

  The tool will look for matching components according to the defined tolerance. The reflected components will be highlighted for convenience.

Lesson 02: Modeling Leon's Body

Note: *This option also controls the Reflection feature of the* **Rotate** *and* **Scale** *tools.*

- **Move**, **Rotate** and **Scale** the vertices in order to match the front and side profile shapes of the torso.

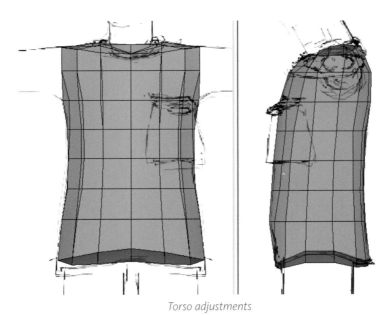

Torso adjustments

The base shape of the torso has now been established. You will notice that the overall form is still cubic. In the next step, you will start adjusting rows of vertices to further round off the shape. You will also adjust rows of edges to better follow lines of topology.

Tip: *You may notice that the image you are working with is not perfectly symmetrical. You should concentrate on just one half of the image.*

4 Adding detail to the upper torso

The torso has been defined as well as possible with the current amount of topology. The next step will be to add detail to better define areas. The best way to do this is to work one area at a time. The first areas will be the shoulder and neck, followed by the upper back and chest.

- Select the two faces at the neck location and **delete** them.
- **Move** the vertices of the neck to properly form the neck's round opening.

  Make sure the vertices at the bottom of the neck follow the line along the shoulder muscle that runs up into the neck.

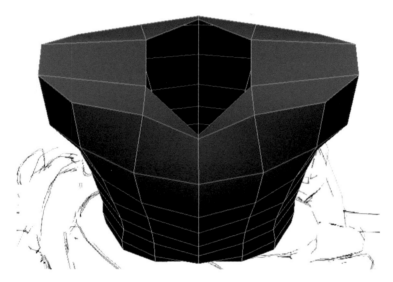

Neck refinements

- Continue tweaking the shape to your liking.

5 Save your work

- **Save** your scene as *02-leon body 02.ma*.

Symmetrical edits

As you have just experienced, a character is typically symmetrical across the center line of the torso. Depending on the tools you are using, it can be tedious to always make sure both halves of your model are identical. A nice workflow to avoid this pitfall is to delete half the torso and create a mirror copy to represent the entire model.

1 Mirror the torso

- Select and **delete** the faces on the right side of the *body*.
- Go to Object mode and with the half torso selected, select **Edit → Duplicate Special → ⬚**, and set the following:

Geometry Type to **Instance**;

Scale X to **−1**.

- Click the **Duplicate Special** button.

Any adjustments done to one side of the torso will simultaneously be done on the other side.

2 Backface culling

Currently, the front and back edges, faces and vertices are all visible in the viewports. This could be confusing when adjusting the topology. The following step will hide any faces that face away from the camera:

- Select **Display** → **Polygons** → **Backface Culling**.

Now only the front faces are visible in the view.

3 Splitting polygons

When refining a model, you get to a point where you need more components to work with. Plenty of polygonal tools will let you do this; for this lesson you will now look into the Split Polygon Tool.

- With the *body* geometry selected, select **Edit Mesh** → **Split Polygon Tool** to create new rows of edges.

- From the top view, **click+drag** on edges to define the line that separates the shoulder and the neck.

Notice how the split was also added to the mirrored half of the body.

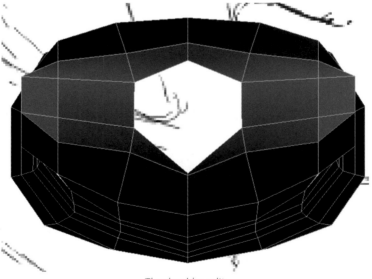

The shoulder split

Tip: *When using the Split Polygon Tool, you can select points that are not necessarily part of the same face. Maya will use the current view to determine the path to take to split across the determined points.*

- Continue to move vertices to better define this new line of detail.

4 Refine the neck

The entire region around the neck does not have enough detail at this point. You will now continue to add as few edges as possible in order to get as much detail as possible.

- Select **Edit Mesh → Insert Edge Loop Tool**.

- **Click+drag** on any horizontal edges right next to the central line of the chest.

This creates a new row of edges traversing any four-sided polygons. Notice that the new row of edges goes underneath the torso, all the way to the other side of the neck.

The edge loop split

- Use the newly added vertices to shape the chest and round the neck.

- **Split** the neck area as follows:

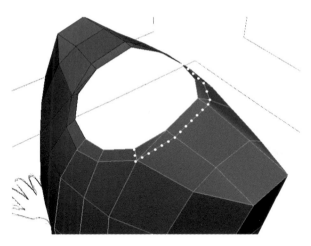

Splitting the chest

5   Delete edges

With the new edges added, some edges have become obsolete. You should remove those edges in order to keep your geometry clean and simple.

- **Select** the following edge:

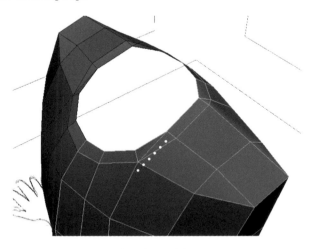

The edge to delete

- **Delete** the edge using **Edit Mesh → Delete Edge/Vertex**.

  *This command will work better than simply pressing **Delete** on your keyboard since it also deletes the unnecessary components associated with the edges.*

Note: *You may notice that with each new split and adjustment, other slight adjustments are needed to keep the topology clean. You will always be going back and moving vertices in order to improve the shape. This is a natural and expected part of the workflow.*

6 Extrude the neck

- **Select** the border edges which are forming the neck opening.
- Select **Edit Mesh → Extrude**.
- Select the **Move tool**.

  Doing so changes the manipulator to global transformation instead of local to each face.

- *Translate* the extrusion down to form the collar.
- Press the **G** hotkey to extrude the edges again.
- This time, **translate** the edges on the **Z-axis** of the local manipulator to space out the shirt collar and the neck.
- Press the **G** hotkey to extrude the edges again.
- Select the **Move** tool.
- **Translate** the edges up to create the neck.

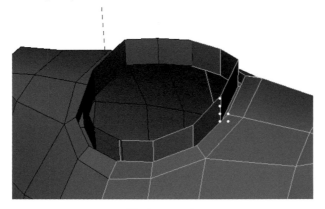

The lower neck

You will now stop extruding the neck since it will be part of the head creation in the next lesson. The initial work is now done for the torso. Additional splitting of edges and tweaking of vertices will be required once the arms and legs are added.

Tip: *If you would like to get a sense of the torso with more topology, you can use* **Mesh → Smooth** *to assess the model and then* **undo** *the Smooth operation before continuing.*

7   Save your work.

- **Save** your scene as *02-leon body 03.ma*.

Model the leg

The character's leg will be modeled
in a very similar fashion to the torso.
Extrusions will be used to establish the
overall shape, and vertices will be moved to
refine the model.

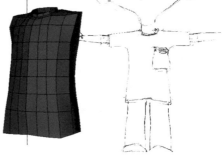

The torso

1   Prepare the pelvic area

Before you can extrude the legs, you need
to extrude the shirt's border and also
create the hips of the character.

- **Select** the faces located under the torso.

- Select **Edit Mesh → Extrude**.

- Select the **Scale** tool and shrink the faces to create the shirt border.

- Press **G** to extrude again, and then **translate** and **scale** the faces with the
  global manipulators.

- **Extrude** the faces one last time and **translate** them down to create the hips
  of the character.

- Use the **Scale** tool to flatten the faces on their **Y-axis**.

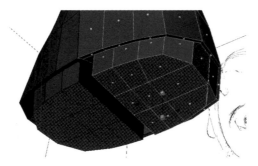

The extruded hips

2   Correct the center line

By doing these extrusions, you have created unwanted faces in the center axis of the model.
Since the hips of the character should not have a space in its center, you will have to fix this.

- Press **4** to display the model's wireframe.

- **Select** the problematic faces located on the inside of the hips and make sure you do not select any other faces on the model.

- Press the **Delete** key.

3 Snap vertices on an axis

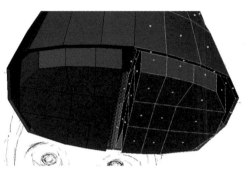

The faces to delete

- While in the *front* view, select all the vertices that should be on the central line of the character.

- **Double-click** the **Move** tool in the toolbox.

- Disable the **Retain component spacing** option.

- Hold down the **X** hotkey to snap to grid.

- **Click+drag** on the **X-axis** arrow to snap the vertices to the grid X-axis.

  The central line of the character is now perfectly straight and aligned with the grid's X-axis.

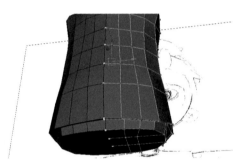

4 Prepare for the leg extrusion

- **Scale** and **move** the face located under the hips to prepare for the extrusion of the leg.

The snapped central vertices

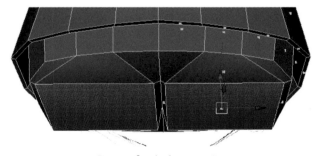

Prepare for the leg extrusion

- **Split** polygons vertically all around the leg so that the lines of the torso flow into the leg.

- **Delete** any unwanted edges.

- **Tweak** the model to get the following rounded shape:

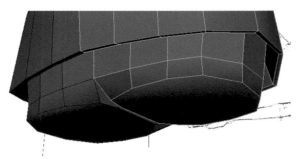

The rounded leg shape

5 Extrude the leg

- **Extrude** the leg down **seven** times: to the middle of the upper leg, the top of the knee, the middle of the knee, below the knee, the middle of the lower leg, the top of the ankle, and the bottom of the ankle.

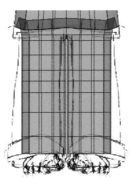

The rough legs

6 Shape the leg

- **Move** the leg vertices to define the shape of the leg, making sure that you keep the rows of vertices perpendicular to the leg. Try to avoid twisting the vertices as they run down the leg.

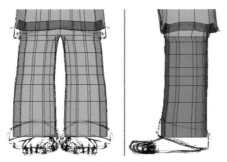

The refined leg shape

> **Tip:** *To flatten a row of vertices, scale them on the axis you want to be flat.*

7 Finalize the legs

- **Move** the vertices to again refine the leg shape, round out the square edges, and better define the knee area.

Refining the legs

- Select the last ring of faces and **extrude** twice to create the pant cuffs.

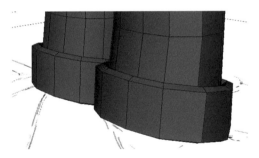

The pant's cuffs

> **Tip:** *As you are extruding, you may want to switch the manipulator to **Global** mode by clicking the small round icon attached to the manipulator. This icon is called the "cycling index".*

- **Move** vertices to continue refinement.

8 Soften the model

- Select *body* and then select **Normals → Soften Edge**.

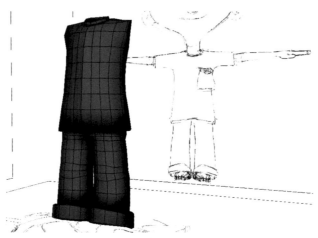

The soften model

9 Save your work

- **Save** your work as *02-leon body 04.ma.*

Model the foot

A series of extrusions will be used to create the foot and the toes.

1 Extrude the foot

- Select the face underneath the cuff.

- **Extrude** it **three** times to create the inside of the pants, the skinny ankle and then down to the top of the toes.

- **Scale** the last extrusion on the **Y-axis** to flatten it.

- **Extrude** once more straight down to the bottom of the foot.

- **Move** the vertices of the foot to spread out the topology and shape the foot.

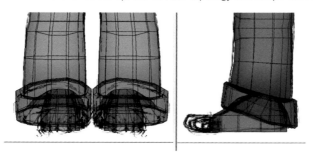

The foot extrusion

- **Refine** the sole of the foot as much as you can.

2   Isolate selected

Working on geometry that is partially inside or hidden by another object can be quite difficult. In order to simplify the foot refinement process, you will isolate the foot geometry. This means that you will tell Maya to display only certain faces in the viewport.

- Select the face underneath the foot.
- Choose **Select → Grow Selection** or press the **>** hotkey.
- **Grow** the selection again until you have selected the entire foot.
- In the perspective view, select **Show → Isolate Select → View Selected**.

  Only the selected faces are now visible in the viewport.

- To exit the **Isolate** mode, simply disable **Show → Isolate Select → View Selected** in the viewport.

3   Refine the foot

- Use the **Split Polygon Tool** and **Delete Edge/Vertex** to clean up the foot geometry. Don't forget to also split the sole of the foot.

Tip: *When splitting polygons, you should try as much as possible to create quads. Quads are polygonal faces with four edges and four vertices. When this is not possible, you should divide faces to create as few triangles as possible.*

- Reconfigure the front portion of the foot in order to have five faces from which to extrude the toes.

The refined foot topology

- When you are done, disable **Show → Isolate Select → View Selected**.

> **Note:** *When creating new polygons, it is possible that they become invisible due to the isolate state. To correct this, you must toggle off* **View Selected***, reselect the proper faces and then isolate the faces again.*

4 Extruding the toes

- Turn **Off** the **Edit Mesh** → **Keep Faces Together** option.

- **Extrude** all five toes at once **three** times, roughly scaling the toes as you are extruding.

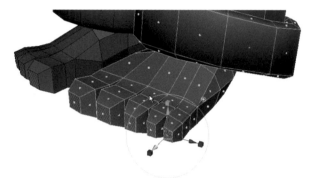

The extruded toes

- **Scale** the toe individually.

- **Extrude** the toe nails.

- **Tweak** the general shape of the foot.

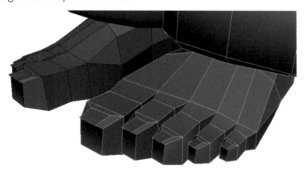

The extruded toe nails

5 Refine the sole of the foot

- Select **Edit Mesh** → **Insert Edge Loop Tool**.

- **Click+drag** on a horizontal foot line to add an edge line across the entire foot, close to the sole.

Once the edge loop is inserted, the new edges are automatically selected. You will use these edges to smooth out the sole.

- Choose **Select → Convert Selection → To Vertices**. Select **Modify → Transformation Tools → Move Normal Tool**.

This tool allows you to move components based on their normals.

- **Click+drag** the manipulator along the **N-axis**.

Doing so moves the vertices along their normals and speed's up the process of rounding up the foot sole.

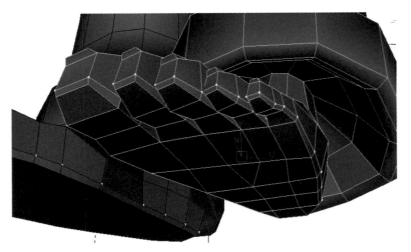

The foot sole refinement

6   **Save your work**
- **Save** your work as *02-leon body 05.ma*.

Model the arm

The arm of the character will be modeled in a fashion similar to the torso and leg. Extrusions will be used to establish the overall form, and vertices will be moved to refine the shape.

1   **Subdivide the arm edges**

Currently, the arm opening has six bordering edges. Ideally, the opening should have eight bordering edges. The top and bottom edges will be subdivided to facilitate this.

- Select the top and bottom edges on the arm opening faces and choose **Edit Mesh → Add Divisions**.

Two new vertices will be added in the middle of these edges.

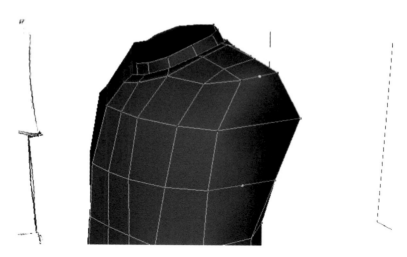

Subdivided edges

- Select the two arm faces and flatten them on the **X-axis** using the **Scale Tool**.
- Rearrange the vertices to make the arm's faces as round as possible.

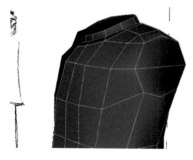

The rounded arm faces

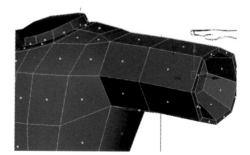

Extruding the sleeve

2 Extrude the arm

- Enable the **Edit Mesh → Keep Faces Together** option.
- **Extrude** the faces out **four** times to the following locations: middle of shirt sleeve, border of sleeve, thickness of border, and the skinny arm inside the sleeve. Use the **Extrude Manipulator** to adjust the arm as you go.
- **Extrude** again **six** times to the following locations: before the elbow, middle of elbow, after the elbow, middle of forearm, beginning of wrist, and end of wrist.
- **Move** vertices to shape the arm as well as possible with the current topology.

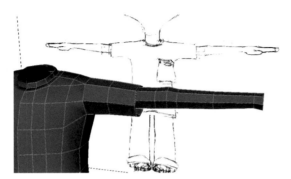

Extruding the arm

3 Split the upper arm

- **Split** the edges connecting the upper arm and the shoulder in order to continue the lines on the top of the arm and in the armpit.

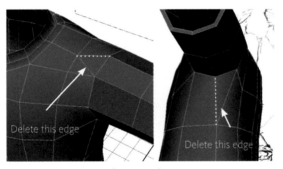

The arm splits

4 Correct chest topology

- **Split** a line of edges that starts from the line in the back up to the middle of the chest.

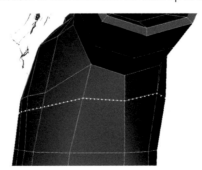

The chest split

Lesson 02: Modeling Leon's Body

- **Tweak** the shape of the shirt to reveal the underlying skin.

5 Extrude the palm

- **Extrude** the two faces at the end of the wrist **twice** to create the palm.
- **Move** vertices as needed to shape the hand.

  Make sure to place the vertices in a way that will allow you to easily extrude the thumb. The vertex in the center of the palm can be pulled up slightly.

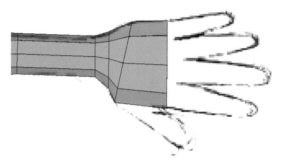

Extrude the palm

6 Split the fingers

- **Split** the faces at the end of the hand to create the four faces that will be used to extrude fingers.

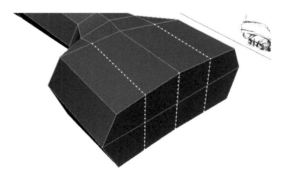

Split for the fingers

- **Move** the row of vertices at the bottom of the hand slightly backwards toward the palm.

  This will round out the flesh at the base of the fingers.

- **Move** the middle row of vertices down.

  This will allow the fingers to be extruded with single faces.

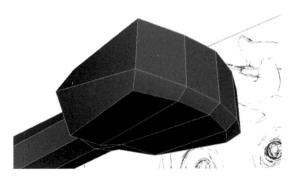

The refined palm

- **Extrude** each finger **four** times.
- **Move** the vertices for each finger as you are extruding to shape them properly.

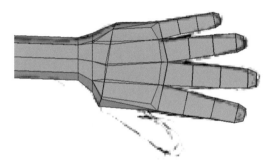

The extruded fingers

- Select the thumb side face, **extrude** it out **four** times, and **move** the vertices to shape it properly.

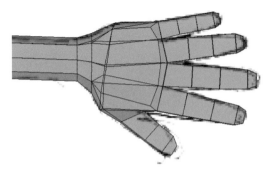

The extruded thumb

Project 01

7 Refine the hand shape

Continue to split edges and move vertices on the hand until you are satisfied with the amount of detail. Concentrate on defining the overall structure of the hand and then refine areas such as the knuckles and nails. Satisfactory results can be achieved with at least six edges to round up the finders. You may need to delete some existing edges in order to maintain clean topological flow.

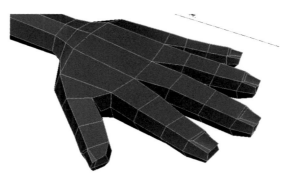

The refined hand

8 Save your work

- **Save** your work as *02-leon body 06.ma*.

9 Preview the high-resolution geometry

- Select **Mesh** → **Smooth** to smooth out the geometry and see how the high-resolution model looks.

- Be sure to select **Edit** → **Undo** to remove the *polySmooth* node before continuing with the lesson.

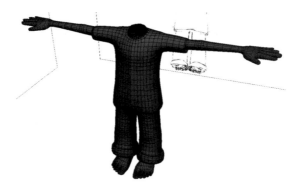

The smoothed model

Refine the entire model

The body has been built with some degree of refinement. At this stage, the topology needs to be assessed and decisions need to be made about how to tie things together. The limbs could be integrated better to enhance the flow of the topology.

You will notice the model has triangles and n-sided faces in several areas. Triangles can cause problems when deforming surfaces. Folds or spikes may appear in areas where you do not want them. Ideally, the model should follow a few rules:

- Quads should be used as much as possible, especially in areas of high deformation.
- Areas of deformation, such as muscles and articulations, should be isolated and defined using loops of edges.
- Loops of edges going through the entire character should be used to tie the model together where you can.

The current character is skinny, wearing clothes, and looking cartoonish, so it is not critical to refine the muscle mass. For other types of characters, it is recommended to spend some time to define the muscles, bones and articulations.

1   Find irregular polygons

Your geometry has been modeled and shaped to define the overall contour. This is a good start. You now need to assess problematic topology.

- Press **F11** to display polygonal faces on your model.
- Choose **Select → Select Using Constraints...**
- Set the following:

     Constraint to **Next Selection**;

     Order to **Nsided**;

- **Click+drag** in the viewport to select all the faces in your model.

  If you have polygonal faces with more than four sides, they will be selected. If you don't have any irregular polygons, nothing will be selected.

- **Locate** the areas with n-sided polygons and **correct** the problem as needed.

> **Note:** *In some cases, you will need to further define an area before cleaning it up. Even though it is always preferable to define quads, sometimes you will have to define triangles where several edges meet.*

- When you are done with the Selection Constraint window, simply click the **Close and Reset** button.

Tip: *Also try to use the selection constraints to locate triangles and fix them if possible.*

2 Add definition

Use the **Edit Mesh** → **Insert Edge Loop Tool** to add definition perpendicular to key deforming areas such as the torso and articulations.

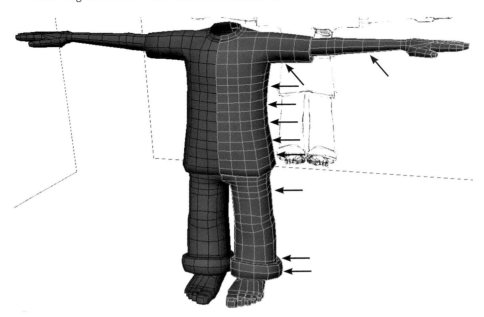

Inserted edge loops

Tip: *Make sure to space out any new edge loops equally. Doing so will greatly improve the model's deformation.*

Mirror geometry

At this point, the body has been developed as far as it will be in this lesson. This does not mean it cannot be refined further. If you wish, continue to use the principles you've learned in this chapter to develop and refine the body more. Focus on greater muscle definition and further refinement of the hand and foot.

1 Delete the instance and the construction history

- Select the right half of the *body* and **delete** it.

- Select **Edit** → **Delete All by Type** → **History** to delete all the construction history in the scene.

2 **Snap the central vertices**

- In the *front* view, select all the vertical central vertices.
- **Double-click** on the **Move Tool** to open its options.
- Make sure the **Retain Component Spacing** option is turned **Off**.
- Still in the front view, hold down **x** to snap to grid and **click+drag** on the **X-axis** in order to snap all the vertices in a perfect vertical line.

  Doing so will close any gaps upon mirroring of the geometry.

3 **Mirror the geometry**

- Select the half body, and then select **Mesh** → **Mirror Geometry** → ☐, and set the following:

  Mirror Direction to **–X**;

  Merge with the original to **Off**.

- Click on the **Mirror** button.

  The full body is now a single piece of geometry, but the central vertices were not merged.

- Select **Edit Mesh** → **Merge** → ☐.
- Make sure the **Threshold** is set to **0.01** and then click the **Merge** button.

  The central line of vertices has been merged together. Any further adjustment to the geometry will now have to be done on both sides of the model unless you want to break the symmetry to have your character look more realistic.

- With the geometry selected, select **Normals** → **Soften Edges** to soften any hard edges.

4 **Save your work**

- **Save** your work as *02-leon body 07.ma*.

Create a pocket

Later in this book, you will place Earl, Leon's little squirrel friend, in his shirt pocket. You will now model this pocket.

1 **Extrude the pocket**

Using what you have learned so far in the lesson, extrude a patch of faces on the character's shirt. Make sure the **Keep Faces Together** option is enabled.

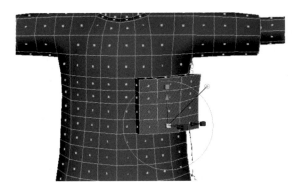

The pocket extrusion

- Turn **Off** the manipulator's **Reflection** option.
- **Refine** the pocket's shape.
- **Extrude** the top faces to form the inside of the pocket.

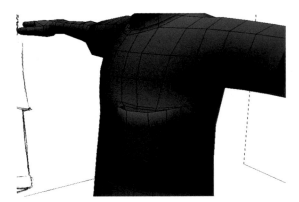

The refined pocket

Tip: *For simplicity, you will want the inside of the pocket to be not very deep, with a good distance from any other geometry. This will prevent interpenetration when deforming.*

Finalize the model

1   Sculpt the model

- If needed, use **Mesh → Sculpt Geometry Tool** to smooth out areas of the model by setting the operation to **Smooth**.

2   Clean up

- Select **Edit → Delete All by Type → History** to delete all the construction history in the scene.

3   Save your work

- **Save** your work as *02-leon body 08.ma*.

Conclusion

In this lesson, you learned how to model starting from a simple cube to create Leon's refined polygon body. Using image planes allowed you to create the body accurately. You learned how to split polygons to create loops of edges that define key areas, as well as how to use extrusions to create limbs. Polygon smoothing was discussed as an option to provide the final overall level of detail.

In the next lesson, you will model Leon's head.

Lesson 02: Modeling Leon's Body

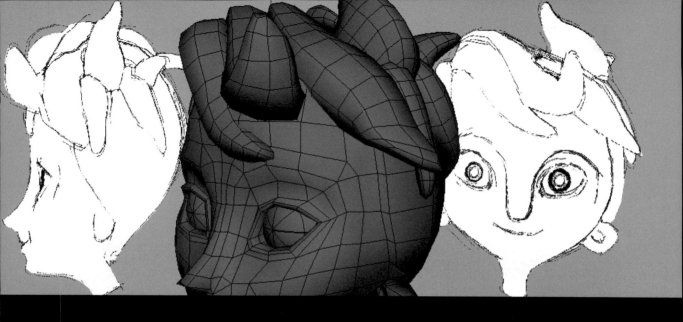

Lesson 03
Modeling Leon's head

Creating a basic polygon head shape

The workflow for modeling a head is very similar to the body; however, the head is a much more complex area and if the proportions and topological flow are not handled correctly, the head will texture and deform improperly.

1   Import image planes

Using the same image plane technique used in the previous lesson, you will now add three image planes for the head using the images *leonHeadFront.tif*, *leonHeadSide.tif* and *leonHeadTop.tif*.

- Select in any viewport **Panels → Saved Layouts → Four View**

- If you moved any camera, you can reset its position by selecting
  View → Default Home.

- In the front viewport, select **View → Image Plane → Import Image...**

  This brings up a file browser that allows you to select the wanted image plane.

- Select *leonHeadFront.tif* from the *sourceimages* directory.

- Adjust the image plane **center** attributes as needed to align it properly above the grid.

- Import and place the remaining head image planes.

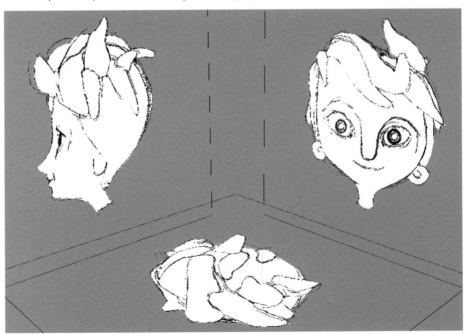

The image planes

Note: *Based on the concept images, it would be easier to start modeling the head using a polygonal sphere, but since this lesson is about how to generate geometry, you will start from a cube. Note that a sphere would also have lots of triangles in the poles.*

2 Create a cube

- A polygon cube will be used initially to create the overall shape of the head. Select **Create → Polygon Primitives → Cube → □**, and set the following:

  Width divisions to **6**;

  Height divisions to **5**;

  Depth divisions to **3**.

  Notice that those numbers of subdivisions were determined by the different facial parts such as the eyes, nose, mouth, and large forehead. The width divisions also took into consideration the need for a central line of edges. If you desire, you can create a default cube, scale it roughly around the head, and then change those attributes in the Channel Box to best suit the reference images.

- **Scale** the head so it fits around the bounding area of the head, based on the image planes.

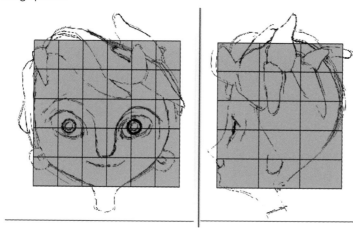

The initial cube

- **Rename** the cube *head*.

3 Work on the basic shape

- **Move** and **scale** vertices in the different views to round off the square edges and define the head shape more accurately. Try to keep your changes symmetrical even though the reference images are not.

Lesson 03: Modeling Leon's Head

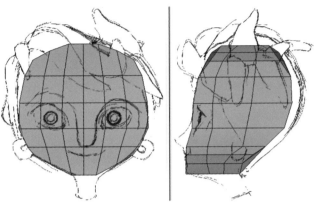

Basic head shape

Tip: *Remember to avoid moving the central vertices of the head away from the center line in the front view to prevent a gap from being created between the object and the mirrored instance.*

4   **Extrude the neck**

- Select the four faces forming the neck base and **extrude** them **twice** using **Edit Mesh → Extrude**.

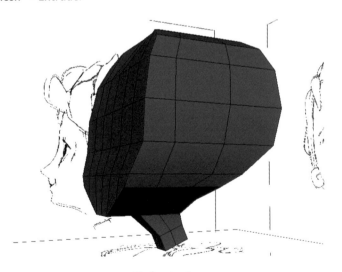

Neck extrusion

- **Delete** the faces under the last neck extrusion since this is where the neck will be connected to the body.

5   Switch to Polygon Proxy Mode

The Polygon Proxy Mode lets you display both the proxy polygonal cage and the smoothed high-resolution object at the same time. By using this feature, you can refine the shape of the low-resolution object, while seeing the results on the high-resolution object, allowing you to get the best final result possible. Once you are done modeling in this mode, you can keep the low-resolution object for skinning and texturing, and then smooth it before rendering to get the optimal results.

- **Delete** the faces on the right side of the face.

  The proxy options will allow you to mirror the geometry automatically.

- With the *head* selected, select **Proxy → Subdiv Proxy → ❏**.

- Set the following in the option window:

  Mirror Behavior to **Full**;

  Mirror Direction to **-X**;

- **Smooth Mesh In Layer** to **On**;

  Smooth Layer Display to **Reference**.

  These options specify that you want to mirror the geometry, and that you need the smooth object to be on a layer that is unselectable to prevent picking it or modifying it by mistake. This layer also allows you to hide the smooth object if needed.

- Click the **Smooth** button.

  The low-resolution object is set to be semi-transparent, and a smoothed duplicate is set to be opaque.

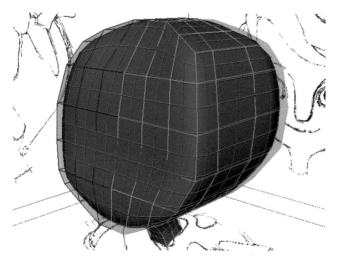

The mirrored proxy and smoothed object

Note: *In the workflow shown here, you must not edit the smoothed object. Any changes on the smoothed object will be lost, since it will not be saved at the end of this lesson.*

6   Refine the head

- **Refine** the head as much as possible with the current proxy topology.

- Don't forget to round up the initial cube in every viewport.

- Try to delimit the eye socket and the ear base with single faces to facilitate their extrusions.

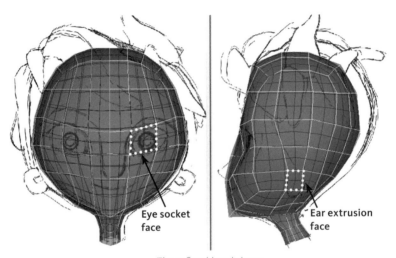

Eye socket
face

Ear extrusion
face

The refined head shape

Tip: *Use the [`] hotkey to toggle visibility between the proxy and the smooth object. Use the [~] hotkey to display both objects at the same time.*

7   Save your work

- **Save** your scene as *03-leon head 01.ma*.

Facial details

Now that the basic shape of the head has been achieved, you can work on adding details and correcting the general flow of edges.

1   Extrude the ear

- Select the face at the base of the ear and **extrude** it **three** times.

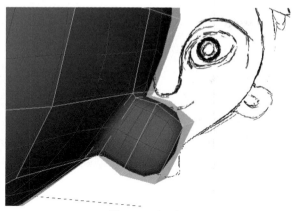

The ear extrusion

> **Note**: *When tweaking the shape of the ear using the proxy geometry, make sure to look at the smoothed geometry to see how it forms the ear.*

- **Extrude** again the two front faces to be used to create the inside of the ear.

> **Tip**: *Toggle the visibility of the headSmoothMesh layer in order to facilitate the selection of components hidden by the smooth geometry.*

2 Add edges

Now that you are running out of vertices to refine the ear, it is time to add some edge loops to your model.

- Select **Edit Mesh → Insert Edge Loop Tool** and add an horizontal edge loop that splits the ear in half and also splits in half the mouth area.

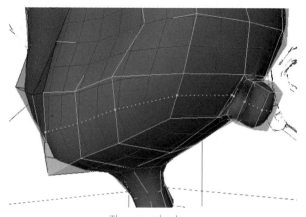

The new edge loop

• **Refine** the head using the new components.

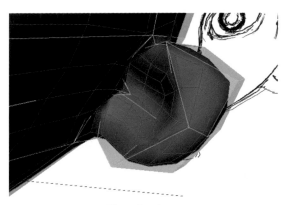

The refined ear

3 Eye socket

In order for the eye socket to be round, you will require at least eight vertices to shape it. You will now extrude the eye socket and then add subdivisions to the head.

• **Extrude** the face, delimiting the eye **three** times. first to create the eyelids, then for thickness to the eyelid, and finally to create the eye socket inside the head.

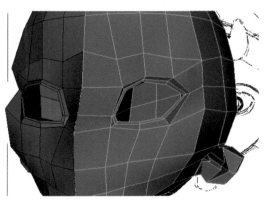

The extruded eye socket

• Insert **two** edge loops running vertically and horizontally in the eye socket.

• **Refine** the new topology.

Tip: *Make sure to have the edges extend from the eye socket radially. Doing so represents the radial layout of muscles that go around the eye.*

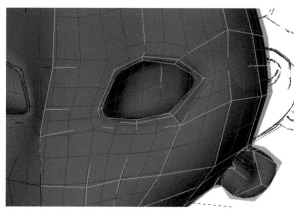

The refined eye socket

4   **Shape the head**

Edge loops have been inserted for the ear and the eye socket but also split faces all around the head, and now is a good time to revise the topology of the head.

- **Refine** the global shape of the head.

- **Split** faces in the lower back of the head and try to define only quads.

> **Tip:**   *If you want to work on the low-resolution model without it being semi-transparent, you can open the head's Attribute Editor, access its Lambert shader tab to the far right, and set the* **Transparency** *attribute to* **black**.

5   **Brows**

- **Split** edges to define the eyebrow as follows:

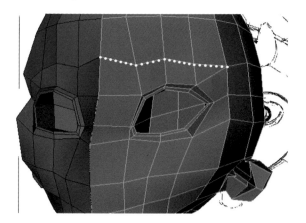

The eyebrow split

6 Nose

- Select the central faces defining the base of the nose and **extrude** them once.
- Pull them out on the **Z-axis** using global translation.
- Since the extrusion has created unwanted faces on the central line, select them and **delete** them.

  You now have a proper extrusion to be used to model the nose.

- **Refine** the nose shape.

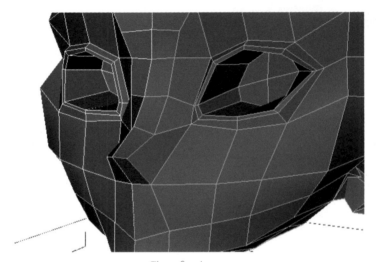

The refined nose

7 Save your work

- Save your scene as *03-leon head 02.ma*.

Model the mouth

Perhaps the most difficult facial part to model is the mouth. This is because there are many things to consider at once. First, you need to add lots of topology to be able to model a proper mouth. Second, you need to take in consideration the radial flow of the topology coming from the mouth muscles. Third, you must not clutter the rest of the model with unnecessary edges. Finally, all this topology needs to deform and animate smoothly.

1 Adding topology

Since you want to avoid splitting edges all the way to the back of the head, you must concentrate on splitting only the mouth region of the model.

- **Split** the mouth area as follows:

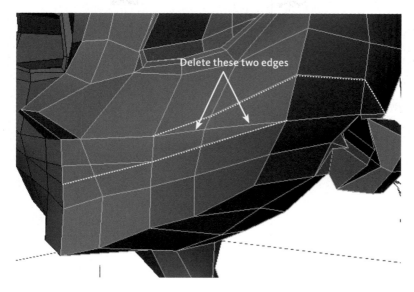

Splits to refine the mouth

- **Refine** the mouth shape according to the image planes.
- Select the two faces defining the lips and **extrude** them.
- **Scale** the extrusion down to create the lips border.
- **Extrude** the same faces again **three** times while moving them on their **Z-axis** to form the inner mouth.
- Select the undesired faces that were created on the central line and **delete** them.

2   Refine the inner mouth

Refining the inner mouth can be quite challenging since visualizing the 3D surface through a wireframe tangle requires a very good understanding of your geometry. The best way to work on the inner mouth is to reverse the head's normals and hide the backfaces. Doing so will allow you to see the inside of the head.

- Select the *head,* and then select **Normals → Reverse**.
- If the backfaces are visible, hide them by selecting
  Display → Polygons → Backface Culling.
- From the front view, snap the central vertices to the **X-axis**.

- **Refine** the inner mouth to achieve a better shape as follows:

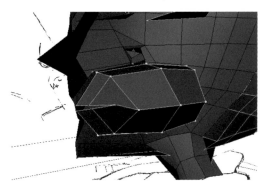

The inner mouth

- When you are done, select the *head* and toggle **Normals → Reverse** and **Display → Polygons → Backface Culling**.

3 **Refine the lips**

- **Split** faces to create edge loops around the lips.

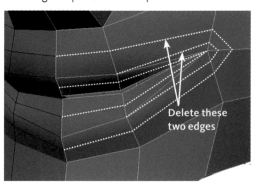

Lip edge loops

- Take some time to adjust the whole mouth to match the image planes.

 Tip: *Make sure to leave a gap between the upper and lower lips. This will prevent merging problems and will greatly help when deforming the lips.*

4 **Add edge loops**

Now that you have more edge loops going around the lips, you will need some radial edges to define the lips even more.

- Select the **Split Polygon Tool**.

- From the front view, **click+drag** on the edge on the neck border, and then **click+drag** on the horizontal edge between the eyebrows.

  Doing so defines a long edge loop going from the neck border, through the chin, all around the inside the mouth, creating the lip crease under the nose, and then finishing on the eyebrows.

- Continue to **split** the polygons to create an arc above the eye, going around to the cheek and then down under the chin.

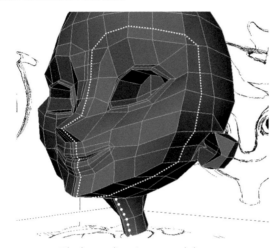

The long split going around the eye

- **Split** another long edge loop that goes from the neck, through the mouth, around the eye, down on the cheek, and ends up in the back of the head.

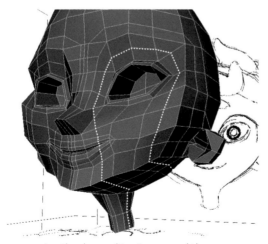

Another long split going around the eye

Lesson 03: Modeling Leon's Head

- The structure of the head is done; however, undesirable topology exists in several areas. Triangles and five-sided faces are evident in areas where they should not exist. Selection constraints can be used to help you identify the problematic areas. Spend time tweaking the current topology as best you can.

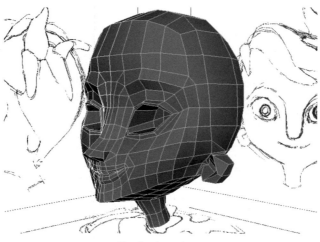

The final topology

Note: *At this stage in the process, it is getting very hard to add topology since any change will have a domino effect through the entire model. This is an expected part of the modeling process which will allow you to improve visualizing modeling approaches.*

5 Save your scene

- **Save** your scene as *03-leon head 03.ma*.

Adding the eyes

Now you will add separate spheres to create the eyes and tweak the eyelids to curve on the surface correctly.

1 Eyeball

In order to refine the eyelid shape, a sphere will be created as the eyeball.

- Select **Create → NURBS Primitives → Sphere**.
- **Rename** the *sphere* to *eyeball*.
- **Move** the *eyeball* where the eyeball should be.
- **Rotate** the *eyeball* by **90** degrees on the **X-axis**.
- **Scale** the *eyeball* appropriately.

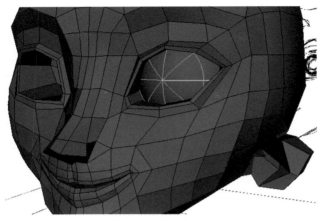

The eyeball in place

Tip: *The eyeball should always be perfectly round.*

2 Duplicate the eye

- With the *eyeball* selected, select **Edit → Group.**
- Select **Edit → Duplicate Special** and set the following:

  Geometry type to **Copy**;

  Scale X to **−1**.

- Click the **Duplicate Special** button.

  Since the group's pivot was placed at the origin, when you duplicate it with an inverse scale, the result is a mirrored version of the eyeball.

3 Reference the eyeballs

- Assign both *eyeballs* to a new layer and set the layer to be a **Reference** layer.

  This will allow you to work on the eyelid without accidentally selecting and moving the eyeballs. You will notice that the eyelid requires adjustment in order to follow the eyeball's curve correctly.

4 Tweak the eyelids

- Use the **Edge Loop Tool** to add an edge loop on the inside of the eyelid.

  This inner eyelid edge loop should be barely visible going through the eyeball.

- **Move** the eyelid vertices to properly follow the *eyeball* surface.
- Round up the eyelid and adjust the surrounding vertices.

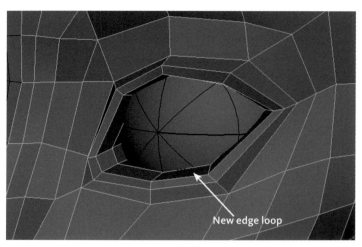

The refined eyelid

> Note: It is normal to see more geometry in the inside of the eye corner just as in a real eye.

5 Clean up

- With the *head* selected, select **Normals → Soften Edge**.
- With the *head* still selected, select **Proxy → Remove Subdiv Proxy Mirror → ⬚.**
- In the options, set **Mirror Direction** to **−X** and click the Remove **Mirror** button.

  Doing so removes the smooth object and automatically merges the mirrored proxy objects together to create a single polygonal object.

- Select **Edit → Delete All by Type → History**.

6 Save your work

- Save your scene as *03-leon head 04.ma*.

Head details

Since you could go on forever improving your head, you need at some point to call the geometry final. You will now stop improving the head's topology and concentrate on adding the final details.

1 Hair extrusion

In order to create the hair, you will extrude the scalp slightly to give it volume.

- Select the faces of the head delimiting the scalp area.

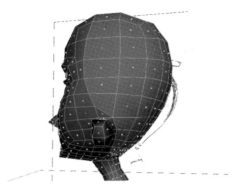

The scalp faces

Note: *You may need to split some faces to get a nice scalp shape. If so, you have to decide whether the scalp should be symmetrical or not. In this case, the scalp will be symmetrical.*

- **Extrude** the faces outward to give volume to the hair.
- **Move** the vertices to smooth out the results.

2 Add the bangs

You will now give the character a hair style by modeling bangs according to the reference images. Those pieces of geometry will be created from a circle extruded along curves.

- Select **Create → EP Curve Tool.**
- From the front view, draw a curve with six points, starting from the hair split and following one of the bangs on the image plane up to its tip.

Try following the curvature of the bangs as much as possible.

Hair curve

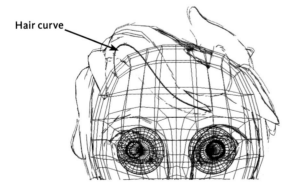

The hair curve

- From the other views, **tweak** the shape of the curve to follow the forehead, leaving a gap between the head and the curve.

- Select **Create → NURBS Primitives → Circle**.

- Select the new circle and **Shift-select** the hair curve.

- Press **F4** to access the **Surfaces** menu set.

- Select **Surfaces → Extrude → ❑**, and set the following options:

  Style to **Tube**;

  Result position to **At path**;

  Pivot to **Component**;

  Orientation to **Profile normal**;

  Output geometry to **Polygons**;

  Type to **Quads**;

  Tessellation method to **Count**;

  Count to **40**.

- Click the **Extrude** button.

  The resulting geometry will be a low-resolution tube that you will use to define the bangs.

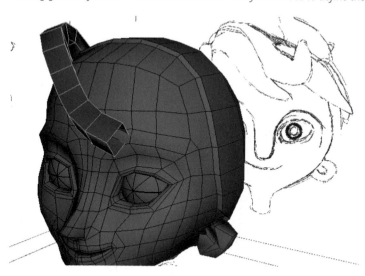

The bangs extrusion

 Tip: *Because of construction history, you can still tweak the curve's shape, which will in turn deform the geometry.*

- **Tweak** the vertices to get a proper shape.
- Select the vertices that define the opening at the end of the geometry; then select **Edit Mesh → Merge to Center.**

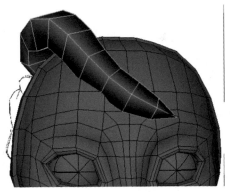

One hair bang

- **Rename** the geometry *hairBang*.

3 Create the rest of the bangs

Using the technique you have just learned, place, extrude, and tweak all the other bangs.

Tip: *Duplicate other bangs to speed up the process.*

- When you are done, select all the bangs and select **Mesh → Smooth.**

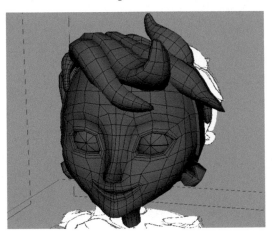

The final hair style

Lesson 03: Modeling Leon's Head

4 Clean up

- With the *head* and *hairBangs* selected, select **Normals → Soften Edge**.
- Select **Edit → Delete All by Type → History**.
- **RMB** on the *layer1* used to reference the eyes, and then select **Delete Layer**.
- Open the Outliner and **delete** any unwanted nodes such as the curves used to create the bangs.

5 Save your work

- Save your scene as *03-leon head 05.ma*.

Combining the body and the head

Leon's body and head can now be combined. This is an easy procedure with only one main consideration: the number of edges on the neck opening needs to be the same as for the head and the body.

1 Delete the image planes

The image planes are no longer needed.

- Open **Window → Rendering Editors → Hypershade**.
- In the top part of the Hypershade, select the **cameras** tab.
- Select the **three** image planes and **delete** them.

2 Group the head

- Since you will have to move the head to fit the body geometry, select all the head geometry and **group** it.
- Select **Modify → Center Pivot**.

3 Import the body

- Select **File → Import** and select *02-leon body 08.ma*.

4 Place the head

- Select the group containing all the head geometry.
- **Scale** and **move** the *head* until it matches the image planes.

5 Match the vertices

The head has fourteen vertices at the neck opening and the body has twelve. Two vertices on the head opening will be merged to match the counts.

The body with the head aligned

- Make sure there are no faces closing the neck openings on both geometries. If there are faces, delete them to leave a hole in the geometry.

- On *head*, select the **three** vertices at the front of the neck and select **Edit Mesh →
Merge To Center**.

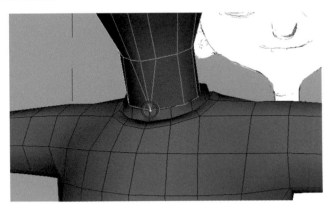

Merged head vertices

6 Attach the pieces

Now that the two openings have the correct number of vertices, the head vertices can be snapped to the body to flow nicely into each other.

- With the **Move Tool** active, hold down **v** to **Snap to Point** and **snap** each head vertex on its correspondent body vertex.

Lesson 03: Modeling Leon's Head

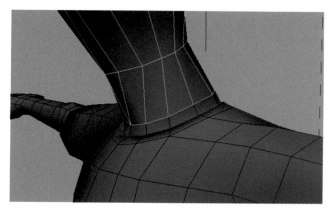

Snapped vertices

- Select the *body* and the *head* and then select **Mesh** → **Combine**.

  The body and head are now one piece.

- Select Leon and then select **Edit Mesh** → **Merge** → ☐.

- In the options, make sure **Threshold** is set to **0.01**.

- Click the **Merge** button.

  The neck vertices are now merged together.

7 Finalize Leon

You may wish to adjust the neck vertices somewhat and add some edge loops, but remember that you need to adjust both sides at once to maintain symmetry.

8 Smooth the model

- Use the **Edit Polygons** → **Sculpt Polygon Tool** to smooth out areas of the model by setting the operation to **Smooth**.

Tip: *You can sculpt equally on both sides of the head by turning on the Reflection option (reflecting against the X-axis), in the Stroke section. Also, you can select vertices on which you want to paint. Lastly, you can click the Flood button to smooth the selection all at once.*

9 Clean up

- **Rename** the geometry *leon*.

- With *leon* selected, select **Normals** → **Soften Edge**.

- Select all geometry pieces, and **group** them under a single group named *geometry*.

- Select all geometry pieces, and then select **Modify** → **Freeze Transformations**.
- Select **Edit** → **Delete All by Type** → **History**.
- **Delete** any obsolete nodes in the Outliner.
- **Delete** the image planes from the Hypershade.
- Select **File** → **Optimize Scene Size** to clean up the scene.

Leon completed

10 Save your work

- Save your scene as *03-leon complete.ma*.

Note: *The final scene can be found in the support files.*

Conclusion

Congratulations – you have now modeled an entire character! In the process, you learned how to model using several polygonal tools. You also learned where to split edges to create edge loops around key areas of the face. Doing so greatly helps when it comes time to deform the model.

In the next lesson, you will texture Leon using several polygonal texturing tools.

Lesson 03: Modeling Leon's Head

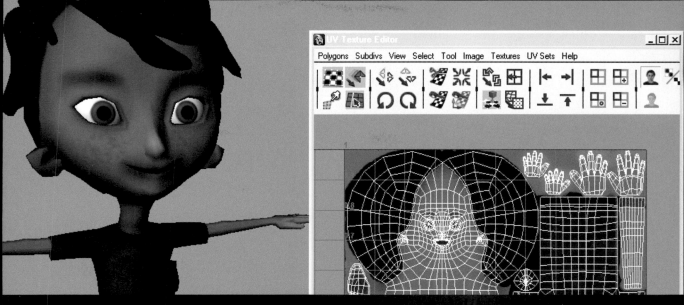

Lesson 04
Polygon Texturing

UVs determine how textures appear on the surface. While NURBS surfaces have predictable UVs, polygonal surfaces, because of the arbitrary nature of their topology, do not. Before you can texture a poly surface, its UVs must be properly set up.

In this lesson, you will texture Leon's geometry.

In this lesson you will learn the following:

- Basic workflow for texturing polygonal surfaces;
- How to project UVs;
- How to cut and sew UVs;
- How to unfold UVs;
- How to organize UVs in the 0–1 UV space;
- How to export a UV snapshot;
- How to create a simple PSD network.

Texturing polygonal surfaces

In this exercise, you will set up the UVs for Leon from the previous lesson.

Note: *Throughout this lesson, your results should be similar to the images shown here, but may vary depending on your model.*

1   **Open Leon's scene file**

- **Open** the scene from the previous lesson called *03-leon complete.ma*.

- **Save** the scene right away as *04-leon texture_01.ma*.

2   **Switch to the Perspective View/Texture Editor layout**

- From the menu bar at the top of the Perspective view, select **Panels → Saved Layouts → Persp/UV Texture Editor**.

3   **Check the UVs for Leon**

- Select *leon*'s geometry and check the layout of its UVs in the UV Texture Editor window.

    As they are right now, the UVs will not provide good coordinates for applying a texture.

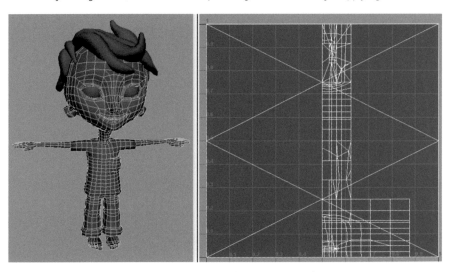

Leon's UVs displayed in the UV Texture Editor

4   **Assign a new material to Leon**

- **RMB** on the geometry and select **Materials → Assign New Material → Lambert**.

    Doing so will automatically create a new lambert material, assign it to the geometry, and open its Attribute Editor.

5 Assign a checker texture to the Color channel

- In the Attribute Editor, click on the **Map** button for the **Color** channel.

  Doing so will display the Create Render Node window, which allows you to create and map a texture to the selected attribute.

- Click on the **Checker** texture in the Create Render Node window.

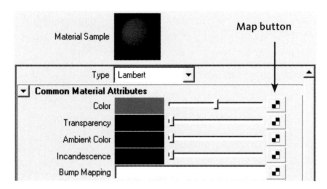

Map button for Color channel

6 Switch to shaded with texture

- Press the **6** key on your keyboard to enable hardware texturing.

  The checker texture should now appear on leon, but because of the poor UV layout, the checker looks irregular.

Irregular texture placement due to poor UVs

7   Change the checker's Repeat values

- In the Attribute Editor, select the *place2dTexture* tab related to the *checker1* texture.
- Change both **Repeat U** and **V** values to **20**.

8   Increase the display quality of the texture

- In the Attribute Editor with the new *lambert* shader selected, open the **Hardware Texturing** section and change **Texture Resolution** to **Highest (256x256)**.

  Doing so will display the texture more accurately in the viewport.

9   Turn off the texture display in the UV Texture Editor

- In the UV Texture Editor menu bar, select **Image → Display Image** to toggle the display of the checker texture **Off**.

10 Apply a planar projection to the body

- Select the body and then select **Create UVs →❏ Planar Mapping → ❏**.
- In the **Planar Mapping** options, make sure **Fit projection to Bounding box** is turned **On** and the **Mapping Direction** is set to **Z-axis**.
- Click the **Project** button.

  Doing so will rearrange the surface's UVs by projecting new UV coordinates on the Z direction.

Leon's UVs using planar mapping

Cut the UVs

In order for the UVs to be properly unfolded, you must first cut the UVs into UV shells, which will define the different parts of the body, such as the head, arms and legs. The shells should be able to lay relatively flat when unfolded without overlapping, much like a cloth pattern is laid flat for a piece of clothing prior to sewing.

The location of the UV cuts requires some planning to obtain the best unfolded result. The better the UV cuts, the better the correlation between the original polygons and their corresponding UV mesh. In addition, you should anticipate that the polygon edge cuts will result in texture mismatches along those edges and plan their locations on the model accordingly so they are less visible. For example, you can make edge cuts under the arms or on the back of the legs of a character.

1 Display UV borders

- With *leon* selected, select **Display** → **Polygons** → **Texture Border Edges**.

  This option will display UV borders with a thicker line so that it can be easily distinguished.

2 Cut the neck UVs

- Choose **Select** → **Select Edge Loop Tool**.

  This tool allows you to double-click on an edge and automatically get its edge loop selected as long as it can find the proper edges to follow.

- **Double-click** the horizontal edge ring at the base of the neck where it is inside the shirt.

  You will cut this edge loop since it is quite well hidden under the shirt.

- Make sure all the edges in that loop are selected while in wireframe.

- Select **Edit UVs** → **Cut UV Edges**.

  By cutting the UVs at the neck, the UVs are now divided into two distinct shells: the head UV shell and the body UV shell.

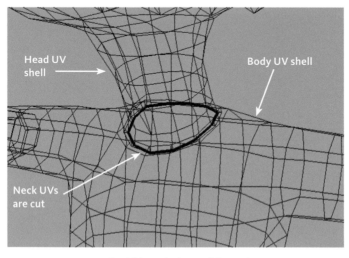

Cut UVs at the base of the neck

Lesson 04: Polygonal Texturing

3 Separate the shells in the Texture Editor

- In the Texture Editor, with the *leon* geometry selected, **RMB** and select **UV**.

- **Click+drag** to select a few UVs that are part of the head.

- Select **Select → Shell**.

  All the UVs from the head shell are selected.

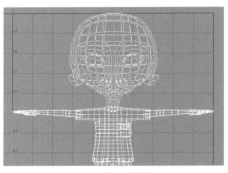

Head UV shell

- Activate the **Move Tool** by pressing **w** on your keyboard.

- **Translate** the head shell next to the body.

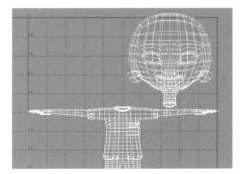

Separate head and body shells

4 Cut the head UVs

To be able to unfold the head UVs, you must cut the head shell again a couple of times. In this step, you will create UV shells for the left and right sides of the head and the inner mouth.

- Select the vertical edges in the middle of Leon's face using either the **Select Edge Loop** tool, the **Select → Select Contiguous Edges** tool or by selecting them manually.

- Select **Edit UVs → Cut UV Edges**.

  The left and right sides of the head are now separated into two UV shells.

- Select the edge loop located in the inner mouth, just behind the lips.
- Select **Edit UVs → Cut UV Edges**.

> **Note:** *Cutting the UVs in the mouth rather than outside the mouth will help hide the seam created by the head and mouth textures meeting along that cut.*

5 Separate the UV shells

- In the Texture Editor, separate each individual shell by selecting a single UV component and using **Select → Shell**.

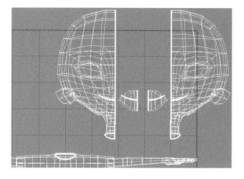

Separate head shells

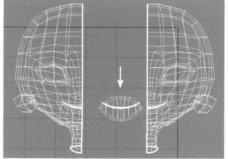

The inner mouth shell

6 Sew the inner mouth UV shells

The inner mouth shells do not need to be separate, so they will be sewn together.

- In the Texture Editor, **RMB** and select **Edge**.
- Select the edges along the vertical center line on one of the inner mouth shells.

  Notice that the same edges are also selected on the other side of the inner mouth shell.

- Select **Polygons → Move and Sew UV edges**.

Unfold the head

The *Unfold UVs* function lets you unwrap the UVs for a polygonal object while it attempts to ensure that the UVs do not overlap. Unfold UVs helps to minimize the distortion of texture maps on organic polygon meshes by optimizing the position of the UV coordinates so they more closely reflect the original polygon mesh.

1 Unfold UVs

- Select the **UVs** of one half of *leon*'s face.

- From the Texture Editor, select **Polygons** → **Unfold** → ☐.

  The tool's options are displayed.

- Make sure to select **Edit** → **Reset Settings**; then turn **On** the **Rescale** option.

- Click the **Apply** button.

  The command will automatically unfold the UV shell as follows:

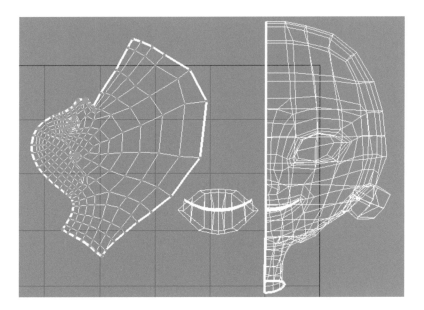

The unfolded face

2   Unfold UVs with pinning

In the previous step, the Unfold command moved and scaled the UV shell, which isn't what you want. To prevent that from happening, you can deselect some UVs so the Unfold solver considers them to be pinned in location.

- **Undo** the previous Unfold command.

- Select the **UVs** of one half of *leon*'s face.

- Deselect any two **UVs** along the central line of the shell. For instance, deselect one UV at the base of the neck and another one in the forehead.

- Select **Polygons** → **Unfold**.

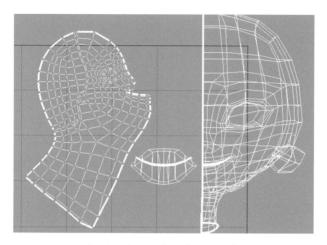

Pinning the unselected UVs result

3 Repeat for other half of head

- **Repeat** the previous step to unfold the other half of the head using the same two pinned UVs.

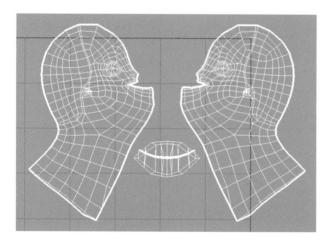

Properly unfolded head

- **Move** the inner mouth UV shell aside.

4 Sew the face shells together

To avoid having a texture seam in the middle of the face, the two head shells can be sewed together starting at the base of the neck up to the tip of the cranium. You will leave a hole for the mouth.

- Select the **border edges** from the bottom of the neck corner up to the tip of the lip corner.
- Select **Polygons → Sew UV Edges**.

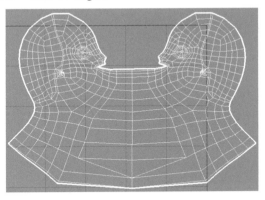

Sewed chin UV edges

- **Repeat** the last steps to sew from the top lip corner up to the scalp line.

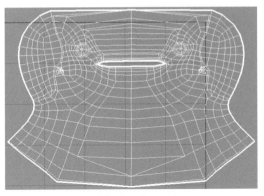

Sewed forehead UV edges

Tip: *Keep in mind that sewing too many edges can cause texture stretching.*

5 Unfold the head shell again

You can make the head UV shell better by unfolding a second time, specifying pinned UVs.

- Select all the UVs of the new united head shell.
- **Deselect** UVs intended for pinning such as the bottom of the neck and the top of the scalp.
- Select **Polygons → Unfold**.

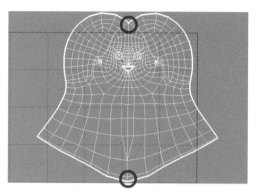

UVs used for pinning

6 Get better results

As you can see, unfolding a UV shell is quite simple, but when you look at the previous image, you can see that the neck area is much bigger than the entire facial area, contrary to the actual model. This is not recommended since the facial area needs much more UV space. You will now have to stretch the UVs and unfold once more.

- Select a UV on the central line near the chin area and move it down slightly.

- Select the entire head shell.

- Deselect the same two UVs used for pinning in the previous step, and also deselect the UV you have just moved.

- Select **Polygons → Unfold**.

  Notice that the neck area is now smaller and the facial area takes up more space.

- Continue moving and pinning UVs to get an acceptable result.

- **Repeat** the previous steps to unfold the inner mouth shell.

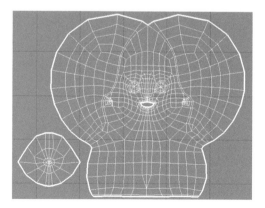

The final head UVs

Tip: *You can move, rotate and scale groups of UVs intended for pinning for the Unfold solver to generate different results.*

Now that the head UVs have been properly unfolded, they are in much better shape for supporting textures.

Head with textures

Tip: *Ideally, a perfect UV layout would have every square in the checker texture about the same size overall the body. In this image, the facial squares are much bigger than those on the neck, which means the neck will have better texture resolution than the face. Although this is not the optimal solution, it will be more than adequate for this lesson.*

7   **Save your work**

- **Save** your scene as *04-leon texture 01.ma*.

Cut and unfold the rest of the body

Now that you have more experience unfolding polygonal geometry, you can unfold the rest of the body. The following steps are similar to what you have done on the head, but there are areas where the unfolding will be somewhat more difficult, such as the fingers and toes.

1   **Unfold the arms**

The arm UVs should be cut on the inside of the shirt and at the wrist. The cut along the arm should be located underneath the arm to reduce visibility. The hands will be in separate UV shells.

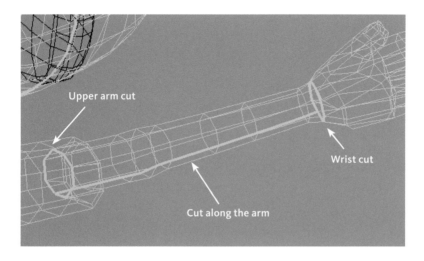

The arm cuts

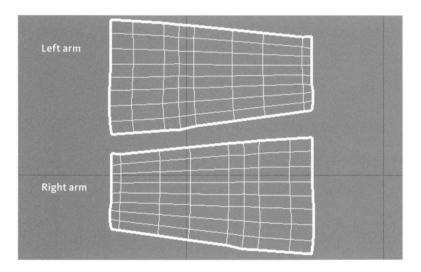

The arm UV shells

2   Unfold the hands

The hands are a little trickier since they cannot be unfolded as easily. The simplest way to unfold them is to cut the hand in half horizontally. You will then have a top and bottom UV shell for each hand.

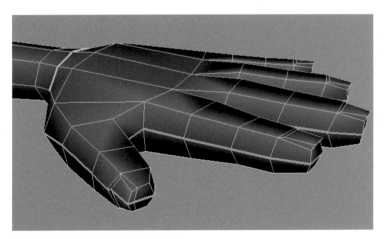

The hand cuts

You should now select each shell's faces and assign planar mapping in the Y-axis. Once that is done, it is easier to unfold the shells using pinning on the wrist and fingers.

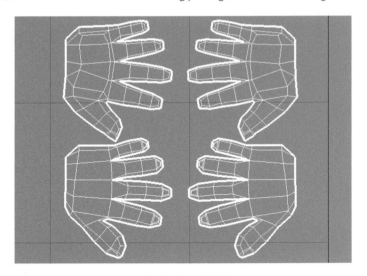

The hand UV shells

Tip: *At certain times you may find it to be easier and more logical to fix the UVs manually instead of always using the Unfold command.*

3   Unfold the feet

The feet are similar to the hands and should be cut to form a top and bottom shell.

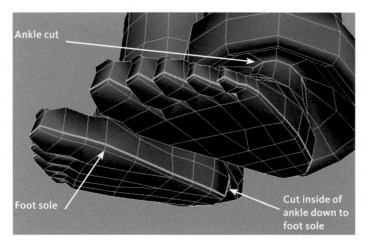

The feet cuts

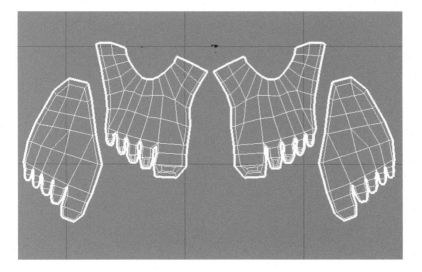

The feet UV shells

4 Unfold the shirt

The simplest solution for unfolding the shirt is to cut vertically in the armpits and horizontally under the shirt at the waist area. This solution will allow the UVs to be unfolded without any seams visible on the shoulders.

Lesson 04: Polygonal Texturing

Project 01

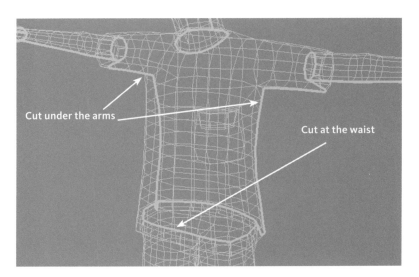

The shirt cuts

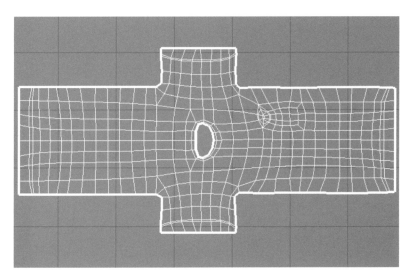

The shirt shell

5   Unfold the pants

The pants will be divided into two shells, similar to cloth panels, dividing the front and back of the pants.

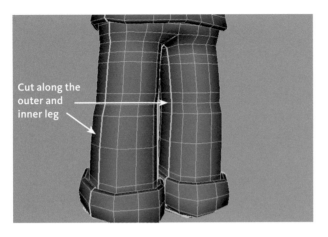

The pants cuts

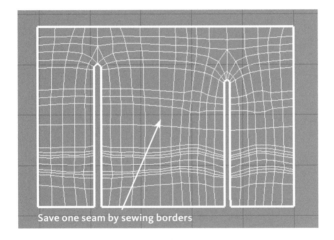

The pants shells

6   Save your work

- **Save** your scene as *04-leon texture 02.ma*.

The 0–1 UV space

Now that the entire character's UVs have been unfolded, you must place all the shells into the *0–1 UV space*. The 0–1 UV space is visible in the Texture Editor and is defined by the upper right quadrant of the grid.

When you load a texture, Maya will normalize it to be in the 0–1 space, thus making it square, regardless of its width and height.

Lesson 04: Polygonal Texturing

If you use one big texture map for your entire character, it is better to place the character's UV shells in the 0–1 space to lose as little as possible of the texture map. On the other hand, if you use multiple texture maps for your character (for instance, one map for the head, one for the body, and one for the arms and legs), you can place the UV shells into different quadrants to avoid having a tangle of UV shells in the same quadrant.

Note: *With texture wrapping, it is possible to use other quadrants besides the upper-right one. Texture wrapping repeats the texture beyond the 0–1 UV space.*

1   Place all the shells in the 0–1 UV space

For this lesson, you will use a single texture map, thus placing all the UV shells in the same quadrant.

Tip: *At the top of the Texture Editor there are buttons to flip and rotate the selected UVs.*

The toolbar buttons to flip and mirror UVs

- Place the shells to optimize usage of the 0–1 UV space.

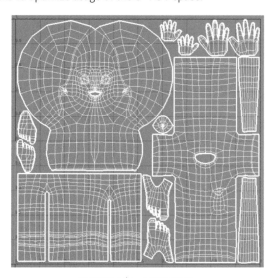

Optimized 0–1 UV space

> **Tip:** *Keep in mind when organizing the shells that some shells need more texture space than others. For instance, the face needs a lot of texture space while the inner mouth doesn't.*

2   Export UVs to paint the texture

- From the Texture Editor panel, select **Polygons** → **UV Snapshot**...

- In the UV Snapshot options, browse for the current project *sourceImages* folder, and name the output image *outUV*.

- Set the following:

    Size X and **Y** to **512**;

    Image Format to **TIFF**.

- Click the **OK** button.

    The UV snapshot image outUV.tif will be saved out to the sourceImages folder.

Open the UV snapshot image in a paint program to paint the character's texture map. When you are done painting the texture, map a file texture instead of the checker and load your new texture.

3   Using a PSD (Photoshop) texture

As an alternative to the UV snapshot, you can use Photoshop (PSD) file textures.

- Press **F6** to change the current menu set to **Rendering**.

- Select *leon*'s geometry and select **Texturing** → **Create PSD Network**.

    Doing so will display the options of the PSD network.

- In the **Attribute** section, select the **color** channel and click the **>** button.

    This will place the color channel in the PSD file.

- Set **Size X** and **Y** to **512**.

- Click the **Create** button.

    There is now a PSD file in the sourceImages folder.

Open the PSD image in Photoshop to paint the character's texture map. When you are done painting the texture, select **Texturing** →❏ **Update PSD Networks** to reload the PSD textures.

Lesson 04: Polygonal Texturing

Project 01

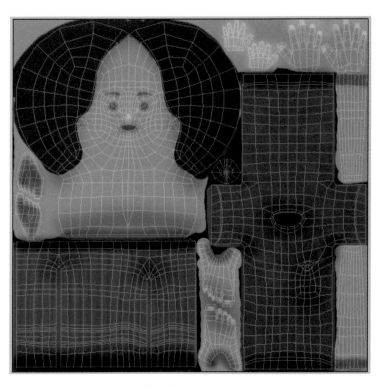

Leon's texture map

Leon with textures

4 Texture the eyes

You can now take some time to texture the rest of Leon's geometry.

- **Assign** to the eyeballs a **Phong** shader.
- **Map** the **color** channel with a **Ramp** texture.
- Set the ramp **Type** to a **U Ramp** and set the colors to your liking.

Since the eyes are NURBS surfaces, they have automatic UVs.

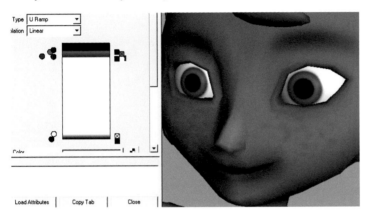

The ramp texture used for the eyes

5 Texture the bangs

Perhaps the simplest solution to texturing the bangs in this case is to simply assign to them the same lambert shader used for the body. You then only have to place the hair UVs in the hair area on the texture.

The UV placement of the bangs

6 Clean up the scene

Since this particular scene will be used later on in this book, you have to make sure it is clean, emptied of any unnecessary objects, well named, and well organized.

- Select **Edit → Delete All by Type → History.**
- **Select File → Optimize Scene Size.**
- Make sure all objects in your scene are correctly named in the Outliner.
- Make sure all the geometry is under a group named *geometry*.

The final character

7 Save your work

- **Save** your scene as *04-leon texture 03.ma*.

Conclusion

You just textured a complete character! You learned about polygonal UV mapping tools such as Planar Mapping, Cut, Sew, and Unfold UVs. You also learned about 0–1 UV space, which is very important for any texturing task. Lastly, you exported a UV snapshot and created a PSD shading network.

In the next project, you will model another character, but this time using NURBS.

Project 02

In Project Two, you are going to model Leon's little friend, the pocket squirrel named Earl. It will be modeled as a full NURBS character. This will give you the chance to explore more in-depth NURBS modeling.

You will start by reviewing the basics of NURBS components. Then you will model the squirrel's body using reference images. Once that is complete, you will model its head and attach it to the body.

These lessons offer you a good look at some of the key concepts and workflows for modeling in NURBS.

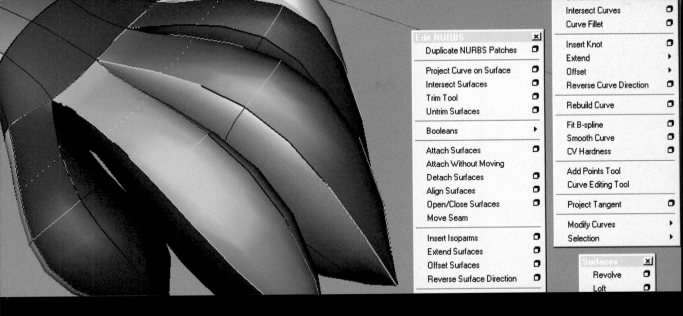

Lesson 05
NURBS Basics

NURBS modeling is a fast and easy way to produce smoothly contoured shapes. NURBS modeling tools and techniques are well suited to both organic shapes, such as people, and industrial designs, such as cars.

In this lesson you will learn the following:

What is NURBS geometry?

NURBS stands for Non-Uniform Rational B-Spline, and it is a method for producing free-form 3D curves and surfaces in Maya. NURBS curves, and the surfaces produced from those curves, are easy to work with and can achieve almost any shape.

Relationship between NURBS curves and surfaces

Essentially, a NURBS surface can be considered a grid of NURBS curves. As a result, most aspects of NURBS curves, such as degree, parameterization, direction, and form, behave the same way in surfaces as they do in curves. Surfaces simply have an additional parametric direction.

Curves

Anatomy of a NURBS curve

Every NURBS curve is made up of:

- Control vertices (CVs), which lie off the curve and define its shape;
- Hulls, which connect sequential CVs as a visual and selection aid;
- Edit points (EPs), which lie on the curve and mark the beginning and end of curve spans;
- Spans, which are the individual sections within a curve defined by edit points.

Degree

Curves in Autodesk® Maya® software can be drawn in first, second, third, fifth, or seventh degree. The higher the degree of the curve, the more complex a single span can be. The degree of a curve refers to the largest exponent value used in the polynomial equation that defines the shape of a span within the curve.

A single-span first-degree curve will be a simple straight line, and it will only be able to cross any given axis once. A first-degree curve with more than one span will look like a jagged line.

A single-span second-degree curve will be a parabola, and it will be able to cross any given axis twice.

Single-span third-degree curves are often described as *simple S's*, because they look like the letter S. Single-span third-degree curves can cross any given axis three times.

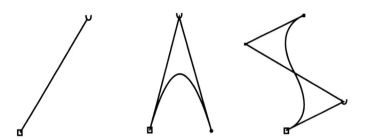

First-, second-, and third-degree single-span curves

When creating curves, the number of CVs you must place before the first span will be created is always one greater than the degree type. So to create a first-degree curve you would have to place two CVs, to create a second-degree curve you would have to place three CVs, and to create a third-degree curve you would have to place four CVs.

Parameterization

Parameterization, also known as knot spacing, refers to how Maya distributes value along the length of a curve. There are two types of parameterization in Maya: *uniform* and *chord* length.

Uniform parameterization distributes value evenly, per span, through the curve regardless of the actual length of the span. For example, a uniformly parameterized curve with 3 spans will have parametric values from 0 to 3, with the value at each edit point being 0, 1, 2, or 3. As a result, curves with uniform knot spacing have very predictable values.

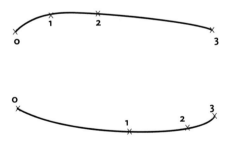

Two uniform curves and their parametric values at EPs

Since the parametric value within each span is equal, regardless of the span's length, the overall distribution of value in curves with spans of greatly different sizes can be uneven. This can lead to texturing problems in surfaces created from these curves.

Lofted surface with texture

 TIP: *While it's not essential, a good rule is to try and keep the spans in your curves roughly the same length.*

Chord length parameterization distributes value through the curve according to the physical distance between the edit points. As a result, parametric value is distributed evenly throughout the entire length of the curve.

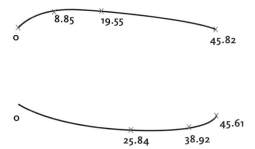

Two chord length curves and their values at the EPs

While chord length knot spacing can solve some texturing problems, the unpredictable value within the curve can lead to surface problems, such as *cross-knot insertion*.

Improved texture display   **Cross knot insertion**

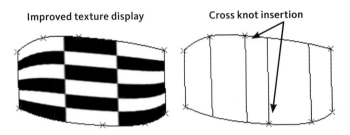

Diagram of lofted surface, with and without texture

While chord length parameterization has its uses, most modelers opt for the predictability of uniform parameterization when creating curves.

Curve direction

All NURBS curves have a U direction. The curve's U direction simply refers to the direction along the curve in which its parametric value increases. The direction of a curve is clearly indicated by the first two CVs of the curve. The CV at the beginning of the curve looks like a little square, while the second CV is indicated by a U.

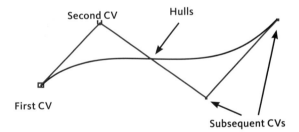

Curve with CVs and hulls displayed

Continuity

Continuity refers to the physical relationship at the intersection between two NURBS curves or surfaces. There are several levels of continuity in Maya. For the purposes of this project, you will examine the two most important levels of continuity:

- Positional continuity (or G0);
- Tangent continuity (or G1).

Positional continuity means that two curves simply intersect at their ends. If surfaces were produced from two curves with G0 continuity there would be no gaps between the surfaces, but there would be a visible seam at the intersection point. In other words, the two surfaces would look like one continuous surface with a corner.

Lesson 05: NURBS Basics

Go continuity is achieved simply by having the first or last CV of one curve on top of the first or last CV of another curve.

Go curves and surfaces

Tangent continuity means that two curves intersect at their ends with the tangent of each curve matching at the intersection point. The tangency of a curve is the direction that a curve is pointing at any given point along the curve. Surfaces produced from curves with G1 continuity will have no gaps at the point of intersection and show no visible seam. In other words, the two surfaces would look like one perfectly smooth continuous surface.

G1 continuity is achieved first by achieving Go continuity, and then by having the neighboring CVs on the curves line up. In short, having four CVs in a row equals tangent continuity.

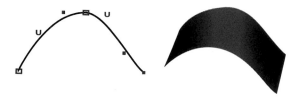

G1 curves and surfaces

G1 continuity is essential to seamless NURBS patch models.

Quality curves

Since NURBS surfaces are often created from one or more NURBS curves, it is essential that those curves be well constructed:

- Opposing curves should have the same parameterization.
- Parameterization should be consistent between curves.
- Appropriate continuity should be achieved between curves and surfaces.

Open, Closed and Periodic geometry

NURBS geometry can exist in three forms: *Open*, *Closed*, and *Periodic*.

Open curves or surfaces typically have their start and end edit points at different locations, creating a curve that looks open. However, if you were to place the first edit point on top of the last edit point so that the curve looped back on itself, it would still be considered open geometry because the edit points could still be moved away from each other.

Closed curves or surfaces are always loops because their start and end edit points lie on top of each other and are seamed together. If you select the first edit point on a closed curve and move it, the last edit point will go with it. Moving the first or last edit point of a closed curve may result in loss of G1 continuity at the seam.

Periodic curves or surfaces are also loops with a seam, but they have two unseen spans that extend past and overlap the first and last visible spans. The overlapping spans maintain G1 continuity at the seam when edit points are moved.

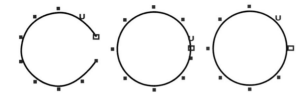

Open, Closed, and Periodic curves

Surfaces

Anatomy of a NURBS surface

Every NURBS surface is made up of:

- Control vertices (CVs), which lie off the surface and define its shape;
- Hulls, which connect sequential CVs in the surface's U and V directions;
- Isoparms, which lie on the surface, denoting consistent parametric value and defining surface spans (or patches);
- Spans, which are the individual sections defined by the isoparms.

U and V surface direction

Like NURBS curves, NURBS surfaces have directions of increasing parametric value. A surface's U and V directions will affect the orientation of a texture applied to the surface. They will also determine which direction the surface's normals face.

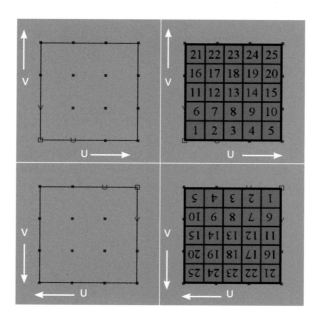

U and V surface direction and texture orientation

Degree

Like NURBS curves, surfaces can be first, second, third, fifth, or seventh degree. However, NURBS surfaces can be different degrees in their U and V directions. For example, a cylinder could be more geometrically economical by making it first degree along its length where it's straight, and third degree around its circumference.

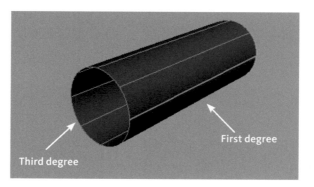

First and third degree cylinder

Normals

Like polygonal surfaces, NURBS surfaces have normals that are perpendicular to the surface. The U and V directions of a NURBS surface will determine which direction the normals face on the surface.

Commonly referred to as the *right-hand rule*, the relationship between U and V directions and a surface's normals can be predicted using your thumb, index finger and middle finger. Using your right hand, simply point your thumb in the U direction of the surface and your index finger in the V direction. Then point your middle finger so that it's perpendicular to your index finger. Your middle finger will now indicate the normal direction of the surface.

Changing surface direction

The increase in either U or V parametric value can be reversed so that it runs in the other direction. Or, the U and V directions can be swapped when necessary to reverse surface normals, reorient textures, or correct rigidbody penetration problems.

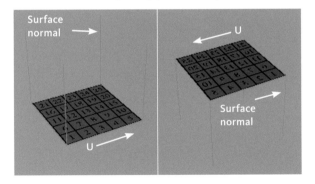

Surface normal reversed because U direction reversed

Isoparms

Isoparms are the flow lines that run through NURBS surfaces in both the U and V direction, defining the surface's shape according to the CVs. In the same way that edit points on a curve define its spans, isoparms on a surface define its patches.

In mathematical terms, isoparms indicate lines of consistent parametric value in the U or V direction of a surface. As a result of this flow of consistent value, isoparms can be used to break, or *detach*, a single NURBS surface into two separate surfaces.

Curves on surface

Like an isoparm, a *curve on surface* is a line that appears on a NURBS surface. Unlike an isoparm, it does not indicate a line of consistent parametric value; rather it defines an arbitrary boundary in the UV coordinates of the surface.

A curve on surface can be created by drawing directly on a *live* NURBS surface, by projecting an existing NURBS curve on to a surface, or by intersecting one NURBS surface with another.

A curve on surface is typically used to cut away, or *trim*, unwanted sections of a NURBS surface.

Trimming NURBS surfaces

While NURBS surfaces are extremely flexible and capable of achieving almost any shape, they are ultimately four-sided patches and, as such, have certain limitations. To overcome these limitations, NURBS surfaces can be trimmed to cut away unwanted sections. If you were modeling a surface that needed to have openings in it, such as the air vents in a bicycle helmet, you would trim those holes out.

While trimming surfaces is well suited for industrial design, it is inappropriate for models that need to deform because the trimmed boundaries will tear apart during deformation, showing gaps in the model.

NURBS tools

NURBS patch modeling relies on the effective implementation of a few tools and techniques. To speed up your workflow, you will create a custom tool shelf and fill it with the tools most commonly used during NURBS patch modeling.

1   **Create a scene file**
    - Select **File → New Scene**.

2   **Create a new shelf**
    - Select **Window → Settings/Preferences → Shelf Editor.**
    - In the displayed window, select the **Shelves** tab and click on the **New Shelf** button.
    - **Rename** the new shelf *patchModeling*.
    - Click the **Save All Shelves** button.

    There is now a new shelf displayed among the shelves of the main interface.

Tip: *If the shelves are not displayed in the main interface, select*
        Display → UI Elements → Shelf.

3 Add the Move Normal Tool to the shelf

- Hold **Ctrl+Shift** and select **Modify** → **Transformation Tools** → **Move Normal Tool**.

  The Move Normal Tool will appear on your custom tool shelf.

  This Tool allows you to move CVs along a surface's U or V direction, or along the surface's normal. The Move Normal Tool is useful for moving CVs to readjust the flow of a surface's isoparms while maintaining the original shape.

4 Attach Surfaces options

- Select the **Surfaces** menu set by pressing the **F4** hotkey on your keyboard.
- Select **Edit NURBS** → **Attach Surfaces** → ❑.
- Reset the settings by selecting **Edit** → **Reset Settings**.
- Set the following options:

      Attach Method to **Blend**;

      Blend Bias to **0.5**;

      Insert Knot to **Off**;

      Keep Original to **Off**.

- Select **Edit** → **Save Settings**.
- Click the **Close** button.

5 Add Attach Surfaces to your shelf

Now that the options for the **Attach Surfaces Tool** are set properly for your needs, you will add the tool to your new shelf.

- Hold **Ctrl+Shift** and select **Edit NURBS** → **Attach Surfaces**.

  The Attach Surfaces tool will appear on your custom tool shelf.

> **Note:** *The **Attach Surfaces** tool joins two separate NURBS surfaces into one surface.*

6 Rebuild Surfaces options

- Select **Edit NURBS** → **Rebuild Surfaces** → ❑.
- **Reset** the settings.
- Set the following options:

      Rebuild Type to **Uniform**;

      Parameter Range to **0 to #Spans**;

      Keep CVs to **On**.

- Select **Edit** → **Save Settings**.
- Click the **Close** button.

7 Add Rebuild Surfaces to your shelf

- Hold **Ctrl+Shift** and select **Edit NURBS** → **Rebuild Surfaces**.

  The Rebuild Surfaces command will appear on your custom tool shelf.

Note: *The **Rebuild Surfaces** command recreates a NURBS surface with good parameterization.*

8 Add Detach Surfaces to your shelf

- Hold **Ctrl+Shift** and select **Edit NURBS** → **Detach Surfaces**.

  The Detach Surfaces command will appear on your custom tool shelf.

  The Detach Surfaces command splits a NURBS surface at the selected isoparm(s).

9 Add Insert Isoparms to your shelf

- Hold **Ctrl+Shift** and select **Edit NURBS** → **Insert Isoparms**.

  The Insert Isoparms command will appear on your custom tool shelf.

  This command allows you to add isoparms defined on the surface.

10 Rebuild Curves options

- Select **Edit Curves** → **Rebuild Curve** → ❑.
- **Reset** the settings.
- Set the following options:

  Rebuild Type to **Uniform**;

  Parameter Range to **0 to #Spans**;

  Keep CVs to **On**.

- Select **Edit** → **Save Settings**.
- Click the **Close** button.

11 Add Rebuild Curves to your shelf

- Hold **Ctrl+Shift** and select **Edit Curves** → **Rebuild Curve**.

  The Rebuild Curve command works just like Rebuild Surfaces except that it works on curves.

12 Add the Rebuild Surfaces Option Window to your shelf

- Hold **Ctrl+Shift** and select **Edit NURBS** → **Rebuild Surfaces** → ☐.

  When you press this shelf button, the Rebuild Surfaces option window will be displayed.

13 Add a Rebuild Curves Option Window to your shelf

- Hold **Ctrl+Shift** and select **Edit Curve** → **Rebuild Curve** → ☐.

  When you press this shelf button, the Rebuild Curve option window will be displayed.

14 Global Stitch options

- Select **Edit NURBS** → **Stitch** → **Global Stitch** → ☐.
- **Reset** the settings.
- Set the following options:

  Stitch Corners to **Closest Knot**;

  Stitch Edges to **Match Params**;

  Stitch Smoothness to **Normals**;

  Max Separation to **0.1**;

  Modification Resistance to **10.0**;

  Sampling Density to **1**;

  Keep Original to **Off**.

- Select **Edit** → **Save Settings**.
- Click the **Close** button.

15 Add the Global Stitch Tool to your shelf

- Hold **Ctrl+Shift** and select **Edit NURBS** → **Stitch** → **Global Stitch**.

  The Global Stitch tool sews multiple NURBS surfaces together to make them appear to be one piece.

16 Label the shelf icons

- Select **Window** → **Settings/Preferences** → **Shelf Editor**.
- Select the **Shelf Contents** tab.
- Highlight the rebuildSurfaceDialogItem item.
- Set the **Icon Name** to *Options*.
- Highlight the Rebuild Curve Option Box item.
- Set the **Icon Name** to *Options*.
- Click the **Save All Shelves** button.

Doing so will save your shelf preferences on disk for your next Maya session.

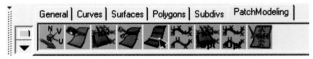

The new custom shelf

Tip: *You can also save your preferences by selecting* **File → Save Preferences.**

Socking

You will now work through a typical NURBS modeling example. Complex shapes, like shoulders, can be difficult to achieve if not approached properly. One of the principal techniques used in NURBS patch modeling is what is commonly referred to as *socking*. Socking is the practice of repeatedly attaching, detaching, and rebuilding NURBS patches to create an integrated network of patches that appear to be seamless. Socking will be used extensively in the next lesson.

Note: *NURBS patches are always four-sided, but borders of CVs can be all at the same location, thus giving the impression of surfaces without four sides.*

1   Create two primitive NURBS surfaces

In a new scene, you will use half a sphere and a cylinder to represent a simplified version of a shoulder and arm.

- Select **Create → NURBS Primitives → Sphere.**

Tip: *If you want Maya to create the primitive at the center of the world, you can toggle Off* **Create → NURBS Primitives → Interactive Creation** *menu item.*

- **RMB** on the sphere and select **Isoparm.**
- Select the vertical isoparm that appears thicker than the other ones.

  This specific isoparm indicates the UV start and end of the surface.

- **Detach** the sphere by clicking on the appropriate shelf button.

  Even if it doesn't look like you detached the surface, you just opened the sphere along that isoparm.

- **Select** the vertical opposite isoparm.
- **Detach** the sphere again by clicking on the appropriate shelf button.

  The sphere is now split into two parts.

Project 02

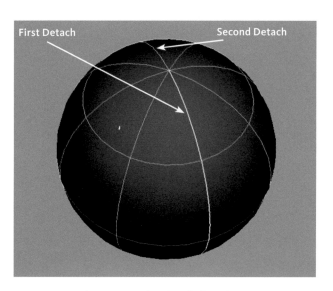

Isoparms used to detach the sphere

- **Delete** one half of the sphere.
- Select the remaining half, and then select **Edit → Delete by Type → History.**
- Select **Create → NURBS Primitives → Cylinder → ▢.**
- n the options, set the following:

   Caps to **None;**

   Sections to **8**.
- **Move** and **rotate** the cylinder as follows:

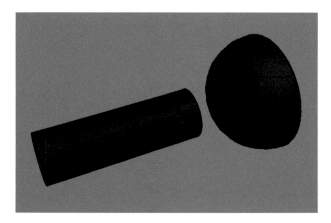

Simple arm and shoulder

TIP: *Change the view's shading mode to display* **WIREFRAME ON SHADED** *to always see the isoparms, even when the surfaces are not selected.*

Because of the layout of each surface's topology, it will be impossible to create a smooth transition between them by simply attaching. To solve this problem, you will detach both surfaces into multiple pieces, and then strategically reattach them to each other.

2 Rebuild the sphere

During the socking process, pieces from the sphere will be attached to corresponding surfaces in the cylinder. As a result, the way each piece is broken up will have a tremendous impact on the final transition between the two surfaces. To facilitate the transition of the topology from the cylinder to the sphere, you will rebuild the sphere to have more spans.

- Select the sphere and then click on **Rebuild Surfaces Opt** from the shelf.
- Set the following:

    Keep CVs to **Off**.

    Number of Spans to **8** in both **U** and **V**.

- Click the **Rebuild** button.

    The sphere now has more spans to work with.

3 Detach the sphere at an isoparm

- **RMB** on the sphere and select **Isoparms.**
- Drag a selection box to select the following **4** isoparms:

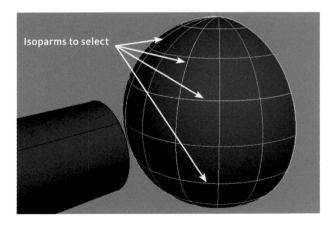

Isoparms to select

Simple arm and shoulder

> **Tip:** *Clicking on an isoparm will select it and highlight it yellow. If you **click+drag** on an isoparm, the selection becomes a dotted yellow line, which means you are defining a new isoparm. By selecting isoparms using the selection box, you are guaranteed to select only existing isoparms and not define new ones.*

- Click on the **Detach Surface** shelf icon.

  By doing so, Maya will detach the selected isoparms one after the other and not all at once. Because of that, the surface will not be entirely cut at once.

- Continue detaching the sphere until it has been divided into **9** pieces.

4 Delete the center surface

- Select the surface at the center of the nine patches and **delete** it.

5 Rebuild the cylinder

- **Rebuild** the cylinder to have **8** spans in **U** and **V**.

6 Detach the cylinder into four slices

- Select the four isoparms on the cylinder that flow into the corners created by the missing surface on the sphere.

- **Detach** the cylinder.

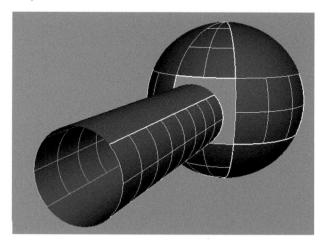

Detached sphere and cylinder

7   Attach the cylinder surfaces to the sphere surfaces

- Select the top surface on both the sphere and the cylinder.

- Click on the **Attach Surfaces** shelf icon.

- Click on the **Rebuild Surfaces Tool** to rebuild the surfaces.

> **Note:** *You should generally rebuild a surface with the **Keep CVs** option after you attach it. Rebuilding with Keep CVs forces the CVs to hold their position, allowing the surface to maintain its shape while the parameterization of the surface is cleaned up.*

8   Repeat for the other surfaces

- **Repeat** the process outlined above to attach each of the remaining cylinder surfaces.

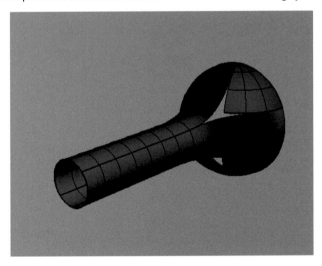

Cylinder surfaces attached to sphere surfaces

9   Detach where you just attached

- Select the isoparm nearest the point where the attachment occurred and **detach** there.

10 Narrow the gap at the top right corner

Attaching the cylinder and sphere surfaces begins the transition between the two, but there are still big gaps at the corners. To correct this, you will now attach, rebuild, and detach the corners.

- Select the top-right surface in the sphere, and then **Shift-select** the adjacent surface below it.

- **Attach** the two surfaces.
- **Rebuild** the new surface.
- Select the isoparm where the attachment just occurred and **detach** there.
- Select the second surface from the last operation, and then **Shift-select** the surface below it.
- **Attach**, **rebuild,** and **detach** the surface.
- **Repeat** this process until you have attached, rebuilt, and detached all of the surfaces in the corner of the sphere and cylinder.

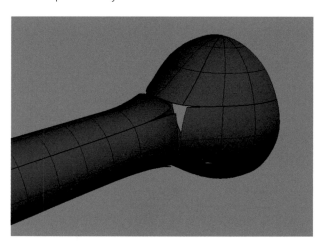

The current patches

11 **Deleting the history**

Each of the commands outlined above will generate a construction history node for the surfaces. In order to keep your scene clean, you should delete the construction history to delete unnecessary history nodes.

- Select all of the surfaces, and then select **Edit → Delete by Type → History**.

12 **Apply a Global Stitch**

- Select all of the surfaces and click on the **Global Stitch** button on your shelf.

> **Note:** *It is possible that the Global Stitch doesn't entirely close the surfaces because the gaps can be too wide. The following step will solve this issue.*

13 Adjust the Max Separation value

If there are still gaps between your surfaces, you may need to adjust your **Max Separation** value.

- Select one of the surfaces just stitched.

- Select *GlobalStitch1* in the **Inputs** section of the Channel Box.

- Increase the **Max Separation** value in small increments until the gaps disappear.

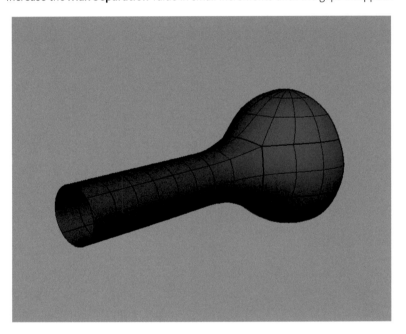

Cylinder and sphere surfaces, once they have been stitched together

Note: *You can delete the history to remove the* **Global Stitch** *from the models' construction history, but the stitch will ensure that gaps never appear between patches as they are moving or deforming.*

Conclusion

In this lesson, you learned about the various principles of NURBS geometry, including curve and surface degree, parameterization, curve direction and quality, and changing curve and surface direction. You have also learned the basics of NURBS modeling, which consist of stitching patches together to create a more complex model.

In the next lesson, you will apply these principles to build Leon's squirrel friend using NURBS patches.

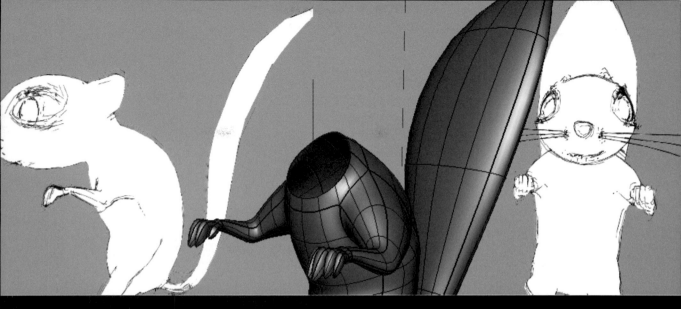

Modeling the Squirrel's Body

In this lesson you will build the squirrel's body out of NURBS patches using an organic modeling technique commonly referred to as socking. Organic NURBS modeling relies more on strategy and technique than on complex tools.

In this lesson you will learn the following:

The torso

The first step in building a NURBS patch body is to block out the character with NURBS primitives, such as cylinders and spheres. You will begin modeling the squirrel by opening a scene file that already has image planes set up.

1   **Scene file**

   • Open the file called *06-squirrel body 01.ma*.

     The squirrel's front, side and top reference image planes have already been set up in this scene.

The reference images

2   **Create a default NURBS cylinder**

   • Select **Create → NURBS Primitives → Cylinder**.

   • Using the *front* and *side* reference images, **move** and **scale** the cylinder so it roughly matches the proportions of the squirrel's torso.

Tip: *You can use* **View Cube** *to quickly change between views.*

The Perspective View Cube

3   Increase the number of spans in the U direction

- Select the *cylinder*'s *makeNurbCylinder1* construction history node in the **Inputs** section of the Channel Box.

- Increase the value for **Spans** to **4**.

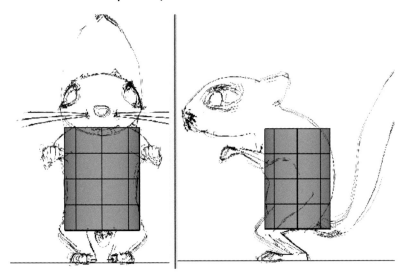

The cylinder in position

Note: *It is important to keep the number of spans in your NURBS surfaces to a minimum during the geometry-blocking process. Keeping your geometry light makes it easier to work with. You should always try to achieve as much shape in the surface as possible with the existing CVs before adding more.*

Lesson 06: Modeling the Squirrel's Body

Shaping the torso

You are about to start editing the torso cylinder by manipulating CVs and hulls directly. In addition to the shape of the surface, the flow of topology will also be adjusted.

1   Delete history from the cylinder

Since changing values associated with the construction history will cause unpredictable results if components are manipulated, you should delete the cylinder's construction history.

- With the cylinder highlighted, select **Edit → Delete by Type → History**.

2   Shape the cylinder

- **RMB** on the cylinder and select **Hulls**.

- One at a time, **LMB** on each hull running horizontally across the cylinder, and then **move**, **rotate** and **scale** them until the cylinder matches the image plane as closely as possible.

You should have the top of the cylinder flowing into the squirrel's neck and the bottom of the cylinder flowing into the squirrel's tail.

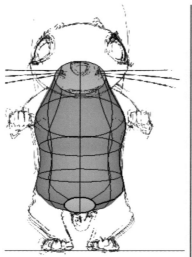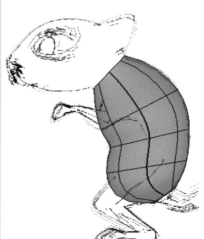

The basic shape of the torso

 Tip: *Remember to work in the front and side views.*

3 Use the Move Normal Tool to adjust the flow of geometry

Once you are satisfied with the shape of the torso, you should adjust the flow of topology by using the **Move Normal Tool** to move CVs. This tool will allow you to move CVs along the surface, minimizing changes to the shape of the surface.

- **RMB** on the cylinder and select **Control Vertex.**

- Select CVs in the chest area of the cylinder.

- Change to the **Move Normal Tool** by clicking on your custom shelf button.

- **Move** the CVs along the surface's **N** direction by **click+dragging** on the manipulator's N handle.

- Continue adjusting CVs until you are satisfied with the flow of the surface's isoparms.

> **Note:** *Good topological flow makes sculpting your surface easier and ensures that your model will deform properly when it is bound. Whenever possible, it is a good idea to establish good topological flow early in the model when the geometry is light. That way, as you increase the number of spans in a surface, the topology is maintained.*

4 Delete one half of the cylinder

- **RMB** on the cylinder and select **Isoparm.**

- Select the isoparm at the front center of the cylinder.

- **Detach** the surface.

- Select the isoparm at the back center of the torso and **detach** again.

  The cylinder should now be divided into two pieces.

- **Delete** the right piece.

The torso starting to take shape

Lesson 06: Modeling the Squirrel's Body

Note: *Later on, you will mirror the geometry on the right side of the character. Doing so will save you a lot of modeling work.*

5 Save your work

- Save the scene as *06-squirrel body 02.ma*.

The arm and leg

Now you will create the squirrel's arm and leg using other primitives. Those primitives will later be modified to be socked to the torso.

1 Create the arm

- Select **Create** → **NURBS Primitives** → **Cylinder** → ❐, and set the following options:

   Axis to **Z**;

   Number of Spans to **2**.

- Click the **Create** button.

- **Move**, **rotate** and **scale** the cylinder to roughly match the arm in the image planes.

- **Tweak** the shape of the cylinder by manipulating its hulls and CVs.

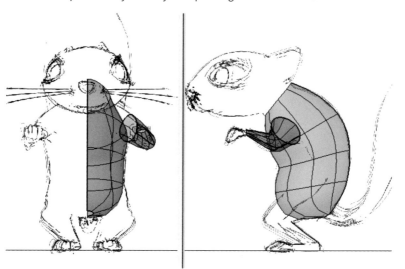

The arm cylinder

> **Tip:** Showing both the hulls and CVs at the same time makes their position relative to each others easier to see.

2 Create the shoulder

You will now create a NURBS sphere to define the character's deltoid and shoulder.

- Select **Create → NURBS Primitives → Sphere**.

- **Move**, **rotate**, and **scale** the *sphere* to match the squirrel's deltoid and shoulder.

  When placing the sphere, you should make sure to place the poles pointing into the arm and attempt to align the isoparms together.

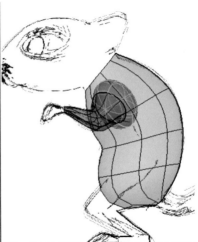

The shoulder sphere

3 Create the leg

- **Create** a default **NURBS cylinder** aligned with the **Y-axis**.

- **Move**, **rotate**, and **scale** the cylinder at the knee location.

- **Tweak** the cylinder to fit the leg from the crotch to the ankle.

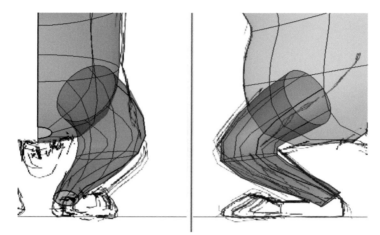

The leg cylinder

> **Note:** *There is only so much you can do with primitive objects. Don't worry about the details yet.*

4 Save your work

- Save the scene as *06-squirrel body 03.ma*.

Refining the torso

Now that all the pieces are in place, you will refine the surfaces' shapes before socking the arm and leg to the torso.

1 Increase the torso's number of spans

As you increase the number of spans on the torso, you have to think about how you will cut the model to connect the arm and leg. It is not good to simply add a bunch of spans since you want to keep the geometry as light as possible.

- With the *torso* selected, click on the **Rebuild Surfaces Opt** shelf button.

- **Reset** the settings.

- Set the following options:

   Rebuild type to **Uniform**;

   Parameter Range to **0 to # Spans**;

   Direction to **U and V**;

   Number of Spans U to **8**;

   Number of Spans V to **6**.

- Click the **Rebuild** button.

  The number of divisions has increased on the torso, giving you more isoparms to use for socking. Notice how there is one patch directly under the shoulder sphere and two patches directly under the leg cylinder. This is where the body parts will be socked to the torso.

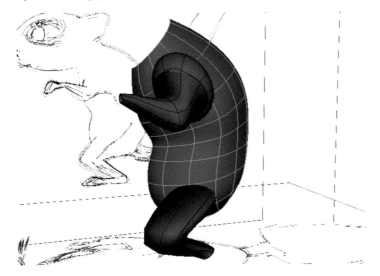

New topology of the torso

Note: *As you build your character, it is a good idea to refine the character as a whole.*

Using lattices for refinements

Sometimes, it is hard to deform a piece of geometry using only the CVs. In this example, you will use a lattice deformer to refine the shape of the shoulder.

1   **Create a lattice**

- Select the shoulder *sphere.*

- From the **Animation** menu set, select **Create Deformers → Lattice**.

- In the Channel Box under the *ffd1LatticeShape*, set the following:

    S Divisions to **3**;

    T Divisions to **5**;

    U Divisions to **3**.

Lesson 06: Modeling the Squirrel's Body

Project 02

2 Shape the deltoid

- **RMB** on the lattice and select **Lattice Point**.
- **Move** lattice points to refine the deltoid into a muscular shape that flows into the arm.

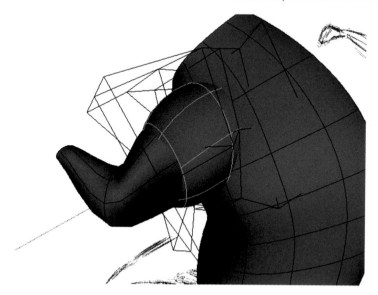

Shoulder deformed by a lattice

3 Remove the lattice by deleting history

- Select the *sphere* and select **Edit → Delete By Type → History**.

> **Note:** *Simply deleting a deformer from a piece of geometry will result in the surface snapping back to its original, undeformed shape.*

Attach the arm and shoulder

You will now sock the shoulder to the arm by doing a series of strategic attachments and detachments similar to the socking example in the last lesson.

1 Detach the shoulder

- **Detach** and **rebuild** the vertical isoparm on the shoulder where it meets with the arm.
- **Delete** the part of the shoulder that is inside the upper arm.

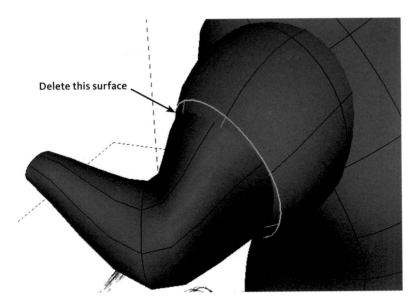

Detach and delete a shoulder section

- **Detach** and **rebuild** the vertical isoparm on the shoulder sphere where it intersects with the torso.

- **Delete** the portion inside the torso.

Tip: *You don't need to always select an existing isoparm on the surface. Instead, you can define a new place to detach.*

2   Moving a seam

At this point, you can attach the arm and shoulder, but if the seams on the two surfaces are not properly aligned, you might get a twisting result. You will now learn how to change the location of a seam.

- Notice the seam location on the arm surface. It is the isoparm thicker than the other ones.

- Select the closest relative isoparm on the shoulder.

- Select **Edit NURBS → Move Seam.**

  The surface will be rebuilt to have a seam at the specified location.

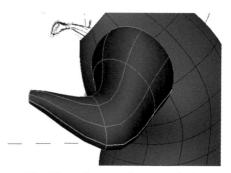

The aligned seams　　　　　　　　*Shoulder and arm surfaces attached*

Note: *If your surfaces attach at edges other than the ones you intended, you will have to indicate where you want the attachment to occur on each surface. Do this by picking an isoparm near the edge where you want the attachment to occur.*

3 **Attach the arm to the shoulder**

- Select the *shoulder* surface and **Shift-select** the *arm* surface.

- **Attach** the two surfaces together.

Note: *When you're attaching surfaces, both surfaces must either have the same number of spans or the number of spans must be multiples of each other. If not, cross knot insertion will occur, resulting in poorly parameterized surfaces.*

Tip: *Just as on polygonal objects, you will want to hide any seams as much as possible to prevent texture problems. Always place seams in hidden locations when possible.*

4 **Blend Bias value**

When attaching surfaces, the Attach tool blends between the two original surfaces in the attachment area. Adjusting the **Blend Bias** value controls which surface's shape exerts more influence over the shape of the new attached surface.

- Select the *attachSurface1* that was created in the previous step in the **Inputs** section of the Channel Box.

- Adjust the **Blend Bias** of the attachment by changing the value between **0** and **1**.

OR

- Highlight the **Blend Bias** attribute and **MMB+drag** in the view to invoke the virtual slider.

5 **Rebuild the surface**

- **Rebuild** the new arm surface.

Note: *If rebuilding your surfaces with Keep CVs set to On results in a poorly parameterized surface, then one or both of the surfaces probably have poor parameterization. Try to undo the attach operation and then rebuild each surface before attaching opened, closed or periodic surfaces*

In the arm case, the surface needs to be closed and periodic in its V direction. You can check this by doing the following.

- Select the *arm* surface.
- Open the Attribute Editor and check its shape characteristic.
- Under the **NURBS Surface History**, you will see the **Form V** is set to **Periodic**.
- This means that the arm surface is properly closed. If it is not a periodic surface, then you need to use the **Edit NURBS → Open/Close Surface** command to close it properly.

Refining the shape of the arm

Now that the arm and shoulder are in one piece, the arm's shape will be refined slightly to develop the elbow area.

1 **Blinn material**

A blinn material is very useful in modeling, since its specular highlights will make it easier to judge subtle contouring in the surfaces.

- Select all NURBS surfaces.
- Press **F6** to change to the **Rendering** menu set.
- Select **Lighting/Shading → Assign New Material → Blinn**.

The new blinn material will be assigned to all selected surfaces and the Attribute Editor will display the material's attributes.

- Notice how the blinn highlights shine on surfaces as you move the perspective camera.
- **Rename** the material to *bodyBlinn*.

2 **Freeze transformations**

When modeling with NURBS surfaces, you may notice darker areas in the surface's shading. This is due to the surface normals being affected by the work you have done. In order to correct the surface's normals, you can do the following:

Project 02

- Select **Edit → Delete All by Type → History**.
- With all the surfaces selected, select **Modify → Freeze Transformations**.

  Notice how the surfaces' highlights are changing.

3 Arm definition

- Highlight an extra circular isoparm near the elbow by **click+dragging** on the arm surface.
- Click the **Insert Isoparm** button in your shelf.

  The new isoparm is defined and is intended to add topology in the elbow area to help for deformation purposes.

- **Rebuild** the surface with **Keep CVs** set to **On**.
- **Move** the CVs to refine the elbow geometry.

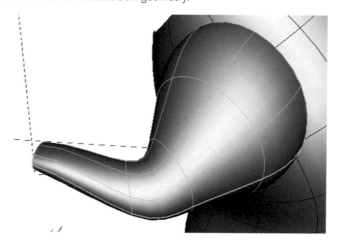

Elbow refinements

4 Save your work

- Save the scene as *06-squirrel body 04.ma*.

Sock the arm to the torso

The process of blocking out your character is generally the longest phase of modeling the NURBS body. Now, at the end of this phase, you should have a series of independent NURBS surfaces with the correct proportions and essentially the proper shape for your character.

Next you will sock the pieces together to create an integrated series of patches.

1   Detach the arm and the torso

When socking, it is important to plan ahead when detaching the pieces to be socked. You should always consider how the two surfaces will flow into each other when they are attached. Generally, the isoparms should flow together in corners. The number of spans on the surfaces is not an important consideration because the surfaces can easily be rebuilt prior to attaching.

- **Detach** the arm horizontally into four sections of two spans each.

    This will allow the attachment of the arm to a square patch on the torso.

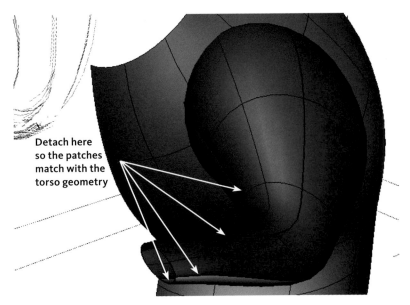

Detach here so the patches match with the torso geometry

Arm patches

> **Note:** *In order to make it easier to see the patches, colored shaders are assigned to the different pieces.*

- **Repeat** to break up the upper torso into **nine** pieces.

    You will have to insert an isoparm at the neck. The four pieces corresponding to the arm surfaces should have two spans each.

- **Delete** the patch of the torso located under the arm.

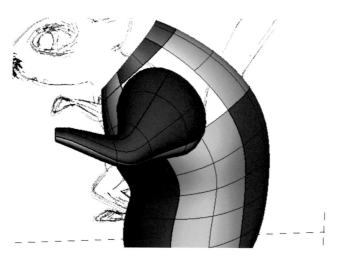

The detached torso

2   Rebuild where necessary

- **Rebuild** detached surfaces so that each one has the same number of isoparms as the surface it is about to be attached to.

> **Tip:**   If one surface has three spans and the other has two, you should rebuild the surface with the lower number of spans to match the surface with the larger number. Otherwise you are likely to lose detail when the denser surface is rebuilt. Remember that surfaces with spans that are evenly divisible don't need to be rebuilt before attaching.

3   Narrow the gaps between the shoulder and torso surfaces

- Working your way around the shoulder, **attach**, **rebuild**, and **detach** the surfaces of the arm and torso to narrow the gaps between them.

4   Apply a Global Stitch

- Once you have attached all around the shoulder, select all of the surfaces and click the **Global Stitch** button on your tool shelf.

5   Adjust the Max Distance value

Chances are there will still be gaps between some of your surfaces after the stitch is applied. If necessary, select the *globalStitch* node in the **Inputs** section of the Channel Box and increase the **Max Separation** value until the gaps close.

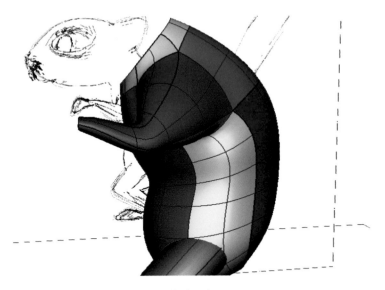

Arm socked to the torso

Note: *In some cases you will find that increasing the **Max Separation** value starts stitching unwanted vertices together before it closes all of the holes. If this happens, there are two things you can do. First, lower the **Max Separation** value until the unwanted stitching is corrected, and then select just the surfaces with the gap. Apply a new global stitch to them, and adjust the **Max Separation** value for this stitching. Second, you could undo the **Global Stitch** and then try narrowing the gap further by repeating the attach, detach, rebuild process in the area with the excessive gap. Following that, apply the global stitch.*

6   Delete the construction history

Delete all the construction history in order to make the changes to the model permanent.

7   Save your work

- Save the scene as *06-squirrel body 05.ma*.

Flow of topology

When building a character, it is essential that the topology flows well to ensure good deformation once the character is bound. While following this lesson, you must make sure to redirect the flow of topology between the different NURBS patches.

1 Arm flow

Take some time to make sure the flow of topology of the arm is adequate. The patch on the top of the shoulder should flow to end up being the patch on top of the wrist. If you notice some twisting, you must correct the situation either by tweaking the CVs or by cutting the arm at the wrist and then offsetting the detach location to finally reattach the arm together.

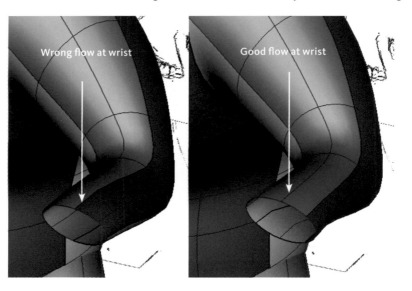

Different flow of topology

Attaching the leg

Getting the topology to flow between the leg and the torso needs much more planning.
It is not uncommon for a patch modeler to start over several times before getting the optimal stitching solution.

1 Insert isoparms to the leg

- **Insert** two isoparms on the leg surface, one in the middle of the upper leg and the other near the ankle.
- **Rebuild** the surface.

2 Detach the torso

- **Detach** the torso horizontally above and below the leg.
- **Rebuild** the resulting surfaces.

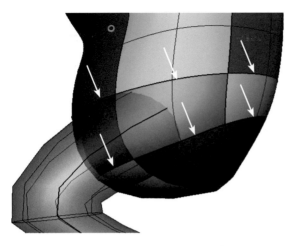

Detach the torso horizontally

3   Outer leg

- **Detach** and **rebuild** a patch with two spans on the outside of the leg.
- **Attach** the new patch to the one on the outside of the torso.

Attached outer leg

- **Detach** where you have just attached and **rebuild** the surfaces.

4   Top of the leg

- **Detach** and **rebuild** a patch with one span on the top of the leg.

Lesson 06: Modeling the Squirrel's Body

- **Detach** and **rebuild** a patch with one span on the front of the torso.
- **Attach** the new patch on the top of the leg to the corresponding one on the torso.
- **Detach** where you have just attached and **rebuild** the surfaces.

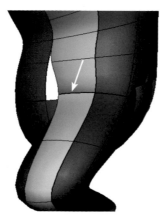

Attached top leg

5 Inner leg

- **Detach** and **rebuild** a patch with two spans on the inside of the leg.
- **Detach** and **rebuild** a patch with one span horizontally on the belly.
- **Attach** the new patch on the inside of the leg to the corresponding one on the belly.

  The patch with one span is automatically rebuilt to have two spans.

- **Detach** where you have just attached and **rebuild** the surfaces.

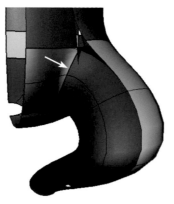

Attached inner leg

6   Under the leg

- **Detach** and **rebuild** a patch with one span under the torso.
- **Attach** the new patch to the two-span neighbor to create a three-span patch.

  The patch with three-spans now fits with the remaining patch on the leg.

- **Attach** the corresponding patches together.
- **Detach** where you have just attached and **rebuild** the surfaces.

Attached under leg

The patch to delete

7   Delete unnecessary pieces

- **Delete** the torso pieces inside the leg that were not attached so far.
- **Delete** the extra patch in the lower back since it is no longer required.
- **Attach** the corresponding lower back patches together.
- **Detach** where you have just attached and **rebuild** the surfaces.

8   Stitch it all together

- Select **Edit → Delete All By Type → History**.
- Work your way into stitching all the body pieces together.
- Select all of the surfaces and apply a **Global Stitch**.
- Adjust the **Max Separation** value as necessary.

> **Tip:**   *If you need to repeat the global stitch, you should first delete all the construction history.*

Lesson 06: Modeling the Squirrel's Body

9 **Refine the geometry**

When a patch model is stitched together, you can use the **Sculpt Geometry Tool** to refine the shape of the geometry further. Select all the patches that you wish to sculpt.

- Select **Edit NURB→ Sculpt Geometry Tool**.

- **Sculpt** the surfaces.

    The Global Stitch applied in the previous step will make sure to keep the patches together as you sculpt the model.

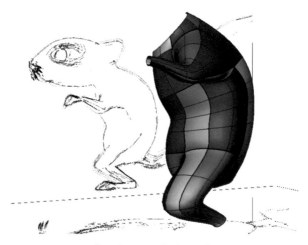

All surfaces stitched together

10 **Save your work**

- Save the scene as *06-squirrel body 06.ma*.

Model the tail

The tail can be thought of as only a cylinder. In this step, you will use a curve to extrude the tail and then you will sock it to the body.

1 **Draw a curve**

- Select **Create → EP Curve Tool.**

- From the *side* view, draw a curve composed of about seven points based on the shape of the tail in the reference image.

2 **Extrude the tail**

- Select **Create → NURBS Primitives → Circle.**

- In the **Inputs** section of the Channel Box, set the *makeNurbCircle1*'s Sections attribute to 12.

  This number of spans will match with the number of spans on the torso.

- Select the *circle* then **Shift-select** the tail *curve*.

- Select **Surfaces → Extrude → ❏.**

- In the options, set the following:

  > **Style** to **Tube**;

  > **Result position** to **At path**;

  > **Pivot** to **Component**;

  > **Orientation** to **Profile normal**;

  > **Curve range** to **Complete**;

  > **Output geometry** to **NURBS**.

- Click the **Extrude** button.

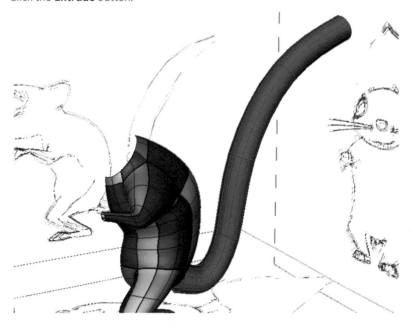

The tail extrusion

3 Shape the tail

- Take some time to shape the tail according to the reference images, using the CVs and hulls, or with a lattice deformer.

- **Scale** the tip of the tail flat on its **X-axis**.

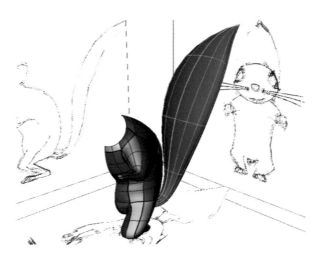

The refined tail

4   Sock the tail

Using what you have learned so far, sock half of the tail to the body and delete the other half.

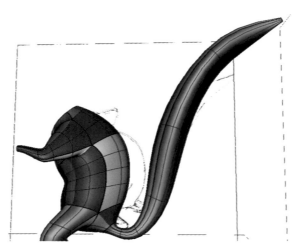

The socked tail

5   Clean up

- **Apply** a global stitch.
- **Delete** all the construction history.
- **Delete** the two curves used for the tail extrusion.

NURBS hands and feet

Building NURBS hands and feet uses the same techniques that have been explored so far, but requires much more time and planning. In order to speed things up, you will import the basic hands and feet from the support files.

1   Import basic hand and foot

- Select **File → Import → □**.

- In the options, turn **Off** the **Use Namespaces** option and set **Resolve Clashing nodes with the file name**.

- Click the **Import** button.

- Select the scene called *o6-squirrel hand foot.ma.*

  The new geometry is now ready to be integrated in your scene.

- Place the hand and the foot to its proper location according to your model and the image planes.

2   Detach the knuckles area

- **Detach** and **rebuild** the fingers.

  The finger patches should have one patch each on top and bottom and two patches each on the sides.

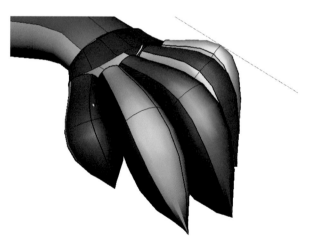

The finger patches

3   Attach the fingers

- **Attach** the surfaces between the fingers to each other.

Tip: *Don't forget to pick the isoparms directly if the surfaces don't attach as you expect.*

- **Detach** and **rebuild** where you have just attached.
- **Repeat** for all the finger in-betweens.
- Since the attach operations moved the surfaces away from the palm, select the CVs affected by the attachments and **move** them closer to the palm.

4 Stitch the fingers and knuckles

- Select all the hand patches that were not involved in the previous step.
- Use a **Global Stitch** to sock the finger and knuckle surfaces to each other.
- Change the **Max Separation** value to **0.08**.

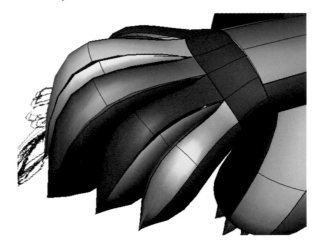

Fingers stitched to the knuckles

5 Stitch the entire hand

- **Delete** all the construction history.
- Select the entire hand surfaces.
- Apply a **Global Stitch**.

  Doing so will collapse the tip of the fingers the wrong way. You will have to change some attributes for the Global Stitch.

- In the **Channel Box**, highlight the *globalStitch1* node and set the following:

Stitch Smoothness to **Off**;

Max Separation value to **0.08**.

- The hand should now be properly stitched. If not, repeat this step or try to get the surfaces closer together.

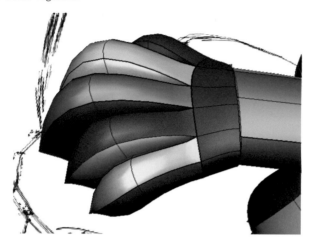

The stitched hand

- **Delete** all the construction history.

6   Attach the hand to the arm

The hand can now be stitched to the arm, but the number of spans on the wrist does not match those of the arm. You will have to propagate a new isoparm on both the top and bottom arm patches, along with all the other patches connected to them. The patches on either sides of the arm do match up to the double of spans on the wrist.

- Select the top patch of the arm.

   You will need to rebuild this patch to have three spans along the arm.

- Select the **Rebuild Surfaces Options** shelf button.

- Change **Direction** for either **U** or **V** depending on your surface's direction.

> **Tip:**   You can easily see which direction to change by openning the Attribute Editor and looking at the Spans UV values.

- Set the **Number of spans U** or **V** to **3**.

- **Propagate** this span change to the neck patch.

- **Redo** this step for the patch under the arm, and propagate the span change all the way to the leg.

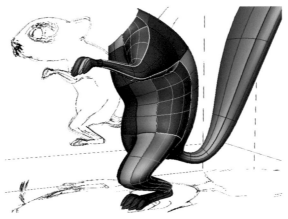

The patches to change the number of spans

> **Note:** *It is not uncommon when modeling in patches to be forced to propagate more spans throughout the entire model. Since this adds a lot of topology to the model, it is the reason why you must keep the resolution of your character to its minimum throughout the modeling process.*

- Apply a **Global Stitch** to all the patches without the fingers.

7   Repeat for the foot

The same process used for the hand can be used to stitch the foot to the leg. The only exception is that this time, you will have to propagate spans only in the inside of the leg onto the belly, where they will add as little topology to the model as possible.

Attached toes and ankle

8   Save your work

- Save the scene as *06-squirrel body 07.ma*.

Final touches

1   Assign a blinn

- Select all the patches.

- Select **Lighting/Shading → Assign Existing Material → bodyBlinn**.

OR

- Select **Lighting/Shading → Assign New Material → Blinn**.

2   Reverse normals

- Select all the patches.

- Select **Display → NURBS → Normals (Shaded Mode)**.

Note: *NURBS normals display only in shaded mode.*

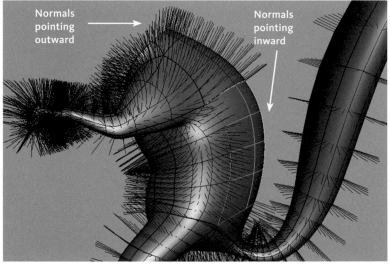

Direction of normals

- Select patches whose normals seem to be pointing inward.

- Select **Edit NURBS → Reverse Surface Direction → ❑**.

- Set the options to reverse either in **U** or **V** and click the **Apply** button.
- **Repeat** until there are no more reversed surfaces on the entire character.
- Select all the patches and turn **Off** the normals' display.

3   **Mirror and stitch**
- Select all the patches and **group** them.
- **Duplicate** the group and set **Scale X** to **-1**.
- If required, **snap** the central CVs to the **X-axis**.
- **Attach** the center surfaces two by two.
- Apply a **Global Stitch** on all the surfaces with the **Stitch Smoothness** set to **Off** and a **Max Separation** value of **0.08**.

4   **Clean up**
- Select all the patches.
- Select **Modify** → **Center Pivot**.
- Select **Modify** → **Freeze Transformations**.
- Select **Edit** → **Delete All By Type** → **History**.
- Select **File** → **Optimize Scene Size**.
- **Group** and **rename** everything properly

The squirrel body

5 Save your work

- Save the scene as *06-squirrel body 08.ma.*

Conclusion

In this lesson you learned how to block out a character with primitives, how to sock geometry together, and how to redirect and propagate topology. The character modeled here was quite simple and without any muscular definition, but in order to create more complex characters, you will need to perfect your skills by progressively increasing the level of difficulty.

In the next lesson you will expand what you have learned so far by creating a NURBS head. Instead of starting with primitive surfaces, you will begin by building a network of NURBS curves that will be used to generate the patches.

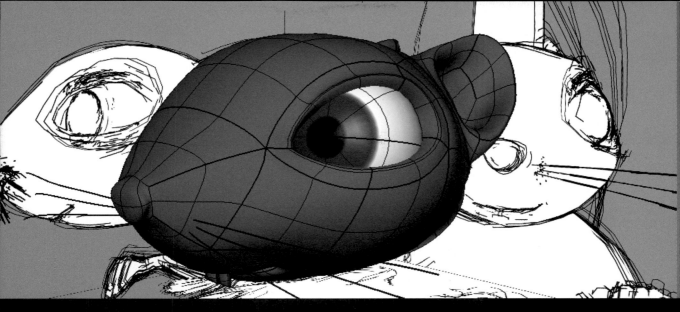

Lesson 07
Modeling the Squirrel's Head

In this lesson, you will build a squirrel's head to attach to the NURBS body built in the previous lesson. First, a network of NURBS curves will be created for the framework of the head. A series of NURBS patches will then be produced from those curves. Finally, the surfaces will be socked together.

In this lesson you will learn the following:

- How to continue modeling from an existing model;

Create profile curves

The first step in creating the NURBS head will be to create a network of curves that will serve as the basis for the final surfaces. You will attempt to make the profile curves follow the natural structure of facial muscles. As a result, the surfaces created from these curves will have good topologies that will help deform them correctly.

1 **Scene file**

   • Open the scene file *07-squirrel head 01.ma* from the support files.

   This scene already has image planes set up for reference. There is also the modeled neck piece from the previous lesson from which you will start modeling.

2 **Duplicate the border curve from the neck surface**

   Since the head needs to conform to the body, you will start by duplicating curves from the isoparm at the top of the existing neck patches.

   • **RMB** and select **Isoparm** on each of the surfaces of the neck.

   • Select the topmost isoparms forming the neck opening.

   • Select **Edit Curves → Duplicate Surface Curves**.

   • **Hide** the *neckLayer* in the Layer Editor.

3 **Rebuild the curves**

   Even though the curves have been duplicated from surfaces with good parameterization, it is recommended to rebuild them anyway.

   • Select all the curves and **rebuild** them with the **Rebuild Curves** button on your shelf.

4 **Draw a profile curve**

   • Select **Create → EP Curve Tool**.

   > **Note:** *The EP Curve Tool is being used rather than the CV Curve Tool because the CV Curve Tool places CVs that lie off the curve, while the EP Curve Tool places edit points that lie directly on the curve. Drawing the curve directly makes it easier to draw following the reference images.*

   • From the side view, hold down **c** to Snap to Curve; then **click** on the back neck curve and **drag** to the back of the neck.

   The first curve point will be created at the very back of the neck curve.

   • Continue placing curve points to draw a curve matching the profile of the head in the image plane.

Note: *The number of CVs is not very important since the curves will ultimately be rebuilt.*

- Once you reach the mouth, draw the inner mouth curve.
- Finish the curve at the throat by pressing **c** to **snap** the last curve point to the front of the neck curve.
- Switch to Component mode and adjust the curve by pulling CVs, if necessary.

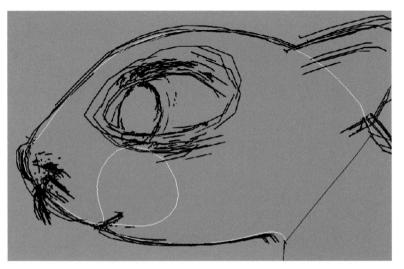

The profile curve with the inner mouth

Tip: *When drawing the profile curve, try to keep it simple. Use as few CVs as possible while still conforming to the basic shape of the head. Also, try to keep the CVs evenly spaced.*

5 Draw the eye curve

You will now create three curves that will be used as the boundaries of the eye. A surface will then be lofted between these curves, creating a surface with radial topology ideal for eye deformations.

- From the side view, use the **EP Curve Tool** to draw a circle curve for the inner boundary of the eye.
- **Snap** the end curve point to the beginning curve point to make a closed circle.
- Pull CVs as necessary to adjust the shape using the reference images.

Lesson 07: Modeling the Squirrel's Head

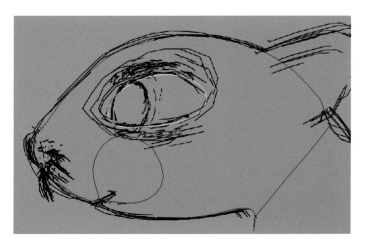

The inner eye curve

6   Close the inner eye curve

Even though the curve appears to form a closed loop because there are no visible gaps, the loop can easily be broken by moving either the first or last CV of the curve. This will make editing the shape of the curve without opening the loop difficult.

You will now close the curve, which will correct this problem. Closing the curve will prevent the loop from opening because it will connect the first and last CVs so that they always move together.

- Select the inner eye curve.

- Select **Edit Curves** →_ **Open/Close Curves** → ❑.

- In the options, set the following:

    Blend to **On**;

    Insert knot to **On**;

    Insert parameter to **0.1**;

    Keep Originals to **Off**.

- Click the **Open/Close** button.

7   Move the curve into position

- Center the curve's pivot by selecting **Modify** → **Center Pivot**.

- In the *front view*, **move** the inner eye curve along the **X-axis** so that it lines up with the eye in the image plane.

- Pull CVs to refine the shape of the inner eye curve, so that it looks good in all the different views.

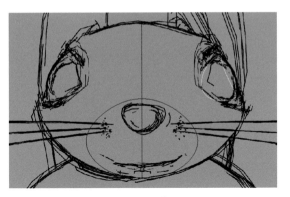

Inner eye curve in front view

Note: *Since the reference images in image planes rarely line up perfectly, you will have to make judgment calls when trying to conform the shape of a curve or surface to front and side images.*

8 **Outer eye curve**

- **Duplicate** the inner eye curve.

- **Scale** the duplicated curve up to match the outer boundary of the eye area, generally defined by the eye socket.

- Pull CVs on the curve to match the image plane.

Note: *The curves you create make up the basic framework of the head. Look at the curves in the Perspective view as you create them and try to picture your model. If the curves seem incorrect, adjust their shape.*

The outer eye curve adjusted in front and side view

9   **Eye inside curve**

• **Duplicate** the inner eye curve.

• **Scale** the duplicated curve down and push it inside the eye socket.

This curve will be used to create geometry inside the eye socket and prevent seeing inside the head.

10 **Draw the boundary for the lips**

You will now create curves for the character's mouth. Once again, these curves will be used as the basis for a radial surface.

• From the front view, use the **EP Curve Tool** to **draw** a curve to match the outline of the lips.

• Make sure to **snap** the first and last points of the curve to the profile curve.

• **Pull** CVs to conform the shape of the curve to the image planes.

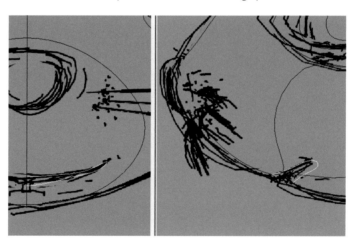

The lips curve

Tip: *Remember that the image planes are only helpful to a point, and that you must use your own judgment to shape the curves in 3D space for best results.*

11 **Draw an outer boundary for the mouth**

• **Draw** a second mouth curve, starting between the lips and the nose and finishing on the chin.

• **Snap** the first and last points to the profile curve and pull CVs to adjust the shape to your liking.

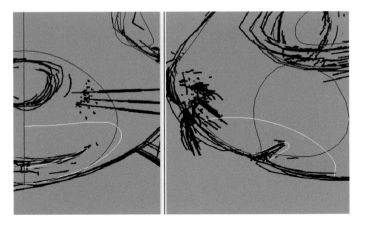

The outer lips curve

12 Nose curve

- **Repeat** the last step to create one profile curve for the nose.

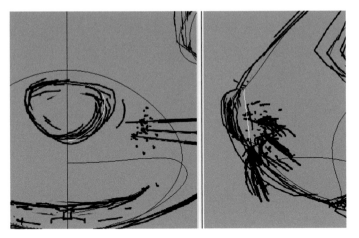

The nose curve

13 Ear curves

- **Repeat** the last step to create three profile curves for the ear. The first curve should delimit the base of the ear where it connects to the head, the second curve should delimit the outer rim of the ear, and the last curve should be a duplicate of the second curve, but scaled down and pushed into the ear.

Lesson 07: Modeling the Squirrel's Head

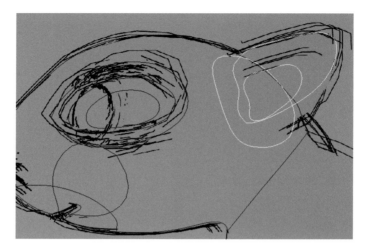

The three ear curves

14 Connect the outer eye curve to the front profile curve

The **EP Curve Tool** is ideal for situations where you want to draw a curve between two existing objects.

- Press **c** to Snap to Curve, and then place a first curve point at the corner of the outer eye curve.

- Draw a second curve point at the center of the front profile curve.

  This curve forms part of the upper boundary for the base of the ear, so the second edit point should line up with the upper base of the ear in the side view.

15 Save your work

- Save your scene as *07-squirrel head 02.ma*.

Create the cage curves

Now that the main components of the head have been addressed, you can start planning how you will cut the head to create square patches. The EP Curve Tool is ideal for this task since it allows you to snap points to two existing curves to create a straight curve to be used for cutting the head in patches.

> **Note:** *This example shows only one of many possible scenarios about how you might cut the head in patches.*

1 Create a connecting curve

- Select the **EP Curve Tool**.

- Press **C** to Snap to Curve, and then **draw** a first point on the front eye corner of the outer eye curve.

- **Snap** a second curve point to the middle of the nose bridge.

- Press **Enter** to complete the curve.

- Select the **EP Curve Tool** again by pressing the **g** hotkey.

- **Snap** a curve point on the top of the outer eye curve; then **snap** another point to the top of the head curve and press **Enter**.

  You have just delimited the first square patch of the head.

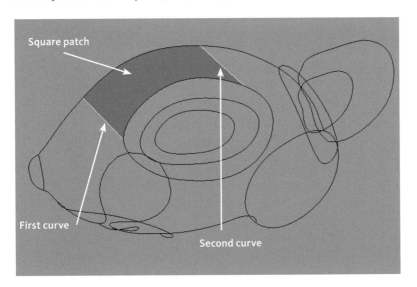

The first square patch

2 Adjust the shape of the curves

- Pull CVs on each of the connecting curves to round up their shape.

Tip: *Do not move the first and last points on the curves, since they are connecting with the profile curve. If they no longer connect, then you must select the CV and snap it to the curve again. Otherwise, the **Cut Curve** tool used later in this lesson will not work.*

3   Draw the remaining profile curves

From this point, you will continue drawing the network of profile curves. Remember to follow the structure of facial muscles. Also, remember that since these curves will be used to generate surfaces, they should always define a four-sided border.

- **Draw** the remaining profile curves.

Tip: *Curves should be intersecting at the same location on a profile curve. This can be easily achieved by snapping a point on an existing intersecting curve rather than on the profile curve itself.*

- Use the illustrations below as a guide for creating the rest of the profile curves.

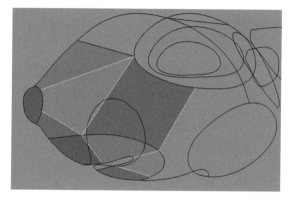

The nose and mouth area

Tip: *Notice in the previous picture how the nose patch has four connecting points.*

The cheek and chin area

> **Tip:** The curves connecting to the base neck curves should be snapped to edit points in order to facilitate the attachment of the head to the body.

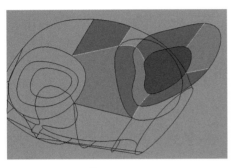

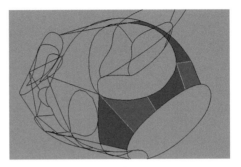

The ear area

The neck area

> **Tip:** Make sure to consider the original neck patches when defining curves at the neck.

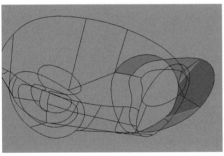

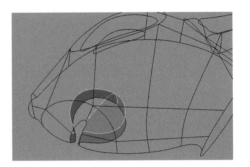

The back of the ear area

The inner mouth area

4   Save your work

- Save your scene as *07-squirrel head 03.ma*.

Rebuilding a curve network

You now have a network of interconnected curves, but many of those curves, like the front and side profile curves, are connected to multiple curves and stretch well beyond the area of any one surface patch. As a result, the parameterization of these curves within any one patch is going to be unpredictable, which could result in poor surfaces. To ensure the best possible surfaces from your curves, you will break the curves into individual pieces, with each piece representing only the area of the surface it bounds. The curves will then be rebuilt to the appropriate number of spans.

Lesson 07: Modeling the Squirrel's Head

1   Open an existing scene file

Before rebuilding the curve network for your head, you will try rebuilding a simpler curve network.

• Open scene file *07-curve network.ma*.

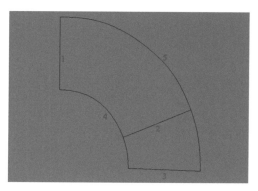

Simple curve network

2   Create a square surface in the upper section

• Select curves **1**, **5**, **2** and **4** in that order.

• Selecting **Surfaces → Square**.

A square surface is created in the area defined by the selected curves.

3   Create a square surface in the lower section

• **Repeat** the process above to create a square surface in the lower section bounded by curves **2**, **5**, **3** and **4.**

Note: *The topology of both surfaces is very uneven, with isoparms at odd intervals. This is known as cross-knot insertion, and it is a result of surfaces being created from curves with mismatched topology.*

4   Display the edit points for all curves

• Select all of the curves, go into Component mode, and display their **Edit Points**.

Notice how the edit points are unevenly spaced on the curves. They indicate the beginning and end of a curve's spans. One isoparm is defined on the surface for each corresponding edit point on a curve.

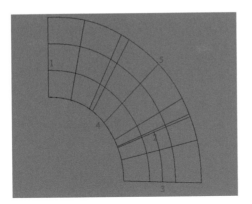

Poor surfaces resulting from poorly parameterized curves

5 Delete the surfaces created earlier

6 Cut the curves

The **Cut Curves Tool** detaches curves wherever they intersect.

- Select all of the curves and select **Edit Curves → Cut Curve**.

7 Rebuild the curves

The curves have been cut into sections representative of the surfaces they will create, but their topology is still inadequate.

- Select the larger piece of what used to be curve 4 and curve 5.
- **Rebuild** it to **4** spans.
- Select **Edit Curves → Rebuild Curve → ☐**.
- **Reset** the options and make sure **Number of Spans** is set to **4**.
- **Rebuild** the smaller pieces of curves 4 and 5 to have **2** spans each.
- **Rebuild** curves 1, 2, and 3 to have **1** span each.

Note: *The number of spans a curve is rebuilt to should be based on how much detail will be required in a given surface, as well as general consistency with the neighboring curves.*

8 Create square surfaces

- Select the four curves delimiting a square in order.
- Select **Surfaces → Square**.

Now that the curve network's topology has been corrected, with the curves on each end of a boundary having the same number of spans, you should get much better results from the square operation.

Lesson 07: Modeling the Squirrel's Head

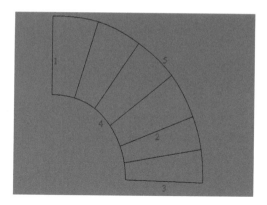

Good surfaces from rebuilt curves

Rebuilding the head's curve network

You will now use what you have just learned to rebuild the profile curves of the squirrel's head.

1   **Scene file**

    • Continue with your own scene.

    OR

    • Open the scene called *07-squirrel head 03.ma*.

2   **Refine the curves**

    Take some time to round up your new curves and make sure to keep the intersecting points together.

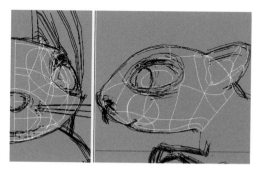

The rounded up curve network

3   **Cut all the curves**

    • Select all the curves in the scene.

- Select **Edit Curves →Cut Curve**.

  Every intersecting curve will now be split into its individual segments.

- Verify that all the curves were cut correctly.

Note: *Just like when detaching isoparms on surfaces, you might have to repeat the operation in order to cut the curves at every intersection point.*

- If some curves were not cut, make sure they intersect properly and cut them again.

4   Detach the eye curves

Because the inner eye curves were not intersecting, they were not cut properly. You will now cut them manually.

- Select the two inner eye curves.

- **RMB** on each one of them and select **Curve Point**.

- Hold down the **Shift** key and select the four curve points on both curves that align with the intersection of the outer eye curve.

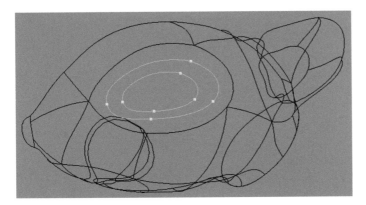

The selected curve points

- Select **Edit Curves → Detach Curves.**

5   Rebuild all the curves

At this time, if you were to create the surfaces from the curves, their topology would not be very good, since the curves have not yet been rebuilt. Since you don't know yet how dense you would like the patches to be, you will simply rebuild all the curves to the same number of spans. This number must be high rather than low so you don't lose any refinements.

- Select all the curves in the scene.
- Select **Edit Curves** → **Rebuild Curve** → ❑.
- In the options, set the following:

  > **Rebuild type** to **Uniform**;
  >
  > **Keep** to **Ends** only;
  >
  > **Number of spans** to **4**.

- Click the **Rebuild** button.

6   Delete history

- Select **Edit** → **Delete All By Type** → **History**.

7   Loft the eye surfaces

- Select three corresponding eye curves in order.
- Select **Surfaces** → **Loft**.
- Increase the loft's **Sections Span** value to **2**.

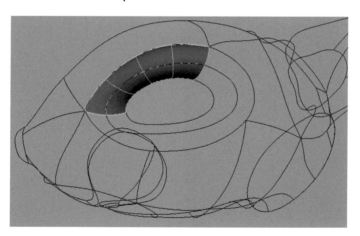

Lofted eye surface

- **Repeat** to loft the remaining eye curves.

Note: *If you get twisting in your geometry, you might have to place some CVs manually or use* **Edit Curves** → **Modify Curves** → **Smooth** *to distribute the CVs equally along the curve. If you still have construction history, the surface will automatically update to reflect your changes.*

8 Create all the patches

You will now generate all the patches for your model.

- Select any four boundary curves in order, and then select **Surfaces → Square**.

- **Repeat** for all the other patches.

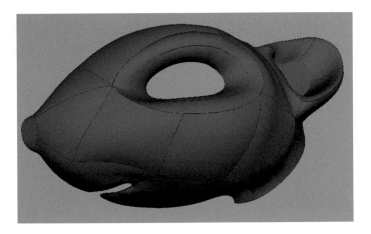

All the patches created

Note: *If you have surfaces with only three sides, it is possible to create a surface out of it anyway, using the* **Surfaces → Boundary** *tool.*

9 Save your work

- Save your scene as *07-squirrel head 04.ma*.

Head topology

It is now time to look at your surfaces and decide how dense they should be. Since you still have construction history, it is easy to select all the curves across the patches and change their number of spans. It is also important to look at the referenced neck faces to determine how the head should flow in the rest of the body.

1 Neck surfaces

- **Show** the *neckLayer* to see the original neck surfaces.

- Enable **Wireframe on Shaded** to see the topology on all the patches.

2   Propagate topology

The head should most certainly have more topology than the body. When looking at the neck patches, keep in mind that the related head patches must have an evenly divisible number of spans in order to connect properly to the body.

- Select all the curves going across the same flow of patches starting at the neck.

You should basically end up with a ring of curves going all around the head.

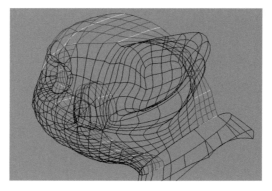

The ring of selected curves

Tip: *Toggle the surface mask button in the Status Line to prevent picking any surfaces.*

- **Rebuild** the curves to have only **2 spans**.

If you still have construction history, all the patches will update to the new topology.

- **Repeat** the process to rebuild all the faces to their minimum acceptable topology.

In the following image, all the curves were rebuilt to have only two spans. The only exceptions are the large forehead area connecting into the eye, which was set to have three spans, and the inner mouth patches, which were refined furtherfor a nice lip border.

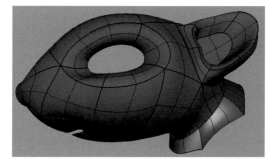

The completely rebuilt curve network

3 Delete the history

- **Delete** all construction history.

- **Delete** all the curves since they are no longer required.

4 Global stitch

- Select all the head surfaces along with the neck surfaces then apply a **Global Stitch**.

- Set the **Stitch Smoothness** to **Tangent** for the *globalStitch1* node.

  Doing so will stitch all the knots and make sure all the patches' tangencies flow into each other.

> **Note:** *Always make sure the surfaces are not pinching after you create a Global Stitch. If they do pinch, undo the stitch and tweak the geometry to prevent the problem.*

5 Clean up

- **Delete** all construction history.

- **Delete** the reference neck patches since they are no longer required.

6 Save your work

- Save your scene as *07-squirrel head 05.ma*.

Refinements

Now that your head topology is final, you can start adding details to it. Here, you will bring refinements to the eyelids and nose, and you'll create the eyeball, teeth, and whiskers.

1 Create an eyeball

It is important for the eyelid and eyeball surfaces to maintain a close relationship, so you will create eyeball to help refine the eyelids.

- Select **Create → NURBS Primitives → Sphere**.

- **Move** and **scale** the sphere into position using the reference images.

- **Rotate** the sphere by **80** degrees on the **X-axis** and by **30** degrees on the **Y-axis**.

- **Assign** a **Phong** material and **map** it with a **Ramp**.

- **Tweak** the *ramp* to define the iris of the squirrel.

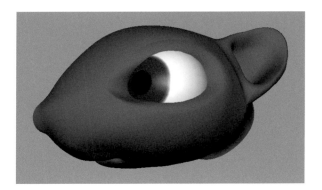

The squirrel's eyeball

- **Rename** the *sphere* to *eyeball*.

2   Refine the eyelids

- **Insert** isoparms in the eyelids to create more definition.

3   Global stitch

Before making any changes to the geometry, it is a good idea to assign another Global Stitch. Doing so will prevent you from accidentally separate two patches.

4   Tweak the eyelids and nose

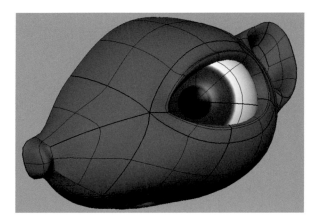

The refined shape

5   Extras

Take some time to model some polygonal teeth and NURBS whiskers.

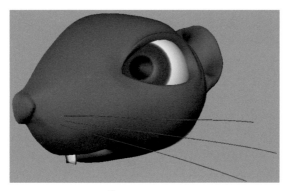

Extra geometry

6   Mirror the head

- **Delete** all the construction history.

- **Group** all the geometry together.

- **Duplicate** the group and set its **Scale X** to **−1**.

- **Attach** all the central patches together two by two.

- Apply a **Global Stitch** on all the head patches.

7   Clean up

- Select all the patches.

- Select **Modify → Center Pivot**.

- Select **Modify → Freeze Transformations**.

- Select **Edit → Delete All By Type → History**.

- Select **File → Optimize Scene Size**.

- **Group** and **rename** everything properly.

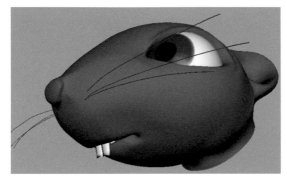

The final head geometry

8 Save your work

- Save your scene as *07-squirrel head 06.ma*.

Import the body

1 Import the body

- Select **File → Import**.

- **Import** the scene file called *06 -squirrelBody_08.ma*.

2 Attach the head to the body

- **Scale** and **move** the head to its proper location on the body.

- Select the head and neck surfaces and apply a **Global Stitch**.

- **Apply** the *bodyBlinn* shader to all the head patches.

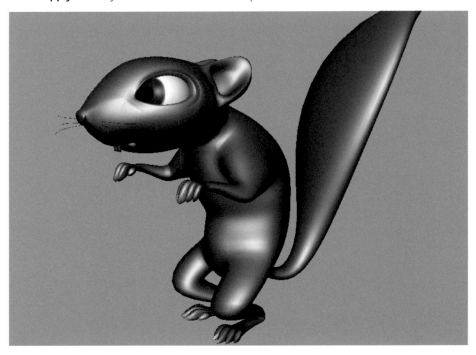

Finished head and body

3 **Reverse normals**

- Select **Edit** → **Select All by Type** → **NURBS Surfaces**.

- Select **Display** → **NURBS Components** → **Normals**.

- Select patches whose normals seem to be pointing inwardly.

- Select **Edit NURBS** → **Reverse Surface Direction**.

- **Repeat** until there are no more reversed surfaces on the entire head.

- Turn **Off** the normals display.

4 **Clean up**

- **Delete** any obsolete nodes in the Outliner.

- **Delete** the image planes from the Hypershade.

- Select **File** → **Optimize Scene Size** to clean up the scene.

5 **Save your work**

- Save the scene as *07-squirrel complete.ma*.

Conclusion

Building a NURBS patch character is a relatively easy task in terms of tools, but it requires lots of visualization experience in order to be perfect.

In this lesson, you learned how to use a curve network to build a patch head. A few basic rules were discussed to simplify the process, such as ensuring that your curves match the facial structure of your character, and that the curve network has clean and predictable topology.

In the next lesson, you will learn about various NURBS tasks, such as conversion, tessellation, and texturing.

Lesson 08
NURBS Tasks

In this lesson, you will examine a number of general tasks related to modeling with NURBS, such as conversion, tessellation, and texturing.

In this lesson you will learn the following:

- How to convert NURBS surfaces to polygonal surfaces;
- How to display and reverse normals;
- How to deal with the tessellation of NURBS surfaces;
- How to use 3D textures when working with NURBS patch models;
- How to create texture reference objects.

Project 02

Converting NURBS to polygons

Depending on the specific needs of your production, you will often need to convert NURBS surfaces into a polygonal mesh. The following exercise shows the workflow of converting NURBS to polygons.

1 Create a new scene file

2 Create a primitive NURBS sphere

3 Convert the NURBS sphere to polygons

- With the *sphere* selected, select **Modify → Convert → NURBS to Polygons → ☐**.
- Set the following options:

  Type to **Quads**;

  Tessellation Method to **General**.

- Under **Initial Tessellation Controls**, set the following:

  U Type to **Per span # of iso params**;

  Number U to **1**;

  V Type to **Per span # of iso params**;

  Number V to **1**.

- Click the **Tessellate** button.

  The polygonal version of the sphere is created.

4 Move the poly sphere to the side

- **Translate** the poly sphere to the side of the original NURBS sphere.

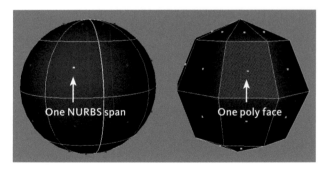

NURBS sphere and converted poly sphere

5   Evaluate the conversion

Using the current tessellation, the polygonal sphere was converted with one quad (four-sided face) for every span in the original sphere. As a result, the poly sphere appears multifaceted. Unlike NURBS surfaces, whose tessellation can be adjusted at render time, what you see is what you get with polygons, so you will need to determine on a case by case basis how precisely the sphere should be converted.

6   Delete the poly sphere

7   Convert with higher tessellation setting

- With the NURBS sphere selected, select **Modify** → **Convert** → **NURBS to Polygons** → ☐, and set the following options:

  Number U and **V** to **3**.

- Click the **Tessellate** button.

  A polygonal version of the sphere, which is much closer to the original sphere, is created.

8   Move the poly sphere to the side

- **Translate** the poly sphere to the side of the original NURBS sphere.

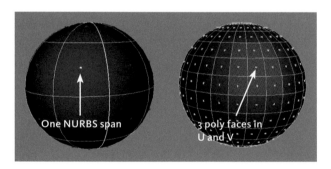

NURBS sphere and higher-resolution poly sphere

9   Evaluate the conversion

This time, the conversion created three faces in the U and V directions for each span on the original sphere, resulting in a polygonal sphere that appears less faceted.

Dealing with border edges

A common workflow is to build a model out of multiple NURBS patches, taking advantage of sophisticated NURBS modeling techniques, and then to convert those patches into a single polygonal mesh before binding or texturing. In order to do this, the NURBS patches must be converted into individual polygonal surfaces, which are then combined into a single poly mesh.

Before converting a multi-patch NURBS model, you will take a quick look at the issues associated with combining multiple polygonal surfaces into a single mesh.

1   **Open an existing scene file**

• Open the scene file *08-simple example 01.ma*.

2   **Combine the two polygonal surfaces**

• Select the **two** polygonal surfaces, and then select **Mesh → Combine**.

The polygonal surfaces are now combined into single poly mesh, with two distinct poly shells.

3   **Display the mesh's border edges**

• With the poly mesh selected, select **Display → Polygons → Border Edges**.

Visually thicker edges appear around the poly mesh faces that have edges not shared by any other face.

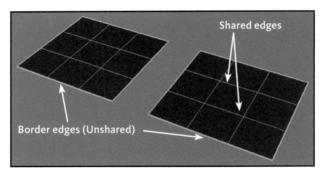

Border edges displayed on poly mesh

4   **Delete the poly mesh**

5   **Make layer2 visible**

Layer2 contains two separate, single-span NURBS surfaces with G1 continuity.

6   **Convert the two NURBS planes to polygons**

• Using the same tessellation settings you set earlier, convert the two NURBS planes to polygons.

7   **Delete the NURBS surfaces**

8   **Combine the poly surfaces**

• Select the two polygon surfaces and **combine** them into a single poly mesh.

9 Display the mesh's border edges

- Display the polygon border edges as you did in the previous example.

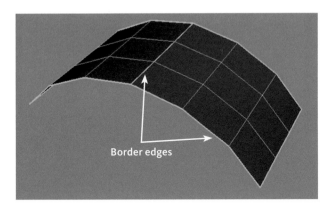

Border edges displayed on poly mesh

Note: *As the previous example, border edges appear wherever there are edges that do not share a face. In the previous example it was easy to see that the border edges didn't share faces. However, in this case the edges in the center of the mesh appear to share faces on each side, when in fact they don't.*

10 Select one vertex on an internal border edge

- **RMB** on the mesh and select **Vertex**.
- Select a single central vertex by clicking once directly on it.

11 Translate the selected vertex

- **Move** the selected vertex on the **Y-axis**.

You will notice that there are in fact two vertices at that location and that you have selected only one of them. As in the previous example, combining the two poly surfaces may have made them into a single poly mesh, but the individual vertices are unaffected. The vertices must be merged to eliminate the border edge.

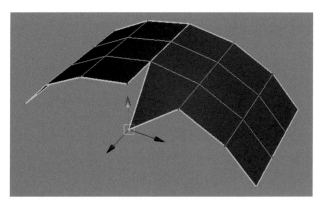

The vertex moved down

- **Undo** the previous move.

12 **Select all of the mesh's vertices**

- Select all of the mesh's vertices.

- Select **Edit Mesh → Merge**.

13 **Adjust the Distance value**

Even if the vertices are right on top of each other they might not actually merge with such a low **Distance** setting, so the border edge will remain. If this is the case, do the following:

- Select the surface and in the **Inputs** section of the Channel Box, increase the *polyMergeVert1* **Distance** attribute in small increments until the border edge disappears.

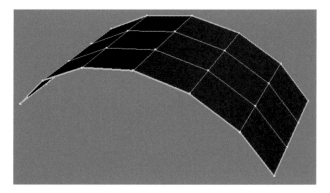

Merged vertices

Note: *Be careful to increase the **Distance** value in small increments or you may end up merging vertices that you don't want to merge.*

Dealing with flipped normals

Depending on how it was built, a network of NURBS patches may have surface normals that do not all face in the same direction. In this case, merging the surface's vertices will not be enough to eliminate internal border edges because the normals must all face in the same direction.

1 Delete the poly surface from the last example

2 Display layer3

- Make *layer3* visible.

  This layer has two pairs of NURBS surfaces.

3 Display the surface normals

- Select the four NURBS surfaces; then select **Display → NURBS → Normals**.

  One pair of surfaces has normals facing the same direction, while the other pair has normals facing in opposite directions.

Tip: *NURBS normals are only visible in shaded mode.*

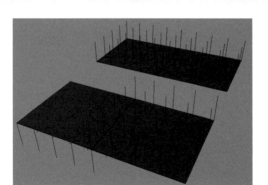

Surface normals

4 Convert the surfaces to polygons

- **Convert** the four NURBS surfaces to polygons.

- **Delete** the original NURBS surfaces.

5 Combine the surfaces

- Select one pair of surfaces and **combine** them.

- Select the other pair of surfaces and **combine** them.

6 Display the border edges and normals

- Display the border edges for both poly meshes.

  Both meshes should have border edges where the center vertices need to be merged.

- Also, select the polygonal normals by selecting **Display → Polygons → Face Normals**.

7 Merge the vertices

- **Merge** the vertices for both meshes.

  The internal border edges disappear on the surface with consistent normals, but not the other mesh with flipped normals.

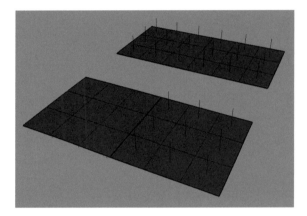

Border edge still visible on mesh with flipped normals

8 Reverse the surface normals

- **RMB** on the surface with incorrect normals and select **Face**.

- Select the faces with flipped normals.

- Select **Normals → Reverse**.

  Doing so will flip the normals of the selected faces. The border edge was merged automatically because of the polyMergeVert1 construction history node.

Converting a NURBS patch model

You will now use the above techniques to convert a NURBS patch model into polygons.

1 Open an existing scene file

- Open the scene file *08-simple example 02.ma*.

  This scene contains the head model with some NURBS patches with reversed surface direction.

2 Convert the NURBS patches to polygons

- Select all of the NURBS patches.

- Select **Modify** → **Convert** → **NURBS to Polygons** → ☐.

- Set the following options:

    Number U to 1;

    Number V to 1.

> **Note:** You can use the **Attach Multiple Output Meshes** option to automatically combine and merge the resulting surfaces.

- Click the **Tessellate** button.

3 Delete the original NURBS surfaces

4 Display the normals and borders

- Select all of the poly surfaces and select **Display** → **Polygons** → **Border Edges** and **Display** → **Polygons** → **Face Normals**.

    Most of the poly surfaces have normals that are facing inward. You could correct that now by reversing the normals for selected surfaces, but you will correct all of the normals later in a single operation.

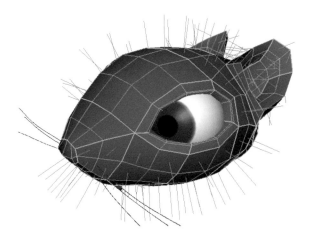

Normals displayed on polygonal surfaces

5 Combine the poly surfaces into a single mesh

- Select all of the converted poly surfaces and **combine** them into a single poly mesh.

6 Merge the vertices

- Select **Edit Mesh → Merge**.

- Set the **Distance** attribute in the Channel Box to **0.1**.

  Some of the border edges will remain. Any neighboring faces with normals that are facing in opposite directions will create a border edge.

7 Conform the normals

You will now conform the surface's normals so they are all facing in the same direction.

- Select the mesh and select **Normals → Conform**.

  The tool will determine how many faces have normals facing out and how many have normals facing in, and reverse the normals of the faces in the minority. With the normals corrected, the border edges should disappear.

8 Make sure the normals are facing out

Since the Conform command reverses the normals of the fewer number of faces, it will not necessarily leave the normals facing in the appropriate direction. Generally speaking, it's best for normals to point outward.

- If the faces of your mesh are currently facing in, select the mesh and then select **Normals → Reverse**.

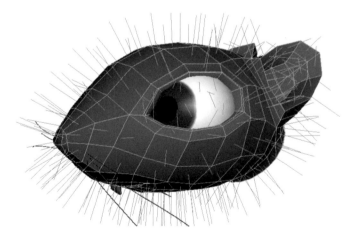

Appropriate normals and borders

9 Soften the normals

Even after merging the vertices and correcting the mesh's normals, you may find that seams appear on areas of your mesh when you render. These seams are caused by *hard* normals from one face to the next. Normals must be softened to eliminate these seams in your render.

- Select the poly mesh, and then select **Normals → Soften Edges**

10 Render the poly mesh

- Click on the **Render Current Frame** button to render the scene into the Render View window.

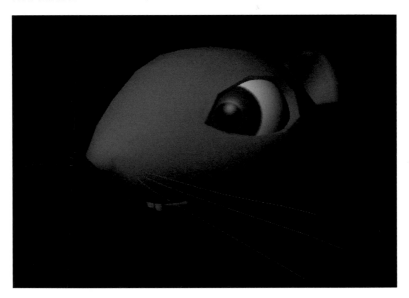

Rendered poly head

Tip: *You can assign a poly smooth on the head geometry to refine it even more.*

Tessellating NURBS surfaces

Tessellation is the process of dividing a NURBS surface up into triangles, either as part of a conversion to a polygon surface or so that it can be rendered.

Note: *NURBS surfaces are always converted to polygons before rendering.*

Polygonal surfaces are pre-tessellated because they are already made up of triangles (four-sided faces are ultimately divided into two triangles). That's why polygonal surfaces tend to look faceted when rendered, unless the mesh is quite dense. NURBS surfaces, on the other hand, are tessellated at render time, so the apparent roundness of a NURBS surface can always be adjusted.

Project 02

In this exercise you will adjust the tessellation of NURBS surfaces to refine how they appear when they are rendered.

1 **Open an existing scene file**

- Open the scene file *09-simple example 03.ma*.

  This scene contains the NURBS head with proper surface direction.

2 **Render the head**

- **Frame** the eye area of the squirrel's head in the perspective view.

- **Render** the scene.

  The rendered image will reveal some problems where the patches meet together.

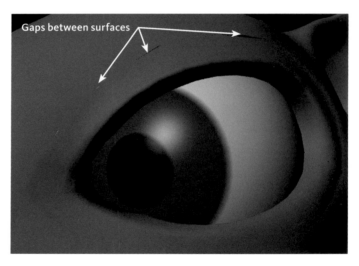

Gaps between surfaces

Problems visible at render time

3 **Display render tessellation**

- Select all the surfaces.

- Select **Window → General Editors → Attribute Spread Sheet**.

- Under the **Tessellation** tab, click on the **Display Render** column header, set the attributes to **1**, and hit **Enter** to set them to **On**.

  The surfaces should now appear according to how they will be tessellated during the render. The same gap that is visible in the software render should now be visible in the view.

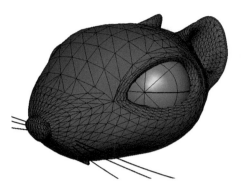

The displayed render tessellation

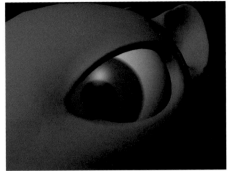

The gaps are now closed

4   Improve the tessellation

There are many tessellation settings that you can change on the surfaces to improve the rendered images, but perhaps the simplest one to use at this time is **Smooth Edge**. This option increases the number of triangles only along the boundary of an object. This lets you smooth the edges or prevent cracks between shared curves of adjacent surfaces without tessellating across the entire object.

- With all the surfaces still selected and with the Attribute Spread Sheet opened, set the **Smooth Edge** column to **On**.

- **Render** the scene.

   The gap between the surfaces should now be gone.

Note: *You can also increase the **U** and **V Division Factors** of the surfaces, but doing so will increase render time. Be judicious when setting tessellation values. Only increase the tessellation until the surface renders acceptably.*

Tweak the squirrel model

Using what you have just learned, you will now fix the normals and tessellation on the complete squirrel model created in the last lesson.

1   Open an existing scene file

- Open the scene file *07-squirrel complete.ma*.

2   Freeze transformations

If some models were mirrored and not frozen, when you freeze transformations the normals might be reversed. Thus, you need to freeze all the geometry before pursuing.

- Select all the surfaces, and then select **Modify → Freeze Transformations**.

3 Normals

- Select all the surfaces, and then select **Display → NURBS → Normals**.
- **Reverse** the direction of any surface in which the normals point inside the body by selecting the surface and choosing **Edit NURBS → Reverse Surface Direction**.
- To hide the normals, select the object and then **Display → NURBS → Normals** again.

4 Tessellation

- Select all the surfaces.
- Select **Window → General Editors → Attribute Spread Sheet**.
- Under the **Tessellation** tab, click on the **Smooth Edge** column and set it to **On**.

The squirrel now renders correctly

5 Save your work

- Save your scene as *08-squirrel normals 01.ma*.

Texturing NURBS surfaces

While NURBS surfaces' inherent UVs generally make texturing them easy, applying a texture to a series of NURBS patches can be a little more difficult. In this exercise you will use a projected texture to place a texture across multiple NURBS patches.

1 Switch view layout

- Select **Panels** → **Saved layouts** → **Hypershade/Render/Persp**.

2 Display the top and bottom tabs in the Hypershade

- Click on the **Show top and bottom tabs** button in the Hypershade.

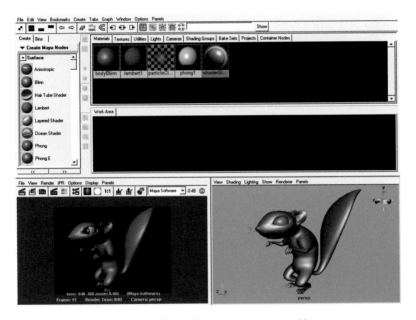

Hypershade, Render and Perspective view panel layout

3 Teeth shader

- **Create** a **Phong** material and **assign** it to the teeth.

Lesson 08: NURBS Tasks

- **Map** a **Marble** 3D texture into its **Color** and tweak it so it looks like the following when rendered:

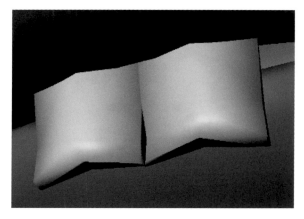

Pearl shader

Using a 3D texture simplifies the task of texturing geometry since you don't have to bother about UVs.

4 **Eye shader**

- **Create** another **Phong** material and **assign** it to the eyes (if it doesn't exist already).

- **Map** a **Ramp** into its **Color** and tweak it so it looks like the following:

Eye shader

 Tip: *Use another ramp in the eye ramp color to create the perpendicular lines found in the iris.*

- If the other eye's iris is located behind the eyeball, you must reverse the surface's direction in order to flip its UVs to show the texture properly.

- In the Attribute Editor for the eye shader, set a small amount of **Glow Intensity** under the **Special Effects** section.

5 Whisker shader

- **Create** a **Ramp Shader** with black color and strong specular and **assign** it to the whiskers.

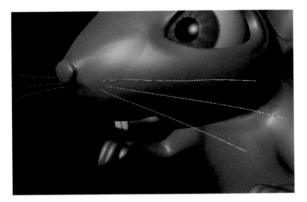

Whiskers shader

6 Nose shader

- Make sure the nose patch clearly delimitates the nose area.

- **Create** a **Blinn** material and **assign** it to the nose patch.

- **Map** a **Leather** 3D texture into its **Color**.

- **Assign** the same leather texture also to the **Bump Map** and **Specular Color.**

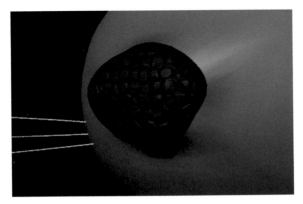

The nose texture

Lesson 08: NURBS Tasks

7 Fur shader

- **Create** a **Blinn** material and **assign** it to all the fur surfaces.
- Click on the **map** button for the **Color** attribute.
- Change the 2D texture option to **As projection** then create a **ramp** texture.

  When you create a texture as a projection, a manipulator lets you change the texture's projection on the surfaces with a 3D manipulator.

- **Rotate** and **move** the new projection manipulator as follows:

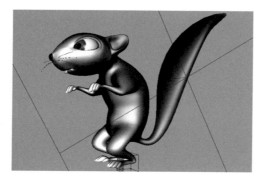

Skin shader

- Change the ramp's colors to get a dark brown on the back and tail and a lighter brown on the paws, belly and face.
- Adjust the ramp to your liking.
- **Map** a **cloud** 3D texture in the ramp's color and set it to have brown color variations.

  The 3D cloud texture will affect the tones of the fur.

- **Assign** the same cloud texture to the **Specular Color** and **Bump Map**.

The fur shader

8   Inner Mouth

- **Create** a **Phong** material and **assign** it to the inner mouth surfaces.
- Change the **Color** of the material to a dark red.

9   Save your work

- Save your scene as *08-squirrel textures 01.ma*.

Texture Reference Object

In order to keep the geometry from swimming in the 3D textures when animating the squirrel, you will have to create *Texture Reference Objects*. Texture reference objects are duplicates of the original surfaces and keep all the texturing information.

1   Create Texture Reference Objects

If you followed the steps of the previous exercise, you now have 3D textures and 3D projections on the squirrel. The objects affected by those 3D textures and 3D projections will need texture reference objects.

- From the Hypershade, **RMB** on the fur material and select **Select Objects With Material**.
- In order to be able to modify them all at the same time, **group** the surfaces together.
- **Rename** the group *skinGroup*.
- With *skinGroup* selected, go in the Rendering menu set and select **Texturing → Create Texture Reference Object**.

   A templated duplicate of skinGroup is created and now serves as a texture reference object.

- **Repeat** the previous steps to create texture reference objects for any other surface using 3D texture, such as the *nose* and *teeth*.

2   Texture objects layer

- Select all the texture reference objects and the *place3dTexture* nodes from the Outliner and **group** them together.
- **Rename** the group *txtGroup*.
- **Create** a new layer and **rename** it *txtRefLayer*.
- **Add** the *txtGroup* to the *txtRefLayer*.
- Make the layer in **reference** and **invisible**.

3   Clean up

- Make sure everything is organized in hierarchies and named appropriately.

Lesson 08: NURBS Tasks

- Select **Edit** → **Delete All By Type** → **History**.
- Select **File** → **Optimize Scene Size**.

The textured squirrel

4   Save your work

- Save your scene as *08-squirrel textures 02.ma*.

Conclusion

Congratulations, you have now finished the squirrel model! In this lesson, you learned about generic workflow when using NURBS surfaces. You also learned about surface normals and tessellation, which will greatly improve NURBS rendering quality. Other lessons learned include how to convert NURBS into polygons, which gives you the freedom of either pursuing with NURBS or polygons for the rest of the character pipeline. Lastly, you textured the squirrel using 2D and 3D textures, and added texture reference objects to prevent the 3D textures from sliding when the surfaces move or deform.

In the next project, you will learn about modeling with subdivision surfaces.

Project 03

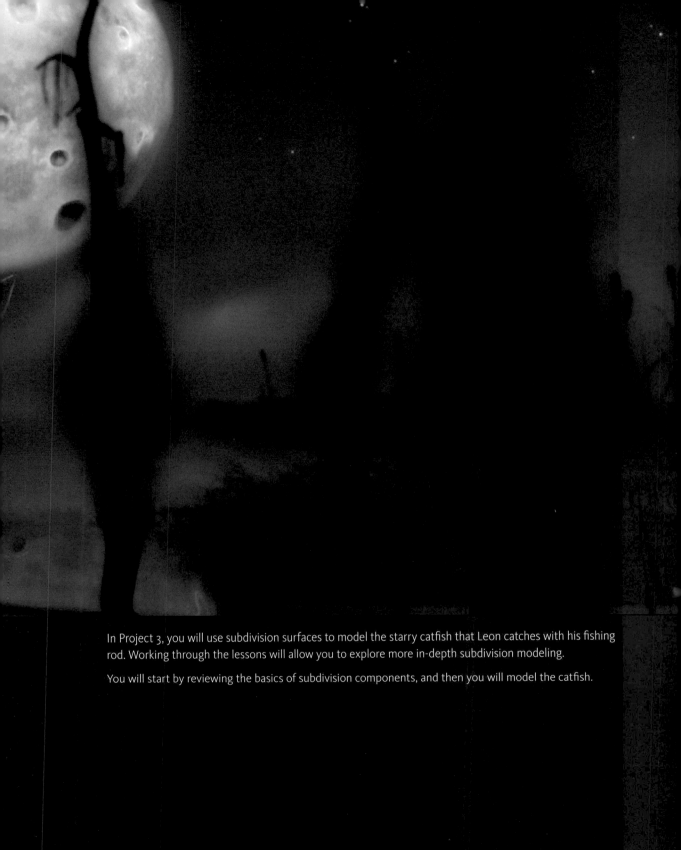

In Project 3, you will use subdivision surfaces to model the starry catfish that Leon catches with his fishing rod. Working through the lessons will allow you to explore more in-depth subdivision modeling.

You will start by reviewing the basics of subdivision components, and then you will model the catfish.

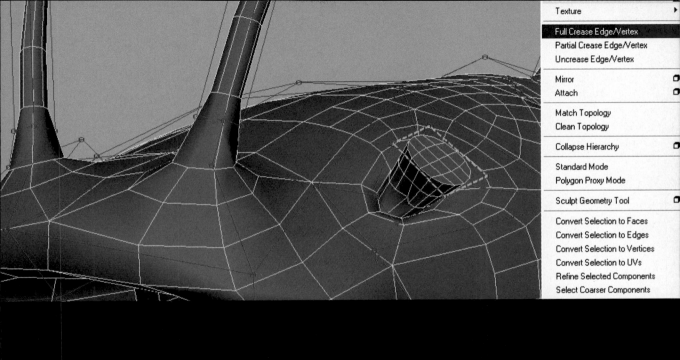

Texture ▶

Full Crease Edge/Vertex
Partial Crease Edge/Vertex
Uncrease Edge/Vertex

Mirror ◻
Attach ◻

Match Topology
Clean Topology

Collapse Hierarchy ◻

Standard Mode
Polygon Proxy Mode

Sculpt Geometry Tool ◻

Convert Selection to Faces
Convert Selection to Edges
Convert Selection to Vertices
Convert Selection to UVs
Refine Selected Components
Select Coarser Components

Lesson 09
Subdivision Basics

What are subdivision surfaces?

Subdivision surfaces (or SubDs) are a combination of some of the best features of both NURBS and polygon surfaces. Subdivision surfaces get their name from the ability to add geometry to localized areas of the surface where greater detail is needed, without affecting the rest of the surface. This ability to add detail just where you need it makes SubDs an excellent choice for complex organic shapes.

SubD surfaces compared to polygons and NURBS

Like polygons, SubDs allow arbitrary topology. This means that you are not restricted by the limitations of a single four-sided patch, or the difficulties presented by a series of four-sided patches, as you are with NURBS modeling.

Like NURBS surfaces, SubDs are not pre-tessellated, so they render smoothly. While the arbitrary topology of polygons makes them easy to model with, the fact that polygons are pre-tessellated means that they tend to appear faceted when rendered.

Anatomy of SubD Surfaces

Hierarchical components

The ability to edit components on different levels of a hierarchy is integral to the idea of working with localized subdivisions of detail. This hierarchical approach to components means that edits applied to a coarse level of the hierarchy affect components on refined levels in the same area. As a result, you can make adjustments on a refined component level to alter fine details (such as the shape of the corner of an eye), and then edit components on a coarser level to change the overall shape of the surface. The fine details will follow along.

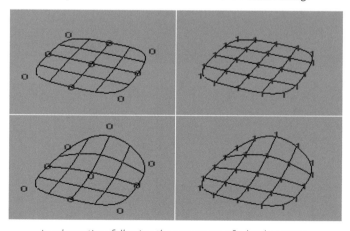

Level 1 vertices following the movement of a level 0 vertex

Note: *You can change the display type of SubD vertices between numbers or points in the* **General Preferences**, *under the* **Subdivs** *category.*

Standard Mode vs. Polygon Proxy Mode

SubDs can be manipulated in two different modes, *Standard Mode* and *Polygon Proxy Mode*, which you can switch between at any time.

In Standard Mode, you work directly with the hierarchical components of the SubD surface itself. Standard Mode is generally used for adjusting the details of a SubD surface.

Switching to Polygon Proxy Mode creates a temporary polygon proxy surface that matches the level o components of the actual SubD surface. Polygon Proxy Mode is mostly used for adjusting the overall shape of a SubD surface. Most of Maya's suite of poly editing tools can be used in Polygon Proxy Mode.

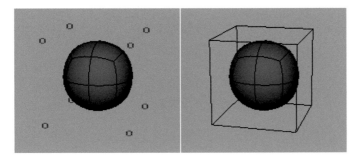

Standard Mode and Polygon Proxy Mode

SubD components

Unlike NURBS or polygonal surfaces where the nature of components is constant, SubD components are associated with the SubD surface itself, or the poly proxy object.

While working in Standard Mode you can select and edit vertices, edges, and faces at any given level of the component hierarchy. While working in Polygon Proxy Mode, selecting or editing vertices, edges, or faces is limited to the level o components of the SubD surface.

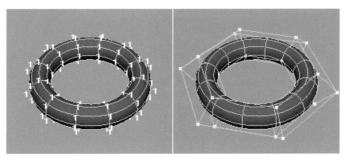

Vertices of level 1 in Standard Mode and level 0 in Polygon Proxy Mode

Basic SubD Workflows

Achieving a basic shape while in Polygon Proxy Mode

Probably the most popular SubD modeling technique is working in Polygon Proxy Mode to achieve the basic shape of your model, and then switching to Standard Mode while working with surface details.

This technique takes advantage of poly modeling's large suite of tools to create the basic shape and uses Standard Mode's hierarchical components to create detail only where necessary.

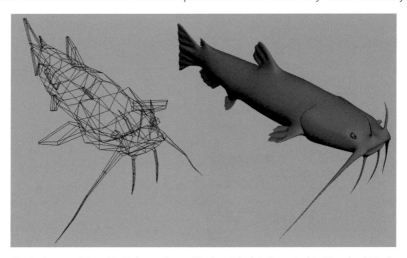

Basic shape achieved in Polygon Proxy Mode, with detail created in Standard Mode

Refining SubDs

Refining is the process of adding detail to a surface by increasing the level of components in a given area of the surface, thus increasing the number of points available in that area.

To refine a SubD surface, select a component on the surface in the area where you want to refine the detail, **RMB** on the surface, and select **Refine**.

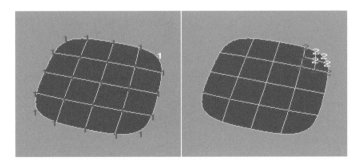

Level 1 vertices refined to level 2

Switching between levels

Switching between levels allows you access to the components associated with a given level of the hierarchy. To switch between levels of the component hierarchy, display the surface's components, **RMB** on the surface, and select **Display Level → 0**

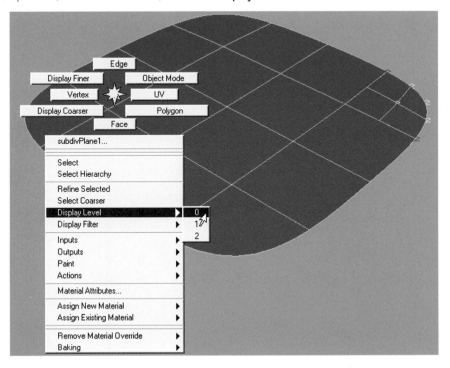

Switching from level 2 to level 0 in the component hierarchy

Lesson 09: Subdivision Basics

Creasing SubD surfaces

SubD surfaces can be *creased* to sharpen corners. *Full creases* move the surface to the selected edge or vertex, creating a hard or sharp corner. *Partial creases* move the surface closer to the edge or vertex than it originally was without moving it all the way to the edge or vertex. This has the effect of creating a sharper inflection in the shape of the surface without creating a visible edge.

Creases are indicated by dotted edges in the poly proxy object.

Creases can be removed after they are created by selecting the creased edge, and then selecting **Subdiv Surfaces → ❑ Uncrease Edge/Vertex**.

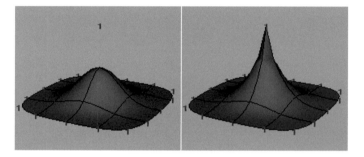

Full crease applied to center vertex

Cleaning up SubDs

Once points are added to a surface by refining, they cannot be removed unless you use the *Clean Topology* command. This will remove added points that have not been edited, and therefore, are not necessary to define detail in the surface.

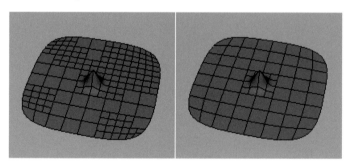

Unnecessary components deleted by Cleaning Topology

SubD smoothness

Just as you can with NURBS surfaces, you can specify the smoothness of SubDs in the viewport by pressing **1**, **2**, or **3** on your keyboard.

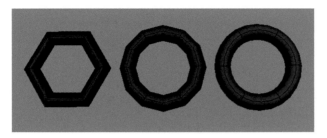

SubD smoothness

Conclusion

Subdivision surfaces are an excellent choice for models that require varying levels of detail. Now that you are familiar with the principles and basic workflows of SubDs, you will apply these ideas and techniques in the next lessons to model a SubD catfish.

Lesson 10
Modeling the Catfish

In this lesson, you will model a subdivision surface catfish. Doing so will allow you to gain experience using SubD surfaces.

In this lesson you will learn the following:

- How to define a shape using Polygon Proxy Mode;
- How to switch between Standard Mode and Polygon Proxy Mode;
- How to refine hierarchical components;
- How to define creases;
- How to clean SubD topology;
- How to mirror and attach SubD surfaces.

Define a shape in Polygon Proxy Mode

The first step in building a catfish is creating the basic shape while in Polygon Proxy Mode.

1   Image planes

- Open the scene file named *10-catfish body 01.ma*.

    This scene contains image planes showing the catfish for reference.

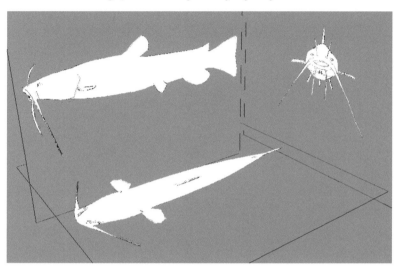

The catfish reference image planes

2   Create a SubD primitive sphere

- Create a SubD sphere by selecting **Create** → **Subdiv Primitives** → **Sphere**.
- With the sphere selected, press the **3** key to increase the sphere's display resolution.
- **Rename** the sphere to *body*.

3   Switch to Polygon Proxy Mode

- **RMB** on *body* and select **Polygon** to switch to Polygon Proxy Mode.

    A temporary polygonal object is displayed, which represents level 0 of the SubD surface's hierarchical components.

> **Note:** *You can also access the* **Polygon Proxy Mode** *through the* **Subdiv Surfaces** *menu in the* **Surfaces** *menu set.*

4   Move the body

- **Move** and **scale** the geometry so the sphere fits the area just under the dorsal fin.

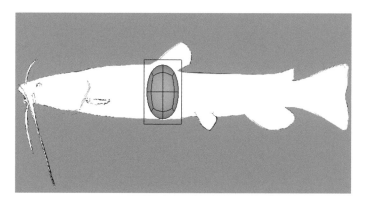

The startup body shape

5   Display the poly object's faces

- **RMB-click** on *body* and select **Face** from the radial menu, or press **F11**.

The faces of the temporary polygon object are displayed.

6   Extrude the lower body

- Select the face on the back of *body*.

- Select **Edit Mesh → Extrude** and extrude it along its local **Z-axis** all the way to the base of the tail fin.

- In the Channel Box for the *polyExtrudeFace1* node, set the **Divisions** to **4** and the **Offset** to **1.4**.

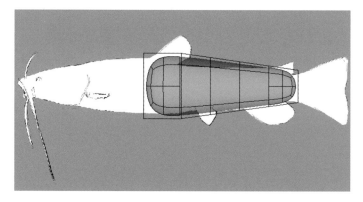

Face of SubD sphere extruded to create the lower body

7 Extrude the upper body

- **Repeat** the previous step to extrude the front of the body.

8 Refine the body

- **Refine** the current polygonal object using the reference image in all views.

> **Tip:** *RMB on the fish body and select **Vertices** to refine the shape of the fish, just as you would do with a polygonal object.*

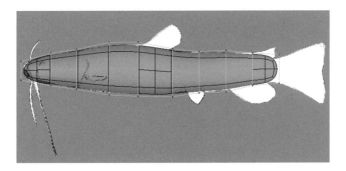

The basic body shape

> **Tip:** *Concentrate on making the subD object accurate by tweaking the polygonal proxy cage. Be aware that just as with NURBS, the subD object will change shape across many vertices as you add and tweak the topology.*

9 Dorsal fin

- **Extrude** the top face three times to create the dorsal fin.

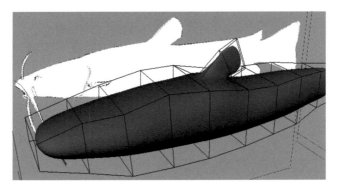

The dorsal fin extrusion

10 **The tail**

- **Extrude** the tail once, moving it on its Z-axis up to the end of the tail.
- **Extrude** the top and bottom faces of the tail to create the long pieces of fin.
- **Tweak** the vertices as shown here:

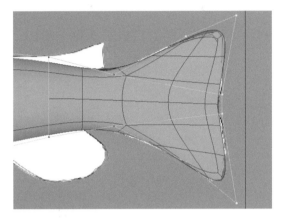

The tail topology

11 **Split central line**

- Use the **Split Edge Loop Tool** to split the model in its central axis.
- Select all the faces on the right side of the model and **delete** them.

12 **Extrude the other fins**

- Take some time to extrude the other fins of the fish.
- If you don't have enough topology to work with, you can simply add edge loops or split polygonal faces, just as you would do on a normal polygonal model.

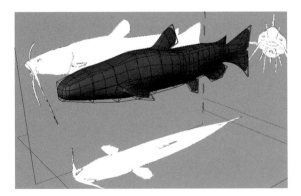

Fish with all its fins

13 Save your work

- Save your scene as *10-catfish body 02.ma.*

Refine the head

So far you have seen all the possibilities that Polygonal Proxy Mode offers with subDs. You will now continue to use polygonal tools to refine the head of the catfish.

1 Extrude the whiskers

- **Insert** a vertical edge loop on the front of the head.
- **Extrude** four times to create the top whiskers.

2 Add topology to the head

- **Split** the head in order to get more faces to extrude.
- **Extrude** the eye socket.

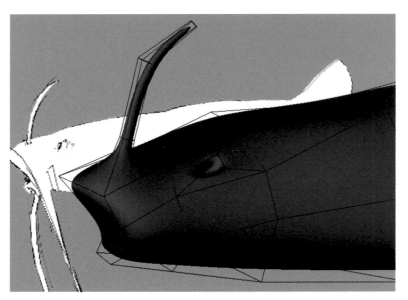

The current head topology

3 Extrude the remaining antennas

- **Extrude** the antennas on the side and bottom of the fish's mouth.

All the whiskers in place

- For each face on the tip of the whiskers, select **Edit Mesh → Merge To Center.**

4 Create the mouth

- **Extrude** the face on the front of the head towards the inside.
- **Delete** the face located on the central axis to fix the mouth opening.
- **Delete** the face located at the back of the inner mouth.

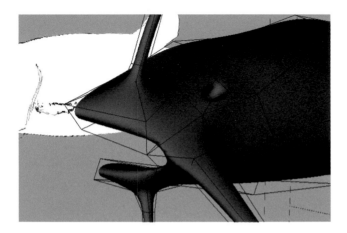

The mouth opening

Lesson 10: Modeling the Catfish

5 **Wedge the gill**

- Select two faces and two edges on the side of the head and use **Edit Mesh → Wedge Face** to create the gill opening.

- **Refine** the gill.

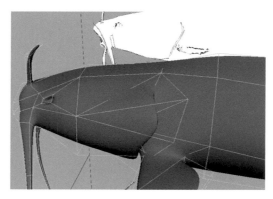

The wedged gill

6 **Save your work**

- Save your scene as *10-catfish body 03.ma*.

Working in Standard Mode

Now that the basic shape of the fish has been achieved, you will switch to Standard Mode and create the surface's details with hierarchical components.

1 **Switch to Standard Mode**

- **RMB** on *body* and select **Standard**.

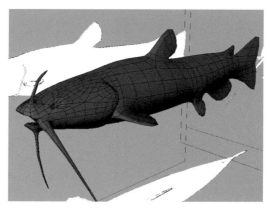

Fish in Standard Mode

2 Display the vertices

- **RMB** on the *body* and select **Vertex**.

  Level 0 vertices of the SubD surface are displayed.

3 View a finer level of the component hierarchy

You are going to pull vertices in the fins to create ridges, but editing the level 0 vertices will cause too broad a change of shape. You will now view a finer level of the component hierarchy to see if it will provide enough detail.

- **RMB** on the *body* and select **Display Level** → **1** from the menu.

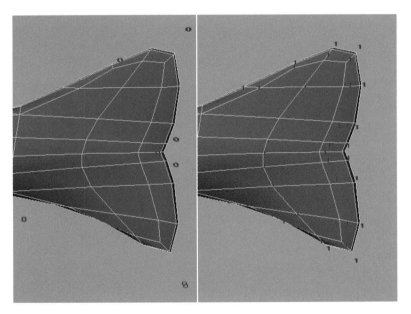

Areas covered by level 0 and level 1 vertices

Note: *You can also select* **Display Finer** *or* **Display Coarser** *from the same menu.*

4 Expand the level 1 components

Currently, there are not many level 1 vertices. Before attempting to refine the existing level 1 components to level 2, you will expand them so that the entire tail area is covered with level 1 vertices.

- Select the current level 1 vertices on the tail and select **Subdiv Surfaces** → **Expand Selected Components**.

Project 03

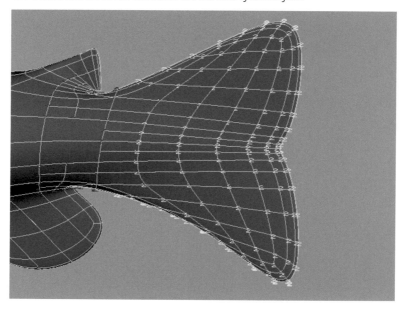

Note: *Depending on how you tweaked the model, it is possible that expanding the selected components has no effect since all the level 1 vertices already exist.*

5   Refine components

Even at the finer level of the hierarchy, there are too few vertices present to provide enough detail to define the shape required. You will now refine the components in the tail so that there are more vertices to work with.

- Select all of the level 1 vertices in the tail; then **RMB** and select **Refine Selected**.

    There should now be level 2 vertices in the tail area of the surface.

Level 1 vertices refined to level 2

6   Tweak the tail shape

- Select every other row of level 2 vertices running along the length of the tail.
- **Scale** and **move** the selected vertices into the tail to create ridges in the surface.

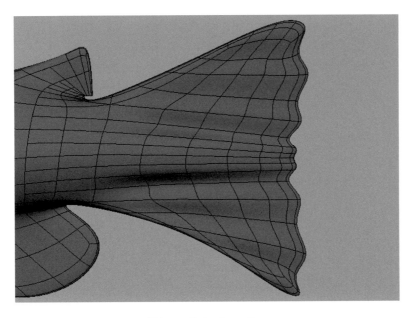

Ridges with level 2 vertices

7 Ridge all the fins

- **Repeat** the previous steps to insert ridges in all the fins.

Refined fins

8 Add a Full Crease to inner gill

- **RMB** on the *body* and select **Display Coarser** until you get to **level 0**.
- **RMB** on the *body* and select **Edge**.

- Select the edges defining the inside of the gill.
- Select **Subdiv Surfaces** → **Full Crease Edge/Vertex**.

  Notice how the subD geometry is sharper when creased.

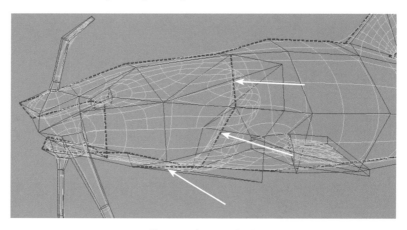

Fully creased inner gill edges

Note: *Full crease edges are displayed with dotted lines in the viewport. Border subD edges are automatically set to full crease.*

9 **Crease the vertices on the extremity of the antennas**

- **RMB** on the *body* and select the level 0 vertices at the tip of each whisker.
- Apply a **Full Crease** to them.

  A creased vertex will affect the subD geometry by creating a spike.

Full Crease applied to level 0 edges

10 **Experiment with the eye**

• Go back into Polygon Proxy Mode and **extrude** the face inside the eye socket to create a bulging eye.

Note: *Avoid changing the topology, such as subdividing a face, in areas where you've edited components in Standard Mode. Changing the topology can alter the surface in unexpected ways. This is not a problem for edits to level o components, however.*

• Go into Standard Mode and **full crease** the edges locate inside the eye socket.

• **Adjust** the shape of the eye to your liking.

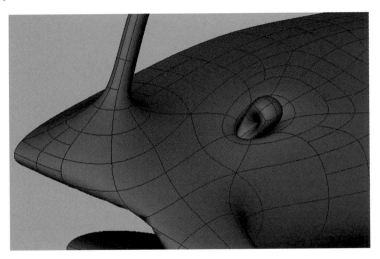

The eyeball

11 **Clean the geometry**

During the SubD modeling process, vertices are often created that end up being unnecessary to express the shape of the surface. While you can't directly delete these vertices, you can use Clean Topology to remove them automatically.

• Select the *body* and then select **Subdiv Surfaces → Clean Topology.**

Any unnecessary components on the surface will be deleted.

12 **Mirror the geometry**

• Select the *body* and then select **Subdiv Surfaces → Mirror → ☐.**

• In the options, set **Mirror** to **X** and click the **Mirror** button.

• Select the entire fish geometry, and then select **Subdiv Surfaces → Attach → ☐.**

- **In the options, set Threshold** to **0.01** and turn **Off** the **Keep originals** option.
- Click the **Attach** button.

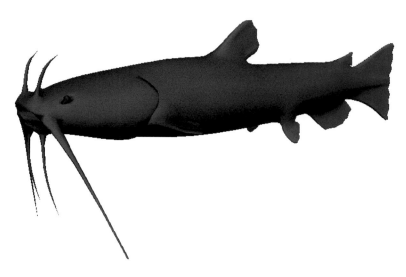

The entire fish geometry

13 **Clean up**

- **Delete** any obsolete nodes in the Outliner.
- **Delete** the image planes from the Hypershade.
- Select **File → Optimize Scene Size** to clean up the scene.

14 **Save your work**

- Save your scene as *10-catfish body 04.ma*.

Conclusion

You are now more familiar with hierarchical components in SubD modeling. You learned how to create a basic shape using Polygon Proxy Mode and how to refine and display various levels of details. Lastly, you creased components, cleaned up topology, and mirrored your entire model.

In the next lesson, you will learn about converting SubDs and texturing them.

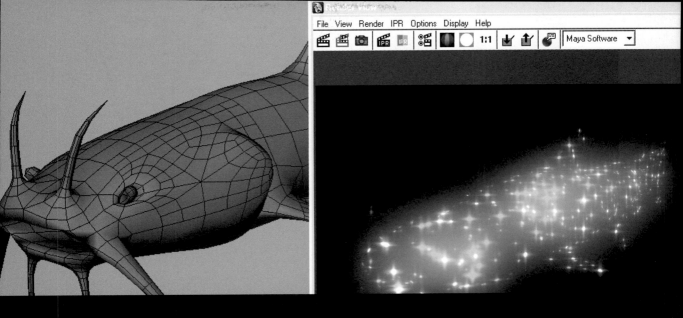

Lesson 11
Subdivision Tasks

In this lesson, you will examine a number of general tasks related to modeling with subdivision surfaces (SubDs).

In this lesson you will learn the following:

- How to convert polygons to SubDs;
- How to convert SubDs to polygons;
- How to map SubD UVs;
- How to assign a ramp;
- How to assign a 3D texture;
- How to assign shaders to portions of a SubD model;
- How to tweak SubD UVs.

Converting polygons to SubDs

In order to create a high-resolution model, it is possible to convert polygon surfaces to subdivision surfaces. While this process is generally problem-free, there are two issues you may typically encounter: the first is an insufficient **Maximum Base Mesh Faces** setting in the Convert Polygon to Subdiv option window, and the second is nonmanifold geometry.

The following exercise demonstrates both of these issues.

1   Open an existing scene file

* Open the scene file *11-poly to subd.ma*.

    The scene contains a modified version of Leon from Project 1.

2   Convert the polygon mesh to SubDs

* Select *Leon*'s geometry, and then select **Modify → Convert → Polygons to Subdiv**.

    An error message should appear informing you that the conversion failed, and that details can be found in the Script Editor.

3   Open the Script Editor

* Click on the **Script Editor** button at the lower-right corner of the interface to open the Script Editor window.

    The Script Editor states that the conversion failed because the resulting surface would have more base mesh faces than the maximum allowed by the conversion settings.

* Take note of the number of base mesh faces the *resulting surface* would have.

4   Increase the Maximum Base Mesh Faces value and convert

* With the mesh still selected, select **Modify → Convert → Polygons to Subdiv → ❑**.

* In the options, increase the **Maximum Base Mesh Faces** to a value higher than that listed in the Script Editor, such as **3000**.

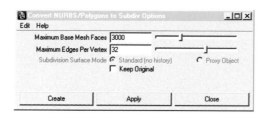

Convert Polygons to Subdiv options

This new setting value will fix the first issue that you may encounter when converting polygons to SubDs.

5 Convert the mesh to SubDs

- Click on the **Create** button.

  Once again, an error message should appear informing you that the conversion failed, and that details can be found in the Script Editor.

6 Open the Script Editor

The Script Editor states that the conversion failed because *one or more edges is non-manifold*. The surface will have to be cleaned up to correct the non-manifold geometry.

7 Clean up the polygonal mesh

- Select the poly mesh, and then select **Mesh → Cleanup...**, and set the options as follows:

- Under **Cleanup Effect**:

    Set **Operation** to **Cleanup matching polygons**.

- Under **Remove Geometry**:

    Set **Nonmanifold Geometry** to **On**.

> **Tip:** *If you don't want the tool to automatically clean up the geometry, set the* **Operation** *option to* **Select matching polygons**. *Doing so will allow you to frame the problematic geometry and correct it manually.*

- Click the **Cleanup** button.

  The tool will correct the nonmanifold geometry.

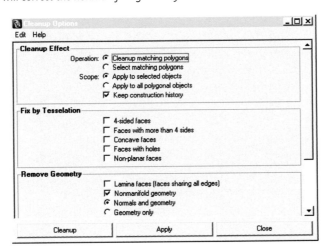

Polygon cleanup options

Note: *The nonmanifold geometry was located in Leon's mouth and was an extracted T-shaped polygon. The Cleanup Tool has simply separated the polygons from the mouth geometry.*

8 Convert the poly mesh to SubDs

- With the mesh still selected, select **Modify → Convert → Polygons to Subdiv**.

This time, the conversion is successful.

The converted geometry

Converting SubDs to polygons

It is not uncommon to take advantage of workflows that are unique to subdivision modeling, such as hierarchical components, and then convert the SubD surface to polygons for texturing and binding. How you choose to convert from SubDs to polygons will depend on your requirements.

1 Open an existing scene file

- Open the scene file *10-catfish body 04.ma* from the last lesson.

2 Check the number of component levels

- **RMB** on the SubD *fish* and check the number of display levels it has.

Note: *The fish should have display levels from 0 to 2.*

3   Convert SubDs to polygons

- Select the *fish*; then select **Modify** → **Convert** → **Subdiv To Polygons** → ▢, and set the following:

  Tessellation Method to **Vertices**;

  Level to **0**.

- Click the **Apply** button.

  The fish will be converted into a polygonal mesh that reflects the level 0 components of the SubD surface.

Polygonal surface after converting the Level 0 faces

- **Undo** the conversion.

4   Convert at higher settings

- In the Convert options, set the **Level** option to **1** and click the **Apply** button again.

  Once again, the SubD surface is converted to a poly surface, this time reflecting the level 1 vertices. The resulting surface is a more accurate representation of the original SubD surface, but the poly mesh is denser.

- **Undo** the conversion, and then repeat the conversion at **Level 3**.

  Converting at level 3 creates a perfectly faithful reproduction, but it also creates an extremely dense mesh.

Note: *When converting from one surface type to another, you will often have to strike a balance between accuracy in the resulting surface and density of the geometry.*

Lesson 11: Subdivision Tasks

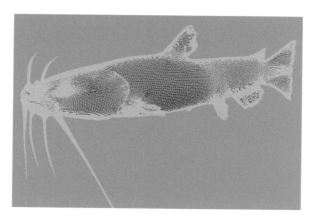

Polygonal surface after converting the level 3 faces

Texturing SubD surfaces

Texturing SubDs is much the same as texturing polygonal surfaces, although there are fewer tools for SubD texturing than the ones available for polygons.

In this exercise, you will apply a texture to the SubD fish from the last lesson.

1   Scene file

 • Open the scene file *10-catfish body 04.ma.*

2   Display the UVs

 • Select the *fish*, and then open the **Window → UV Texture Editor**.

 The polygonal surface UVs are in poor shape for texturing.

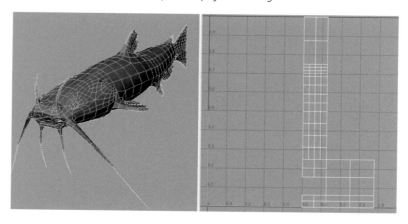

UVs viewed in the Texture Editor

3   **Map the subdivision surface's UVs**

- Select all the *fish*'s **Level 0** faces.

- Select **Subdiv Surfaces** → **Texture** → **Planar Mapping** → ❑.

- Set **Mapping Direction** to **X-axis**.

- Click the **Project** button.

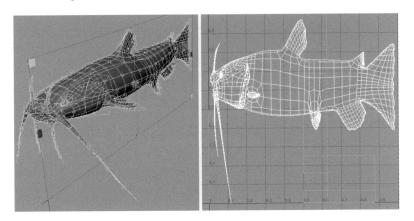

Corrected UVs

As you can see, subD UVs are very similar to polygonal UVs.

4   **Map a granite 3D texture**

- **Assign** a **Lambert** shader to the fish.

- Open the Attribute Editor for *lambert2* and **map** a **granite** 3D texture for the **Color** attribute.

- In the Hypershade, **MMB+drag** the *granite* texture on the *lambert* shader and map it to the **Incandescence** attribute.

  Since you will be using the granite shader to simulate stars, it will look much better if the stars are incandescent.

5   **Tweak the shader**

- In the Attribute Editor for the *granite* texture, set the following:

    Color 1 to **black**;

    Color 2 to **white**;

    Color 3 to **light blue**;

    Filler Color to **black**;

    Cell Size to **1.0**;

Lesson 11: Subdivision Tasks

Density to **0.6**;

Mix Ratio to **0.2**;

Spottyness to **1.0**;

Creases to **Off**.

This will result in a texture similar to a starry night sky.

> **Note:** *You will only see a texture preview in the viewport. You will need to render the model in order to see the result of the shader on the geometry.*

- In the Attribute Editor for the *lambert* shader, set **Glow Intensity** to **1.0** under the **Special Effects** section.

  This will make the stars glow.

- In the **Hypershade**, under the **Materials** tab, select the *shaderGlow1*.

- In the Attribute Editor for the *shaderGlow1*, under the **Glow Attributes**, set the **Glow Star Level** to **6.0**.

6 Test render

- **Test render** the *fish* to see the result of the star shader on the geometry.

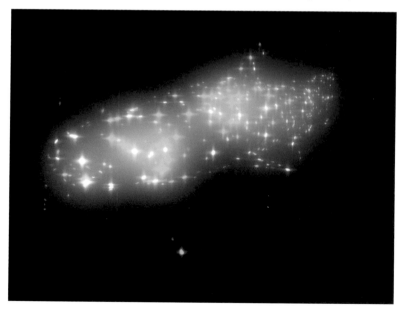

The rendered fish

7 Create Texture Reference Objects

Since the star shader is a 3D texture, you will need to create a texture reference object for the fish.

- With *fish* selected, go into the **Rendering** menu set and select **Texturing → Create Texture Reference Object**.

- Select the texture reference object and the *place3dTexture* nodes from the Outliner and **group** them together.

- **Rename** the group *txtGroup*.

- **Create** a new layer and **rename** it *txtRefLayer*.

- **Add** the *txtGroup* to the *txtRefLayer*.

- Make the layer a **reference** and **invisible**.

8 Clean up

- Make sure everything is organized in hierarchies and named appropriately.

- Select **Edit → Delete All By Type → History**.

- Select **File → Optimize Scene Size**.

9 Save your work

- Save your scene as *11-catfish texture 01.ma*.

Conclusion

You are now able to convert polygons to SubDs or SubDs to polygons. Doing so will allow you to decide whether you want to work with SubDs or polygons. You also learned about SubD UV mapping and how similar to polygon mapping it is.

In the next project, you will set up a character rig for Leon.

Project 04

In Project 4, you will create a character rig for Leon from Project 1. You will start by reviewing the basics of character rigging nodes, such as bones, IKs, locators and constraints. You will then build a complete rig. By the end of this project, you will have a full rig ready to be bound to Leon's geometry for animation.

Setup Leon's Skeleton

To begin, you are going to set up Leon's skeleton, which will help you prepare him for movements as well as provide a framework for applying deformations. This is done by drawing a series of joint nodes to build a skeleton chain.

To create the greatest flexibility for animating, you will set up the character's skeleton by combining several techniques.

In this lesson you will learn the following:

Layers

The Layer Editor is a good tool for organizing the various parts of a character. It provides an easy way to separate all the parts of Leon—geometry, skeletons, IK, etc.—into logical groups. In the Layer Editor, you can hide, show, template and reference selected layers to speed up interactivity by reducing the visible and modifiable elements in the scene.

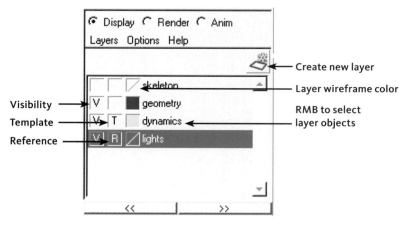

The Layer Editor

1 **Element visibility**

The more elements you can hide in your scene, the quicker you can interact with it. Layers can greatly accelerate the process of hiding and showing scene elements.

2 **Element selection**

It can be difficult to select objects and groups of objects efficiently in the interface. Layers offer various options in order to make the selection of objects easier.

3 **Template elements**

When you template layers, you still see a transparent representation of their elements, but they are not selectable.

4 **Reference elements**

When you reference layers, you see their elements, but they are not selectable. This enables you to view your scene normally, but you cannot select or modify referenced objects. A referenced object will also allow you to snap points to its wireframe.

Selecting and displaying only the elements of the scene you are working on is crucial to operating successfully in a scene.

Layers can also be used to break down your scene logically. You can make your background elements one layer and your foreground elements another layer. You can also create render layers that will render separately as compositing passes. By using this feature, you can render elements such as characters, background, and effects separately.

Prepare Leon's geometry

You are going to use Leon's body to help position the skeleton properly. You will first prepare the geometry for rigging. Once you begin creating the skeleton, you don't want to accidentally modify Leon, so you will create a layer just for the geometry, allowing you to template it.

1   Open Leon's geometry file

- Open the file called *04-leon texture 03.ma* from project 1.

2   Double-check the file's content

Depending on who created the character, the file might have some nonstandard nodes and leftovers lying around in it. It is recommended to always double-check how clean the file is before going on with the rigging, because once you start, it will be complicated to come back later on.

- Make sure all of Leon's geometry is grouped under a *geometry* group.
- Make sure Leon's scale is appropriate.
- Make sure that Leon's geometry is facing the **Z-positive axis**.
- **Move** the geometry in the **Y-axis** to place the feet on the grid.
- With *geometry* selected, select **Modify → Freeze Transformations**.

All the geometry is now frozen, meaning that their transform attributes are reset to their default values with the objects in the current position.

> **Note:** *Freezing transformations makes it easier to reset the geometry to its orignal position if needed later in production.*

- Open the Outliner and make sure all nodes are properly named.
- Select **Edit → Delete All by Type → History**.
- This will delete any unwanted construction history.

> **Tip:**   *Make sure you don't have a smooth applied on Leon before deleting the history.*

- Select **File → Optimize Scene Size**.

This will remove any unused nodes in the scene.

5   **Create a new layer for Leon's geometry**

  • Click the **Create a New Layer** button in the Layer Editor.

Tip: *If the Layer Editor is not visible, enable the* **Channel Box/Layer Editor** *button under* **Display → UI Elements**.

  • **Double-click** on the *layer1* to open the **Edit Layer** window.

  • Name the layer *geometryLayer* and click on the **Save** button to confirm the changes.

  • In the Outliner, select the *geometry* group.

  • **RMB** on the *geometryLayer* and select **Add Selected Objects.**

  The selected objects are now a part of the geometryLayer.

Note: *You can see the layer's connection in the* **Inputs** *section of the Channel Box for the selected elements.*

6   **Template the layer**

  • Click on the middle box next to the *geometryLayer* to see a **T**, which means the layer is templated.

  You can now see Leon's geometry in wireframe. The geometry also cannot be selected in any viewports.

Note: *The geometry is still selectable through editors such as the Outliner or the Hypergraph.*

7   **Save your work**

  • Save your scene as *12-skeleton 01.ma*.

Drawing the skeleton

A skeleton chain is made up of *joints* that are visually connected by *bones*. A skeleton chain creates a continuous hierarchy of joint nodes that are parented to each other. The top node of the hierarchy is known as the *root* joint. The joints and bones help you visualize the character's hierarchy in the 3D views but will not appear in renders.

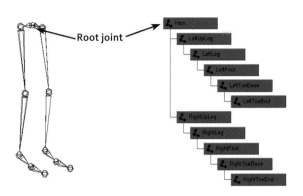

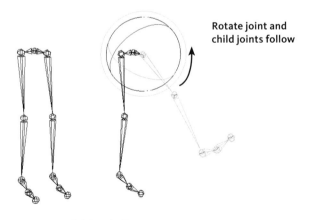

Joints and bones in the viewport and the Hypergraph

Joint hierarchies let you group or bind geometry. You can then animate the joints, which in turn, animates the geometry. When you transform the joints you will most often use rotation. If you look at your own joints you will see that they all rotate. Generally, joints don't translate or scale unless you want to add some squash-and-stretch to a character's limbs.

When you rotate a joint, all the joints below it are carried along with the rotation. This behavior is called forward kinematics and is consistent with how all hierarchies work in Autodesk® Maya® software. In Lesson 14, you will learn how to use inverse kinematics to make it easier to animate joint rotations.

**Rotate joint and
child joints follow**

Joints rotations

Tip: *Use the up, down, left, and right arrow keys to traverse through a hierarchy.*

Lesson 12: Setup Leon's Skeleton

The leg joints

Using the geometry as a guide, you will begin by creating Leon's left leg skeleton. You will then mirror the joints to create the right leg skeleton. Later in this lesson you will build the upper body, which will be connected by the *Hips* joint.

1   **Draw the left leg**

• From the side view, frame Leon's legs.

• Press **F2** to display the **Animation** menu set, and then select
Skeleton → Joint Tool → ❑.

• In the options, set **Orientation** to None.

Note: *Joint Orientation will be discussed in the next lesson.*

• Starting at the hip, place **five** joints for the leg, as shown in the next image.

• **Rename** the joints to *LeftUpLeg, LeftLeg, LeftFoot, LeftToeBase,* and *LeftToeEnd.*

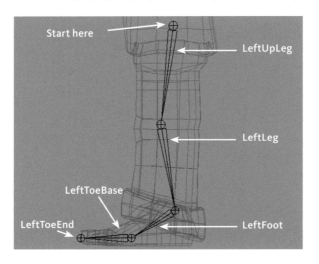

Left leg joints

Tip: *Always make sure to draw the knee in a bent position. This will make it easier to apply an IK solver to the chain.*

2 Change the joint display size

- If you find the joint display size to be too big or too small, you can change the default setting under **Display** → **Animation** → **Joint Size...**

3 Move the joint chain to Leon's left side

The *LeftUpLeg* joint is now the *root* node of the leg's joint chain hierarchy. If you pick this node you can move the whole chain at once.

- From the front view, select the *LeftUpLeg* joint and **move** it along the **X-axis** so it aligns with the position of Leon's left hip bone.

- Still in the front view, **move** if needed the *LeftLeg* and *LeftFoot* joints along the **X-axis** so they align with the position of Leon's left knee and ankle.

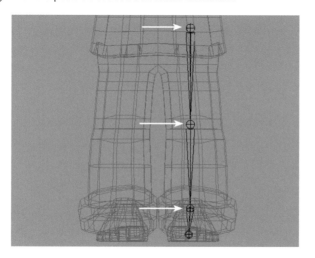

Moving the joint chain into Leon's left leg

4 Mirror the leg to create the right leg

- Select the *LeftUpLeg* joint.
- Select **Skeleton** → **Mirror Joint** → ❐.
- In the options, set the following:

    Mirror across to **YZ**;

    Mirror function to **Behavior**.

- Click the **Mirror** button.

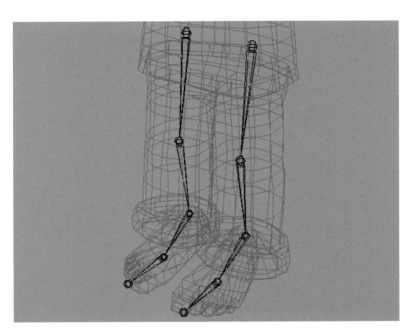

Mirrored leg

5   Rename the right leg

Always take the time to name your objects so they are easy to find and select.

- **Rename** the right leg joints to *RightUpLeg*, *RightLeg*, *RightFoot*, *RightToeBase* and *RightToeEnd*.

> **Tip:**   *This type of task is perfect for using MEL scripting to rename all the joints automatically. Execute the following MEL command to rename the currently selected node's Left for Right:*
>
> ```
> for($each in `ls -sl`) rename $each `substitute "Left" $each
> "Right"`;
> ```

The spine joints

You will now create another skeleton hierarchy for Leon's pelvis, spine, neck, and head. The hierarchy will start from the hips, which will be the root of the skeleton. The root joint is important since it represents the parent of the hierarchy. Using the hips as the root, the upper body and the legs will branch off from this node. You can then move the whole skeleton hierarchy by simply moving the root.

1   **The pelvis joint**

- Select **Skeleton** → **Joint Tool** → ▢.

- In the options, set **Orientation** to **XYZ**.

  *By creating the joints with **Orientation** set to **XYZ** and the **Second Axis World Orientation** set to **+y**, you have made sure that the X-axis of the joint will always point towards the child joint and the Y-axis will point in the world-positive Y-axis direction. You set the orientation to **XYZ** so that the local rotation axis of the joints will be aligned in the direction of the spine. This topic will be covered in more detail in the next lesson and throughout the book.*

- From the side view, **click+drag** the pelvis bone just above the hip joint.

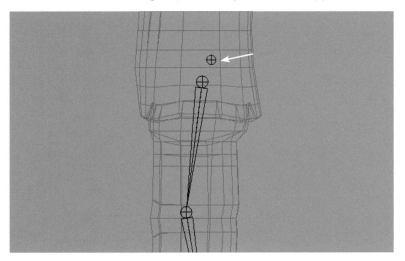

The pelvis joint

Tip: *While placing joints, you can use the **MMB** to modify the placement of the last created joint. When using the **Move Tool** on a joint hierarchy, all the child joints will move accordingly. Press the **Insert** key to toggle the **Move Pivot Tool**, which will move only the selected joint and not its children.*

2   **The spine joints**

- Draw equally spaced joints until you reach between Leon's shoulders.

Tip: *Try to follow the shape of Leon's back to create a joint chain similar to the spine under his skin. Since Leon's back is hyperextended while standing straight, the spine will have a slight curve in it.*

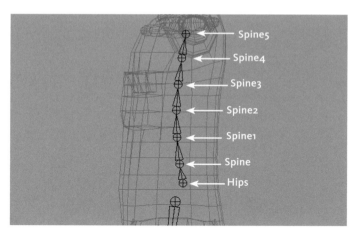

Joint names for the spine

- Press **Enter** on your keyboard to complete the joint chain.
- **Rename** the joints according to the illustration.

3 Neck and head joints

- Press **y** to activate the **Joint Tool**.
- Click on the last joint between Leon's shoulders to highlight it.

  Doing so will specify that the Joint Tool should continue drawing from that joint.

- **Draw** the neck and head joints as follows:

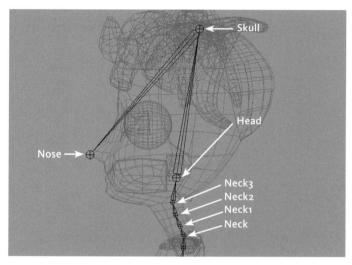

Joint names for neck and head

> **Tip:** There are no strict rules about how many joints are needed to create the upper body spine; it really depends on how you want to animate the motion in the back. You could use an IK Spline for the back to simplify the control of such a large number of joints. Here are some guidelines for determining the number of joints to use in a typical biped character: spine (3 - 10 joints), neck (1 - 5 joints).

- **Rename** the joints according to the previous illustration.

Parenting skeletons

You now have three separate skeleton hierarchies: one for each leg and the spine. To make them one hierarchy, you need to parent the legs to the root joint.

There are several rigging approaches to the hip/spine relationship. The method you use depends on what the animation requires and how much control you need. For Leon, you will create a setup that provides natural lower body motion and easy control.

1 Add a single joint

- Press **y** to activate the **Joint Tool**.
- Click on the *Hips* joint to highlight it.
- Hold down **v** to Snap to Point and draw a single joint over the *Hips*.
- Press **Enter** to confirm the joint creation.

   If you open the Outliner, you will see that you have just created a single joint, which is a child of the Hips. Both legs will be parented to this new joint.

- **Rename** the new joint *HipsOverride*.

2 Parent the legs to the override

- Open the Outliner.
- Select the *LeftUpLeg* joint; then hold **Ctrl** to select the *RightUpLeg*.
- Hold **Ctrl** again and select the *HipsOverride* joint.
- Select **Edit** → **Parent** or press the **p** key.

> **Note:** The HipsOverride was selected last since it has to be the parent of the two legs. You could have also used the Outliner to parent these joints by **MMB+dragging** the child node onto the intended parent.

3 **Test the lower body**

- **Rotate** each leg to see how it reacts.

- **Rotate** the *Hips* and *HipsOverride* to see how they react.

Note: *You will notice that the HipsOverride bone gives you independent control of the hip rotation.*

- When you are finished testing the lower body rotations, select the *Hips* joint, and then select Skeleton → Assume Preferred Angle.

Tip: *You can also select the **Assume Preferred Angle** command with the **RMB** in the viewport when a bone is selected.*

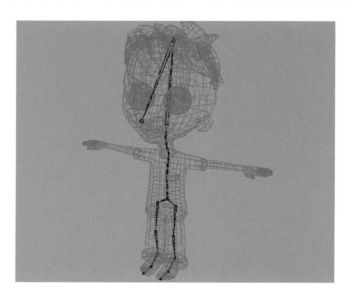

Leon's skeleton so far

4 **Save your work**

- Save your scene as *12-skeleton 02.ma*.

The arm joints

You will now create Leon's arms and hands using the character's geometry to aid the joint placement.

In this exercise, you will learn about an arm technique that will set up special skinning characteristics in the forearm area. You will do this by creating a roll joint between the elbow and the wrist. When you later skin Leon, this extra forearm joint will cause the forearm to twist when the wrist rotates, just like a human arm.

When you create the roll bone, it is important to ensure that the forearm joints are created in a straight line.

1 **Left arm joints**

- Select the **Skeleton → Joint Tool**.

- From the Perspective view, click on the last spine joint to highlight it.

> **Tip:** *If you don't know which spine joint is the last one, click on any spine joint, use the* **Up** *and* **Down** *arrows to walk in the hierarchy to find the appropriate joint.*

- In the top view, place one joint at each of the following articulations: the clavicle, the shoulder, the elbow, the middle of the forearm, and the wrist. Hold down the **Shift** key as you place the *roll bone* and *wrist* joints to make sure they are in a straight line with the elbow.

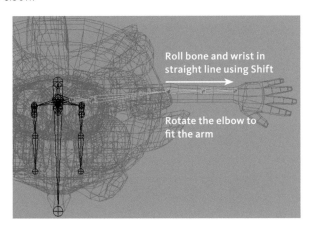

The arm joints

- **Rename** the joints *LeftShoulder, LeftArm, LeftForeArm, LeftForeArmRoll,* and *LeftHand.*

2 **Place the arm joints**

- Still from the top view, **rotate** and **scale** the *LeftForeArm* joints to achieve proper alignment with Leon's forearm. You can also **scale** the *LeftForeArmRoll* to reach Leon's wrist.

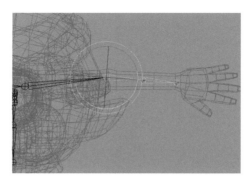

Arm joints aligned in top view

- Select the *LeftShoulder* joint.

- Press the **w** key to enter the **Move Tool**, and then press the **Insert** key (**Home** on Mac) to enter the **Move Pivot Tool**.

- From the front view, **translate** the *LeftShoulder* joint down so that it is closer to the center of the chest.

Note: *Since you will be reorienting the joints in the next lesson, it is okay to translate the specified joints.*

- Press the **down** arrow key to change the selection to the *LeftArm* joint.

- Press the **Insert** key (**Home** on Mac) again, to toggle back to the **Move Tool**.

- **Translate**, **rotate** and **scale** the *LeftArm* joint **up** to fit Leon's arm.

Note: *Make sure to keep the arm joints in a straight line in the front view.*

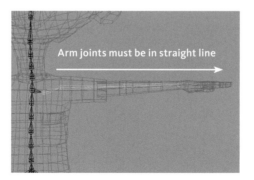

Arm joints aligned in front view

3   **Left hand joints**

- Select **Skeleton** → **Joint Tool**.

- Click on the *LeftHand* joint to highlight it.

- In the top view, place the following index joints:

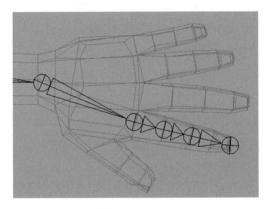

The index joints

- Press the **up** arrow **four** times to put the selection on the *LeftHand* joint.

- **Repeat** the previous two steps to create the rest of the fingers.

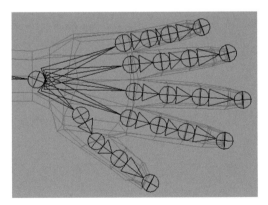

All fingers created

- Press **Enter** to exit the **Joint Tool**.

4   **Place the fingers**

- Place the fingers in Leon's geometry by **translating** and **rotating** the first joint of each finger. Only **rotate** the other finger joints.

Lesson 12: Setup Leon's Skeleton

5   **Rename the fingers**

- Select the first index joint.

- Select **Edit → Select Hierarchy**.

- Locate the **Input Line** at the top right of the main interface and change its setting to **Rename**.

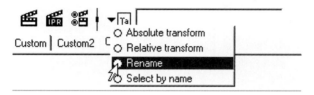

The Input Line

- Type *LeftHandIndex* in the **Field Entry,** and then hit **Enter**.

  The selected joints will be renamed like this:

  LeftHandIndex1, LeftHandIndex2, LeftHandIndex3, LeftHandIndex4;

- **Repeat** the previous steps to select and rename all the middle finger joints to *LeftHandMiddle*.

- **Repeat** the previous steps to select and rename all the ring finger joints to *LeftHandRing*.

- **Repeat** the previous steps to select and rename all the thumb joints to *LeftHandThumb*.

6   **Mirror the arm joints**

- Select the *LeftShoulder* joint and mirror it by selecting **Skeleton → Mirror Joint → ❏.**

- In the options, set the following:

    Mirror across to **YZ**;

    Mirror function to **Behavior**;

    Search for to *Left*;

    Replace with to *Right*.

- Press the **Mirror** button.

  Leon's right arm skeleton is created.

Completed skeleton

Note: *Make sure the right arm is named properly.*

7   Save your work

- Save your scene as *12-skeleton 03.ma.*

Conclusion

This lesson introduced the use of joints for building skeletal structures. Joints are objects specially designed to live in hierarchies and maintain the parent-child relationship. They also contain special attributes to control their orientation, which is important for character animation. These joints, as you will see in following lessons, can be animated using controls such as inverse kinematics and Set Driven Key.

In the next lesson, you will learn the importance of knowing how joints operate with respect to their orientation, specifically their local rotation orientation.

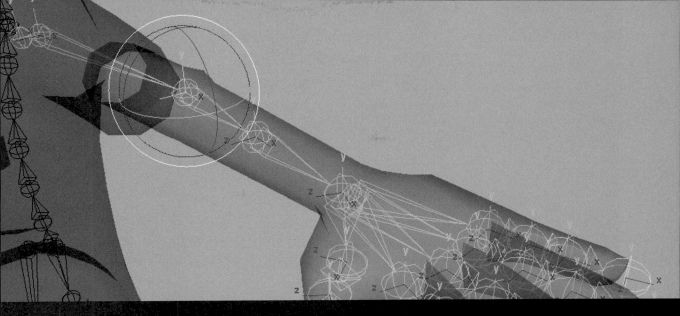

Lesson 13
Joint Orientation

In this lesson, you will learn about the local rotation axis and how to tweak axes on Leon's
skeleton from the last lesson. Having the proper local rotation axis for each joint is crucial when
setting up and animating a character.

In this lesson you will learn the following:

Joint orientation

Each joint has a *Local Rotation Axis* that defines how the joint will react to transformations. For most parts of a character, the default orientation is fine. When setting up more complex situations, it is important to make sure that all the joints' axes of rotation are aimed in a consistent manner.

By using *Orientation*, you ensure that all local rotation axes of new joints are aligned with the bones that follow. This will help control the joints' transformations when using forward kinematics.

Following are some simple examples that explain the basics of local rotation axes:

1   **Open a new scene**

2   **Turn Orientation off**

- Select **Skeleton** → **Joint Tool** → ☐ and set the following:

    Orientation to **None**;

    Second axis world orientation to **None**.

- In the front view, draw joints in an **S** pattern.

    You will see that the round joint icons are all aligned like the world axis.

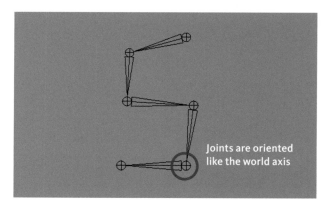

Joint orientation set to None

3   **Orientation turned On**

- Select **Skeleton** → **Joint Tool** → ☐ and set the following:

    Orientation to **XYZ**;

    Second axis world orientation to **None**.

- In the front view, draw joints in an **S** pattern.

  The joint icons are all aligned with the first bone that follows. Only the last joint in the chain is aligned with the world axis because there is no child bone to align to.

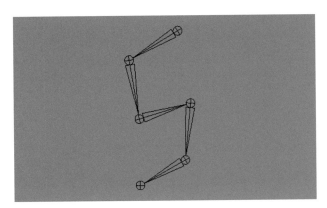

Joint orientation set to XYZ

4 Draw joints with World Axis Orient turned On

- Select **Skeleton → Joint Tool →** ☐ and set the options back to default values like the following:

  Orientation to **XYZ**;

  Second axis world orientation to **+y**.

- In the front view, draw joints in an **S** pattern.

  As with the last skeleton, each joint icon is aligned with the bone that follows it. The only difference is the Y-axis, which has been aligned to the world-positive Y-axis. The only way you can see the difference is by either rotating the joints or displaying their local rotation axes.

5 Display the joint axes

- Select the fourth joint in all three of the hierarchies.

- Press **F8** to go into Component mode.

- Enable the **?** mask button in the Status Line.

  This will display the local rotation axes of the selected hierarchies.

The first skeleton has its axes aligned with world space. The second skeleton has its X-axis pointing down the bone. The third skeleton has its X-axis pointing down the bone and its Y-axis pointing in the world-positive Y direction.

Lesson 13: Joint Orientation

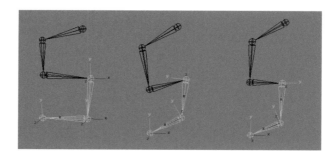

Displayed local rotation axes

Note: *Local rotation axes are aligned according to the right-hand rule. For example, if you select an orientation of XYZ, the positive X-axis points into the joint's bone and towards the joint's first child joint, the Y-axis points at right angles to the X-axis and Z-axis, and the Z-axis points sideways from the joint and its bone.*

6 Rotate joints around the X-axis

- Go back into Object mode and click on the **Rotate X** channel in the Channel Box to highlight it.

- **MMB+drag** in the view to invoke the virtual slider and change the **Rotate X** value interactively.

  The second and third skeletons rotate nicely around the bone while the first skeleton is rotating in world space with no relation to the bone at all.

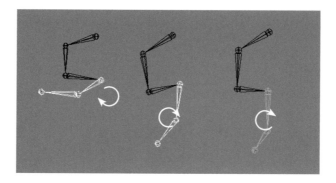

The first two skeletons' joints rotated around their local X-axes

- Press the **z** key to **undo** the rotations.

Joint edits and joint orientation

In the last lesson, you repositioned joints using several techniques, such as translating, rotating, and scaling the joint pivot. Some of these techniques can offset the local rotation axis from its child bone, which could be problematic when animating. Following is a review of the four techniques and their effect on the local rotation axis:

Rotating joints

When you rotate a joint, its local rotation axis is not affected, but the bone's rotation values change. Attempting to keep zero rotation values makes it easy to reset joints' rotations. This issue can be resolved by freezing transformations on the joints.

Rotating joints

Scaling joints

Scaling joints

Of all the techniques described here, scaling a bone is the most unobjectionable, but it will alter the default scaling values. These values can be reset by freezing transformations.

Translating joints

When a joint is translated, the parent joint's local rotation axis will offset from pointing to its child bone and can create inappropriate rotations when animating. This issue can be resolved either by manually tweaking or automatically reorienting the local rotation axis.

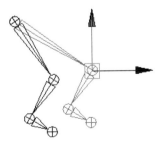

Translating joints

Translating joint pivots

When translating a joint pivot, both the parent and the translated joints' local rotation axes will offset from pointing to its child bone and can create inappropriate rotations when animating. This issue can be resolved either by manually tweaking or automatically reorienting the local rotation axis.

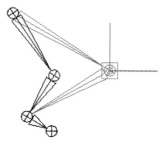

Translating joint pivots

Reorient local rotation axes

When you use the Joint Tool with Orientation set to XYZ, the tool forces the X-axis to point down to the bone toward the first child joint. If the joints' placements are adjusted, you might need to also adjust their local rotation axes so they will correctly point down the bone. One solution is to simply reorient the joints, as if they were just drawn.

1   **Translating joints**

- **Select** and **translate** the joints of the second **S**-shaped skeleton created earlier to create a clear offset on their local rotation axes.

- Select the *root* joint, and then select **Skeleton → Orient Joint → ❑.**

- Set the options as follows:

> **Orientation** to **XYZ**;
>
> **Second axis world orientation** to **+y**;
>
> **Orient child joints** to **On**;

- Click the **Orient** button.

  Notice that all joints of the selected hierarchy now have proper default rotation axes.

> **Note:** *If you notice that some joints are not properly aligned, you might have to fix the flipped local rotation axis manually. You will learn how to do this in the next exercise.*

Project 04

It is important to note what happens in the Attribute Editor when the joint orientation is changed:

Rotation doesn't change.

Joint Orient changes so that the **Rotate** attributes don't have to change.

Editing local rotation axes

In addition to making sure that one axis always points down the bone, you also want to make sure that the other axes relate to the skeleton in the same way.

1   Selecting local rotation axis component

- Select the root joint of the last **S**-shaped skeleton created earlier.

- Press **F8** to go into Component mode, and make sure the **?** selection mask button is enabled.

    All the local rotation axes of the selected joints are displayed. Notice the orientation in which the Z-axes are pointing. Some are pointing in one direction while others are pointing in the opposite direction.

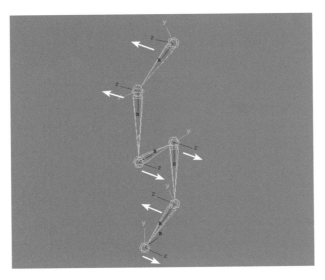

Joints rotated around X-axis.

2   The problem

- Go back into Object mode.

- With the root joint still selected, select **Edit → Select Hierarchy**.

- **Rotate** the bones on their **Z-axis**.

  Notice how the bones rotate unexpectedly since they are not all rotating in the same direction. This is the problem you want to fix.

- **Undo** the rotations.

3   **Rotate the joint axes interactively**

- Go back into Component mode.

- Select one of the local rotation axes pointing in the opposite direction to the root.

- **Rotate** the axis by about **180 degrees** on its **X-axis**.

Tip: *Make sure the **Rotate Tool** option is set to **Local**. When you drag an axis, an indicator in the middle of the **Rotate Tool** will show the rotation angle. You can also enable the **Snap rotate** option to rotate by a prefered angle step.*

4   **Rotating the joint axes using a script**

You can also rotate the axes more accurately by entering a simple MEL script in the command line. Because the joints were created with the **Orientation** set to **XYZ**, if an axis is flipped, it needs to be rotated by **180 degrees** on the **X-axis**.

- Select the remaining local rotation axis pointing in the opposite direction to the root.

- In the command line, enter the following command:

```
rotate -r -os 180 0 0;
```

Note: *Don't worry about the last joint. Its local axis is not oriented toward anything and does not affect how the skeleton works.*

Note: *The **Second axis world orientation** option, which is available when creating or reorienting joints, will eliminate the need to worry about flipped secondary axes in most cases.*

Freeze joint transformations

When you use the **Rotate Tool** or **Scale Tool** to alter the placement of a joint, it is good to reset the rotation and scale attributes to their default values at the rigging stage. This will allow the skeleton to be quickly reset into its default position.

1   **Freezing joints**

- **Select**, **rotate** and **scale** the joints of the last **S**-shaped skeleton created earlier to change their values in the Channel Box.

- Select **Modify** → **Freeze Transformations**.

   Notice that the altered rotation and scale values in the Channel Box are reset back to their default values with the joint chain still in the current position.

Note: *The translation values of joints cannot be reset to their default values, or they would be moved to their parent position. Another way of resetting joints is to re-create a complete skeleton, using Snap to Point.*

When to be concerned about local rotation axes?

To determine the proper axis for your joints, you need to understand what you are going to do with the joints. The following options explore some of the possibilities discussed throughout the rest of the book. You may want to return to this list when you are more familiar with the options available:

Forward kinematics (FK)

For FK, it is important for joints to be able to rotate correctly, local to their direction. How a joint rotates is directly linked to the orientation of its local rotation axis. This is very apparent when animating fingers, and you will be looking at this in more detail later in this lesson.

Expressions and Set Driven Keys

If an expression is created to rotate multiple joints simultaneously around a specific axis, you want the joints to rotate in a consistent direction. If one of the axes is flipped, the task of writing an expression is much more difficult.

Inverse kinematics (IK)

The differences are not as apparent when an IK goes through the joints. But in many cases, joints will only need to rotate around the proper axis, and having the local rotation axis set before adding IK will help, especially when you intend to allow blending between IK and FK.

Constraints

With constraints, any rotation results will depend on whether the objects involved in the constraint have similar orientation.

Correcting Leon's skeleton

Next, you will correct Leon's local rotation axes. With all the joint orientations set correctly, you will not have to worry about them anymore.

1 Open an existing scene file

- Open the scene file from the last lesson called *12-skeleton 03.ma.*

2 Delete right side joints

At this time, you need to bother only with one half of Leon's skeleton. There is no need to correct the entire left arm and then the entire right arm. The Mirror Joint command will take care of this for you.

- Select the *RightShoulder* and the *RightUpLeg* joints.

- Press **Delete** on your keyboard.

3 Reset the skeleton

Since you used several techniques in the last lesson to place your joints in Leon's geometry, it is a good idea to reorient all the local rotation axes of each joint.

- Select the *Hips* joint and then select **Modify → Freeze Transformations.**

  This will reset any nondefault values on the joints.

- Select the *Hips* joint and then select **Skeleton → Orient Joint.**

  Doing so will reorient all the local rotation axes to XYZ.

4 Display the local rotation axes

- Select the *Hips* joint and press **F8** to go into Component mode.

- Make sure the **?** selection mask button is enabled.

5 Verify the joint alignment

When looking at Leon from the front, all the vertical joints, such as the pelvis, spine, head and leg, should have their Z-axes pointing on the same side. All horizontal joints, such as the arm and hand, should have their Y-axes pointing on the same side.

- Locate any problematic local rotation axes, select them, and rotate them around their **X-axes**.

 Tip: *The Hips and HipsOverride local rotation axes should be oriented like the world axis. This will greatly simplify the animation tasks on the pelvis.*

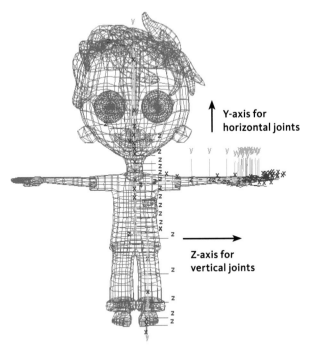

Y-axis for
horizontal joints

Z-axis for
vertical joints

Correct local rotation axes

6 Mirror the joints

- Go back in Object mode.
- Select the *LeftShoulder* joint.
- Select **Skeleton → Mirror Joints → ❏**.
- In the options, set **Search for:** *Left* and **Replace with:** *Right*.

  Doing so will automatically rename the joints correctly.
- Click **Apply** to leave the option window open.
- Select the *LeftUpLeg* joint.
- Select **Skeleton → Mirror Joints**.

Note: *If you look at the mirrored joints' local rotation axes, you will notice that their X-axes and Y-axes are pointing in opposite directions. This is the desired effect and will make animation tasks easier.*

The mirrored local rotation axes

7   Set the preferred angle

- Select the *Hips* joint.

- Select **Skeleton → Set Preferred Angle**.

    The skeleton's current pose will be kept in memory as the preferred angle and can be recalled at any time using the **Assume Preferred Angle** *command.*

8   Test rotations

Take some time to test orientation by selecting multiple joints simultaneously. For instance, select the shoulders on both arms and notice the effect of the mirrored local rotation axis. When you are done, select the *Hips* joint; then **RMB** and select **Assume Preferred Angle**.

9   Save your work

- The final scene is called *13-orientation 01.ma*.

Conclusion

Creating joints, orienting them appropriately, and naming them correctly are the trademarks of a good rigger. Understanding why Maya assigns orientation based on child joint orientation can help predict where a *flip* of local rotation orientation may occur.

There are many tricks to setting up joints quickly including snapping, parenting, and duplicating. Riggers can usually speed up repetitive tasks by using MEL macros, commands, and scripts.

In the next lesson, you will learn about the basics of *inverse kinematics*.

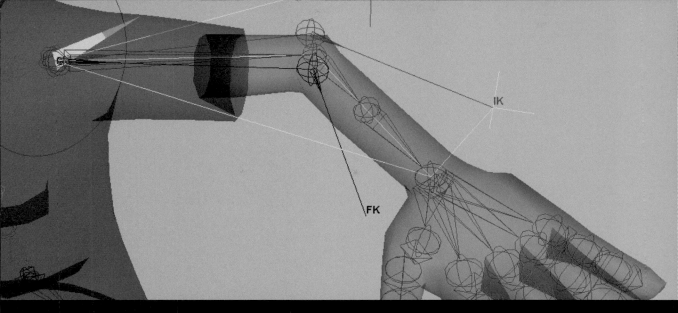

Lesson 14
Inverse Kinematics

In this lesson, you will learn about inverse kinematics (IK). You will see that IK can provide control over a joint chain that would be very difficult to achieve using forward kinematics (FK).

In this lesson you will learn the following:

- The difference between IK and FK;
- The different IK solvers;
- How to set up Single Chain IK solvers;
- How to set up Rotate Plane IK solvers;
- How to use the preferred angle;
- How to change the IK stickiness and priority;
- Important IK attributes;
- How to use the Pole Vector and Twist attributes;
- How to animate IK handles and joints;
- How to use IK/FK blending.

Forward vs. inverse kinematics

In the previous lesson, you used *forward kinematics* (FK) by rotating joints manually. While FK is very powerful, it has some limitations when it comes to animating a complex setup such as a character. Since all of the animation is accomplished using the rotation of joints, if you rotate a parent joint in the hierarchy, all of its children will also be moved. For instance, if you were to rotate a character's foot so that it plants on the ground, any movement in the pelvis area would move the foot out of place.

Inverse kinematics (IK) solves this problem by controlling a series of joints using an IK handle. Moving either the handle or a parent joint evokes the IK solver, which calculates the appropriate joint rotations to achieve the desired pose.

Autodesk® Maya® software contains three main IK solvers:

Single Chain IK solver

This solver provides IK in its simplest form. When you move the IK handle, the chain will update so that the joints lie along a plane relative to the IK handle's rotation. The Single Chain IK solver will be used with Leon's reverse foot setup.

Rotate Plane IK solver

This solver gives you more control and is the most commonly used IK solver. You can use the IK handle so that the joints lie along a plane and then you can rotate the plane using a Twist attribute or by moving a pole vector handle. The Rotate Plane IK solver will be used to rig Leon's arms and legs.

Spline IK solver

This solver lets you control the joint rotations using a spline curve. You can either move the chain along the curve or update the shape of the curve using its CVs. The Spline IK solver will be used to control Leon's spine.

Forward kinematics example

The following example shows a simple leg being controlled by FK:

1 **Create the leg joints**
   • In the side view panel, draw three joints representing a leg.
   • In front of the leg, place two cubes as follows:

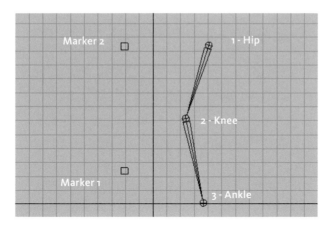

Leg joints and positioning markers

These will help you visualize what is happening as you work with the joints.

2   **Rotate the joints**

- **Rotate** the *hip* and *knee* joints so that the *ankle* joint is positioned at *marker1*.

  With FK, you must rotate the joints into place to position the ankle.

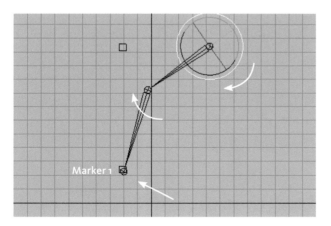

Positioned leg

3   **Move the hip joint**

- **Move** the *hip* joint forward to place it on *marker2*.

  You will see how the knee and ankle joints also move. Now the ankle joint is no longer on the first marker. You would have to rotate the joints back to return the ankle into its previous position.

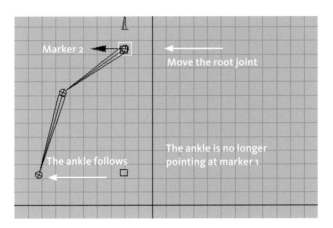

Moving the hip joint

Inverse kinematics example

The following example shows a simple leg being controlled by IK:

1   **Single Chain IK handle**

  - **Undo** the previous moves to get back to the original leg position.

  - Select **Skeleton → IK Handle Tool → □**.

  - In the option window, set the following:

      Current Solver to **ikSCsolver**;

      Sticky to **On**.

  > **Note:** *The **Sticky** option will be explained later in this lesson.*

  - Click the **Close** button.

  - Click on the *hip* joint to establish the root of the solver.

  - Click on the *ankle* joint to place the IK handle.

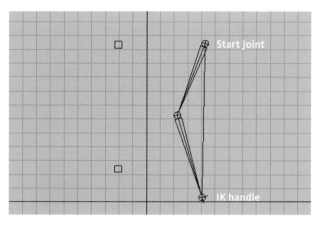

The IK handle

2   Move the IK handle

- **Move** the IK handle so that it's placed on *marker1*.

  Notice how the knee and hip joints rotate to achieve the proper pose.

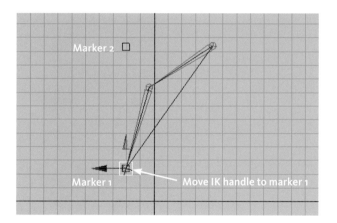

Moved IK handle

3   Move the hip

- Select the *hip* joint.

- **Translate** the *hip* joint to place it on *marker2*.

  The IK handle keeps the ankle joint on the first marker as you move the hip joint forward. The ankle will pull away from the IK handle if you pull the hip too far.

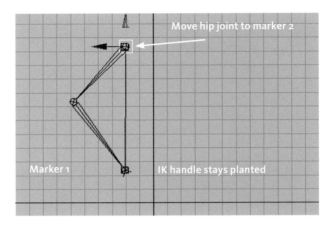

Moved hip joint

Preferred angle

The IK solver will use a joint's preferred angle to establish the direction a joint should bend. It can be thought of as a default bend direction. For example, if you create a straight up and down leg joint, run IK through that joint and try to manipulate it. The solver will not be able to bend the joint. By setting the preferred angle, you provide the solver with a guideline to follow.

1   Create straight leg joints

- In a new scene, draw three joints in a straight line, holding down **x** to **Snap to Grid**.

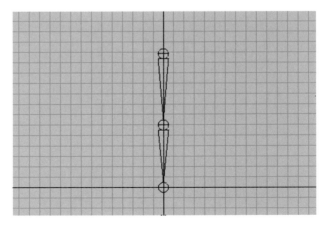

New leg joints

2   Add a Single Chain IK handle

- Select **Skeleton → IK Handle Tool**.

- Select the *hip* joint as the root and then the *ankle* joint to place the IK handle.

3   Move the IK handle

- **Move** the IK handle to affect the chain.

  Notice that the knee does not bend. This is because there is no bend in the bones on either side of the knee. Therefore, the solver is not able to figure out which direction to bend.

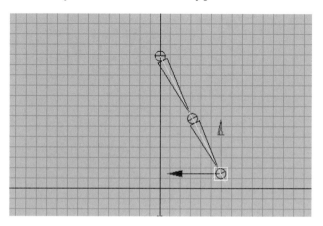

Moved IK handle

4   Undo

- **Undo** the last move on the IK handle to return the chain to its original position.

- **Delete** the IK handle.

5   Set the preferred angle

- Select the *knee* joint.

- **Rotate** the *knee* to bend the leg.

- With the *knee* still selected, select **Skeleton → Set Preferred Angle → ❑.**

- In the option window, turn **Selected Joint** to **On**.

- Press the **Set** button.

- **Rotate** the *knee* joint back to **0**.

6   Add another IK handle

- Press the **y** key or select **Skeleton → IK Handle Tool.**

- Select the *hip* joint as the root and then the *ankle* joint to place the IK handle.

7   Move the IK handle

- **Move** the IK handle to affect the chain.

  Now the knee should be bending since the preferred angle tells the solver in which direction to bend.

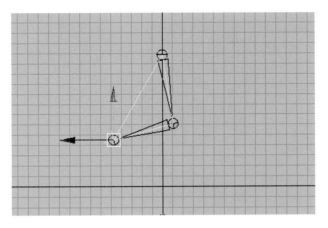

Moved IK handle

Stickiness

In the previous examples, you turned on IK's stickiness in order to plant the IK handle in one place. Without this, an IK handle will move when you move the root joint of a chain and this might not be what you expect. For instance, with stickiness on, a foot will stay planted on the ground and not move if you move the character's hips. The foot would move if stickiness was set to off.

> **Note:** *As soon as a keyframe is set on the IK handle, the IK's behavior will change, just as if stickiness is turned On.*

1   Turning On or Off stickiness after its creation

- Select the IK handle.

- Open the Attribute Editor.

- Under **IK Handle Attributes**, set **Stickiness** to **Sticky**.

IK priority

IK priority is the order in which IK solvers are evaluated. A solver with a priority of **1** is evaluated before a solver with a priority of **10**. This is important to keep in mind as you build up the controls for a character. For instance, an IK solver in the hand or fingers should be evaluated after the IK solver in the arm. The joints in the finger are lower in the skeleton hierarchy, as they depend on the joints in the arm for their placement.

Note: *If it seems that an IK chain is not updating properly in the interactive display or you notice differences between your interactive and final renderings, you should check the IK priority of the solvers.*

1 **Changing an IK handle's priority on creation**

  • Select **Skeleton** → **IK Handle Tool** → ❑.

  • In the option window, set **Priority** to the desired value.

2 **Changing an IK handle's priority**

  • Select an IK handle.

  • Open the Attribute Editor.

  • Open the **IK Handle Attributes** section and set the **Priority** attribute to the desired value.

Tip: *You can change multiple IK handles' priority by selecting the IK handles and typing the following MEL command:* `ikHandle -edit -autoPriority;`

The **autoPriority** *flag will automatically prioritize the selected IK handles based on their position in the hierarchy.*

Rotate plane IK solver

So far, you have only used the Single Chain IK solver. This type of IK lets you easily control the bending of a joint chain, but it doesn't give you good control over the orientation of the chain. For instance, if you set up a Single Chain IK on a character's knees, you could not easily spread the knees outward.

The Rotate Plane IK solver enables you to specify the orientation of the joint chain, using a *Twist* attribute or *Pole Vector* attributes. These attributes will define the rotate plane vector, which runs between the start joint and the end effector. The rotate plane acts as the goal for all joint rotations. By default, the IK handle will manipulate the joint chain so that it follows the default rotate plane. You can then rotate the plane by either editing a Twist attribute or by moving a Pole Vector handle.

The following example shows an arm being controlled by the Rotate Plane IK solver:

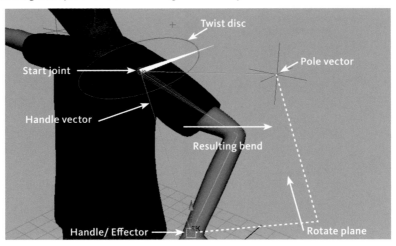

Diagram of Rotate Plane IK

1   Create arm joints

- In a new scene, draw three joints as shown here:

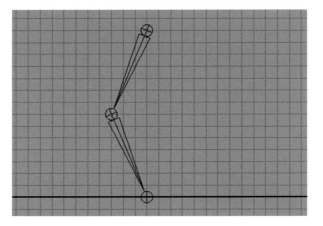

New joints

2   Add a Rotate Plane IK handle

- Select **Skeleton → IK Handle Tool → ▢**.

- In the option window, set the **Current Solver** to **ikRPsolver**.

- Click on the *shoulder* joint to set the start joint of the IK handle.

- Click on the *wrist* joint to place the IK handle.

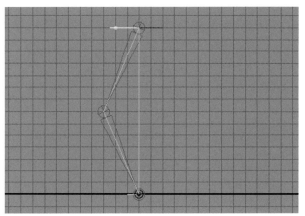

Rotate Plane IK handle

3 Move the IK handle

- **Move** the IK handle.

  The IK handle appears to be working in a similar manner to the Single Chain IK solver. Basic IK handle manipulation is the same for both solvers.

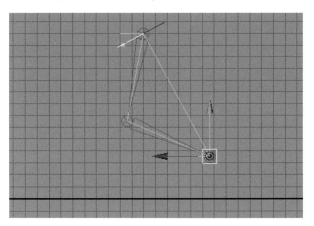

Moving the IK handle

4 Control the handle's Pole Vector

- Select the **Show Manipulator Tool**.

  A series of manipulators appear, to let you control the IK handle's Pole Vector and Twist attributes.

- In the Perspective view, **click+drag** on the **Pole Vector's** handle to rotate the IK solver's plane.

This lets you control the joint chain orientation solution.

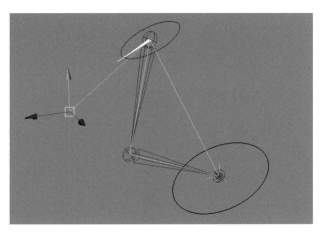

Pole Vector manipulator

5 **Manipulate the twist disc**

- Still with the **Show Manipulator Tool** enabled, **click+drag** the twist disc to alter the IK solution away from the rotate plane.

The Twist attribute can be considered an offset from the plane defined by the Pole Vector.

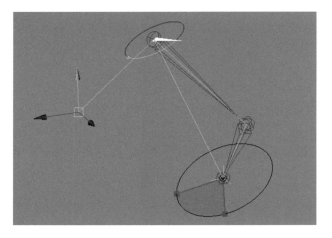

IK handle's Twist attribute modified

Pole vectors

Sometimes when manipulating IK handles, the solver can flip the joint solution by 180-degrees. Flipping occurs when the end effector is moved past the plane's pole vector axis. To solve a flip issue, you need to move the Pole Vector handle out of the way. You may need to set keys on the Pole Vector handle in order to control flipping during a motion.

To give you easy access to the Pole Vector, you can constrain it to an object. By doing so, you don't have to use the Show Manipulator Tool in order to edit the Pole Vector location. You will be using Pole Vector constraints in the next two lessons.

IK/FK blending

While IK animation of a skeleton chain is an excellent way to control goal-oriented actions like a foot planting on the ground or a hand picking something up, simple actions like an arm swinging as a character walks are typically easier to accomplish with FK animation. For this reason, IK/FK blending makes it easy to switch seamlessly between IK and FK control of a skeleton chain.

In this exercise, you will animate a skeleton chain using IK, switch to FK animation for a few poses, and then switch back to IK animation.

1   Open the demo scene file

  • Open the scene file *14-IkFkBlending.ma*.

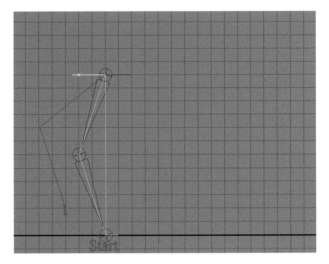

14-IkFkBlending.ma

2 Turn On the Ik Fk Control attribute

- Select the IK handle and open its Attribute Editor.

- In the **IK Solver Attributes** section of the **ikHandle1** tab, turn **On** the **Ik Fk Control** attribute.

This attribute tells the solver that you want to use the IK/FK blending functionality.

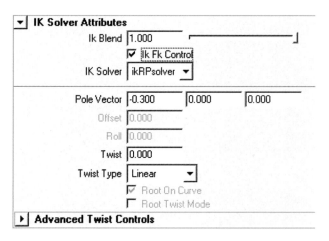

Ik Fk Control attribute turned On

3 Animate the IK

- Make sure that you're at frame **1** on the **Time slider**.

- Select the IK handle and **keyframe** it by hitting the **s** key.

- Advance to frame **10**.

- **Move** the IK handle to the first marked position.

- Set a **keyframe**.

- Advance to frame **20**.

- **Move** the IK handle to the second marked position and set a **keyframe**.

- Advance to frame **30**.

- **Move** the IK handle to the third marked position and set a **keyframe**.

Note: *When switching between IK and FK, the affected joints change to orange in IK and green in FK when nothing is selected. If the IK handle is selected, you will see three distinct joint chains: one for the IK, one for the FK, and another one for the result of the blending.*

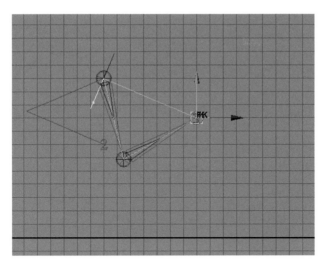

Current position of IK handle

> **Tip:** *You can change the size of the IK/FK joints under* **Display → Animation → IK/FK Joint Size...**

4 Switch from IK to FK

You will now switch from IK to FK control of the arm between frames **30** and **40**.

> **Note:** *When blending from IK to FK animation, you must set keys for both the skeleton joints and the IK handle during the transition period.*

- Make sure that you are still at frame **30**.
- Select the shoulder and elbow joints in the arm and **keyframe** them.

> **Note:** *Setting keys for the joints at the same frame where you stopped using IK is necessary to define the transition range for the blend from IK to FK.*

- Advance to frame **40**.
- Select the IK handle again.
- Find the **Ik Blend** attribute in the **Channel Box**.
- Set its value to **0**.

- Set a **keyframe** for the IK handle.

  By keying the IK Blend value at 0 at frame 40, you are specifying that you want to control the arm using FK at that frame.

5   **Animate the arm using FK**

- While still at frame **40**, pose the arm in the fourth marked position by **rotating** the joints.
- Set a **keyframe** for both the *shoulder* and *elbow* joints.
- Advance to frame **50**.
- Pose the arm in the fifth marked position by **rotating** the joints.
- **Keyframe** both joints again.
- Advance to frame **60**.
- Pose the arm in the sixth marked position by **rotating** the joints.
- **Keyframe** both joints again.

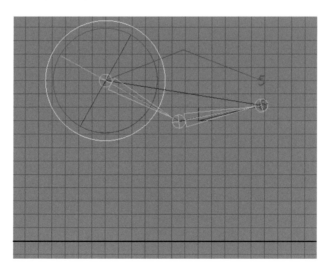

Joints rotated to position

6   **Switch back from FK to IK**

Now that you are finished animating the arm using FK animation, you will switch back to IK control.

- Select the IK handle.

Note: *The IK handle should still be where you left it at frame* **30** *when you changed its IK Blend value to* **0**.

- Set another **keyframe** for the IK handle at frame **60**. This is the last frame where you set keys directly on the joint rotations.
- Advance to frame **70**.
- Set the IK handle's **Ik Blend** value back to **1**.

  The arm can now be controlled with the IK handle.

- **Move** the IK handle to the seventh marked position and set a **keyframe** for it.
- Advance to frame **80**.
- **Move** the IK handle back to the original start position and set a **keyframe**.
- Play the animation.

  The skeleton chain should achieve each position, animating seamlessly between IK and FK as it goes.

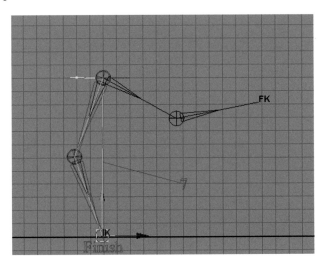

IK handle moved back to its first position

Note: *Maya will display the position of the FK joints so you know where they are when you want to blend back to FK.*

Lesson 14: Inverse Kinematics

IK/FK blending in the Graph Editor

When you switch between IK and FK and vice versa, the Graph Editor can display the animation curves of an IK handle and its joints partly as solid lines and partly as dotted lines.

That allows you to see the animation curve of an IK handle as a solid line when IK is on and as a dotted line when IK is off. In other words, the solid lines show where the joint chain gets its animation from.

This functionality of the Graph Editor is enabled only when you use the **Set IK/FK Key** command.

1 **Select the IK handle**

- Select the IK handle and go to frame **30**.

2 **Open the Graph Editor**

- Display the IK handle's animation curves by selecting **Window** → **Animation Editors** → **Graph Editor**.

- Select **View** → **Frame All** or press the **a** hotkey.

   Notice that the curves appear normal.

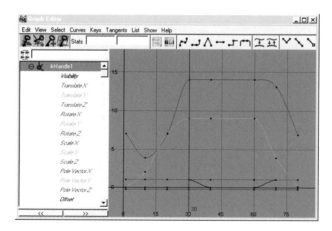

IK handle's normal animation curves

3 **Set IK/FK Key**

- Still with the IK handle selected, select **Animate** → **IK/FK Keys** → **Set IK/FK Key**.

   The Graph Editor now displays the curves with dotted lines where the IK handle does not control the joint chain.

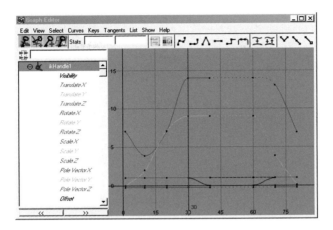

IK handle's dotted animation curves

The Set IK/FK Key menu item sets keys on all the current IK handle's keyable attributes and all the joints in its IK chain. When you use Set IK/FK Key, Maya performs additional operations to ensure a smooth transition between IK and FK.

When you want to key IK and FK animation on the same joint chain, you can use this menu item instead of setting a traditional keyframe. It is recommended that you use Set IK/FK Key when animating a joint chain with both forward and inverse kinematics.

> **Note:** *Keys that are bordered by a solid curve on one side and a dotted curve on the other should be edited with caution, since adjustments will likely cause the skeleton chain to pop as the IK and FK might no longer match.*

Conclusion

In this lesson, you learned about both the Single Chain and Rotate Plane IK solvers. The Rotate Plane solver is well suited for working situations where more control is needed, like for arms and legs, and it is a superset of the Single Chain solver. The Rotate Plane solver contains attributes that add a further level of control for the animator and help prevent inappropriate solutions such as those that result in flipping or illogical rotations.

IK animation of joint hierarchies requires understanding of the different types of IK solvers available in Maya and their benefits and limitations. Some animators will prefer to use FK for some situations and IK for others.

In the next lesson, you will implement IKs on Leon's lower body.

Lesson 14: Inverse Kinematics

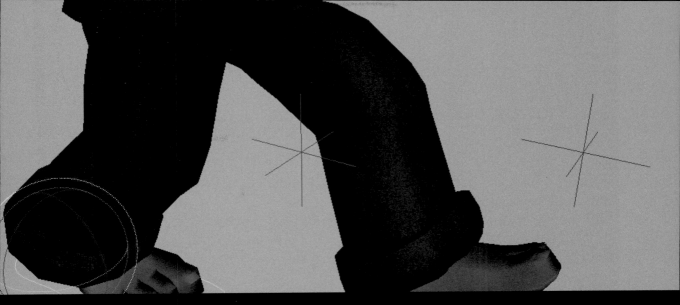

Lesson 15
Leg Setup

In this lesson, you will set up Leon's lower body. You will start by creating IKs, which will then be parented into a separate skeleton chain used for manipulating the foot. You will also create pole vectors to offer more control over the leg placement. The goal of this setup is to create a simple control mechanism for driving the action of the legs and feet.

In this lesson you will learn the following:

- How to set up IK on leg joints;
- How to build a reverse foot setup;
- How to parent IK handles in a hierarchy;

Adding IK to Leon's legs

The first thing to know when creating an IK chain is that you should never create a single IK handle on joints you intend to animate on their own. The joints in an IK chain should always be moving all together, unless you are using IK/FK blending. For instance, if you have a single IK chain starting from the hip going down to the toes, the IK will prevent you from animating the ankle and toes.

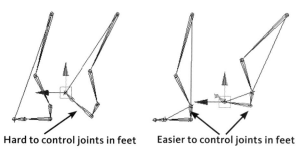

Hard to control joints in feet   **Easier to control joints in feet**

Different IK chains

In this lesson, you will create a more complex setup using several IK chains to control the different parts of the leg. One chain will work from the hip to the ankle and two more will define Leon's foot. The three IK handles will be part of a more complex hierarchy, which will allow you to achieve a nice heel-to-toe motion.

Create the IK handles

You will now set up Leon's controls using one Rotate Plane IK solver for the leg and two Single Chain IK solvers for the foot.

1   **Open the scene**

   • Open the scene file *13-orientation 01.ma* from Lesson 13.

2   **Hide Leon's right leg**

   In order to not confuse the left and right leg, you will temporarily hide the right leg.

   • Select the *RightUpLeg* joint.

   • Select **Display** → **Hide** → **Hide Selection** or press the **Ctrl+h** hotkey.

3   **Set up a rotate plane IK**

   • Select **Skeleton** → **IK Handle Tool** →❑.

- In the option window, set the following:

    Current Solver to **ikRPsolver**;

    Sticky to **On**.

- Select the *LeftUpLeg* to establish the start joint of the IK chain and then the *LeftFoot* to establish the end effector of the IK chain.

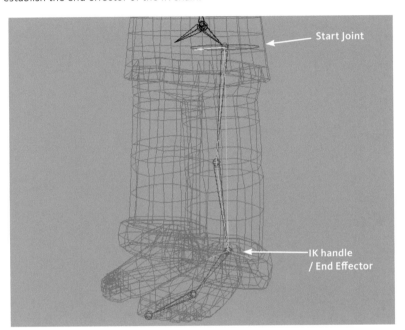

Start Joint

IK handle / End Effector

IK added to the leg

- **Rename** the IK handle to *leftLegIK*.

4 **Set up single chain IKs**

- Select **Skeleton → IK Handle Tool → ☐**.

- In the option window, set the following:

    Current Solver to **ikSCsolver**;

    Sticky to **On**.

- Click on the *LeftFoot* joint and the *LeftToeBase* joint to create your next IK chain.

- Create the last IK chain starting from the *LeftToeBase* joint to the *LeftToeEnd* joint.

- **Rename** the IK handles to *leftAnkleIK* and *leftToeIK*.

Lesson 15: Leg Setup

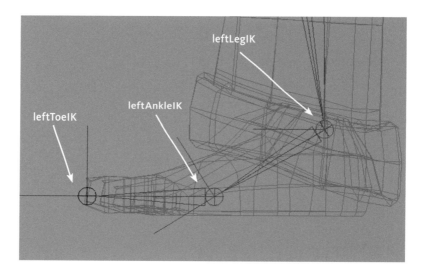

Foot IK handles

Create the reverse foot

You will now create the skeleton chain that will control the IK handles.

The reverse foot skeleton will allow you to use simple joint rotations to control the character's foot. Just as with any other set of joints, it is important to set their local orientations properly.

1   Draw the joints

- Select **Skeleton** → **Joint Tool** → ☐ and set **Orientation** to **XYZ**.

- From the side view, hold down the **v** key to Snap to Point, and then **click+drag** the first joint in order to snap it to the existing LeftToesBase joint.

- Click the **MMB** to display the **Move Tool** without exiting the Joint Tool.

- **MMB+drag** the newly created joint to the base of Leon's heel.

> **Note:** *The reason you used **Snap to Point** and **MMB+dragging** is that this method created the new joint in line with the foot joints, rather than snapping the joint on the world grid.*

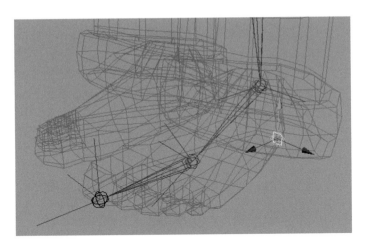

The new joint is aligned at the heel

- Still in the side view, hold down **Shift** to place another joint in a straight line on the tip of the toe geometry.

- Using **Snap to Point**, place **two** new joints, one on the *LeftToeBase* and one on the *LeftAnkle*.

- **Rename** the reverse joints as follows:

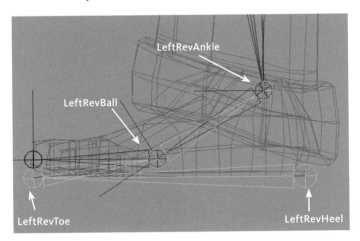

The reverse joints

Note: *The joint LeftRevToe could be snapped onto the LeftToeEnd joint, but having it placed at the very tip of the sole will give proper toe rotation.*

2   **Check the local rotation axes**

- Select the *LeftRevHeel*, and then press **F8** to go in Component mode and enable the selection mask button.

- Make sure to align all **Z-axes** on the local rotation axes in the same direction.

3   **Parent the IK handles**

You will now parent each IK handle to its respective joint in the inverse foot. Doing so will allow you to control the IK handles' position by rotating the reverse foot joints.

- Through the Outliner, select an IK handle and **Ctrl-select** the corresponding joint in the inverse foot; then press the **p** hotkey to parent them.

- The final hierarchy should look like this in the Outliner:

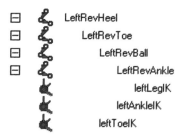

The appropriate hierarchy

- **Test** the rotation of the different reverse joints to see their effect on the leg IKs.

4   **Save your work**

- Save your scene as *15-leg setup 01.ma*.

Create a manipulator

One of your goals in setting up Leon is to create a system of puppet-like controls that will be easy to identify and select, and will provide logical centralized controls for all aspects of Leon's behavior.

While the reverse joint chain could be used as the main foot object for Leon's left leg, in order to keep the selection process consistent, and ultimately easier, the reverse foot will be parented to an easy-to-select curve.

1   **Create a manipulator for Leon's foot**

- Select **Create → NURBS Primitive → Circle**.

- **Rename** it *leftFootManip*.

- Go to Component mode and display the **Control Vertex**.
- **Move** the CVs to match the following illustration:

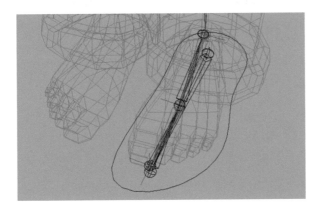

Left foot manipulator

2   Snap the pivot

- Back in Object mode, select the *leftFootManip*.
- Press **w** to invoke the **Move Tool**, and then press **Insert** on your keyboard.

  *The manipulator will change to the **Move Pivot Tool**.*

- Press the **v** key to Snap to Point, and then **MMB+drag** the pivot on the *LeftRevHeel* joint.

  The pivot will snap to the LeftRevHeel joint.

- Press the **Insert** key again to switch back to the **Move Tool**.

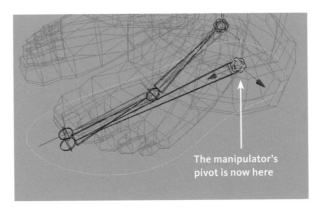

The manipulator's new pivot position

3 Freeze the transformations

Now that *leftFootManip* is well placed, it's a good idea to freeze its transformations, which will make it easy for an animator to reset its position.

- Select *leftFootManip*, and then select **Modify → Freeze Transformations**.

4 Parent the reverse chain to the manipulator

- Select the *LeftRevHeel* joint, **Shift-select** the *leftFootManip*, and then press **p** to parent them.

Adding custom attributes

For the *leftFootManip* to be an effective control object, it should provide control for all aspects of Leon's foot and leg. To this end, you will now add a series of custom attributes to the *leftFootManip* object.

1 Add a custom attribute

- Select the *leftFootManip* node.

- Select **Modify → Add Attribute...**

- In the Add Attribute window, set the following:

   Attribute Name to *heelRotX*;

   Data Type to **Float**.

> **Note:** *Minimum and maximum values could be added at this time, but since you don't know what your minimum and maximum values will be, attribute limits will be set later.*

- Click **Add**.

   A new attribute appears in the Channel Box called Heel Rot X. At this time, the attribute is not connected to anything, but you will use the Connection Editor later to make it functional.

> **Note:** *The Channel Box can show attributes in three different ways: Nice, Long, and Short. If the attribute translateX was displayed in the Nice setting, it would look like Translate X. In the Long setting, it would look like translateX and the Short setting would display it as tx. You can change these settings within the Channel Box by selecting* **Channels → Channel Names**.

2 **Add additional attributes**

As long as the **Add** button is pressed in the Add Attribute window, the window will remain open. Clicking the **OK** button will add the attribute and close the window.

- **Add** the following attributes to the *leftFootManip*:

  heelRotY;

  heelRotZ;

  ballRot;

  toeRotX;

  toeRotY;

  toeRotZ.

3 **Lock and hide channels**

Now that you have added a series of custom attributes to the manipulator, it's a good idea to lock, and make non-keyable, any attributes that should not be used by the animator.

- Select *leftFootManip*.
- In the Channel Box, highlight the **Scale X, Y, Z** and **Visibility** attributes.
- **RMB** in the Channel Box and select **Lock and Hide Selected**.

These attributes are now locked and therefore can't be changed accidentally. They have also been made nonkeyable, which removes them from the Channel Box.

Note: *In general, you should lock and make nonkeyable all attributes on your control object that you don't want the animator to change. This will simplify the animator's work and also make Character Set creation much easier.*

Connecting custom attributes

Now that you have defined a custom manipulator with attributes, it is time to connect those attributes to their corresponding channels on Leon's foot.

1 **Connect the first attribute**

- Open the Connection Editor by selecting **Window → General Editors → Connection Editor**.
- Select *leftFootManip* and click the **Reload Left** button; then select the *LeftRevHeel* joint and click the **Reload Right** button.
- In the left column, select the *Heel Rot X* attribute and in the right column, open the *Rotate* section and select the *Rotate X* attribute.

The two attributes are now connected with a direct relationship. Changing the value of leftFootManip Heel Rot X will also change the value of LeftRevHeel Rotate X.

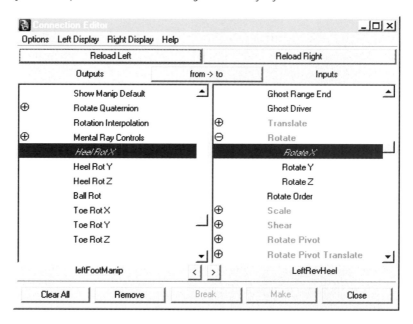

Heel Rot X connected to Rotate X

2   **Connect the rest of the custom attributes**

Use the Connection Editor to connect the rest of the custom attributes:

Heel Rot Y to *leftRevHeel Rotate Y*;

Heel Rot Z to *leftRevHeel Rotate Z*;

Ball Rot to *leftRevBall Rotate Z*;

Toe Rot X to *leftRevToe Rotate X*;

Toe Rot Y to *leftRevToe Rotate Y*;

Toe Rot Z to *leftRevToe Rotate Z*.

3   **Test the connections**

At this point, it is a good idea to make sure the connections are made properly and the foot is behaving the way you expect.

- Select *leftFootManip* and try **translating** and **rotating** it to test the basic leg motion.

- **Undo** the last transformations, or simply enter values of **0** for all of *leftFootManip*'s attributes.

- **Test** each of the custom attributes in the Channel Box by highlighting them and then **MMB+dragging** in the viewport to invoke the virtual slider.

  You should notice that some of them behave properly within a certain range of values, but cause unwanted actions outside of that range. You'll solve that problem next by adding limits.

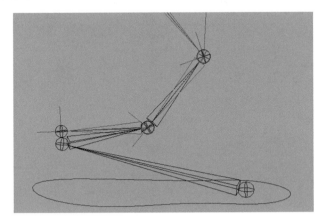

Testing the foot's behavior

- **Reset** the foot's position and rotation.

Adding limits

In order to control the internal actions of the foot, it is necessary to add limits to *leftFootManip*'s attributes.

Note: *It would also be possible to set limits on the rotations of the joints themselves, but that would result in the joints stopping at a given value while the custom attributes continue to change. Setting limits on the manipulator's attributes will give more predictable results.*

1 Range of motion

- Select *leftFootManip*.

- Highlight the *Ball Rot* attribute in the Channel Box.

- **MMB+drag** in the viewport to invoke the virtual slider.

  The foot acts properly as long as the Ball Rot value is greater or equal to **–10**, *but when it goes lower than* **–10** *the foot bends inappropriately.*

- **Reset** *Ball Rot* back to **0**.

2   **Set a minimum limit**

- Select **Modify → ☐ Edit Attribute...**

- In the **Edit Attribute** window, select ballRot.

- Check **Has Minimum** to **On** and set the maximum value to **–10**.

3   **Set limits for the other attributes**

- **Test** each of the other custom attributes and set limits accordingly.

- Set limits as follows:

> *Heel Rot X* Min **–90**, Max **90**;
>
> *Heel Rot Y* Min **-90**, Max **90**;
>
> *Heel Rot Z* Min **–45**, Max **45**;
>
> *Ball Rot* Min **–10**, Max **30**;
>
> *Toe Rot X* Min **–90**, Max **90**;
>
> *Toe Rot Y* Min **–90**, Max **90**;
>
> *Toe Rot Z* Min **–45**, Max **45**.

Final touches

Now that you have a good control system for Leon's foot, it's time to finalize the setup.

1   **IK/FK blend**

If you intend to use IK/FK blending, add the following to your foot manipulator:

- Select the *leftFootManip* node.

- Select **Modify → Add Attribute...**

- In the Add Attribute window, set the following:

> **Attribute Name** to *ikFkBlend*;
>
> **Data Type** to **Float**;
>
> **Minimum** to **0**;
>
> **Maximum** to **1**;
>
> **Default** to **1**;

- Click **OK**.

- Through the Connection Editor, connect this new attribute to the *Ik Blend* attributes of all three IK handles of Leon's leg.

- Under the section **IK Solver Attributes** in the Attribute Editor, turn **On** the **Ik Fk Control** checkbox for all three IK handles.

2 Lock and hide unnecessary attributes and objects

To prevent unwanted manipulation of the reverse foot setup, it is recommended to lock and hide all the attributes and objects that are not intended for animation.

- Select the *LeftRevHeel* joint.

- Set its **Visibility** attribute to **Off**.

- Highlight all the attributes visible in the Channel Box, and then **RMB** and select **Lock and Hide Selected**.

> **Tip:** *For proper locking, you should repeat the last step for all the objects and attributes in the reverse foot setup, but for simplicity reasons, here you will only lock and hide the LeftRevHeel joint. You can also use the* **Window** → **General Editor** → **Channel Control** *to lock and hide attributes.*

Repeat for Leon's right leg

Now that the left leg is set up, unhide the right leg and repeat the lesson. Following are some tips to speed up the process.

> **Note:** *This is a good example of a task that could be automated using MEL scripting.*

1 Duplicate and mirror the left foot setup

- Select the *leftFootManip* and **duplicate** it.

- Press **Ctrl+g** to group the setup and set its **Scale X** attribute to **–1**.

  Doing so will mirror the foot setup for the other leg.

2 Freeze transformations

- **Unparent** the new *LeftRevHeel* from its temporary manipulator.

  These temporary bones are unfortunately not usable in the new setup. You will use them later to create new joints using Snap to Point.

- Select **Window** → **General Editor** → **Channel Control** to unlock the *leftFootManip1* scaling attributes.

- **Unparent** the new *leftFootManip1* from its temporary group.

- With the *leftFootManip1* selected, select **Modify** → **Freeze Transformations**.

  This will reset the new manipulator's attributes to their defaults.

- **Rename** *leftFootManip1* to *rightFootManip*.

3 **Create the new reverse joint chain**

- **Unhide** the new *LeftRevHeel*.

Tip: *Use the* **Window** → **General Editor** → **Channel Control** *to unlock the visibility attribute.*

- Select **Skeleton** → **Joint Tool**.
- Hold down **v** to Snap to Point, and then create a new reverse foot joint chain for the right foot.
- **Rename** the new joint chain accordingly.
- **Parent** the new *RightRevHeel* to the new *RightFootManip*.
- **Correct** the local rotation axes to be similar to the left reverse foot.

4 **Clean up**

- From the Outliner, **delete** all unnecessary nodes.

5 **Rebuild the setup**

- **Unhide** the right joints.
- **Create** all the right leg IK handles.
- **Parent** the IK handles accordingly.
- **Connect** all the custom attributes.
- Double check all the custom attributes' limits to see if they require any changes.

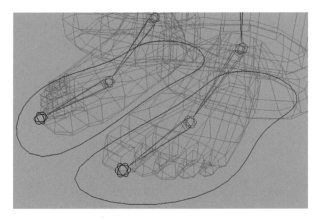

Completed foot setups

Pole vectors

In order to have fully functional legs, the last thing to add are pole vector objects. These will give maximum control to the animator for any leg manipulations.

1 Create locators

- Select **Create → Locator**.

- Hold down **v** to Snap to Point and **move** the locator onto Leon's knee.

- Press **Ctrl+d** to duplicate the locator and snap it to the other knee.

- Select both locators and **move** them in front of the knees on the Z-positive axis.

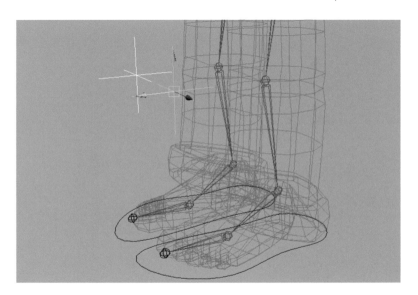

The locators

- **Rename** the locators to *leftPoleVector* and *rightPoleVector*.

2 Add the pole vector constraints

- In the Outliner, select the *leftPoleVector*; and then **Ctrl-select** the *leftLegIK*.

- Select **Constrain → Pole Vector**.

  If the left leg moves when you create the pole vector constraint, you can translate the locator on the X-axis in order to keep the skeleton as close as possible to its default position.

- **Repeat** for the other leg.

3 **Freeze transformations**

- Select both the *leftPoleVector* and *rightPoleVector*.

- Select **Modify** → **Freeze Transformations**.

4 **Lock and hide attributes**

- With both the *leftPoleVector* and *rightPoleVector* locators selected, highlight all the **Rotate**, **Scale** and **Visibility** attributes in the Channel Box; then **RMB** and select **Lock and Hide Selected**.

5 **Save your work**

- Save your scene as *15-leg setup 02.ma*.

Test the setup

You can now hide the *geometryLayer* and test your setup using five main controls:

leftFootManip controls the left leg and foot's heel-to-toe motion.

rightFootManip controls the right leg and foot's heel-to-toe motion.

leftPoleVector controls the rotate plane for the left leg IK.

rightPoleVector controls the rotate plane for the right leg IK.

hips controls the root joint of the entire skeleton.

Explore how these objects work together. Move Leon forward and begin experimenting with the leg manipulators. You may even set keys to preview how the Leon skeleton will animate.

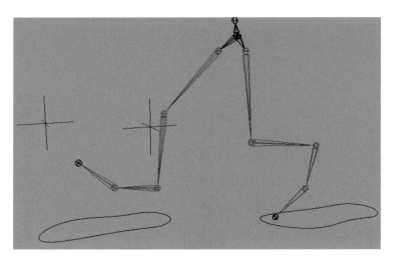

Lower body setup

Conclusion

In this lesson you created a reverse foot setup that uses different IK types and NURBS curves as control objects. You also added several custom attributes and pole vector objects to gain maximum control over Leon's legs.

The foot setup created in this lesson is just one among several other popular foot setups. You should keep your eyes open to all types of solutions, as no clear standard for the *best* foot setup exists today. It usually depends on the situation the character is placed in.

In the next lesson, you will ready Leon's arms and hands for animation.

Lesson 16
Arm Setup

In this lesson, you will create Leon's arm and hand setup. To do so, you will define manipulators, add rotate plane IKs, and create pole vector objects, extending the work you did in the previous lesson.

In this lesson you will learn the following:

- How to set up IK on arms;
- How to work with the solver's end effectors;
- How to drive objects with manipulators;
- How to add constraints;
- An optional roll bone automation technique;
- How to add utility nodes;
- How to use Set Driven Keys.

Arm IK

You will use Rotate Plane IKs for the arm. One special thing to mention is that rather than placing the IK handle on the wrist joint, you will place it at the forearm roll joint. You will then move the chain's end effector to the wrist. This will allow the IK to control the arm as usual, but it will also allow the forearm roll bone to be free for setup.

1   Scene file

- Open the last lesson's scene file *15-leg setup 02.ma*.

2   Rotate plane IK

- Select the **Skeleton → IK Handle Tool → ☐**.
- In the options, set the following:

    Current Solver to **ikRPsolver**;

    Sticky to **Off**.

- **Create** an IK handle from the *LeftArm* joint to the *LeftForeArmRoll* joint.
- **Rename** the IK handle *leftArmIK*.

3   Rename the effector

- Select the *LeftForeArmRoll*.
- In the Outliner, press **f** to frame the selection.

    You will see the end effector, which is parented under the LeftForeArm joint.

- **Rename** the end effector *leftArmEffector*.

End effector

When you create an IK handle, you also create another node called an *end effector*. The end effector defines the end of an IK solver chain. By default, the end effector is hidden and connected to a child joint of the last joint controlled in the IK chain, as if it were a sibling of that child joint. So when you move the end effector, the IK handle will go along for the ride. IK is not invoked when an end effector is moved. This gives you the ability to reposition the IK chain/IK handle without invoking IK.

As you will see, this is what you want to happen for Leon's forearm. Because you want to control Leon's arms from his wrist, you will need to translate the end of the IK chain from the forearm to the wrist. By changing the position of the effector, you are changing the end position of the IK handle down to the wrist without running IK through to the wrist.

 Tip: *If you move the end effector, it is advisable to save a new preferred angle.*

1   Move the end effector

- In the Hypergraph or Outliner, select the *leftArmEffector*.

- Select the **Move Tool**, and then press the **Insert** key to invoke the **Move Pivot Tool**.

- Hold down **v** to Snap to Point, and then **move** the end effector pivot to snap it on the *LeftHand* joint.

Note: *If the arm joints move when you move the effector, the IK's stickiness was enabled and should not be. To fix the problem, simply* **undo** *the move, open the Attribute Editor for the IK handle, and set* **Stickiness** *to* **Off***.*

- Press the **Insert** key to return to standard manipulator mode.

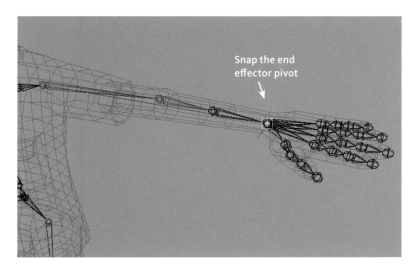

Move the end effector

2   Set the stickiness

- Select the *leftArmIK*.

- In the Attribute Editor, under the **IK Handle Attributes**, set **Stickiness** to **Sticky**.

3   Move the IK handle

- Select the *leftArmIK*.

- **Move** the IK handle along the **X-axis** to confirm that the forearm roll joint does not bend.

The IK handle can now be translated, bending the arm without bending the forearm roll bone. This is a necessary technique that enables you to rotate the hand while creating realistic movement and deformation on the forearm joints and skin. You will eventually drive the rotation of the roll bone joint based on the wrist rotation.

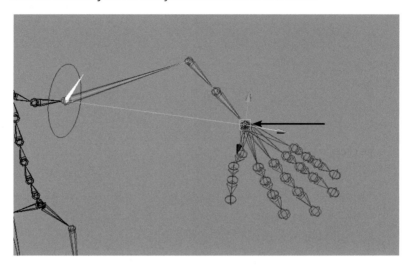

The forearm roll bone doesn't bend

- **Undo** the previous move.

Constraints

Constraints are objects that you assign to control specific aspects of other objects' transformations. Following are descriptions of the constraints that will be used for the arm setup:

Point constraint

A point constraint is used to make one object move according to another object.

Orient constraint

An orient constraint is used to make one object rotate according to another object. An orient constraint will be set on a wrist manipulator to control rotation of the hand.

Parent constraint

A parent constraint is used to make one object behave as if it was parented to another object. A parent constraint will be used to constraint the clavicle to a manipulator.

Pole vector constraint

A pole vector constraint always points an IK's pole vector to the specified object. A pole vector constraint will be used to control the rotation of the arm and will provide a nice visual aid for positioning the elbows.

Hands and elbows

Similar to the lower body setup, you will now create a manipulator and pole vector to control the arm IK efficiently.

1   Wrist manipulator

- Select **Create → NURBS Primitives → Circle**.

- **Rename** circle to *leftHandManip*.

- Press **v** to Snap to Point; then place the *leftHandManip* vertically over Leon's left wrist.

- **Rotate** and **scale** the circle appropriately.

- Select **Modify → Freeze Transformations**.

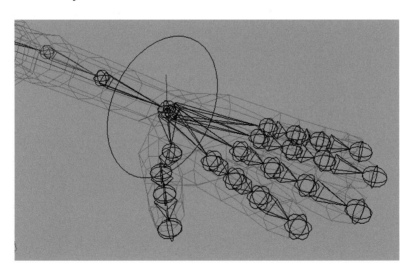

Left hand manipulator

2   Parent the IK handle

- Select *leftArmIK*; then **Shift-select** the *leftArmManip*.

- Press **p** to parent the IK to the manipulator.

3   **Orient constrain**

- Select the *leftArmManip*; then **Shift-select** *LeftHand* joint.

 Tip: *Always select the object that you want to constrain last.*

- Select **Constrain** → **Orient** → ☐.
- In the option window, make sure the **Maintain Offset** checkbox is set to **On**.

   *The **Maintain Offset** option will make sure the wrist stays with its current rotation instead of snapping to the circle's rotation.*

- Click the **Add** button.

   Constraining the LeftHand joint to the leftArmManip will keep the joint aligned with the control object. This will allow you to easily plant the hand.

4   **Lock and hide attributes**

Since *leftArmManip* is one of Leon's control objects, you should lock and make nonkeyable any channels that should not be changed. This will prevent users from manipulating the arm setup in ways that you did not intend.

- **Lock** and **hide** the *leftArmManip*'s **scale** and **visibility** attributes.

5   **Pole vector object**

- Select **Create** → **Locator**.
- Using **v** to Snap to Point, **move** the locator to the left elbow.
- **Translate** the locator behind the elbow on its **Z-negative axis**.
- Select **Modify** → **Freeze Transformations**.
- **Rename** the locator to *leftArmPV*.

6   **Pole vector constraint**

- Select *leftArmPV*, and then **Shift-select** the *leftArmIK*.
- Select **Constrain** → **Pole Vector**.

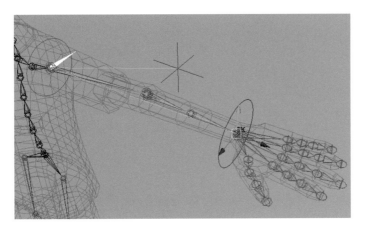

Pole vector object

7   **Lock and hide attributes**

   • **Lock** and **hide** the *leftArmPV*'s **rotation, scale** and **visibility** attributes.

8   **Repeat for the right side**

Both arms set up

9   **Save your work**

   • Save your scene as *16-arm setup 01.ma*.

Clavicles

Now that you have set up an effective system for Leon's arms, you will create a control to easily manipulate the clavicles.

1   Draw a manipulator

- Select **Create → EP Curves → ⬜**.
- In the option window, set the **Curve Degree** to **Linear**.
- From the front view, hold down **X** to snap to grid and **draw** an arrow pointing up as follows:

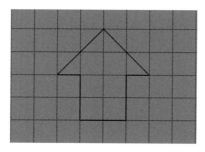

Clavicle manipulator

- Press **Enter** to exit the Curve Tool.
- **Rename** the arrow *leftClavicleManip*.
- **Move** and **scale** the arrow so it is above the left shoulder.
- **Parent** the *leftClavicleManip* to the *Spine5* joint.

2   Adjust the manipulator's pivot

- Select the *leftClavicleManip*.
- Press **Insert** to switch to the **Move Pivot Tool**.
- Press **v** to snap the pivot to the *LeftShoulder* joint.
- Press **Insert** again to toggle off the **Move Pivot Tool**.
- With the *leftClavicleManip* selected, select **Modify → Freeze Transformation**.

3   Parent Constrain

- Select *leftClavicleManip*, and then **Shift-select** the *LeftShoulder* joint.
- Select **Constrain → Parent → ⬜**.
- In the option window, make sure the **Maintain Offset** is set to **On**.

4   Lock and hide attributes

- **Lock** and **hide** the *leftClavicleManip*'s **Translate, Scale,** and **Visibility** attributes.

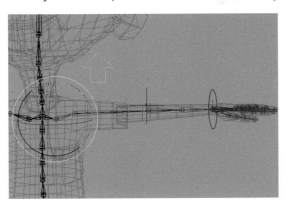

Left clavicle manipulator

5   Repeat for the right arm

IK handles

Now that Leon's arms are set up, some final touches must be added to the manipulators. First, you will add the IK/FK blending functionality. Then you will lock and hide the IK handles to prevent them from accidentally being manipulated.

1   Add an IK FK Blend attribute

- Select both the left and right arm manipulators.
- Select **Modify → Add Attributes.**
- Set the following:

    Attribute Name to *ikFkBlend*;

    Data Type to **Float**;

    Minimum to **0**;

    Maximum to **1**;

    Default to **1**;

- Click **OK.**
- Through the Connection Editor, connect this new attribute to the *Ik Blend* attribute of its respective IK handles.
- In the Attribute Editor, turn **On** the **Ik Fk Control** checkbox for both IK handles under the section **IK Solver Attributes.**

Lesson 16: Arm setup

2   Connect the orient constraint

Since the IK blending will allow you to animate the arms with rotations, it is necessary to turn *off* the orient constraints on the wrists at the same time. Doing so will also allow you to manually rotate the wrist instead of using the manipulator.

- Through the Connection Editor, connect the *Ik Fk Blend* attribute to the *Wo* attribute found on the *LeftHand_orientConstraint1* and *RightHand_orientConstraint1* nodes.

  The Wo attributes stands for weight at index 0 and is usually prefixed with the name of the object it is constrained to. This attribute defines the weighting of the constraint; 1 for enabled and 0 for disabled.

Tip: *The constraints are always parented to the constrained nodes. You can find them easily through the Outliner.*

- Set the **Ik Fk Blend** attribute to **0** to see if you can rotate the bones appropriately.
- When you are done, **undo** any rotations and reset the **Ik Fk Blend** attribute to **1**.

3   Hide the IKs

- Select both the left and right arm IK handles.
- Set their **Visibility** attribute to **Off**.
- Highlight all the attributes listed in the Channel Box; then **RMB** and select **Lock and Hide Selected**.

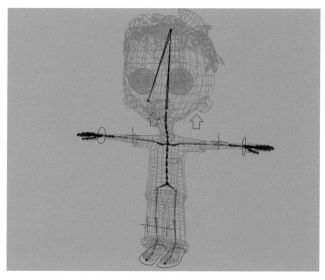

The rig so far

4 Save your work

- Save your scene as *16-arm setup 02.ma*.

Roll bone automation

If you like automation, you can make connections in order to automate the roll bone. This is done by adding a utility node, which will give some wrist rotation to the roll bone.

> **Note:** *The technique shown in this exercise works well only when using the hand manipulators in IK and will not automate the roll bone when animating the arm in FK. To have this setup work for both IK and FK, you would need to write a MEL expression and control a separate roll bone.*

1 Create the utility node

- Select **Window → Rendering Editor → Hypershade**.

  The Hypershade is a good place to create and connect utility nodes.

- Scroll down to the **General Utilities** section in the **Create** bar and locate the **Multiply Divide** node.

- **MMB+drag** a **Multiply Divide** node into the Work Area.

  This will create the utility node in the scene.

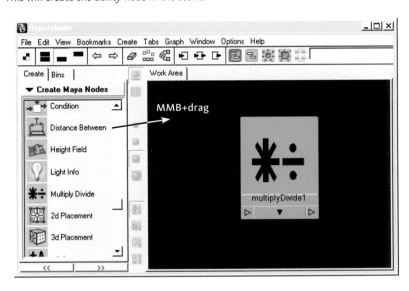

Multiply Divide utility node

2   Connect the utility node

- Select **Window → General Editor → Connection Editor**.

- Select the *leftArmManip* and load it on the left side of the Connection Editor; then select the *multipliDivide1* and load it on the right side.

- **Connect** the *Rotate X* attribute of the manipulator to the *Input1 X* attribute of the utility node.

- **Double-click** on the *multiplyDivide1* node in the Hypershade to open its Attribute Editor.

- In the **Multiply-Divide Attributes** section, set the *Input2 X* to **0.5**.

  This specifies that half of the rotation from the wrist will go on the roll bone.

- In the Connection Editor, load the *multiplyDivide1* node on the left side; then load the *LeftForeArmRoll* joint on the right side.

- **Connect** the *Output X* attribute of the utility node to the *Rotate X* attribute of the roll bone.

  You have now connected half of the wrist rotation to the LeftForeArmRoll rotation.

3   Repeat for the right arm

Tip: *Since you used only the X attribute on the utility node, you don't need to create another one. Just use the Y or Z attribute for the right arm.*

Set Driven Keys

When you want to control attributes based on the animation of another attribute, you can use *Set Driven Keys*. A Set Driven Key is a curve relationship between two attributes. In the Graph Editor, the horizontal axis represents the driver attribute values and the vertical axis represents the driven attribute values.

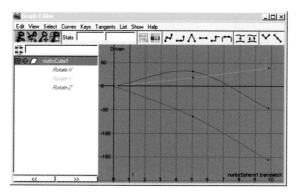

Graph Editor view of Set Driven Key

Because a Set Driven Key is a curve relationship, it is possible to adjust the tangents of this curve and add additional keys. This can help you achieve some interesting behavior. For example, if the rotate attribute of an elbow is driving the size of a bicep muscle, the curve could be edited so that when the elbow is about to reach its maximum bend, the bicep shakes a little as it is flexed.

Finger manipulator

You will add another NURBS circle to the hand to use as a manipulator for articulating the fingers. It is a good idea to create another manipulator for the fingers in addition to the existing one for the arm because the arm's manipulator will be left behind when the arm is controlled in FK.

> **Note:** *This exercise should be applied to your character only if you intend to automate the hand completely. Since the driven keys on the fingers will connect their attributes, it will not be possible to manually animate the fingers. One way to both use the driven keys and manually animate the fingers would be to create overrides for joints in each finger. Creating an override means that every articulation needs two bones overlapping: one for the driven keys and another one for manual rotation.*

1   Create the manipulator

- Select **Create → NURBS Primitives → Circle** and name the circle *leftFingersManip*.

- Press **v** to Snap to Point and **move** the manipulator to the *LeftHand* joint.

- **Adjust** the CVs so the manipulator looks like the following:

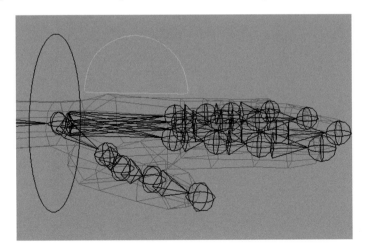

Finger manipulator

Project 04

2 Parent and freeze transformations

- **Parent** the *leftFingersManip* to the *LeftHand* joint.

- **Freeze** the *leftFingersManip* transformations.

3 Lock and hide the attributes

- Highlight all the **translate**, **rotate**, **scale**, and **visibility** attributes in the Channel Box for the *leftFingersManip*; then **RMB** and select **Lock and Hide Selected.**

4 Add custom attributes

You will now add attributes to *leftFingersManip* to control the fingers.

- Select *leftFingersManip*.

- Select **Modify** → **Add Attribute**. Set the following:

   Attribute Name to *indexCurl*;

   Make Attribute Keyable to **On**;

   Data Type to **Float**;

   Minimum Value to **0**;

   Maximum Value to **10**;

   Default Value to **0**.

- Click the **Add** button.

- **Repeat** the steps outlined above to add the following attributes:

   middleCurl;

   ringCurl;

   pinkyCurl;

   thumbCurl.

Tip: *You can also use the Script Editor to execute the* addAttr *MEL command like this:*
```
addAttr -k 1 -ln middleCurl -at double -min 0 -max 10 -dv 0
leftFingersManip;
```

- **Add** the following attributes to the *leftFingersManip* with their **Min**, **Max**, and **Default** values set to **–10**, **10**, and **0**, respectively:

   thumbRotX;

   thumbRotZ;

   fingerSpread.

   All of these custom attributes will be controlled with Set Driven Keys.

> **Tip:** *You can always edit the custom attribute's name, its keyable state, and its min/max values after they have been created by selecting* **Modify** → **Edit Attribute.**

Finger Set Driven Keys

Now that you have all the attributes to control the fingers' rotations, you need to connect the two together. In the case of bending the index finger, you can have its joints rotate when you change the value for the *indexCurl* attribute. When *indexCurl* is set to **0**, none of the index finger joints will be rotated, but when you change *indexCurl* to **10**, the finger will rotate to its maximum. For motions like spreading the fingers, the **Min** and **Max** should range from **–10** to **10**, where **–10** moves the fingers closer together and **10** moves them farther apart.

The following exercise will set up the *indexCurl* attribute to rotate the index finger. You will have to repeat these steps for Leon's remaining fingers.

> **Note:** *The technique used for setting up driven keys is the same for any other driven keys you want to create.*

1 Open the Set Driven Key window

- Select the **Animate** → **Set Driven Key** → **Set...**

  The Set Driven Key window is displayed. It is divided into two parts, driver and driven. The attributes you just created will be the drivers and the joint rotations on the fingers will be the driven attributes.

2 Select the Driver node and attribute

- Select *leftFingersManip.*

- Click **Load Driver.**

  Notice that leftFingersManip appears in the list of drivers, along with all of its keyable attributes.

- Select *indexCurl* from the list of keyable attributes.

3 Select the Driven nodes and attributes

The **rotateZ** attribute of the index joints will be the driven attributes.

- **Select** the three index joints (*LeftHandIndex1, LeftHandIndex2, LeftHandIndex3*).

- Click **Load Driven.**

  Notice that the selected objects appear in the driven list.

- Highlight all the driven objects, and then select *rotateZ* from the list of attributes.

Note: *The local rotation axis must be set up so that the fingers only need to rotate around one axis to curl.*

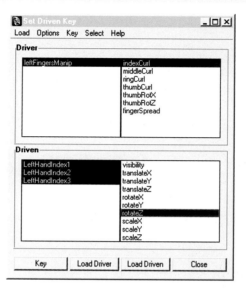

The Set Driven Key window

4   Set an initial key position

- Click on the *leftFingersManip* in the Set Driven Key window to make it active and make sure that *indexCurl* is set to **0** in the Channel Box.

- Click **Key** in the Set Driven Key window.

  Doing so sets keys on all three index joints.

Tip: *You can select the driver and driven objects by selecting them in the Set Driven Key window.*

5   Set a second key position

- Click on the *leftFingersManip* in the Set Driven Key window, and set *indexCurl* to **10** in the Channel Box.

- **Rotate** all the index joints on their **Z-axis** by about **–70** degrees.

Note: *The **Rotate Tool** should be set to **Local**.*

The tip joint of the index should touch the palm of Leon's geometry.

- Press **Key**.

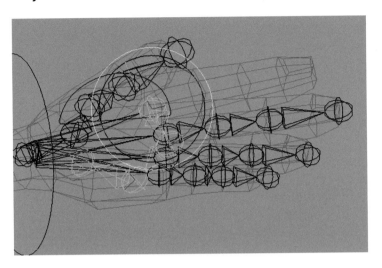

The index joints rotated

Tip: Since the geometry does not deform at this time, you will need to visualize when the finger tip will touch the palm. It is better to over-rotate the joints than to under-rotate them. If you don't rotate the joints enough, you may have to edit them later. If required, you will be able to change the driven key values through the Graph Editor.

6 Test the values

- Select *leftFingersManip*.
- In the Channel Box, highlight the *indexCurl* attribute.
- In the viewport, **MMB+drag** to invoke the virtual slider and change the selected attribute's value.

7 Use Set Driven Key for the other fingers

- **Repeat** this exercise to set up the curl for the *middle finger, ring finger, pinky finger* and *thumb*.

Note: The fingers have three joints to curl while the thumb has only two.

Finger spread

You also want the hand to be able to spread its fingers. Use Set Driven Key again to control the action. This time, you'll use attributes that have a range between –10 and 10, with 0 being the rest position, or preferred angle.

1   Finger spread

- Load the *leftFingersManip* with its *fingerSpread* attribute as the **Driver.**
- **Select** *LeftHandIndex1*, *LeftHandMiddle1*, *LeftHandRing1* and *LeftHandPinky1* joints.
- Click **Load Driven**.
- Highlight the joints and their **rotateY** attribute.
- Set a **key** with **fingerSpread** at **0** with the finger joints at their default positions.
- Set the *fingerSpread* attribute to **10**.
- Select the finger joints and spread them apart; then set a **key** for them.

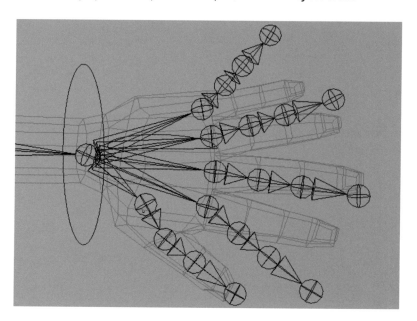

Fingers spread out

- **Rotate** the finger joints in a closed position, and then set a key with *fingerSpread* at **–10**.

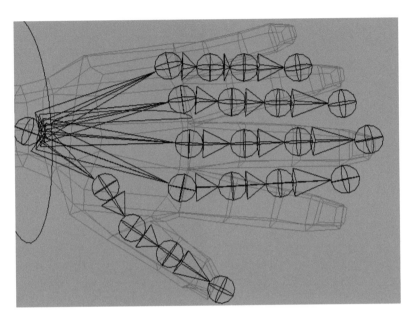

Closed finger spread

2   **Test the results**

- Test the range of motion between **−10** and **10** by changing the *fingerSpread* attribute.

Thumb rotation

The thumb is different from the other fingers in that its base pivots on a saddle joint and has much more freedom of movement than the finger joints. When you set up the thumb motion, you need to allow for flexible articulation that mimics the orbiting provided by a saddle type joint. To do this, you need to use both the *thumbRotX* and *thumbRotZ* attributes.

1   **Drive the rotation Y of the thumb**

- Select *leftFingersManip* and click **Load Driver**.
- Select *LeftHandThumb1* and click **Load Driven**.
- Select *thumbRotX* as the **Driver** attribute and *rotateX* as the **Driven** attribute.
- Set a key with *thumbRotX* at **0** and the *LeftHandThumb1* joint at its default position.
- Set *thumbRotX* to **10**.
- **Rotate** the *LeftHandThumb1* on the **X-axis** in one direction.
- Click **Key**.

2 **Set the second key position**

- Set *thumbRotX* to **–10**.

- **Rotate** the *LeftHandThumb1* in the **X-axis** in the opposite direction.

- Click **Key**.

3 **Drive the rotation Z of the thumb**

- Select *thumbRotZ* as the **Driver** attribute and **rotateZ** as the **Driven** attribute.

4 **Set Keys on the Z-axis**

- Set a key with *thumbRotZ* at **0** and the *LeftHandThumb1* joint at its default position.

- Set a key with *thumbRotZ* at **10** and **rotate** the *LeftHandThumb1* joint down on the **Z-axis**.

- Set a key with *thumbRotZ* to **–10** and **rotate** the *LeftHandThumb1* on the **Z-axis** in the opposite direction.

5 **Test the operation of the hand**

Note: *A good test to do is to try to position the fingers and thumb to for diferent expressions such as a fist, a flat hand, a thumb up, etc.*

Right finger manipulator

You must now re-create the finger manipulator and all its driven keys for the right hand.

Clean the scene

Since the rig is almost done, it is now time to do some cleanup in your scene.

1 **Delete history**

- Select **Edit → Delete All by Type → History**.

2 **Optimize scene size**

- Select **File → Optimize Scene Size**.

3 **Save your work**

- Save your scene as *16-arm setup 03.ma*.

Test the character rig

Leon's rig is starting to take shape. You now have the basic control points for blocking out motion. Test the character's behavior by using the manipulators you created.

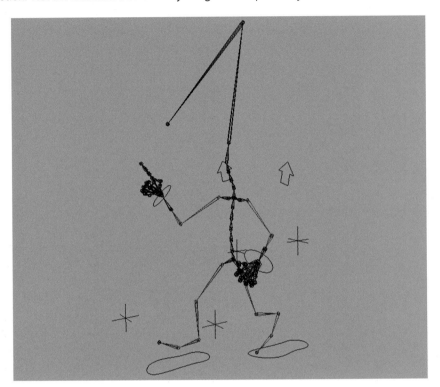

A pose for Leon

You can also experiment with other setups. For instance, you could attempt to parent the pole vectors to the *root* joint. Maybe you would rather use the **Twist** attribute on the IK handles and create a custom attribute on the manipulators for it.

Conclusion

This lesson explored the use of rigging techniques associated with setting up arms. You learned how to add constraints in order to simplify your rig. You also learned about the multiply and divide utility nodes, which can be used instead of writing a MEL expression. Lastly, you implemented finger automation using driven keys.

In the next lesson, you will implement Spline IKs on Leon's spine and you will finalize the setup hierarchy.

Lesson 17
Spine Setup

In this lesson, you will add an IK spline solver to Leon's spine. This will control how his back and neck sway and bend when he moves. It will also provide you with a realistic relationship between the pelvis and spine. Once the IK is in place, you will cluster points on the spline to help create manipulators.

Once that is done, you will finalize the rig in order to proceed to the next project, where you will set up geometry deformations.

In this lesson you will learn the following:

- How to set up a basic IK spline solver;
- How to use clusters to gain control over the spline curve;
- How to parent the clusters to manipulators;
- How to associate Leon's spine and pelvis motion;
- How to create global and local control mechanisms;
- How to create an eye-aiming setup.

IK spline

When you use an IK spline, there are several things to keep in mind:

- Keep the spline curve as simple as possible for the IK spline. For the most part, the default of four CVs works well. Note that the curve created when setting up the IK spline solver will attempt to stay as simple as possible by default.

- Create clusters for the CVs to make selecting and animating easier. Clusters have translation, rotation, and scale attributes, while CVs have only position attributes. This means that clusters can be keyframed more accurately than CVs, which will help for the animation.

- The IK spline should not be starting from a *root* joint. Also, as a rule, it should not cross any branching joints.

In Leon's case, you do not want the IK spline to start at the *Hips* joint, but rather at the first *Spine* joint. It should not start at the *root* joint because that would rotate not only the back but the hips as well. While the hips and back do rotate together in real life, this motion can be difficult to animate and control.

You could also create a single IK spline on Leon starting from the *Spine*, going up to the *Head*, but this will create problems when you need to rotate the neck separately from the back. The best solution for Leon would be the following:

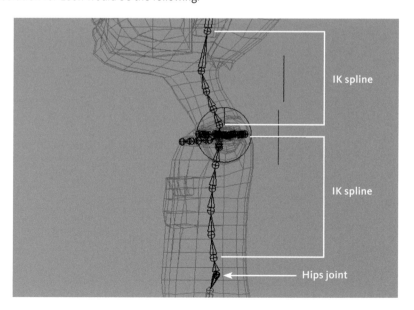

IK splines for Leon

Adding the IK splines

The IK spline solver allows you to control a chain of joints, like Leon's spine, with only a few control points. Animating a flexible back with forward kinematics requires you to keyframe the rotation of each joint individually. With a spline IK, you will control all of the back joints with three control points.

1 Scene file

- Continue with your own scene.

OR

- Open the last lesson's scene file *16-arm setup 03.ma*.

2 Add the first IK spline

- Select **Skeleton → IK Spline Handle Tool → ▢**.

- In the option window, click the **Reset Tool** button.

- Turn **Off** the **Auto Parent Curve** option.

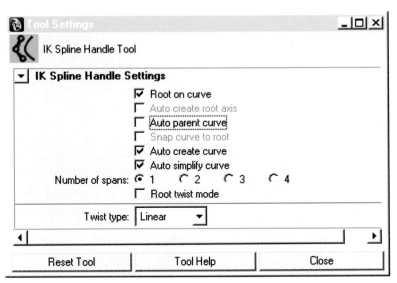

IK spline options

- Select the Spine joint above the *Hips* joint to define the start joint of the chain.

- Select the last spine joint, *Spine5*, to place the IK handle.

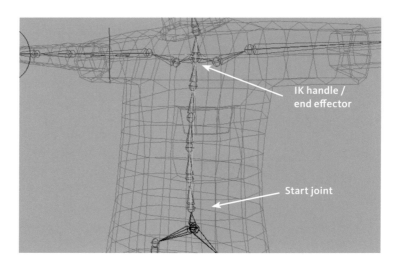

First IK spline

An IK system is created with a curve running through the selected joints. You can control the joints by selecting the CVs of this curve and translating them.

3   Add the second IK spline

- Press **y** to make the **IK Spline Handle Tool** active.
- Select the *Neck* joint to define the start joint of the chain.
- Select the *Head* joint to place the IK handle.

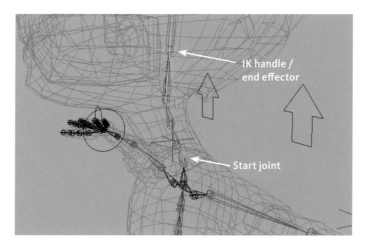

Second IK spline

4   Rename the new nodes

- **Rename** the new IK handles *backSplineIK* and *neckSplineIK*.
- **Rename** the new spline curves *backSpline* and *neckSpline*.

Test the IK splines

There are two ways to operate IK splines. The *Twist* attribute will rotate each of the joints in the solution around the *X-axis*, causing a twisting action up Leon's spine or neck. Moving CVs in the *backSpline* or the *neckSpline* will allow you to pose Leon's back or neck in a serpentine manner. Try both methods in order to understand how the IK spline operates.

1   The Twist attribute

- Select the *backSplineIK* handle.

> **Note:** *The feedback line may let you know that some items cannot be moved in the 3D view. This warning simply means that Spline IK handles cannot be moved the same way that other IK handles are.*

- In the Channel Box, highlight **Twist**
- **MMB+drag** in the viewport to change the value with the virtual slider.
- Reset the **Twist** value back to **0** when you are done.
- With the *backSplineIK* handle still selected, press **t** to show the manipulator for the back.
- **Click+drag** the top manipulator ring to twist the back.

  This manipulator is another way to access the twist.

> **Note:** *Experiment with the **Twist Type** attribute, which is accessible through the Attribute Editor.*

2   Moving CVs

- Select the *backSpline*.

> **Tip:** *You can use the selection mask buttons to select the curve in the viewport. In Object mode, select **All Objects Off**, and then toggle **On** the **Curve** icon.*

- Switch to Component mode.
- Select any CVs on the curve and translate them.
- **Undo** until the *backSpline* is back to its original shape.

> **Note:** *You may notice that the lower CV in the curve should not translate, since it causes the first joint to be translated. You may also notice that translating the top CV in the back curve does not move the neck. Both of these issues will be resolved in the next exercise.*

Clusters

Both curves used by the IK spline solver have four CVs. Currently, the only way to select these CVs is in Component mode. To make selection easier and consistent with the rest of Leon's rig, you will add clusters to the CVs of the curves. The clusters will then be parented to NURBS manipulators.

1 **Select the top CV**

   - Select the *backSpline*.

   - Change to Component mode and set the selection mask to **CVs** and **Hulls**.

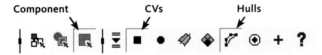

Selection mask buttons

   - Select the top two CVs.

Top CVs selected

2 Create a cluster

- With the CVs still selected, select **Create Deformers** → **Cluster** → ☐.

- Make sure to reset the option window.

- Click **Create**.

  A small **c** *will appear in the viewport.*

- **Rename** this cluster *backTopCluster*.

You have created the top cluster using the first two CVs, allowing you to use the deformer to its maximum capability. As well, You can also rotate it to get the desired orientation of the upper back.

3 Create another cluster

- Now select the bottom two CVs and create a **Cluster** with them.

- **Rename** the cluster *backBottomCluster*.

4 Parent the bottom cluster

- Select *backBottomCluster* and **parent** it to the *Hips* joint.

> **Note:** *It is likely that a warning will let you know that the cluster was grouped to preserve its position. This is normal and you can safely ignore this message.*

5 Lock and hide the bottom cluster

Since the bottom cluster will be used only to keep the tangency of the spine with the pelvis, you should not move this cluster. Therefore, you need to hide and lock it.

- Select *backBottomCluster* and set its **Visibility** to **Off**.

- Highlight all of its attributes in the Channel Box, and then **RMB** and select **Lock and Hide Selected**.

6 Create two other clusters for the neck

You will now repeat the previous steps, but this time to cluster the *neckSpline*'s CVs.

- Select *neckSpline* and display its CVs.

- Select the top two CVs and create a **Cluster** with them.

- **Rename** the cluster *neckTopCluster*.

- Select the bottom two CVs and create a **Cluster** with them.

- **Rename** the cluster *neckBottomCluster*.

- **Parent** the *neckBottomCluster* to the *Spine5* joint.

- **Hide** the *neckBottomCluster* and **lock and hide** all of its attributes.

7 Test the skeleton

- **Translate** and **rotate** the top neck cluster to test movement of the head.
- **Rotate** the *Spine5* joint to see the effect of the cluster on the lower neck.
- **Translate** and **rotate** the top back cluster to test movement of the upper back.
- **Rotate** the *Hips* joint to see the effect of the cluster on the lower back.

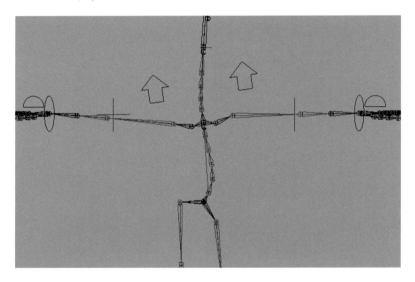

Hips joint rotated

8 Save your work

- Save your scene as *17-spine setup 01.ma*.

Manipulators for the clusters

To continue with the manipulator scheme for Leon, you will now create NURBS curves to be used as manipulators for the clusters.

1 Create NURBS manipulators

You will create two curves using the Text tool—one for *Spine* and one for *Neck*.

- Select **Create → Text → ▢**.
- In the options window type "*S N*" in the text field.
- Make sure that **Curves** is selected in the **Type** section.
- Click on the **Create** button.

2 Rotate the text object

- **Rotate** the text object **90** degrees on the **Y-axis**.

3 Unparent and rename the curves

- Select the *S*.

- Select **Edit** → **Unparent** or press **Shift+p**.

- **Rename** the *S* to *spineManip*.

- Select the *N*, **unparent** it, and **rename** it to *neckManip*.

- **Delete** the original group node from the Outliner.

4 Position the text curves

- In the side view, **move** and **scale** the two new manipulators next to their respective body parts.

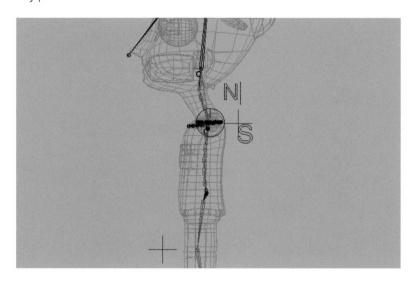

New manipulators

5 Move the manipulators' pivots

- **Snap** the *spineManip*'s pivot to the *Spine5* joint.

- **Snap** the *NeckManip*'s pivot to the *Head* joint.

6 Parent spine and neck manipulator

- **Parent** the spine manipulator to the *Hips* joint and **parent** the neck manipulator to the *spine5* joint.

7   Freeze Transformations

- Select **Edit** → **Freeze Transformations** for both manipulators.

8   Parent the clusters

- **Parent** the clusters to their respective manipulators.

Note: *Maya will automatically group the cluster before parenting it to the manipulator.*
This is normal behavior since the cluster needs to preserve its relative position in space.

9   Lock and hide attributes

- From the Outliner, select all children of the *spineManip*, and then **Ctrl-select** all children of the *neckManip*.
- Set their **Visibility** to **Off**, and **lock and hide** all of their attributes.
- **Lock and hide** the **scale** and **visibility** attributes for the *spineManip* and *neckManip*.

10   Add custom attributes

- Select both the *spineManip* and *neckManip*.
- Select **Modify** → **Add Attribute**...
- Set the new attribute as follows:

    Attribute Name to *twist*;

    Data Type to **Float**.

- Click the **Add** button.
- Add another custom attribute as follows:

    Attribute Name to *ikFkBlend*;

    Data Type to **Float**;

    Minimum to **0**;

    Maximum to **1**;

    Default to **1**.

- Click the **OK** button.

11   Connect the custom attributes

- **Connect** both the *twist* and *ikFkBlend* attributes to their respective IK handles.
- Through the Attribute Editor, turn **On** the **Ik Fk Control** attribute for both IK spline handles.

12 Lock and hide the IK handles and splines

- Set the *backSplineIK*, *neckSplineIK*, *backSpline* and *neckSpline* **Visibility** to **Off**; then **lock and hide** all of their attributes.

13 Test the motion

- **Move** and **rotate** the new manipulators to see their effect on the characters.
- Set the manipulators back to their default attributes when you are done experimenting.

Hips manipulators

In order to complete Leon's back setup, you will need manipulators for the hips. You will need one manipulator for the *Hips* root joint, and another one for the *HipsOverride* joint.

1 Create a NURBS circle

- Select **Create → NURBS Primitives → Circle**.
- **Rename** the circle *hipsManip*.

2 Position the maniplator

- **Move** and **scale** the *hipsManip* to fit Leon's belly.
- Snap the pivot of the manipulator onto the *Hips* joint.

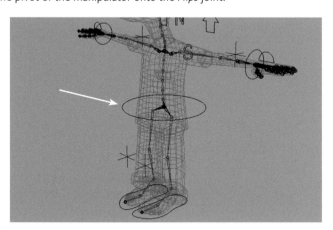

The hips manipulator

3 Duplicate the manipulator

- Select *hipsManip* and **duplicate** it.
- **Rename** the new manipulator to *hipsOverrideManip*.
- **Parent** the *hipsOverrideManip* to the *hipsManip* and **scale** it down.

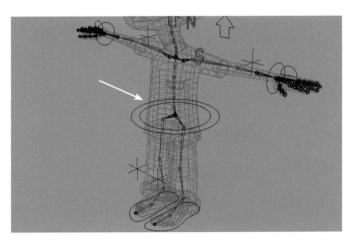

The hips override manipulator

4 Freeze and delete history

- **Freeze** the *hipsManip* and *hipsOverrideManip* transformations.

- Still with *hipsManip* and *hipsOverrideManip* selected, select **Edit** → **Delete by Type** → **History**.

Note: *It is important at this stage not to delete all the history in the scene because that would delete important history, such as the clusters.*

5 Parent constraint the hips

- Select the *hipsManip* and the *Hips* joint; then select **Constrain** → **Parent**.

Note: *Make sure* **Maintain Offset** *is set to* **On**.

6 Orient constraint the HipsOverride

- Select the *hipsOverrideManip* and the *HipsOverride* joint; then select **Constrain** → **Orient**.

Note: *Make sure* **Maintain Offset** *is set to* **On**.

7 Lock and hide unnecessary attributes

Master node

You will now add an additional level of control to Leon's rig by creating a *master manipulator*. When this master node is moved, the entire rig should be moving forward.

1 Create the master manipulator

- Select **Create → EP Curve → ❑**.
- In the option window, make sure **Curve Degree** is set to **Linear**.
- From the *top* view, draw a four-point arrow as follows:

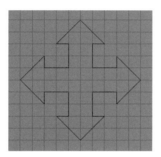

The master manipulator

- **Rename** the curve to *master*.

2 Position master at the center of the world

- With the *master* selected, select **Modify → Center Pivot**.
- **Snap** the *master* to the world origin.
- **Scale** it appropriately under Leon.
- **Freeze** its transformations.

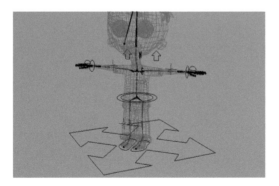

The well placed master node

3   **Lock and hide attributes**

 • **Lock and Hide** the *master*'s **scale** and **visibility** attributes.

4   **Parent the rig to the master**

Everything in the world used to move the rig must now be parented to the *master* node.

 • **Parent** all manipulators, pole vectors, and the root joint to the master node.

 • **Move** the *master* to confirm that everything follows.

5   **Save your work**

 • Save your scene as *17-spine setup 02.ma*.

Final touches

You will now parent everything that is part of Leon's rig to a rig group and place that group on a rig layer. You will also see here how to *color code* the various manipulators so they are easy to see and differentiate.

1   **Group all top nodes together**

In order to have a clean rig scene, you will group all the top nodes together under a single *rig* node.

 • From the Outliner, select all the *splines* and *Spline IKs* and the *master;* then press **Ctrl+g** to group them together.

Note: *Do not group the geometry as it will be in a separate hierarchy.*

 • **Rename** the new group *rig*.

 • **Lock and hide** all the attributes of the *rig* group since the rig must never move.

2   **Create a rig layer**

 • **Create** a new layer in the Layer Editor and name it *rigLayer*.

 • **Add** the *rig* group to the new *rigLayer*.

 You can now easily toggle the visibility of either the geometry layer or the rig layer.

3   **Color code manipulators**

 • Select the *master* node.

 • In the Attribute Editor, open the **Object Display** section and then the **Drawing Overrides** section.

- Turn **On** the **Enable Overrides** checkbox.

  Doing so will prevent the object from getting its color from the layer it is currently in.

> **Note:** *If you cannot enable the checkbox, it's because it has an input connection. In that case, simply* **RMB** *on the* **Enable Overrides** *checkbox and select* **Break Connection***; then turn it* **On.**

- Change the **Color** slider to yellow.

  By changing the color override, you ensure that the object wireframe will have that color in the viewport.

> **Note:** *The object must be deselected in order to see the effect of the color override.*

- **Repeat** the steps outlined here for any other objects.

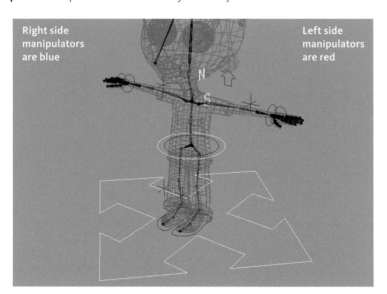

The color coded manipulators

Foolproof the rig

You have been conscientious about restricting access to Leon's attributes, but it is a good idea to double-check every single node in the scene to ensure that any attribute that can potentially break the rig is hidden and locked. You can also display the selection handles of objects that are intended for animation but are not controlled by a manipulator.

1 **Lock and hide potentially harmful objects and attributes**

- Open the **Hypergraph: Hierarchy**.

- Enable **Options → Display → Hidden Nodes**.

- Disable **Options → Display → Shape Nodes**.

- Go over each rig node one by one and **lock** and **hide** every attributes not intended for animation.

Note: *You should not lock any rotation of joints controlled by IKs since they can be animated in FK if wanted.*

Tip: *You can lock and hide multiple attributes on nodes of the same type.*

2 **Display selection handles**

A selection handle is a small cross that appears in the viewport, and that you can see and pick over any other type of node. This is a good alternative to a separate manipulator.

- Select any objects for which you require a selection handle, such as the *head* and *spine5* joints.

- Select **Display → Transform Display → Selection Handles**.

- While in Component mode, enable the **Selection Handle** mask and **move** them anywhere around your character.

3 **Save your work**

- Save your scene as *17-spine setup 03.ma*.

Other Leon setup

All the basics of the Leon rig are final, but many more things can be implemented. The last setup you will create for Leon is the eye setup. For characters more complex than Leon, you might want to add control for the jaw, tongue, ears, clothing, hair bangs, etc., but those are all intended for secondary animation, which is not required here.

The following will finalize the rig.

1 **Eye joints**

- **Draw** a single joint next to the eye geometry in the side view.

- **Parent** the new joint to the *Head* joint.

- **Rename** the new joint to *LeftEye*.
- Select Leon's left eye geometry; then **Shift-select** the *LeftEye* joint.
- Select **Constrain** → **Point Constraint**, making sure **Maintain Offset** is set to **Off**.

  Doing so will snap the new eye joint exactly in the middle of Leon's eye.
- **Delete** the constraint object that was just created.

Note: *The goal of the point constraint was not to constrain the joint, but only to place the joint in the middle of the eye geometry for you.*

- **Mirror** the joint for the right eye.

  You now have two well-placed eye joints that will be used for the eye setup.

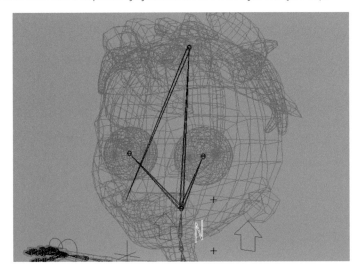

The eye joints

- Make sure the new joint is named *RightEye*.

Note: *The eye joints will also be useful to see the eye location when animating without geometry.*

2   **Eye setup**

- **Create** a NURBS circle and rename it *eyeLookAt*.
- **Place** and **edit** the *eyeLookAt* object so it looks as follows:

Project 04

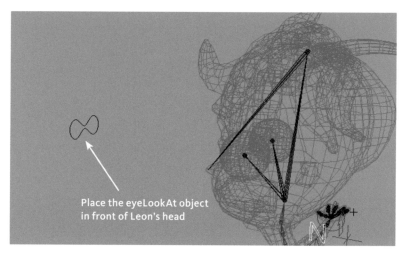

Place the eyeLookAt object
in front of Leon's head

The eyeLookAt object

- **Create** two locators and **snap** each one on its respective eye joint.

- **Move** both locators on their **Z-axes**, next to the *eyeLookAt* node.

- **Parent** both locators to the *eyeLookAt* node.

- **Rename** the locators to *leftEyeLookAt* and *rightEyeLookAt*.

- **Freeze** the transformations of *eyeLookAt* and the two locators.

- **Delete** the history of t*eyeLookAt* and the two locators.

- Select the *leftEyeLookAt* locator; then **Shift-select** the *LeftEye* joint.

- Select **Constraint** → **Aim** → ❏.

- Make sure the **Maintain Offset** option is set to **On**; then **add** the constraint.

- **Create** an aim constraint for the other eye joint and locator.

- **Lock** and **hide** the appropriate objects and attributes.

 Tip: *Don't lock the rotation and scale X attributes of the eyeLookAt node, as they can be
used to simulate crossed eyes.*

- **Parent** the *eyeLookAt* node to the *master* node.

- **Assign** proper coloring overrides to the new nodes.

3 Save your work

- Save your final scene file as *17-spine setup 03.ma*.

The final rig

Conclusion

The spline IK solver is ideal for controlling a long chain of joints such as those found in a snake, an animal's back, or a tail. It is based on the use of a NURBS curve and therefore is a powerful link to other parts of Maya. A NURBS curve, for example, can be deformed using non-linear deformers or animated as a soft body, which utilizes dynamics to generate its animation. For Leon, you used the cluster deformer, which allows you to move the individual NURBS CVs and keyframe his animation.

In the next project, you will set up all the deformation required for Leon to be animated with his rig.

IMAGEGALLERY

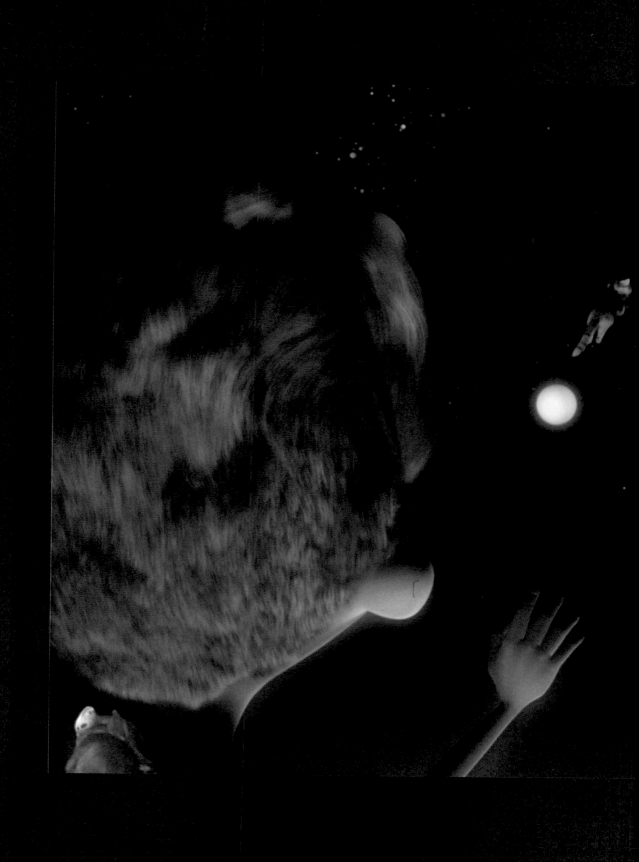

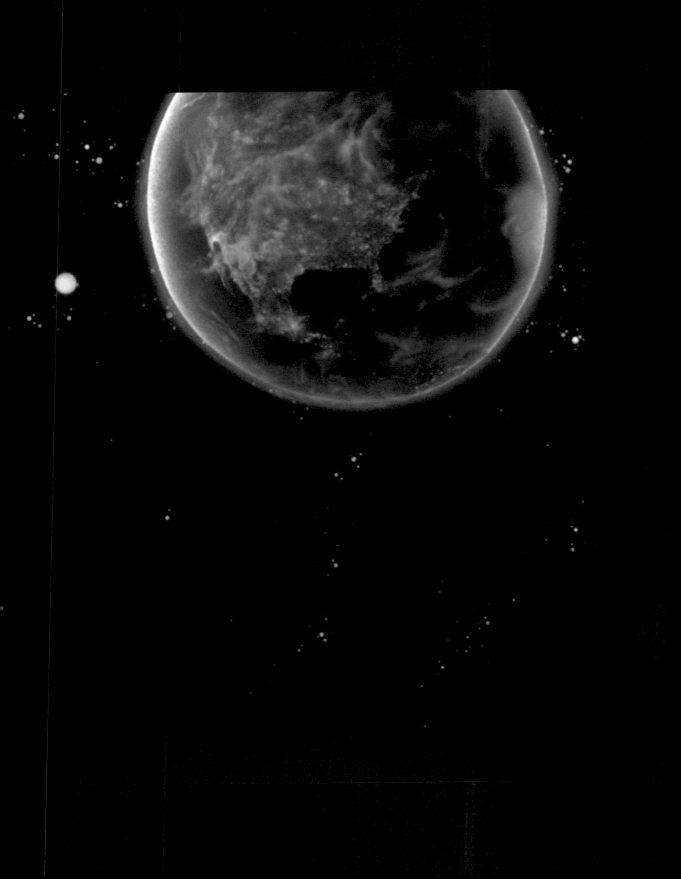

Project 05

In Project 5, you will finalize Leon's geometry and attach it to the character rig from Project 4. First, you will generate all the blend shapes required for Leon's facial expressions, and then you will bind his skin to the rig using smooth binding. You will also create influence objects and assign various deformers to Leon. Finally, you will create a low-resolution model for real time animation.

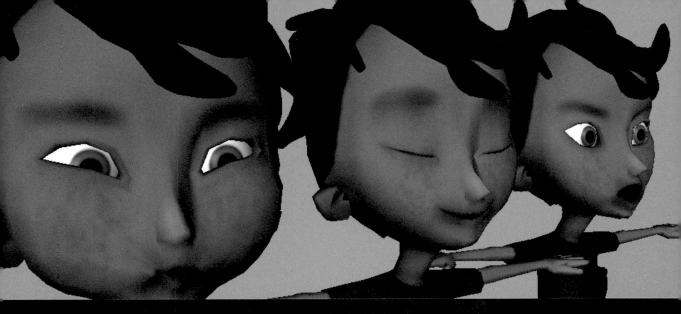

Lesson 18
Blend Shapes

In this lesson, you will bring Leon to life by creating facial expressions. You will do this by creating a blend shape node to morph the head. Once that is done, you will set up a facial manipulator that will give the animator control over Leon's facial expressions.

In this lesson you will learn the following:

- The basic phonemes;
- How to create blend shape targets;
- How to sculpt facial expressions;
- How to use wire deformers;
- How to set up blend shape nodes;
- How to use in-between targets;
- How to edit a deformer set;
- How to connect the blend shape attributes to a manipulator

Blend shape deformers

A *blend shape* is a powerful deformer that allows you to blend several target shapes onto a base shape. When computing the resulting blended shape, the deformer calculates the differences between the base and target shapes. The blend shape attribute values, which range from 0 to 1, define the percentage of the target shapes to assign to the base shape.

The node has one attribute for each of the target shapes, which can be animated to get smooth transitions between shapes.

Blend shape deformers are usually used for facial expressions, but they can also be used in lots of other cases. For instance, you might want to use blend shapes to bulge muscles. You could also use blend shapes along with driven keys to correct geometry as it is being deformed. For Leon, you will concentrate mostly on facial animation.

Facial animation

Facial animation can be broken down into several categories:

Mouth, cheeks and jaw

For lip-synching, phonemes are very important and must be created carefully so they can blend together without breaking the geometry. Generic phonemes such as *A*, *E*, *O*, *U*, can be used to establish mouth shapes that are formed repetitively while talking. Along with the lips, the cheeks must also deform. The jaw must move down for phonemes that require an open mouth. The tongue must also be deformed to follow the different phonemes, such as *TH* and *L*.

Eyes and eyebrows

Eye animation is critical when animating a character, since the eyes are what a viewer will be looking at the most. Shapes for blinking, squinting, or to widen the eyes are very important. The eyebrows must also be taken care of, since they will describe all the emotions of the character. Most shapes in this category should be split to deform either the left or the right side of the face.

Nose

Even though some nose movement comes as a result of other facial motion, the nose blend shapes are often forgotten. Having shapes for breathing in and out or flaring the nostrils will add realism to the facial animation.

Expressions

Sometimes, when facial expressions are repetitive for a character, it is worthwhile to create entire facial expressions rather than using a blend of multiple shapes. Doing so will allow the expressions to be perfect and blend without breaking the geometry. It is especially good when the expressions are extreme.

Collisions

It is a good idea to add blend shapes for when the character's face is touched by something. Even if it is not possible to plan for every geometry collision, you should take some time to determine whether the character will be pulling its ear or receiving a punch on the nose, for example, and create those shapes. This will also add realism to the animation.

Additional shapes

You must not forget about additional shapes that could be useful for facial animation, such as the neck muscles contracting, swallowing, or a bulging thorax as a character breathes in.

Phonemes

Below is a simple chart of the basic phonemes used in the English language. You can use this list to create the different target shapes for your character, and also as a guide to break down the phonetics of a speech.

Note: *Since Leon does not have a tongue or teeth, the phonemes shown here are based only on the lips' position.*

A

As found in words like *alright*, *autumn,* and *car.*

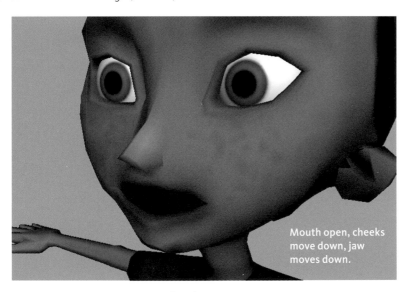

Mouth open, cheeks move down, jaw moves down.

The phoneme A

Project 05

E

As found in words like *he, tree,* and *believe.*

Lips stretched back, cheeks go up, jaw doesn't move.

The phoneme E

O

As found in words like *flow, go,* and *toy.*

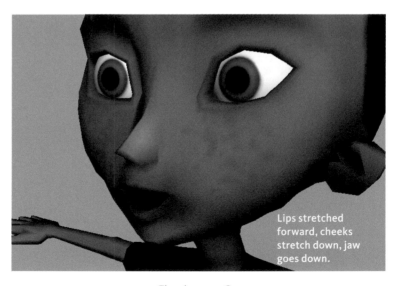

Lips stretched forward, cheeks stretch down, jaw goes down.

The phoneme O

U

As found in words like *you*, *stew*, and *noodle*.

Lips form a pout, cheeks stretch far down, jaw goes down a little.

The phoneme U

V and F

As found in words like *very* and *fabulous*.

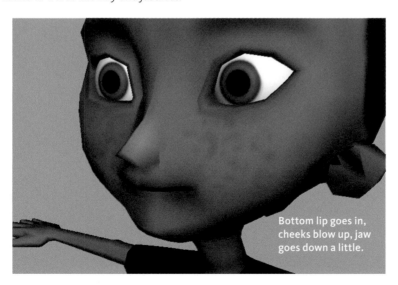

Bottom lip goes in, cheeks blow up, jaw goes down a little.

The phonemes V and F

B, M and P

As found in words like *big*, *mat*, and *put*.

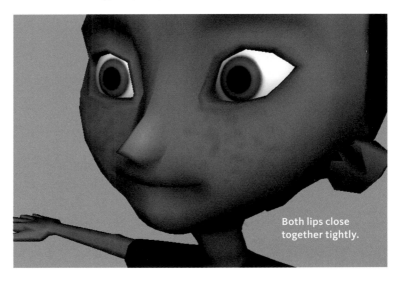

Both lips close together tightly.

The phonemes B, M and P

Tip: *For characters with a full inner mouth, other phonemes such as L, Th and Sh can be added.*

From these basic shapes, you can achieve most mouth shapes in the English language. The tricky part is getting all these shapes to transition properly from one shape to the next. In order to achieve an appropriate blending, you will need to study how each phoneme is formed.

Leon's first blend shape

You will now create Leon's first blend shape target. By doing this, you will learn the workflow for the rest of the shapes to be created.

1   Scene file

• Continue with your own scene.

OR

• Open the last project scene file called *17-spine setup 03.ma*.

2   Set the layers

- Set the *rigLayer*'s **Visibility** to **Off**.

- Set the *geometryLayer* to be displayed normally.

3   Duplicate Leon's geometry

You will now duplicate Leon's geometry in order to sculpt the shape in a different geometry, while keeping the base shape untouched.

- Select the *geometry* group from the Outliner.

> **Tip**:   *If the Translate attributes are hidden and locked, you may need to retrieve those from the Channel Control editor.*

- Press **Ctrl+d** to duplicate it.

- **Translate** the new group on the **X-axis** by **15** units, in order to have two heads side by side.

> **Note:** *The geometry group is duplicated in order to keep the eyes with the duplicate. This will make it easier to shape the area around the eye once you get there.*

4   Rename the duplicate geometry

When you create the blend shape node, it uses the name of each target shape to name the corresponding blend attribute. Because of this, you should always give your blend shape targets concise and informative names.

- **Rename** the duplicated head geometry to E.

> **Note:** *Rename the geometry and not the geometry group.*

5   Wire deformer

There are several ways to sculpt the target shape. For instance, you might want to use a wire deformer, a cluster, or a sculpt deformer. For Leon's blend shapes, you will first tweak the facial geometry using a wire deformer to get broad deformation. You will then sculpt the geometry using the *Sculpt Geometry Tool*.

- Select the *Leon* geometry, and then click the **Make Live** button in the status bar (the magnet icon), or select **Modify → Make Live**.

- Select **Create → EP Curve Tool → ❑** and set the tool to create a CubicDegree curve**.**

- Draw a curve following the mouth line.

- Turn **Off** the Make Live feature.

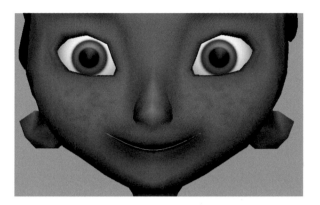

The mouth curve

- Select **Create Deformers → Wire Tool.**
- Pick the geometry and press Enter.
- Pick the curve and press Enter.

  The wire deformer is now created.

- Go into Component mode and tweak the shape of the curve as needed.

  Since the wire's influence is too broad, you must reduce it so it doesn't affect the nose and chin.

 Tip: *Press 5 or 6 to be in shaded mode while deforming or sculpting.*

- In the Channel Box, highlight the *wire1* input node and change its **Dropoff Distance** attribute to a lower value.

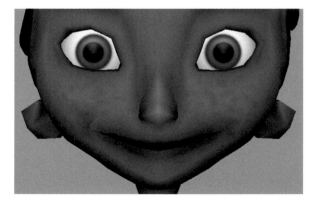

The basic E shape

- When you manage to get a basic *E* shape, select the geometry and then choose **Edit → Delete by Type → History.**

- Delete the curves from the Outliner since they are no longer used.

6 Sculpt Geometry Tool

As you can see, you cannot refine the shape with only a wire deformer. You will now sculpt the geometry using the Sculpt Geometry Tool.

- Select **Mesh → Sculpt Geometry Tool → ☐**.

- In the **Stroke** section, set the **Reflection** checkbox to **On** and specify the **Reflection axis** to **X**.

By enabling this option, you ensure that any sculpting will be reflected on the other side of the geometry.

Tip: *If you need to the reflection to pull vertices in the opposite direction, simply turn On the Invert Reference Vector in the Stroke section of the Sculpt Geometry Tool.*

7 Sculpt the E shape

Using the various sculpt operations, sculpt the *E* shape as best you can. First, smooth the lips that were stretched by the wire deformer, and then open them slightly. Make sure to also move the cheeks and cheekbones up.

Tip: *Always keep a mirror close to you when scultping facial shapes.*

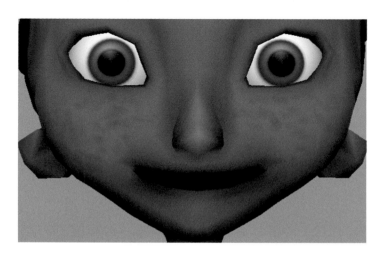

The E shape

Lesson 18: Blend Shapes

Note: *When sculpting a shape, try to keep your edits localized. For instance, don't sculpt the eye area. Also, try not to sculpt other parts of the body by mistake.*

Test the shape

You will now test the effect of the *E* shape on Leon's original head by creating a temporary blend shape deformer. This will allow you to see how the shape is blending in. Since construction history will be kept, you will be able to bring modifications onto the target shape, which will automatically update the blend shape deformer.

1   **Create the blend shape deformer**

    • Select the *E* target geometry, and then **Shift-select** *Leon*'s original geometry.

Note: *The base shape must always be selected last.*

    • Under the **Animation** menu set, select **Create Deformers → Blend Shape → ☐**, and make sure the options are reset to their default values.

    • **Create** the blend shape deformer.

2   **Test the blend shape**

    • Select **Window → Animation Editor → Blend Shape**.

    The Blend Shape window will appear, listing a single slider for the target E.

    • Use the slider to see the effect of the blend shape on the original Leon geometry.

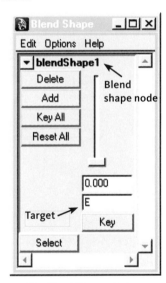

The Blend Shape window

Note: *You can also access blendShape1's attributes through the Input section of the Channel Box.*

> **Tip:**   *It is better to see the wireframe over the geometry in order to see the subtle movement of Leon's skin.*

3   Make corrections

- If needed, make corrections on Leon's *E* target shape using the Sculpt Geometry Tool.

Doing so will automatically update the blend shape node because of construction history.

4   Delete the blend shape deformer

Since the blend shape deformer created above was only temporary, you will now delete it.

- In the **Input Line** located at the top-right corner of the main interface, select the **Select by name** option.
- Type *blendShape1* and hit **Enter**.

The blend shape node is selected.

> **Tip:**   *You can also click the Select button in the **Blend Shape** window.*

- Press **Delete** on your keyboard to delete the blend shape deformer.

5   Add a targets layer

- **Create** a new layer called *targetsLayer* and **add** the shapes to it.
- Set layer's **Visibility** to **Off**.

Doing so will keep your scene refresh fast as you create more and more geometry.

6   Save your work

- Save your scene as *18-blend shapes 01.ma*.

Model all blend shapes

You are now ready to create all the remaining blend shapes required for Leon's animation.

1   Create a target shape

- **Duplicate** the original Leon's *geometry* group, and **move** it aside.
- **Rename** Leon's target geometry to the desired shape name.
- **Sculpt** the target shape.

> **Tip:** Turn **Off** the **Sculpt Polygons Tool**'s **Reflection** option for shapes that are separate for each side of the face.

- **Test** the blending if required; then **delete** the blend shape node.
- **Hide** the target shape.
- **Save** your work.

2 Repeat step 1 for all the shapes

Next is a list of the different shapes you can create:

- **Phonemes**: *A, E, O, U, V, M*;
- **Mouth shapes**: *jawDown, smile, blowCheeks*;
- **Eyebrows**: *leftBrowUp, leftBrowSad, leftBrowMad, rightBrowUp, rightBrowSad, rightBrowMad*;
- **Eyes**: *leftWideOpen, leftLowerLidUp, leftBlinkMid, leftBlinkMax, rightWideOpen, rightLowerLidUp, rightBlinkMid, rightBlinkMax*;
- **Others**: *breath*;

All the target shapes

> **Tip:** *Your shapes will look more natural if they are not all perfect. For instance, moving one eyebrow up can move the cheeks and stretch the other eyebrow; and not necessarily symmetrically.*

3 Save your work

- Save your scene as *18-blend shapes 02.ma*.

In-between targets

The blend shape deformer has the ability to have *in-between* targets. This means that you can have multiple target shapes placed one after the other in the same blend shape attribute. This kind of blending is said to be in *series*, and the in-between shape transition will occur in the order in which you added the target shapes. The effect will be that the blend shape will be able to change from the first target object shape to the second, and so on.

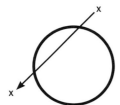

The blend shape interpolation is linear

The blend shape interpolation with in-between targets

The difference between linear and in-between blend shapes

In the last exercise, you created two different blend shapes for the eyes blinking: a blink *mid* shape and a blink *max* shape. You had to do this because if you blend from the eye open straight to the eye closed, the vertices of the eyelid could go straight through the eye rather than following the eye curvature.

1 Scene file

- Continue with your own scene.

OR

- Open the scene file *18-blend shapes 02.ma* from the support files.

> **Note:** *This scene file contains all of Leon's shapes. For simplicity reasons, the rest of the exercise will explain a workflow starting from this file.*

2 In-between targets

- Show the *eyeLayer* and the original *geometryLayer*.

  Doing so displays the original Leon geometry along with only the eye-related blend shape targets.

- From the Outliner, select the *leftBlinkMid* target shape, which is child of the *leftBlinkMidGroup*, under the *eyeGroup*.

- **Ctrl-select** the *leftBlinkMax* target shape, which is child of the *leftBlinkMaxGroup*, under the *eyeGroup*.

- **Ctrl-select** the original *leon* geometry.

  You should now have three objects selected in the following order: leftBlinkMid, leftBlinkMax and leon.

- Select **Create Deformers → Blend Shape → ❑**.

- In the option window, make sure the **In-Between** checkbox is turned **On**.

- Click the **Apply** button.

3 Test the blink blending

- Select the original *Leon* geometry.

- In the Channel Box, highlight the *blendShape1* node in the **Inputs** section.

- Highlight the *leftBlinkMax* attribute, and then **MMB+drag** in the viewport to invoke the virtual slider.

  *You will notice Leon is shaped like leftBlinkMid at **0.5** and shaped like leftBlinkMax at **1**.*

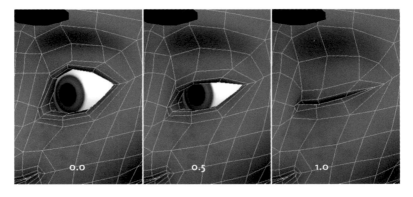

The in-between blending

4 Rename the attribute

Since the blink attribute is named *leftBlinkMax*, rename it to *leftBlink* by typing the following MEL command:

```
aliasAttr leftBlink blendShape1.leftBlinkMax;
```

Note: *You could also give the last target selected a proper name before creating the blend shape node.*

5 Add to a blend shape node that already exists

You will now add the right blink target to the blend shape node.

- Select the following objects in order: *rightBlinkMax* and *leon*.
- Select **Edit Deformers** → **Blend Shape** → **Add**.

  A new Blend Shape attribute is now added to the original blendShape1 node.

- **Rename** the attribute by typing the following MEL command:

```
aliasAttr rightBlink blendShape1.rightBlinkMax;
```

6 Add in-between to a blend shape node that already exists

- Select the following objects in order: *rightBlinkMid* and *leon*.
- Select **Edit Deformers** → **Blend Shape** → **Add** → ☐.
- In the option window, set the following:

    Specify Node to **On**;

    Add In-Between Targets to **On**;

    Target Index to **2**;

    In-Between Weight to **0.5**.

Note: *The* **Target Index** *denotes which blend shape attribute the in-between should be added to, and the* **In-Between Weight** *is the position in the attribute in which it should reach that shape.*

- Click the **Apply** button.

  The right eye now has proper blinking with in-betweens.

Finalize the blend shape

You will now finalize Leon's blend shapes by adding all the remaining shapes to the current blend shape node. In order to have coherence in the list of attributes of the blend shape node, you will have to select all the new targets in the order you want them to appear.

Once the blend shape node is final, you will optimize it by removing unused vertices from the blend shape deformer set. Once that is done, you will delete all the target shapes.

1   Add the targets

- Select the following objects in order:

    leftWideOpen, rightWideOpen, leftLowerLidUp, rightLowerLidUp, A, E, O, U, F, M, jawDown, smile, blowCheeks, leftBrowUp, rightBrowUp, leftBrowSad, rightBrowSad, leftBrowMad, rightBrowMad, breath and *leon.*

- Select **Edit Deformers → Blend Shape → Add → ☐**.

- In the option window, reset all of the options to their default values.

- Click the **Apply** button.

2   Remove unwanted vertices from the deformer set

When you created the blend shape node, it listed all the vertices of Leon's geometry in order to blend them, even if the vertices would never be affected by the deformer. For this reason, you will edit the deformer set in order to remove any vertices that will not be moved by any of the targets.

- Select the *Leon* geometry.

- Select **Windows → Relationship Editors → Deformer Sets**.

The Relationship Editor will be displayed with the deformer sets on the left panel and the scene objects in the right panel.

- Highlight the *blendShape1Set* on the left panel.

INPUTS

blendShape1	
Envelope	1
leftBlink	0
rightBlink	0
leftWideOpen	0
rightWideOpen	0
leftLowerLipUp	0
rightLowerLidUp	0
A	0
E	0
O	0
U	0
V	0
M	0
jawDown	0
smile	0
blowCheeks	0
leftBrowUp	0
rightBrowUp	0
leftBrowSad	0
rightBrowSad	0
leftBrowMad	0
rightBrowMad	0
breath	0
tweak3	

The blend shape node finalized

Project 05

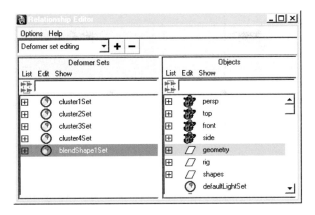

The Relationship Editor

- Select **Edit → Select Set Members** from the left side panel in the Relationship Editor.

  Doing so will select all the vertices of Leon that are currently being affected by the blend shape deformer.

- From the front and side views, while in Component mode, select all the vertices that are not affected by any of the blend shapes.

Note: *Don't select the vertices of the chest and back, since the* breath *shape affects these vertices.*

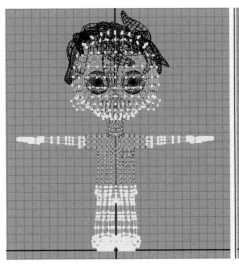
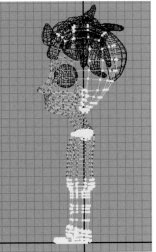

Vertices to remove from the deformer set

- In the Relationship Editor, still with the *blendShape1Set* highlighted, select **Edit → Remove Selected Items** from the left side panel.

3 Make sure the deformer set is good

- **Deselect** all the vertices.
- **RMB** on the *blendShape1Set* to display its context menu, and then select **Select Set Members**.

  Only the remaining vertices deformed by the blendShape1Set get selected.

4 Test the blend shapes

- **Test** Leon's blend shapes and make sure all of them still work correctly.

5 Delete the targets

- Select the *shapes* groups from the Outliner and **delete** it.

> **Note:** *You might want to keep a version of the scene with all the target shapes in case you need them later on. Otherwise, the target shapes can be extracted from the blend shape deformer.*

- Select **File → Optimize Scene Size** to remove any obsolete nodes and layers.

6 Save your work

- Save your scene as *18-blend shapes 03.ma*.

Blend shape manipulator

To continue with the manipulator theme and to make it easy for the animator to access Leon's blend shapes, you will create a manipulator that will list all of Leon's blend shapes.

1 Create a manipulator

- Select **Create → NURBS Primitives → Circle → ❐**.
- In the options, set **Degree** to **Linear** and change the **Number of Sections** to **16**.
- Click the **Create** button.
- **Rename** the circle to *blendShapesManip*.
- **Edit** the manipulator so it looks like the following and place it above Leon's head:

The blend shape manipulator

2 **Place the manipulator in the rig**

- Enable the **Visibility** of the *rigLayer*.

- **Parent** the manipulator to the *Head* joint.

- **Freeze** the manipulator's transformations.

- Select **Edit → Delete by Type → History**.

- **Lock and hide** all of its attributes.

- **Assign** a color override to the new manipulator.

3 **Add custom attributes**

- Add a custom attribute for each shape in the blend shape deformer with the following values:

    Data Type to **Float**;

    Minimum to **0**;

    Maximum to **1**;

    Default to **0**.

Tip: *Add the attributes in the appropriate order. Use MEL to speed things up.*

- Through the Connection Editor, connect all the blend shape attributes to the manipulator's attributes.

Tip: *You can either select the blend shape node or highlight its name in the Channel Box to be able to load it in the Connection Editor. The* **Blend** *attributes are listed under the* **Weight** *attribute.*

- Use the following MEL script to automate the entire task. Be careful about any difference between the names used here and the names in your scene.

```
int $nBS = `getAttr -s "blendShape1.weight"`;
for($i = 0; $i < $nBS; $i++)
{
        string $name = `aliasAttr -q ("blendShape1.weight[" + $i +
"]")`;
        addAttr -k 1 -ln $name -at double -min -0 -max 1 -dv 0
blendShapesManip;
        connectAttr -f ("blendShapesManip." + $name)
("blendShape1." + $name);
}
```

4   **Save your work**

- Save your scene as *18-blend shapes 04.ma*.

Conclusion

In this lesson, you learned how to channel the power of the blend shape deformer. You saw that you could create as many target shapes as needed to control a base shape. You also learned about in-between targets, which can refine the deformation for complex blends. Then you learned how to edit a deformer set, which is an essential concept to understand when dealing with deformers.

This lesson also covered specific facial behavior intended for lip-synching. Generating the appropriate facial expressions will breathe life into your character as it expresses itself.

In the next lesson, you will bind Leon's skin to its skeleton.

Lesson 19
Skinning

In this lesson, you will explore the smooth bind deformer. Smooth binding provides smooth deformations around joints by allowing multiple joints to have influence on the same vertex.

Binding

Bound geometry points (CVs, vertices, lattice points) can be thought of as *skin points*. There are two ways to attach geometry to skeletal joints. Smooth binding is the most common technique; it allows the skin points to be weighted across many different joints. With rigid binding, a skin point is fully assigned to a particular joint. This lesson uses smooth binding for all of Leon's geometry except his bangs, which you will attach with rigid binding.

You can then refine a point's binding by changing the weights coming from each of the influences. These points should all have a total weight of 1.0, which is 100% influenced, but the weights can be shared between many different joints and influences.

The weight or participation of a skin point's influences can be locked or held to a specific value. This will inhibit the weight from changing as adjacent skin weights are adjusted and a total value of 1.0 is maintained.

1 Scene file

- Continue with your own scene from the last lesson.

OR

- Open the last lesson scene file called *18-blend shapes 04.ma*.

2 Hide what doesn't need to be bound

- In the Perspective view, select **Show** → **None**; then select **Show** → **Polygons** and **Show** → **Joints**.
- **Hide** the bangs.

3 Preferred angle

- Make sure the skeleton's preferred angle is properly set by selecting the *Hips*; then **RMB** in the view and select **Set Preferred Angle**.

This will be Leon's default position.

4 Select the appropriate skeleton joints

In order to keep the skinning as simple as possible and to reduce the number of influences to be calculated in Leon's skinning, you will manually pick the joints that will influence the geometry.

- Select all the joints that you judge important to be part of the influences of the binding. For instance, don't select the *Hips* joint, but rather the *HipsOverride* joint. Also, any joints at the tip of a joint chain don't need to be selected.

Tip: *Do your selection from the Outliner to ensure you don't forget any important joints.*

5 Select the surface

• **Shift-select** *leon*'s skin.

6 Smooth Bind Leon

• Select **Skin** → **Bind Skin** → **Smooth Bind** → ❑.

• **Reset** and set the following in the option window:

> **Bind to Selected joints**:

> **Remove unused influences** to **Off**.

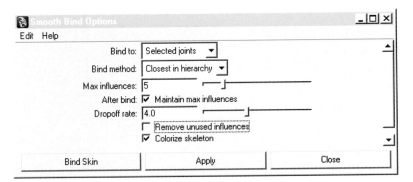

Smooth Bind Options

Following are some explanations on the Smooth Bind Options:

As a Bind method, **Closest in hierarchy** *specifies that joint influence is based on the skeleton's hierarchy. In character setup, you will usually want to use this binding method because it can prevent inappropriate joint influences. For example, this method can prevent a right leg joint from influencing nearby skin points on the left leg.*

Max influences *are the number of joints that will have influence on an individual skin point. Setting the* **Max influences** *to* **5** *means that each skin point will have no more than five joints affecting it.*

Setting the **Dropoff rate** *is another way to determine how each skin point will be influenced by different joints. The dropoff rate controls how rapidly the influence of each joint on individual skin points is going to decrease with the distance between the two. The greater the dropoff, the more rapidly the influence decreases with distance. Max influences and dropoff rate are described in greater detail later in this lesson, under the heading: Paint Weight Tips.*

> **Tip:** *The dropoff rate can be adjusted on individual joints after the character is skinned. The max influences can also be adjusted after the character has been skinned; however, the new setting takes effect only on selected surfaces instead of the entire character with multiple surfaces. When enabled, the* **Remove unused influences** *option will remove any joint with no influence assigned to it. Since you have manually selected the joints you want, this option can be turned off.*

- Press the **Bind Skin** button to attach the skin to the skeleton and establish weighting.

7 Set IKs to FK

In order to test the skinning, you should first disable the IK handles. You want to rotate each bone individually in FK and watch the effect on the geometry.

- Set the **Ik Fk Blend** attribute to **0** for the arms, legs, back, neck, and tail manipulators.

  You can now rotate each bone using FK.

> **Tip:** *You could also select* **Modify → Evaluate Nodes** *and turn* **Off** *the* **IK Solvers** *and* **Constraints** *evaluation.*

8 Test the results

- Test the results of the smooth binding by rotating Leon's arms and legs. Pay particular attention to Leon's articulations.
- Return Leon to his original pose by selecting **Assume Preferred Angle**.

9 Save your work

- Save your scene as *19-skinning 01.ma*.

Editing weights

Weighting a character has traditionally been a long and tedious task. Fortunately, the Paint Skin Weights Tool eases the burden of this process by allowing you to paint weights directly on the geometry using visual feedback.

When a character is bound, a skin cluster node is created for each of the surfaces that is bound to the skeleton. A skin cluster holds all the skin points' weights and influences, and you can edit the assignment of each point to different joints to achieve better deformations.

After moving Leon around in the last exercise, you may notice that the settings you used for the smooth binding provide good quality deformations, but there are some problem areas such as the pelvis and shoulder. These areas will be improved by editing the weights of the skin points for the different influence joints.

Paint Skin Weights Tool

You will now use the Paint Skin Weights Tool to refine the arms' binding. To ensure that you are improving the skinning as you are painting, you will put Leon into various poses that will bring out problematic areas.

1   Pose Leon to show problem areas

A good technique for simplifying the painting process is to keyframe Leon while in extreme poses. This allows you to scroll in the time slider to see the deformations.

- Select the *LeftArm* joint.

- Start at frame **1** and set a keyframe.

- Establish several arm poses every **10** frames:

  Arm up at frame **10**;

  Arm down at frame **20**;

  Arm forward at frame **30**;

  Arm backward at frame **40**;

Arm poses

Tip: *You can create poses that are extreme, but try to keep them within range of the intended for animation.*

2   Paint Tool

- Select the *Leon* geometry.

- Select **Skin → Edit Smooth Skin → Paint Skin Weights Tool → ☐**.

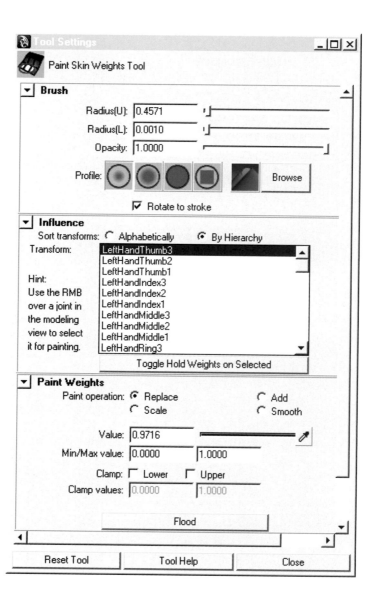

The Paint Skin Weights window

- Within the **Influences** list, find and highlight *LeftArm*.

- Within the **Display** section, set **Color Feedback** to **On**.

This allows you to see a grayscale representation of the weighting values associated with the surface being painted. White corresponds to a value of 1, black a value of 0. The shades of gray represent a value between 0 and 1.

Visual feedback

Note: *In the previous image, the* **Show Wireframe** *option was set to* **Off**.

3 Painting weights

If you look closer at the shoulder area, you will notice gray color on the side of the chest. This kind of influence will deform the chest as you rotate the arm in an up position, such as the one at frame 10. You will now fix this.

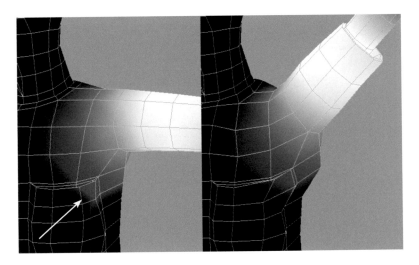

Chest influence at frame 0 and 10

- Select the second **Profile** brush.
- Set the **Paint operation** to **Replace**.

- In the **Paint Weights** section, set **Value** to **0.0**.

  By setting the painting value to 0, you are telling the tool to remove any weight coming from this bone and to reassign the removed weights to other bones already influencing this area, such as the spine bones.

- **Paint** the chest and armpit until the chest is no longer deformed by the *LeftArm*.

Tip: *Hold down* **b** *and* **click+drag** *to increase or decrease the brush size.*

- **Scroll** in the time slider between frame **1** and **10**.

  You will notice that even though you have painted the entire chest area black, some of the chest vertices are still moving. This is because there are weights assigned on other bones of the arm.

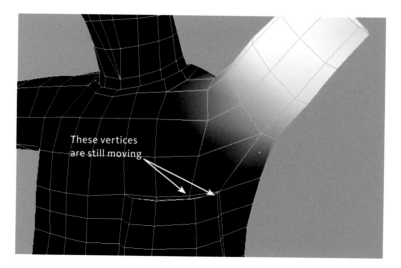

Corrected chest influence

- Select the *LeftForeArm* in the **Influence** section.
- Select the third **Profile** brush.
- Attempt to paint some black on the problematic vertices to see if that fixes the problem.

Note: *With the values so close to 0, you might not see the color difference with the color feedback.*

- If the previous step did not entirely fix the problem, try to paint the other arm joints black as well.

> **Note:** *Painting weights on a character is an iterative process, so there will generally be some going back and forth between the influences.*

4 MMB+dragging

Another quick and easy technique to test the influence of the different bones is to use the middle mouse button and drag in the viewport.

- Go to frame **1**.

- Select the *LeftArm* joint.

- Select **Edit → Delete by Type → Channels**.

  Doing so will remove the animation on the arm.

- Select the **Paint Skin Weights Tool** with the *Leon* geometry selected.

- With the *LeftArm* influence selected, click the **MMB** in the viewport.

  Doing so tells the tool that you wish to rotate the selected influence to test it.

- **MMB+drag** on any of the rotation manipulator axes.

  By dragging the mouse, you rotate the influence accordingly.

- When you are done testing the rotations, you can either **Undo** or **RMB** and select **Assume Preferred Angle** to reset the joint's rotation.

- Click the **LMB** to continue painting weights.

5 Smoothing weights

- Switch the **Paint Weight** operation to **Smooth**.

- **Paint** the shoulder and armpit area to smooth the *LeftArm* influence.

  Smoothing will help to even out the deformation.

6 The clavicle

You are now ready to refine the influence on another part of the body.

- Select the *LeftShoulder* influence.

  There is probably too much influence coming from this joint on the entire chest area.

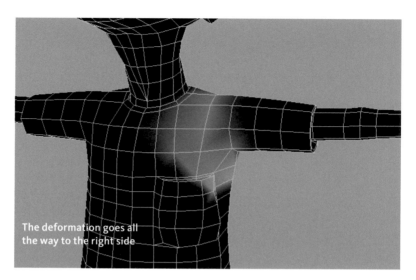

Bad clavicle influence

- Set the operation to **Replace** and paint black on the chest. This will contain the influence to the pectoral muscle and the top of the shoulder.

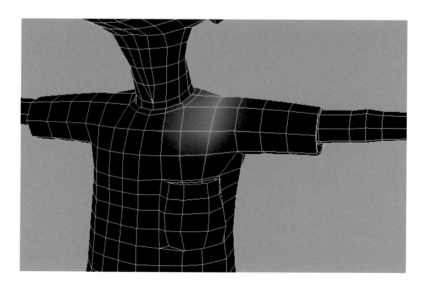

Corrected clavicle influence

Note: *Since the clavicle's rotation is used by the leftClavicleManip, you will not be able to use the* **MMB+drag** *technique. Use the manipulator to test the influence.*

7 Adding weights

So far, you have been painting the influences by painting zero weights (black). Doing so establishes the general influence of a joint, but you might not always be sure of where the removed influence will go. For instance, now that you have removed weights from the clavicle influence, it is not clear where the influence went.

Tip: *As a general workflow, you should remove weights only when roughing out the weights on the entire character. Once that is done, you can start refining the influences by adding weights. If you stick to this, you will be certain to get the best possible results from the Paint Skin Weights Tool.*

- With the *LeftShoulder* influence still selected, set the **Paint Operation** to **Add**.
- Set the **Value** to **0.1** and select the second **Profile** brush.
- **Add** and **smooth** the influence to the clavicle by painting the shoulder blade.

  Doing so will greatly improve the clavicle influence by simulating the shoulder blade moving under the skin.

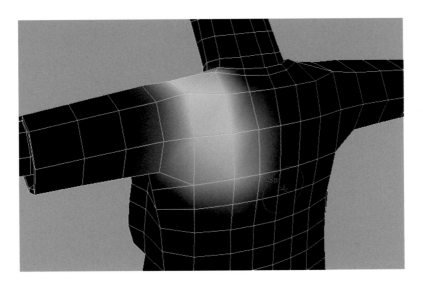

Shoulder blade influence

Tip: *Make sure you don't add too much weight, as it will result in a harsh deformation.*

8 Flooding weights

The Paint Skin Weights Tool has the ability to flood the entire geometry with the specified operation. For instance, if a joint has no influence at all on the geometry, you can set the paint operation to Replace with a value of 0, and then click the Flood button. Another great way of using the Flood button is to smooth the entire influence of a joint in one click.

- Select the *Spine* influence.
- Set the **Paint Operation** to **Smooth**.
- Click on the **Flood** button.

The entire Spine influence was smoothed.

- Click the **Flood** button multiple times in order to really smooth an influence.

Tip: *You should especially flood smooth values after roughing out the entire character's influences, to avoid reassigning some weights onto other, unknown influences.*

A workflow for painting weights

Now that you have learned the basics about painting weights, you can proceed to rough out the entire character. Once that is done, you can start smoothing the weights using the flood technique. Finally, when you have managed to assign adequate influences everywhere, you can add and smooth the localized area.

Following are the primary steps to take in order to weight the entire character perfectly:

1 Roughing out the entire character

The following images show the roughing stage for all the influences. This was achieved by going through them one by one, and painting with the **Operation** set to **Replace** with a value of **1**. You can then precisely define the regions you want certain influences to act upon.

Tip: *Since Leon is symmetrical, don't bother painting the right side of the geometry since you will be using* **Mirror Skin Weights** *to copy the weights from the left side to the other.*

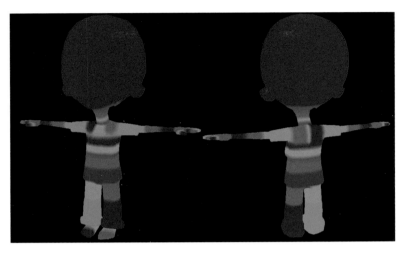

Character roughed influences

> **Note:** *In the above images, joints were colorized using the* **Display** → **Wireframe Color** *tool. Leon is displayed using the* **Multi-color Feedback,** *which is available in the* **Display** *section of the Paint Skin Weights Tool, with the* **Wireframe** *turned* **Off**.

2   Mirror the influences

- With the *Leon* geometry selected, select **Skin** → **Edit Smooth Skin** → **Mirror Skin Weights** → ❑.

- In the option window, set the **Mirror Across** option to **YZ** and turn **On** the **Positive to Negative** checkbox.

- Click the **Mirror** button.

3   Save your work

- Save your scene file as *19-skinning 02.ma*.

4   Flood smoothing

Now that the entire character is weighted correctly, but with skin points influenced by only one joint, it is time to smooth out the weighting. If you were to bend Leon at this time, the binding would look like rigid binding, causing the geometry to crack as it is being folded.

In order to smooth out the binding, you will use the flood smoothing technique starting from the extremities of Leon's limbs, working your way toward the pelvis.

- In the **Paint Skin Weights Tool**, select the **Smooth** operation.

- Starting from the tip of the left fingers, press the **Flood** button for each finger influence.

Tip: *Rather than pressing the **Flood** button multiple times, go back and forth among the finger influences to smooth the binding.*

- Press the **Flood** button again, going from the left palm to the left clavicle.
- Press the **Flood** button again, going from the head down to the base of the neck.
- Keep going down to the first spine bone.

Tip: *Since many bones are meeting in the hip area, you might have to repeat the smooth process, going back and forth between the influences.*

- Do the same, going from the left toes up to the hips.
- Lastly, do the reverse process, going from the hips to the extremities, smoothing only if needed.

  You should now have fairly smooth influences throughout the body.

Tip: *Once again, do not bother with influences on the right side of the body, since you will be mirroring the weights.*

5 **Prune small weights**

Pruning small weights will reassign weight from all the influences that are below a specified threshold.

- Select the *Leon* geometry.
- Select **Skin → Edit → Smooth Skin → Prune Small Weights → □**.
- In the option window, set the **Prune Below** value to **0.1**.

  The idea here is to prune fairly big weights in order to keep the skinning somewhat rough, and to be able to refine the influences manually later on. Toward the end of the painting process, you will use a much smaller value for pruning.

- Click the **Prune** button.

Note: *Without weights lower than 0.1 on your character, it is more likely you will notice zones of skin points that are not well assigned, appearing gray.*

6 Mirror the influences

- With the *Leon* geometry selected, select **Skin** → **Edit Smooth Skin** → **Mirror Skin Weights**.

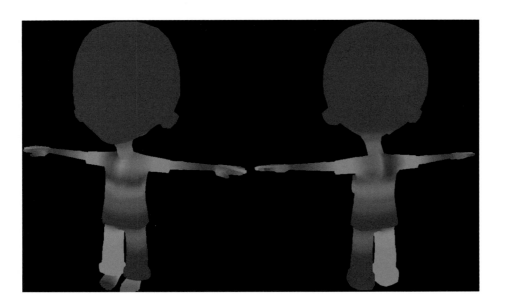

Character smoothed influences

7 Test the influences

- **Rotate** the various joints to see their individual effects, and note the places creating problems.

> **Tip:** *Using the IK splines to test the deformation of the spine and neck might yield better results.*

- If necessary, do another pass of smoothing on the entire character or only on specific body parts where you find the influence to be too rough.

8 Save your work

- Save your scene as *19-skinning 03.ma*.

9 Refining

It is now time to refine all the influences by hand. Use the **Add** and **Smooth** operations as much as possible along with the **MMB+drag** technique to test the deformation. Try to bend your character in all humanly possible ways as you refine folds, but keep in mind that your character can have limitations. It is almost impossible to generate geometry, rigging, and skinning that look good in all possible extreme positions.

Tip: *You can use the* **Alt+b** *hotkey to cycle the background color between the default gray and black. A black background color along with the gray feedback of the Paint Skin Weights Tool will make the influence area more apparent.*

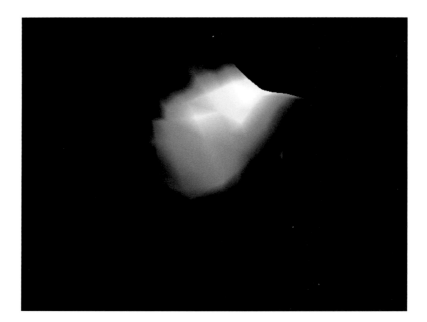

Shoulder influence with gray feedback and black background

Tip: *When you are happy with the weighting of an influence, you can click the* **Toggle Hold Weights on Selected** *button to lock the weights for that influence. Be careful using this feature, because when Maya cannot find an unlocked influence to put weight on, it might end up adding it to unwanted places.*

10 Prune small weights

- Select the *Leon* geometry**.**
- Select **Skin → Edit → Smooth Skin → Prune Small Weights → ❑.**
- In the option window, set the **Prune Below** option to **0.02**.
- Click the **Prune** button.

  You are now sure that very small weight values won't influence the geometry in unintended ways.

11 Mirror the influences

- With the *Leon* geometry selected, select **Skin → Edit Smooth Skin → Mirror Skin Weights**.

12 Save your work

- Save your scene as *19-skinning 04.ma*.

Final touches

There is only few more things to add to Leon for him to be fully animatable. You must skin the eyes to the eye joints and the bangs to the head joint. Once that is done, you will see Leon come to life.

1 Bind the eyes

- Select the left eye geometry, and then **Shift-select** the *LeftEye* joint.

Tip: *Make sure that* **Show → Nurbs Surfaces** *as well as* **Show → Nurbs Curves** *are turned* **On** *in the viewport.*

- Select **Skin → Bind Skin → Smooth Bind**.
- **Repeat** for the other eye.

Note: *You cannot use rigid binding on end joints. This is why smooth binding is used.*

Lesson 19: Skinning

2 Test the eye motion

- Press **6** to see Leon's textures.
- Select and **move** the *eyeLookAt* manipulator.
- Try to **scale** and **rotate** the *eyeLookAt* manipulator to see the effect on Leon.

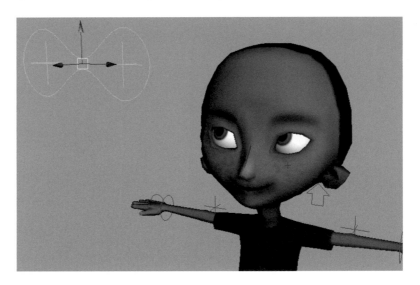

Leon can now look where he wants

3 Skin the hair

The bangs need to be skinned only to a single joint, the *Head* joint. In order to optimize the binding, it is recommended to use rigid binding since there is only need for one influence.

- Select all the bangs, and then **Shift-select** the *Head* joint.
- Select **Skin → Bind Skin → Rigid Bind → □.**
- In the options, set **Bind to Selected joints** and click the **Bind Skin button.**

4 Test the skinning

- For all the manipulators that have the *ikFkBlend* attribute, set them back to **1**.
- Attempt to pose Leon to see if everything follows and deforms properly.

Final skinned Leon

5   Save your work

- Save the scene as *19-skinning 05.ma*.

Paint weight tips

Although smooth binding and the Paint Skin Weights Tool simplify the process of deforming a character, you may still encounter some pitfalls, depending on the character you are working with. The following section provides some general tips and guidelines for making the smooth skinning process more efficient, and also summarizes some of the key points of the workflow you just completed.

Paint Scale Operation

The Scale Operation in the Paint Skin Weights Tool was not mentioned in this lesson, but you might find it very handy. Scaling weights at a value of 0.9, for instance, will remove 10% of the weight of the selected influence and redistribute it proportionately among the other influences in the painting area. This is a good feature to use since the tool will not attempt to add all the removed weights to other influences, but it will rather scale the values you have already defined.

Numeric Weighting

Each skin point has a total weight value of **1.0**, but that weight can be spread across many influences. If a group of skin points isn't behaving the way you want it to, it is possible they are getting weights from different (and perhaps unwanted) influences.

To check or modify the assignments of weights of each skin point, do the following:

- Select some bound vertices or CVs.
- Select **Window** → **General Editors** → **Component Editor**.
- Select the **Smooth Skins** tab.
- Enable **Option** → **Hide Zero Columns** to hide any influences that don't affect the selected skin points.

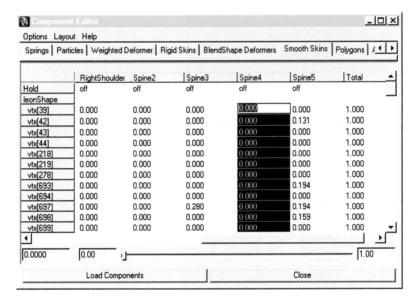

The Component Editor

> **Tip:** *Highlight entire columns by clicking on their influence label; then set the focus on any weight field and type **0**. Then press **Enter** to remove any weight coming from the selected influences. This is very useful when you want to select many points and ensure they are not affected by unwanted influences.*

Adjust the Dropoff Rate

When you initially smooth- bind the skin, you can set the **Dropoff Rate** for each of the influences manually. The dropoff rate determines how much the weighting decrease as the distance between the influence and the skin point increases. Increasing the dropoff rate helps localize the weighting for the selected joint.

To adjust the dropoff rate after skinning, do the following:

- Select the desired joint.
- Adjust the **Dropoff** in the **Smooth Skin Parameters** section of the Attribute Editor.
- Click the **Update Weights** button.

Adjusting the selected joint's Dropoff Rate

Adjust the Max Influences

You can set the number of **Max Influences** on each bound surface. For Leon, in the Smooth Bind options you initially set the **Max Influences** to **5**, which means that a total of five influences can participate in the weighting on a given skin point. This adds up to a lot of weighting and re-weighting since changing the weighting of one skin point has a *rippling* effect on the weights of the other skin points. As the number of max influences increases, so does this complexity of interdependent weighting.

In many cases, it is easier to lower the **Max Influences** of each surface than trying to track down which influence controls which skin point. Lower max influence settings will help to localize the control of the weighting.

Project 05

To change the max influence setting, do the following:

- Select a smooth bound surface.
- Select **Skin** → **Edit Smooth Skin** → **Set Max Influences...**
- Set the new number of maximum influences allowed.
- Click the **Apply and Close** button.

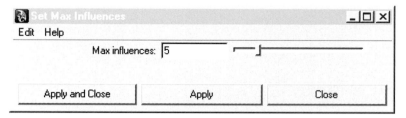

Adjusting the max influences

> **Note:** *A* **Max Influence** *setting of* **1** *causes the surface skinning to behave like rigid binding.*

Equalize weights on multiple surfaces

If the tangency between two NURBS patches is giving you problems, it is often easiest to set the same weighting value on the two surfaces to get a uniform weight across the seam. You can then smooth out the weighting between the two surfaces. This technique is helpful because all of the values are set to a uniform state before the smoothing process begins.

Using a wrap deformer

Another technique used to bind a NURBS patch model is to convert the NURBS patches to a single combined polygonal object and then use a wrap deformer to deform the patches. Doing so greatly simplifies the weighting process of a model since there is only a single poly object to bind and weight.

> **Note:** *You will have the chance to try this out when skinning the squirrel in the next project.*

Holding weights

There are times you can feel like you are chasing your tail when weighting complex surfaces and influence objects. You can toggle **On** and **Off** a **Hold** flag for each influence object. This will lock the value and prevent it from changing.

When you add an influence object to a skinned object, it is a good idea to lock this influence object to a value of 0 when it is created. This will help prevent the new influence object from disrupting your existing weighting. This will be explored in further depth in the next lesson.

Flood values

As you have seen, depending on the number of **Max Influences** set when the original smooth bind is applied, there can be many joints affecting the same skin point. At times, it is easiest to select the surfaces and an influence and replace all weighting values with a common value using the **Flood** button.

This is particularly useful for removing unwanted weighting applied to the root joint, or other joints that should not have any influence on the surface.

> **Note:** *You can also flood only selected skin points.*

Prune small weights

After spending time weighting a character, you might notice that a small amount of weight might be added to many different influences. Generally, the amount of weight is very small and hard to detect, but it does affect where weights are distributed when they are adjusted on a particular influence. When you take weight away from an influence, the weight gets distributed to every influence that has a weight, even if it is only a small weight. This also might have a significant influence on speed, performance and the size of the file.

Pruning small weights will remove weight from all influences below a specified threshold. To prune weights, do the following:

- Select all of the surfaces that you would like to prune.
- Select **Skin** → **Edit** → **Smooth Skin** → **Prune Small Weights** → ❑.
- In the option window, specify the value of small weight to prune as needed.
- Click the **Prune** button.

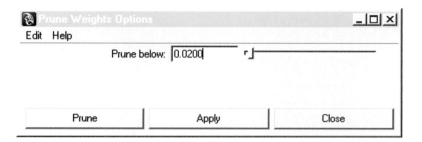

Prune Small Weights options

Copy skin weights

The **Copy Skin Weights** command can greatly speed up a weighting task. For instance, you could weight a lower resolution model and copy the skin weights to a higher resolution model. This would provide a good starting point to refine the higher resolution model.

Import and export skin weights

It's possible to export and import skin weights if needed. Doing so will generate one grayscale image per influence object and write it to disk. The images exported are relative to the model's UVs, so if your model doesn't have proper UVs or has overlapping UVs, importing the weight maps might give undesirable results.

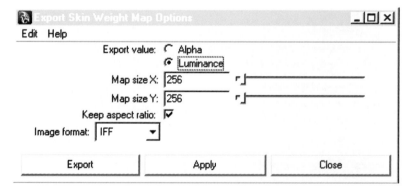

Export Skin Weight Map options

> **Tip:** *If you want to transfer skin weights based on spatial location rather than UVs, use* **Copy Skin Weights**. *With this tool, your source and target skinned geometry do not need to have the same UVs.*

Conclusion

Smooth and rigid skinning are the two basic types of skinning available in Maya. Smooth skinning allows for more control over the skinned surface using influence objects, while rigid skinning relies on clusters of points to be deformed by the influence objects.

In this lesson, you learned how to bind a character and how to use the Paint Skin Weights Tool. You also experienced a typical weighting workflow and learned several tips and tricks for speeding up the weighting process.

In the next lesson, you will learn about influence objects.

Lesson 20
Deformers

In this lesson, you will examine how you can enhance the deformations of geometry using deformers. Deformers can be used on top of other deformers to increase the level of realism and interactivity of a model. You will first implement simple deformers such as clusters and jiggle; you will then implement influence objects and sculpt deformers. Once that is done, you will overlay multiple types of deformers to achieve a more complex setup used to manipulate Leon's shirt pocket.

In this lesson you will learn the following:

- How to create and paint cluster influence;
- How to set up a jiggle deformer;
- How to add influence objects;
- How to weight influence objects;
- How to automate deformations using Set Driven Keys;
- How to mirror influence weights;
- How to use a sculpt deformer;
- How to use a motion path with a custom attribute;
- How to change the deformation order;
- How to bind a lattice deformer;
- How to overlay deformers to achieve maximum control

Clusters

A *cluster* deforms a cluster of points. In order to refine the deformation clusters provide, you can paint and smooth out the affected region. Implementing these deformers can greatly help the animator to insert subtle secondary animation and to gain control over specific regions of the geometry.

You will now insert clusters on Leon's ears, which will give you the potential to animate the ears separately.

1 Scene file

- Open the scene file *19-skinning 05.ma* from the last lesson.

2 Create clusters

- While in Component mode, select the left ear lobe vertices.
- Select **Create Deformers → Cluster → □.**
- **In** the **option window, set Relative** to **On** and click the **Create** button.

  Since you will be parenting the clusters to the Head joint, the deformation needs to be relative to the cluster's parent rather than in global coordinates.

- Repeat for the right ear.

3 Manipulators

- **Create** manipulators for the ears from NURBS circles.
- **Rename** them to *leftEarManip* and *rightEarManip*.
- **Snap** the circles to their respective ear clusters.

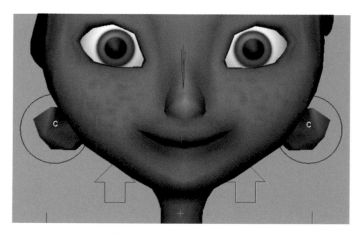

The ear manipulators in place

- **Parent** the manipulators to the *Head* joint.
- **Freeze** their transformations.
- **Delete** their construction history.

4 Set up the clusters

Since the clusters are set to be relative, they need to take their transformations relative to their parent. If you simply grouped a cluster to a manipulator, the cluster would not receive any transformations, and there would be no deformation. To work around this, you will need to parent the clusters to the *Head* joint, and then constrain the clusters to the manipulators. Doing so will directly move the cluster and deform the geometry as intended.

- Select the new clusters and **group** them.
- **Parent** the new group to the *Head* joint and rename it to *earClustersGroup*.
- Select the *leftEarManip*, and then **Shift-select** its cluster.
- Select **Constrain** → **Parent** → ❑.
- Make sure the **Maintain Off**set option is set to **On**; then click the **Add** button.
- Repeat for the other ear cluster.
- **Assign** color overrides to the manipulators.

  You should now be able to pull Leon's ears.

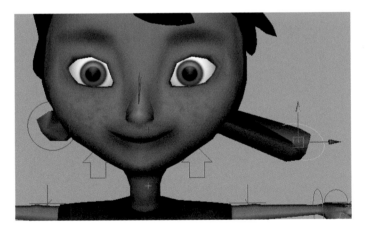

Leon's ear deformation

5 Lock and hide

- **Hide** the *earClustersGroup*.
- **Lock** and **hide** all the attributes not intended for animation on the *earClustersGroup*, the clusters and the manipulators.

Lesson 20: Deformers

6 Smooth the deformation

As you can see, every cluster point is deformed at 100% by default. Even if this is sometimes what you want, it might be better to smooth out the deformation so it doesn't break the geometry.

- Select the *Leon* geometry.
- Select **Edit Deformers** → **Paint Cluster Weights Tool** → ☐.

  The option window is very similar to the Paint Skin Weights Tool.

- Under the **Paint Attributes** section, click the first button and select **Cluster** → **cluster#.weights.**

  Doing so will display on the geometry a grayscale map of the cluster's deformation.

- Set the **Paint Operation** to **Smooth** and click the **Flood** button twice.

  The influence is now smoother for this cluster.

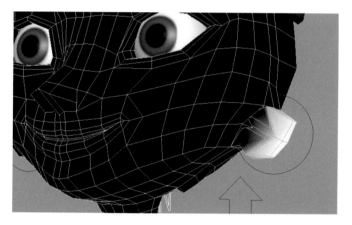

The smoothed cluster influence

- Select the other cluster influence in the paint tool and smooth its influence, too.

  Now when you pull the ear manipulators, the deformation is much smoother.

7 Save your work

- Save your scene as *20-deformers 01.ma*.

Jiggle deformer

Jiggle deformers cause points on a surface or curve to shake as they move, speed up, or slow down. You can apply jiggle to specific points or to the entire object. In the context of jiggle deformers, the term *points* means CVs, lattice points, or the vertices of polygonal or subdivision surfaces.

In this exercise, you will use the jiggle deformer on Leon's bangs.

1   Assign jiggle

- While in Component mode, select the vertices on the bangs that you want to be susceptible to jiggling when Leon's head moves, as follows:

The hair vertices selected

Tip: *You can use the Lasso Tool to select the vertices.*

- Select **Create Deformers → Jiggle Deformer**.

  Jiggle deformers are now added to all selected bang and will affect only the selected vertices.

2   Paint jiggle weights

Just like skin or cluster weights, you can paint jiggle weights by using the Paint Tool.

You will now smooth the jiggle's influence to smoothly deform the hair.

- Select all of the bangs.
- Select **Edit Deformers → Paint Jiggle Weights Tool → ☐**.

  You should see the influence of the jiggle on all the bangs.

- Set the **Paint Operation** to **Smooth** and press the **Flood** button several times to get the following result:

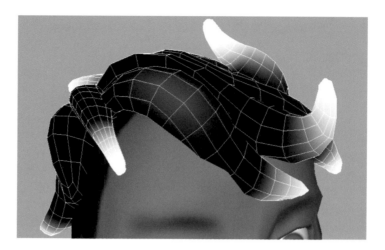

The hair jiggle weights

3 Test the motion

In order to test the motion of the jiggle, you need to move the head so that the jiggle affects the geometry.

- Select the *Head* joint.
- Set **keyframes** at frame **1**, **5**, **10** and **15** with different head rotations going up and down.
- **Playback** the results.

  You should see the jiggle affecting Leon too much.

Too much jiggle

4   Adjust jiggle settings

You will now change the jiggle attributes to adjust the different dynamic settings and even out the jiggling of the hair.

- With the Input Line set to **Select by Name**, type `jiggle*` and press **Enter**.

  Doing so will select all the jiggle nodes in the scene. The different attributes of the deformer are displayed in the Channel Box.

- Set the following to change all the deformers at once:

     Stiffness to **0.2**;

     Damping to **0.1**;

     Jiggle Weight to **0.8**.

- **Playback** the results.

  The jiggle should be much more subtle and realistic.

> **Note:** *You can get more jiggling by increasing the* **Jiggle Weight**.

5   Remove the head animation

- Select the *Head* joint.
- In the Channel Box, highlight the **Rotation** attributes.
- **RMB** and select **Break Connections**.
- Set the **Rotation** attributes back to **0**.

6   Save your work

- Save your scene as *20-deformers 02.ma*.

Influence objects

Influence objects are external sources used to deform a smooth-bound skin. These objects can be any type, such as geometry or locators, and they can behave in a similar way to joint influence. You will see later in this lesson that using geometry as an influence object can really improve your skin deformation. An influence object's default setting uses the transform of an object to affect the skin surface, but it can be set to use components, such as vertices or CVs, to determine the offset of skin points.

For instance, you can add an influence object to simulate a bicep bulging while the arm bends, and the skin vertices would bulge along. You could also use an influence object that is affected by any type of dynamics or deformers. The potential uses of influence objects are endless.

Biceps

Despite the fact that Leon is a pretty skinny character, it might be a good idea to add a bulging bicep as he bends his arm. To do so, you will use a locator as an influence object.

1 Create a locator

- Select **Create** → **Locator** and **rename** it to *leftBicepInfluence*.

Tip: *Make sure that* **Locators** *is turned* **On** *in the* **Show** *menu.*

- **Parent** the *leftBicepInfluence* to Leon's *LeftArm* joint.
- **Move** the *leftBicepInfluence* in the bicep area of the arm.

2 Add the influence

- Select the *Leon* geometry and **Shift-select** the *leftBicepInfluence*.
- Select **Skin** → **Edit Smooth Skin** → **Add Influence** → ❏.
- In the option window, **Reset** the settings; then set the following:

  Use geometry to **On**;

  Lock weights to **On**;

  Default weight to **0.0**.

Note: *The* **Lock weights** *option specifies that the influence object should not get any weights at this time for the surface. You will be painting the weights manually.*

- Click the **Add** button.

  When the influence object is created, the object is duplicated and hidden. That object is a base object, which stores the original shape and position information of the influence object. Without the base object, you would not see any deformation.

  The locator is now part of Leon's influences with zero weight.

3 Paint the influence

- With the geometry selected, select **Skin** → **Edit Smooth Skin** → **Paint Skin Weights Tool** → ❏.
- In the option window, scroll to the bottom of the influence list and highlight the *leftBicepInfluence*.
- Click the **Toggle Hold Weights On Selected** to disable the locking of its weight.

- **Zoom** on the bicep region and **paint** weights as follows:

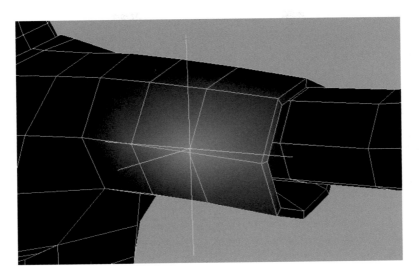

The leftBicepInfluence weights

4   Set Driven Keys

You now want the locator to bulge the bicep as the forearm bends. The best way to do this is by setting driven keys that will automate the bulging animation.

- Select **Animate** → **Set Driven Key** → **Set...**
- Load the *LeftForeArm rotateY* as the **Driver**.
- Load the *leftBicepInfluence* as the **Driven** and highlight all of its **translation** attributes.
- Click the **Key** button to set the default position of the influence object.
- **Rotate** the *LeftForeArm*.

Tip: *The arm must be in FK to rotate the joint manually.*

- **Move** the *leftBicepInfluence* to bulge the bicep.
- Click the **Key** button to set the bulge position of the influence object.

Project 05

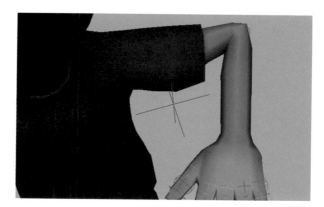

The bulged position of the leftBicepInfluence

5 Test the influence

- **Rotate** *LeftForeArm* back and forth to see the effect of the influence object on the bicep.

6 Set Driven Keys

The bulging of the bicep should look pretty good, but you might notice snaps when it starts and stops moving. This is because the Set Driven Keys are linear. You will now change the influence's animation curve to ease in and ease out.

- Select the *leftBicepInfluence*.

- Select **Window → Animation Editors → Graph Editor**.

- Press **A** to frame all the animation curves.

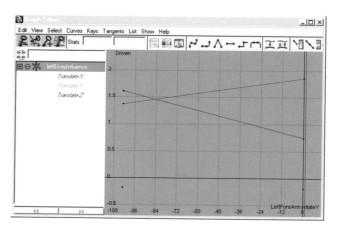

The leftBicepInfluence animation curves

- Select all the animation curves, and then select **Tangents** → **Flat**.

  The animation curves now have flat tangents, which will help for progressive animation of the influence object.

- Bend the arm to see the animation of the locator.

Mirror influences

You could repeat the last exercise for the other arm of Leon's body, but fortunately, you don't have to redo everything. The influence objects can be duplicated and the weighting of the influence can be mirrored, just like bone influences.

1 Mirror the influence objects

The following steps will duplicate the locator and mirror it to the other arm.

- Select *leftBicepInfluence*.
- Press **Ctrl+d** to duplicate it.
- Press **Shift+p** to unparent it.
- Press **Ctrl+g** to group it.
- Set the **Scale X** value for the new group to **−1**.
- Select the new *leftBicepInfluence1* object on the right arm of Leon, and rename it to *rightBicepInfluence*.
- Select the *rightBicepInfluence* then **Shift-select** the *RightArm* joint.
- Press **p** to parent the locator to the joint.
- In the Outliner, **delete** the temporary group used to mirror the locator.

2 Add the influence object

- Select the *rightBicepInfluence*, then **Shift-select** the *Leon* geometry.
- Select **Skin** → **Edit Smooth Skin** → **Add Influence**.

3 Unlock the weighting for the influence objects

You are about to mirror the weighting from the left side of Leon's body to the right side. Before you can do that, the new influence object must have its weight unlocked so that it can receive the new weighting values.

- Select the *Leon* surface.
- Open the **Paint Skin Weights Tool** window.
- Press the **Hold Weights On Selected** with *rightBicepInfluence* highlighted to unlock its weighting.

4 Mirror the shirt's weighting

Now that the duplicate locator has been made an influence object and its influence weight is unlocked, you can mirror the weighting from the left side of Leon's body to the right side.

- Select the *Leon* surface.
- Select **Skin → Edit Smooth Skin → Mirror Skin Weights**.

 Tip: *Make sure that* **Mirror Across** *is set to* **YZ**, *and that* **Direction Positive to Negative** *is toggled* **On**.

- Double-check that the influences of the biceps were mirrored.

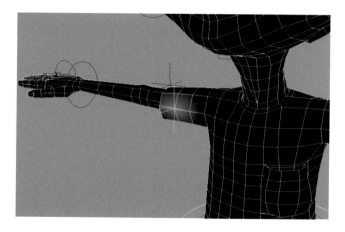

Bicep weight mirrored correctly

5 Recreate the Set Driven Keys

As in the last exercise, use Set Driven Keys and the rotation of the *RightForeArm* to control the bulging of the bicep. Also change the animation curves to have flat tangents.

6 Lock and hide objects and attributes

- Select the *leftBicepInfluence* and *rightBicepInfluence*.
- Set their **Visibility** attribute to **Off**.
- **Lock and hide** all of their attributes from the Channel Box.

7 Save your work

- Save your scene as *20-deformers 03.ma*.

Sculpt deformer

In this exercise, you will add swallowing capability to Leon. To do so, you will create a sculpt deformer and animate it along a path following the throat. You will then edit the order of deformation so the sculpt deformer is evaluated before any other deformers. Doing so will allow the swallowing motion to be accurate when Leon is animated.

1 Sculpt defomer

- With the *Leon* geometry selected, select **Create Deformers** → **Sculpt Deformer**.

  A sculpt deformer will be created.

- In the Outliner, **parent** the *sculpt1StretchOrigin* node to the *sculptor1* node.

  Doing so will allow you to slide the deformer under Leon's skin.

2 Place the sculpt deformer

- Select the *sculptor1* node.

- **Place** the deformer in Leon's throat as follows:

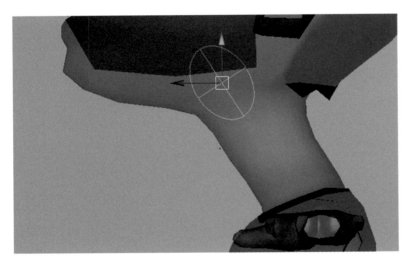

The deformer into Leon's throat

3 Path curve

Now that the sculpt deformer is in place, you need a way to animate it along Leon's throat, even when he is moving around and bending his neck.

- Select **Create** → **EP Curve** → ❑ and make sure the **Curve Degree** is set to **Cubic**.

- **Draw** the curve in Leon's throat, following where the sculpt deformer should pass.

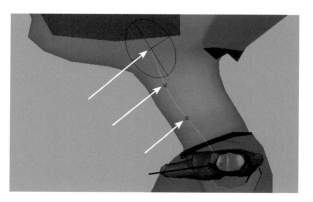

The throat curve

Tip: *Leon must be in his default position.*

- **Rename** the curve to *throatPath*.

4   Motion path

You must now attach the sculpt deformer to the curve as a motion path.

- Select *sculptor1* and **Shift-select** the *throatPath*.
- Select **Animate** → **Motion Paths** → **Attach to Motion Path** → ❑.
- In the option window, set the **Front Axis** to **Y**.
- Click the **Attach** button.

5   Custom attribute

The rig needs a custom attribute so you can control the position of the sculptor in the throat. The best place to add such an attribute is on the *blendShapesManip*.

- Select the *blendShapesManip*.
- Select **Modify** → **Add Attribute**.
- Set the following:

    Attribute Name to *swallow*;

    Data Type to **Float**;

    Minimum to **0**;

    Maximum to **1**;

    Default to **0**.

- Click the **OK** button.

6 Connect the attribute

Right now, the sculpt deformer is animated along its path over the length of the Time slider. Since you want to control the sculpt deformer using the attribute you just added, you will need to break the time connection.

- Select **Window → General Editor → Connection Editor**.
- Load the *blendShapesManip* on the left side.
- Load the *motionPath1* on the right side.

> **Tip:** You can use the Input Line to select the object or highlight it in the Channel Box when the sculptor is selected.

- **Connect** the *Swallow* attribute to the *U Value* attribute of the motion path.

  Doing so will break the time connection of the motion path automatically.

7 Test the swallowing motion

- Select the *blendShapesManip* and change the **Swallow** attribute to see if the sculpt deformer works appropriately.

> **Note:** The swallowing motion works well at this time, but it will stop working as soon as you animate Leon. To fix this, you must change the order of deformation, which is covered in the next exercise.

8 Throat setup

- From the Outliner, select the *sculptor1* and the *throatPath*.
- Press **Ctrl+g** to group them together.
- **Rename** the new group *throatSetup*.
- **Parent** the *throatSetup* to the *rig* group.
- **Hide** the *throatSetup*.
- **Lock and hide** all the throat setup attributes.

Deformation order

It is important to understand that deformers are executed sequentially, before achieving the final deformation of a piece of geometry. In the previous exercise, the sculpt deformer was inserted after all other deformers, which will cause unwanted results as soon as the character moves away.

Currently, Leon is first affected by his blend shapes, then the skinning is evaluated, then the clusters and jiggle kicks in, and last, the sculptor deforms the surface. In order for the sculpt deformer to work properly, you need the character to be in its original position. It would be logical to change the order of deformation so the sculpt deformer is evaluated first.

Fortunately, it is possible to switch the deformation order around quite easily. The following shows how to view and change a model's deformation order:

1   View the deformation order

- **RMB** on the Leon geometry and select **Inputs → All Inputs**.

    This opens up a window that shows the list of deformers currently affecting the geometry.

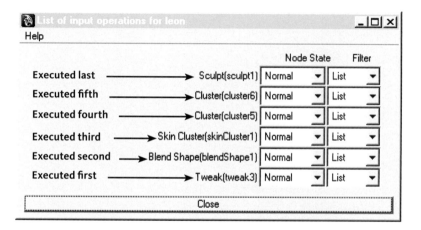

Order of deformation

Note: *The Tweak is a Maya-related node that should not be reordered.*

2   Reorder the deformers

- **MMB+drag** the *Sculpt* deformer over the *Blend Shape* deformer item in the list.

    Doing so will swap and reorder the deformers.

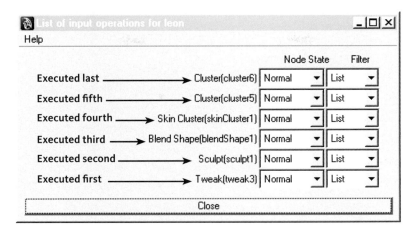

Node State and Filter columns with the following rows:

	Node State	Filter
Executed last → Cluster(cluster6)	Normal	List
Executed fifth → Cluster(cluster5)	Normal	List
Executed fourth → Skin Cluster(skinCluster1)	Normal	List
Executed third → Blend Shape(blendShape1)	Normal	List
Executed second → Sculpt(sculpt1)	Normal	List
Executed first → Tweak(tweak3)	Normal	List

Reordered deformers

3 Pose the rig and test the swallowing

4 Save your work

- Save your scene as *20-deformers 04.ma.*

Pocket setup

Now that you have gone over several deformer types, you can get into a more complex setup that will show how you can overlay deformers. In this exercise, you will create a pocket setup where a NURBS plane influences the pocket vertices. Once that is done, you will deform the NURBS plane with a lattice, for which you will control the points with clusters and manipulators.

Note: *This setup could be implemented in various ways and perhaps simpler than what is shown here, but this exercise will let you experiment with several deformers. Later on you can try to figure out simpler solutions that will fulfil your needs.*

1 Create a NURBS influence object

- **Create** a NURBS plane and set the **Patches U** and **V** to **2**.
- **Rename** the plane to *pocketInfluence.*
- Place the plane in front of Leon's pocket.
- While in Component mode, tweak the plane as follows:

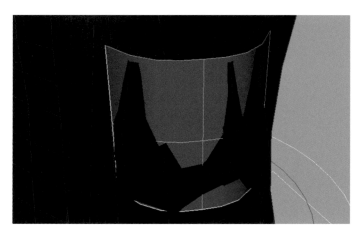

The plane to be used as an influence object

2 **Add the influence object**

- Select the *Leon* geometry, and then **Shift-select** the *pocketInfluence*.

- Select **Skin → Edit Smooth Skin → Add Influence.**

3 **Paint the influence**

- With the geometry selected, select **Skin → Edit Smooth Skin → Paint Skin Weights Tool → ❑**.

- With the *pocketInfluence* highlighted, click the **Toggle Hold Weights On Selected** to disable the locking of its weight.

- **Paint** weights to a full influence of **1.0** as follows:

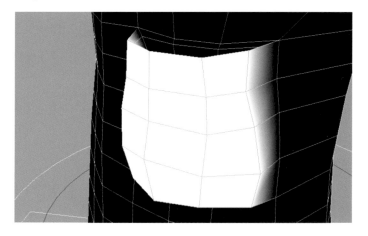

The pocket influence

- **Flood smooth** the influence once.

4   Use components

If you attempt to move the influence object's CVs at this time, you will notice that the pocket points do not move. This is because the smooth skin node doesn't know you want to use the components of the influence object to drive the points and it is using the transform information instead. Since the transform of the *pocketInfluence* stays still (only the CVs are moving), the skin points end up not moving.

There is an attribute in the smooth skin node that allows you to select between using the object's transform node or its components as the driving force to create the deformations. In this case, you will use its component information to get the desired deformations.

- Select the *Leon* geometry.
- In the Channel Box, highlight the *skinCluster1* node.
- Change the **Use Components** attribute to **On**.

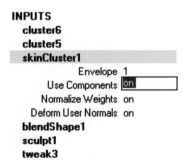

Enable the Use Components attribute

5   Lattice deformer

Now that the pocket deforms using the plane influence, you need to be able to manipulate the plane for animation. One smooth way of doing this is by controlling it with a lattice box.

- Select the pocketInfluence.
- Select **Create Deformers → Lattice.**

  The lattice is created around the pocketInfluence.

- In the Channel Box, set the following for the *ffd1LatticeShape*:

  S Division to **3**;

  T Division to **2**;

  U Division to **3**.

- Select the pocketInfluence and press **Ctrl+h** to hide it.

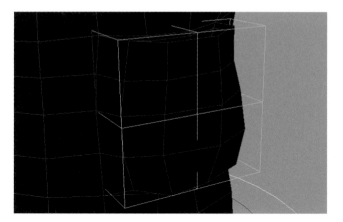

The lattice deformer

6 Bind the lattice

You are going to smooth-bind the lattice to the skeleton so it moves with the rest
of the skeleton.

- Select the joints to bind the influence object to, such as *Spine*, *Spine1*, *Spine2*, *Spine3*,
  Spine4 and *Spine5*.

- **Shift-select** the lattice deformer.

- Select **Skin → Bind Skin → Smooth Skin**.

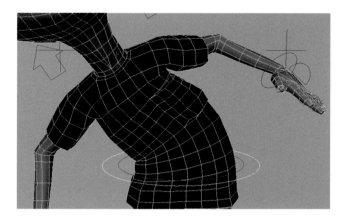

The lattice deforms the influence object

> **Note:** *The default skinning should be good enough, but if you need to edit weights on
> lattice points, you need to do it manually in the Component Editor.*

7 Clusters

The final requirement for the pocket setup is to be able to pull lattice points for animation. One easy way is to create clusters with the lattice points. Those clusters will then be assigned to manipulators, similar to the ear setup.

- **RMB** on the lattice box and select **Lattice Point**.
- Select a single lattice point on the front of the pocket.
- Select **Create Deformers → Cluster.**

Tip: *The cluster option should be set to relative.*

- Repeat for all the other lattice points on the front of the pocket.
- Hide the lattice deformer.

8 Manipulators

As you did with the ear setup, you can now implement manipulators to animate the pocket as you would like.

- **Create** one NURBS circles for each cluster and place them appropriately.

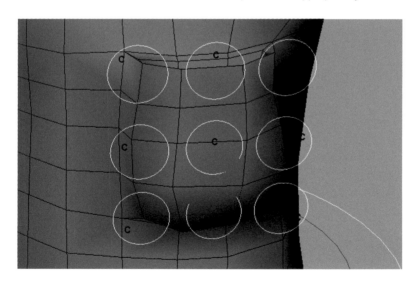

The manipulators in place

Lesson 20: Deformers

- **Rename** all the manipulators to *pocketManip#*.
- **Parent** each manipulator to its closest spine joint and **freeze** their transformations.
- **Parent** each cluster to its closest spine joint.
- **Parent constrain** each cluster to its respective manipulator.
- **Hide** all the clusters and **lock and hide** all of the unneeded attributes.
- **Assign** color overrides to the manipulators.

9 **Final touches**
- In order to keep the scene clean, **group** the influence nodes and lattice nodes together and **parent** them in the *rig* hierarchy.
- Lock all their attributes to prevent erroneous manipulations.

The final setup

10 **Save your work**
- Save your scene as *20-deformers 05.ma*.

Conclusion

In this lesson, you learned about deformers and their workflows. Most importantly, you learned how to use influence objects, which can be any transforms, such as locators, curves, or geometry that get carried along with the animation setup. Very powerful rigs can be established with influence objects using dynamics, soft bodies or even other deformers as you have seen in this lesson. Establishing secondary or reactive movements of a character will greatly help adding the little touch of realism to your animations.

In the next lesson, you will finalize Leon by building a low-resolution model that will react in real-time as the animator plays with it. You will also apply a poly smooth to generate a higher-resolution model that you will be able to turn on or off before rendering.

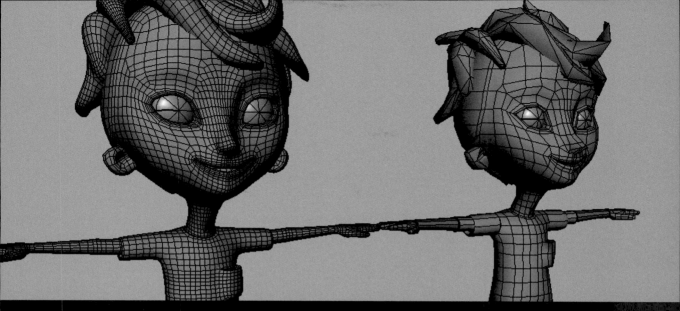

Lesson 21
Final Touches

In this lesson, you will finalize the Leon character by creating both a low-resolution and a high-resolution file to use as references when animating.

In this lesson you will learn the following:

- How to create a low-resolution version of the model;
- How to copy skin weights;
- How to detach skin;
- How to re-create a blend shape deformer;
- How to reduce poly count on meshes;
- How to delete non-deformer history;
- How to remove unused influences;
- How to create a high-resolution version of the model.

Low-resolution geometry

Now that you have an awesome character rig to play with, you should think about creating a low-resolution version of Leon to speed up loading and playback time. This scene will not need things like deformers or influence objects, but it will require all animated items to stay in the scene. Doing so will allow you to switch a reference from the low-resolution model to the high-resolution model without any problems.

1 Scene file

- Continue with your own scene.

OR

- Open the scene file called *20-deformers 05.ma*.

2 Save scene under another name

- **Save** the scene right away under the name *21-leon lores.ma*.

3 Low-resolution layer

- **Create** a new layer.

- **Rename** the layer *loresLayer*.

- Make the *geometryLayer* **templated**.

- **Hide** the *rigLayer*.

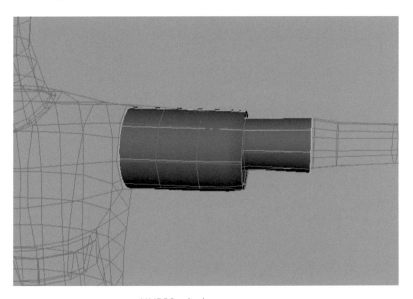

NURBS cylinder upper arm

4 Generate the low-resolution model

There are several ways to create a low-resolution model. One simple technique is to *primitive up* a model. To do this, you must take primitive objects, such as cylinders, and simplify the different limbs of the character to their minimum.

- **Create** a new NURBS cylinder.
- **Move** and **edit** the *cylinder* to fit Leon's upper arm.
- **Rename** the cylinder to *loLeftUpperArm*.
- **Add** the model to the *loresLayer*.
- **Repeat** the previous steps to create low-resolution models for the following body parts:

  loLeftForeArm;

  loLeftUpperLeg;

  loLeftShinLeg.

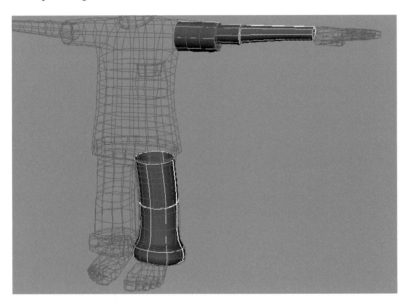

NURBS cylinder leg

5 NURBS cylinder limbs Low-resolution hand

Since it is important to keep the hands accurate on the low-resolution model, you will duplicate the geometry and keep only one hand, which you will rebind later in this exercise.

- Set the *geometryLayer* to normal display.
- Select *Leon*'s geometry and **duplicate** it.
- Press **Shift+p** to unparent the new model.

- **Rename** the new model *loLeftHand*.
- **Add** the new model to the *loresLayer*.
- In Component mode, delete the faces on the *loLeftHand* model, keeping only the hand.

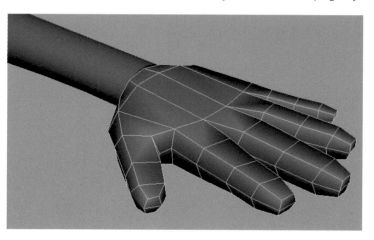

The low- resolution hand model

 Tip: *Delete details at will, but try to keep the shape and proportions of the hand.*

6 Low-resolution foot

- **Repeat** the previous step, but this time to generate the *loLeftFoot* model.

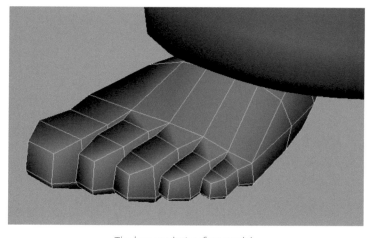

The low-resolution foot model

7 **Low-resolution torso**

- **Repeat** the previous step, but this time to generate the *loTorso* model.

- Simplify the torso using the **Select → Select Edge Loop Tool** and deleting edges using **Edit Mesh → Delete Edge/Vertex**.

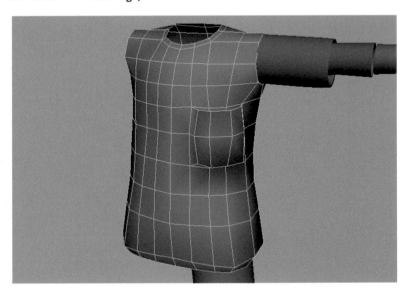

The low- resolution torso model

8 **Mirror on the other side**

- Select all the left low-resolution models.

- Press **Ctrl+d** to duplicate them.

- Press **Ctrl+g** to group the new models.

- Set the **Scale X-axis** of the new group to **–1** to mirror the geometry on the right side of Leon.

- Select all the right low-resolution models; then press **Shift+p** to unparent them.

- **Rename** the models to *loRight*.

9 **Clean up**

- Select all the low-resolution models; then select **Modify → Freeze Transformations**.

- Select **Edit → Delete by Type → History**.

Project 05

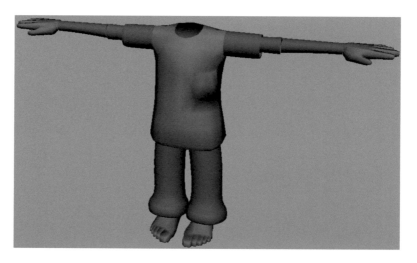

The low-resolution body

10 **Copy skinning**

Now that the low-resolution body is created, you can bind it to the skeleton and copy the weighting of the high-resolution model to the low-resolution model.

- **Delete** the *deformerGroup* and the *bicepInfluences*.

  Deleting the influences tells Maya to remove their weights from Leon's skinning and reassign them to their default joint influences.

> **Note:** *The pocket setup will need to be corrected later in this lesson to represent its behavior correctly.*

- **Delete** the now obsolete pocket cluster groups that are children of the spine joints.
- Enter the following MEL command in the command line:

  ```
  select `skinCluster -q -inf leon`;
  ```

  This command tells Maya to select all the joints that influence the Leon geometry.

- **Shift+select** the *loTorso*.
- Select **Skin → Bind Skin → Smooth Bind**.

  Doing so will bind the selected geometry to the selected joints, which are exactly the same as the higher-resolution model.

- Select the original *Leon* geometry and then **Shift-select** the *loTorso*.

- Select **Skin** → **Edit Smooth Skin** → **Copy Skin Weights**.

  Since the low-resolution geometry was bound to the same joints as the high-resolution geometry, copying the weights will give similar skinning on the low-resolution model.

- **Repeat** the previous steps to copy the original skinning to the hands and feet.

11 Recreate the pocket set up

When you deleted the pocket deformers, the weightings that used to be on the influence object were reassigned back to the default joints. You will now use the pocket manipulators to get back a good representation of how the pocket used to deform.

- Select all the pocket manipulators.
- **RMB** in the Channel Box and select **Channel Control**.
- Set the default **Translation**, **Rotation**, and **Scale** attributes to **keyable** and **unlocked**.

  Since you will add those manipulators as influences, their default attributes need to be unlocked in order to be registered as their default values.

- Select all the pocket manipulators; then **Shift-select** the *loTorso* geometry.
- Select **Skin** → **Edit Smooth Skin** → **Add Influence.**
- Use the Paint Skin Weights Tool to add back influence to the pocket manipulators.

Tip: *Since the low-resolution pocket deformation will not reflect the higher-resolution behavior perfectly, you must use the higher-resolution model to refine the animation of the pocket.*

12 Rigid bind

- Select the remaining unbound geometry one by one and select **Skin** → **Bind Skin** → **Rigid Bind** to rigid bind them to their respective joints.

Low-resolution head

You have now bound the low-resolution model, which is missing a head. Since the head needs as much detail as possible for accurate facial animation, you will need to keep all of its details along with all of its blend shapes.

1 Delete faces

- Show the *geometryLayer*.
- **Hide** the *rigLayer* and *loresLayer*.
- Select and **delete** all the lower body faces, keeping only the head and neck.

The head and neck only geometry

- **Rename** the *Leon* geometry to *loHead*.

2   **Delete deformers**

- **Delete** the *throatSetup* group.

- **Delete** the *earClustersGroup* found as a child of the **Head** joint.

- With the *loHead* selected, select **Skin → Detach Skin**.

    The loHead now only has the blendShape1 and deleteComponent1 inputs.

3   **Replicate the blend shapes**

At this point, since you have deleted the body faces from the original *Leon* geometry, only the head is displayed, but the entire body is still in memory. The *deleteComponent1* history node created in the previous steps simply deletes the faces after applying all the deformers found in the **Inputs** of the model. You now need to replicate the blend shapes to reflect the new head geometry.

- Select the *blendShapesManip*.

- For each blend shape attribute, do the following:

    Set the blend shape attribute to **1**;

    Make sure all the other attributes are set to **0**;

    Duplicate the *loHead*;

    Rename the duplicate to the blend shape attribute's name;

    Hide the blend shape target.

    Doing so will recreate each blend shape target with the new head topology.

4   Create the new blend shape deformer

Now that you have all the blend shapes in the scene, you can safely delete the history from the *loHead* and simply recreate the blend shape deformer.

- Make sure all the attributes on the *blendShapesManip* are set to **0**.
- **Delete** the construction history of the *loHead* geometry.
- Select all the blend shape targets in order; then **Shift-select** *loHead*.
- Select **Create Deformers → Blend Shape → ❑**.
- **Reset** the options and **create** the deformer.
- **Delete** the blend shape targets.
- **Reconnect** the attributes from the *blendShapesManip* to the new *blendshape1* deformer.

  You should now have properly recreated the blend shape deformer for the new head topology.

5   Skin the head

- Select the *Head* joint along with all four the *Neck* joints.
- **Shift-select** the *loHead* geometry.
- Select **Skin → Bind Skin → Smooth Bind**.

  The head now has default skinning.

6   Copy the skinning

Sometimes when rigging a character, you will need to copy the skinning from a model found in another scene file. In this example, you have Leon's head to skin back onto its skeleton, but you no longer have the original skinned character. You will now import the skinned character and copy its weights onto the *loHead*.

- **Save** you scene in case something goes wrong.
- Select **File → Import → ❑**.
- In the options, set **Resolve All nodes** with the file name and then click the Import button.
- Select the file *20-deformers 05.ma*, which contains the correct skinning.

  Notice that the content of the imported file is now in the current file and all nodes have been prefixed with "deformers_05_".

- Select the *deformer_05_leon* geometry, and then **Shift-select** the *loHead*.
- Select **Skin → Edit Smooth Skin → Copy Skin Weights**.

  The loHead is now properly skinned.

- **Delete** the imported character prefixed with *deformers_05_* since it is no longer required.

7 Hair jiggle

- Type *jiggle* in the **Input Line** to select the jiggle nodes created for the bangs **0** to **9**.

Tip: *The Input Line can select objects using wildcards such as * and ?.*

- **Delete** the selected jiggle deformers.
- Type *jiggle* in the **Input Line** to select all the jiggle nodes created for thebangs **10** to **11**.
- **Delete** the selected jiggle deformers.

8 Reduce poly count

The bangs have quite a lot of geometry, and you might prefer them to have a lower polygonal count. You will now reduce the number of polygons using an automated command.

- Select all the bangs.
- Select **Mesh → Reduce → □.**
- In the options, make sure to reset the option and click the **Reduce** button.

The bangs are now reduced by 50% of their initial amount of polygons.

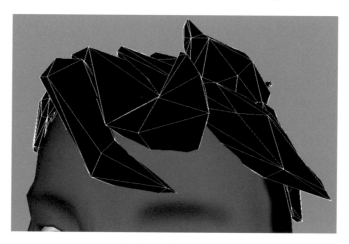

The low-polygon bangs

9 Delete non-deformer history

Since the bangs are bound to the head, you now have *polyReduce* history nodes in the Inputs of the bangs. This means that the original geometry is still in memory. You will now delete the non-deformer history, thus removing the *polyReduce* nodes while keeping their skinning.

- Select all the bangs.

- Select **Edit → Delete by Type → Non-Deformer History.**

  Confirm in the Channel Box that the polyReduce nodes have been deleted.

10 Ear clusters

- **Recreate** the ear clusters from the last lesson.

11 Remove unused influences

In the previous steps, you skinned the geometry to many joints in the skeleton. Many of those joints, however, have no influence on the geometry. You will now remove any unused influences from the skin clusters.

- Select the *loTorso* geometry.

- Select **Skin → Edit Smooth Skin → Remove Unused Influences.**

- Open the Paint Skin Weights Tool to confirm that only important influences remain in the *loTorso* skin cluster.

12 Final touches

- **Parent** all the low-resolution models to the *geometry* group.

- **Delete** the *loresLayer.*

- Select **File → Optimize Scene Size**.

- **Texture** the low-resolution model if wanted.

The low-resolution Leon

Note: *Even though this character is quite simple, the low-resolution scene is about one-third its original memory size, which is quite a considerable saving.*

13 Save your work

- Save the final low-resolution scene file as *21-leon lores.ma*.

High-resolution geometry

In order to create the high-resolution Leon, all you have to do is add a polygonal smooth to the setup.

1 Scene file

- Open the scene file called *20-deformers 05.ma*.

2 Save scene under another name

- **Save** the scene right away under the name *21-leon hires.ma*.

3 Polygonal smooth

- Select **Edit → Select All by Type → Polygon Geometry**.
- Select **Mesh → Smooth**.

The smooth applied to Leon's geometry

4 Create a custom attribute

- Select the *master*.
- Select **Modify → Add Attribute**.

- Set the following:

    Attribute Name to *smooth*;

    Data Type to **Integer**;

    Minimum to **0**;

    Maximum to **3**;

    Default to **1**.

- Click the **OK** button.

Tip: *In order to preserve the value of this attribute when switching from the high-resolution model to the low-resolution model, you will have to add this same attribute to the low-resolution file.*

5 **Connect the custom attribute**

- Select **Window** → **General Editor** → **Connection Editor**.

- Load the *master* on the left side.

- Load the *polySmooth* node that is on the *Leon* geometry on the right side.

- Connect the **Smooth** attribute to the **Divisions** attribute.

- **Repeat** for all the other polygonal objects.

    The rig now has a special attribute just for smoothing the geometry before rendering.

6 **Eye tessellation**

- Select the *lEye* and open its Attribute Editor.

- Under the **Tessellation** → **Simple Tessellation Options** section, set the following:

    Curvature Tolerance to **High Quality**;

    U and V Division Factor to **5.0**.

- **Repeat** for the *rEye*.

7 **Save your work**

- Save the final high-resolution scene file as *21-leon hires.ma*.

Conclusion

In this lesson, you learned about the importance of generating low- and high-resolution versions of your character. Having done so will let you interchange the two scenes between animation and rendering tasks.

In the next project, you will reuse Leon's rig for the squirrel model.

Lesson 21: Final Touches

Project 06

In Project 6, you are going to set up the squirrel's rig. You will start by reusing and modifying Leon's rig. Once that is done, you will convert the NURBS geometry to polygons and skin it, so that everything follows as you animate the rig. Along the way, you will also create basic blend shapes so that the squirrel can have facial expressions.

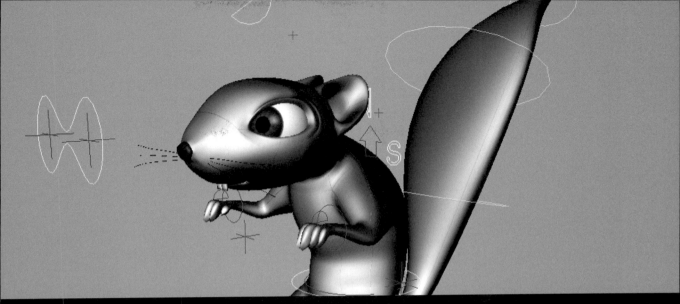

The Squirrel Rig

In this lesson, you will take Leon's rig and modify it for the squirrel. Doing so will save you some valuable time in the rigging operation.

In this lesson you will learn the following:

- How to reuse an existing setup;
- How to scale bones in an IK chain;
- How to connect joints;
- How to delete custom attributes;
- How to use MEL scripting to lock attributes.

Import Leon's rig

You will now import Leon into the Squirrel scene and set the two characters to scale. You will also need to modify several joints on the rig, but the overall process will be much faster than rebuilding an entire rig from scratch.

1   Open an existing scene file

- Open the last scene from Project 2 called *08-squirrel textures 02.ma*.

2   Import Leon

- From Project 5, import the Leon scene file called *21-leon lores.ma*.

Note: *In the import options, make sure to resolve only the clashing names with a prefix. If the import operation did prefix some node names, they will not be specified.*

3   Scale the squirrel

- Select the squirrel's geometry group.

- **Scale** it down and **move** it placed so the hind paws stand on the world grid.

Leon imported into the squirrel scene

Note: *In the above image, Leon was moved beside the squirrel. If you do so, make sure to place Leon back at the origin before continuing.*

4   Delete Leon's geometry

- **Delete** Leon's *geometry* group.

- Select **File → Optimize Scene Size** in order to also remove any nodes and material related to Leon.

5   Freeze the squirrel's transformations

- Select the squirrel's geometry group.

- Select **Modify → Freeze Transformations**.

- Change the **Shading** of the view to **X-Ray**.

- Add the squirrel's geometry to a *geometryLayer* and set it to **reference**.

6   Delete obsolete rig parts

- **Delete** rig parts such as the pocket and ear setups.

7   Make the rig to scale

- Select the *master*, **unlock** its **scale** attributes, and **scale** the rig down to the size of the squirrel geometry.

- **Move** the *hipsManip* until the *Hips* joint is located appropriately in the squirrel geometry.

- **Move** the *armManips* to fit the squirrel's wrists.

Tip: *Try to keep any changes symmetrical.*

- **Move** the arm *poleVectors* so they line up with the squirrel's elbow.

- **Move** the *neckManip* until the *Head* joint fits the squirrel's head.

- **Move** and **rotate** the *footManips* so they line up with the squirrel's feet.

- **Move** the leg *poleVectors* so they line up with the squirrel's knee.

The manipulators moved to fit the squirrel's geometry

Lesson 22: The Squirrel Rig

8   Scale joints

Now that most manipulators have been moved to better locations, you will scale the bones up to suit the squirrel's geometry.

- Select **Edit → Select All By Type → Joints**.
- Select **Window → General Editors → Channel Control**.
- Make sure the checkbox **Change all selected objects of same type** is set to **On**.
- Select the **Locked** tab.
- Move all the **Scale** attributes from the **Locked** side to the **Non Locked** side.
- Select the **Keyable** tab.
- Move all the **Scale** attributes from the **Nonkeyable Hidden** side to the **Keyable** side.

Note: *Since the rig was carefully locked in order to prevent unintended manipulation, several steps outlined next will require you to unlock attributes. A nice workflow is to create macro buttons to lock and unlock the attributes of the selected nodes.*

9   Scale the hips

- Select the *HipsOverride* and **scale** it uniformly to enlarge the pelvis.

Tip: *Since the scale pivot is off center, it is important to scale the joint uniformly by click+dragging the middle manipulator of the Scale Tool.*

10   Reverse feet

- Select both *RevHeel* joints and make them visible.
- Select the reverse foot joints, and **scale** and **move** them to fit the squirrel's feet.

The reverse feet should now fit the squirrel's feet perfectly. Now you must scale the legs and foot joints to reach them.

11   Scale leg joints

- **Scale** the *UpLeg* and *Leg* joints on their **X-axis** until the knees are in proper position.

12   Scale foot joints

- Select both *Foot* joints.
- **Scale** them on the **X-axis** until they reach their respective reverse foot joints.
- Select both *ToeBase* joints.

- **Scale** them on the **X-axis** until they reach their respective reverse foot joints.

13 Feet manipulator shape

- **Hide** the reverse foot chains.
- While in Component mode, modify the *footManips* CVs to be visible around the feet geometry.

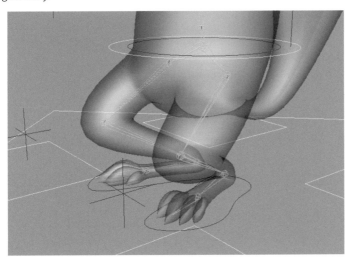

The legs and feet are now well suited for the squirrel

14 Spine joints

- Select the *backSpine* curve and make it visible.
- Change the shape of the curve by moving CVs to round up the squirrel's back.
- Select all the *Spine* joints and **scale** them to place the shoulders appropriately in the squirrel's geometry.
- Tweak the top CV of the *backSpline* so it aligns with the *Spine5* joint.

15 Arm joints

You will now place the clavicle, arms, and fingers in the squirrel's geometry.

- Select the *clavicleManips*, and then **move** them to fit the shoulders.

> **Note:** *IK handles must be set to **Sticky** to update correctly while scaling joints.*

- **Scale** the *Arm*, *ForeArm*, and *ForeArmRoll* joints.

16 Hand joints

- **Scale** the *Hand* joints uniformly to fit the palm area.
- **Scale** and **move** the *finger* joints appropriately.

> **Note:** *Translating finger joints will offset their local rotation axes, but it will allow you to conserve their driven keys animation.*

17 Neck joints

Since Leon has a pretty long neck, you do not require as many joints for the squirrel's neck.

- **Delete** the *neckSpline* and *neckSplineIK*.
- Select the *Head* joint, make sure its translation is unlocked, and **unparent** it temporarily.
- **Delete** all the *Neck* joints except the first one: Neck.

Doing so will leave you with only a single neck joint, which should be enough for this character.

- Select the *Head* joint; then **Shift-select** the *Neck* joint.
- Select **Skeleton** → **Connect Joint** → ❒.
- In the option window, select **Parent joint** and click the **Connect** button.

This step is different than simply parenting a joint since it recreates a special connection that compensates for the parent's scaling. Without this connection, if you were to scale the neck joint, the entire head would deform.

- **Scale** and **move** the *Neck* and *Head* joints appropriately.
- Reuse the *neckManip* for the remaining *Neck* joint by snapping its pivot to the joint.
- **Unlock** all its attributes and **freeze** its transformations.
- Create a **Parent** constraint between the *Neck* joint and the manipulator.

18 Head joints

- **Delete** the *Nose* joint.
- **Move** the *Skull* joint to the tip of the nose for reference.
- **Rename** the joint to *Nose*.
- Use a **Point** constraint on the *Eye* joints to center them in the eye geometry.

Just as with Leon, this is only a trick to center the joints within the eye. The constraint must be removed.

- **Delete** the point constraints.

Project 06

19 Eyes manipulator

- **Move** the eye*LookAt* **down** to align it with the squirrel's eyes.

20 Manipulators

- In Component mode, **tweak** the shape of all the manipulators to better suit the squirrel's geometry.

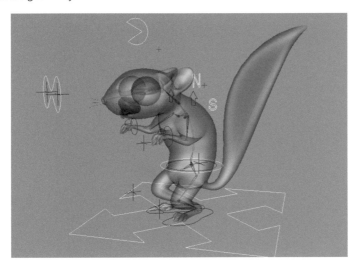

The updated squirrel rig

21 Save your work

- Save the scene as *22-squirrel rig 01.ma*.

Add squirrel controls

Now that you have changed Leon's rig for the squirrel, you must add specific extra controls. In this exercise, you will add joints for the tail and ears.

1 Setup the tail

- **Draw** joints starting at the base of the tail going to the tip of the tail.

- **Rename** all the joints to *tail#* using the **Input Line**.

- **Parent** the first *tail* joint to the *Hips*.

> **Note:** *An extra transform group node is created in the hierarchy for the joints to maintain their positions after scaling the Hips joint.*

Lesson 22: The Squirrel Rig

- **Rename** the new tail group to *tailGroup*.
- Snap the pivot of the *tailGroup* on the *Hips* joint.
- Select **Modify** → **Freeze Transformations**.
- With the first tail joint selected, select **Skeleton** → **Orient Joint**.

  Doing so will ensure that the joints' local rotation axes point toward their first child correctly.

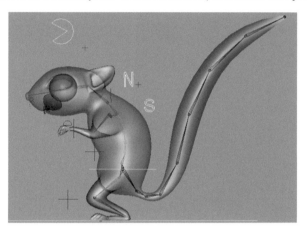

The tail joints

- **Create** an IK spline running through all tail joints.

Tip: *Increase the **Number of Spans** to **3** in the **IK Spline Handle Tool** options to give more definition to the tail curve.*

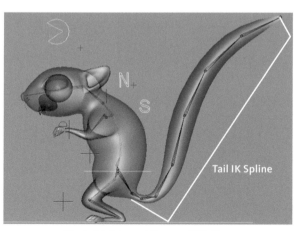

The tail joints and the new IK Spline

- **Create** clusters with the tail curve CVs.
- **Create** manipulators for the clusters, **parent** them to the *master,* and **freeze** their transformations.

Tip: *The cluster at the base of the tail doesn't need a manipulator.*

- **Rename** all the new nodes accordingly.
- **Lock and hide** the appropriate objects and attributes.
- **Assign** color overrides.

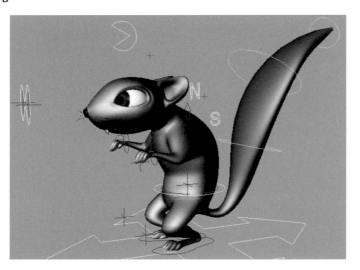

The tail setup

2 **Ear setup**
- **Draw** two joints going from the base of the ear to the tip of the ear in the side view.
- **Place** the joints within the squirrel's left ear geometry in the Perspective view.
- **Rename** the joints to *LeftEar* and *LeftEarEnd.*
- **Parent** the joint to the *Head.*
- Select the group that was automatically created and select **Modify → Freeze Transformations.**
- You can now **parent** the *LeftEar* directly to the *Head* joint and **delete** the transform group.

- With the first ear joint selected, select **Skeleton** → **Orient Joint**.
- **Mirror** the joints for the other ear.
- **Lock and hide** the joints and their attributes.

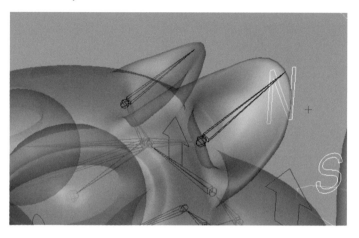

The ears to be animated in FK

3   Save your work

- Save the scene as *22-squirrel rig 02.ma*.

Final touches

Throughout the process of modifying the rig, you have unlocked, shown, and moved quite a lot of nodes and attributes. You should now look at each node and make sure all are properly frozen and locked to prevent erroneous manipulation by the animator.

1   Freeze transformations

Since you moved most of the manipulators while placing the rig, it is a good idea to freeze their transformations so they are at their default positions with default attributes. In order to be able to freeze transformations, you must unlock the attributes to be frozen of the node and its children. Following is the workflow to use while freezing transformations:

- Select the object to be frozen.
- **Unlock** the attributes to be frozen, which are usually **rotation**, **translation**, and **scale**.
- **Unlock** the same attributes on all children of the object.
- **Freeze** the transformations of the object.

    All the children will also be frozen.

> **Tip:** *If you don't need to freeze the transformations of the children, unparent them temporarily while you freeze the transformations. If the objects move as you unparent them, make sure to unlock their attributes first. If the child nodes don't behave as expected when parented back on the frozen object, you can simply keep the tranform group that was automatically created or create one yourself as an override.*

- **Repeat** for all the objects to be frozen, such as manipulators and locators.

> **Tip:** *If an object's attributes are all to be locked to prevent the animator from using it, you do not need to freeze its transformations.*

2   Set preferred angle

- Select the *Hips*; then select **Skeleton → Set Preferred Angle**.

  Doing so will ensure that all the joints have a proper, saved preferred angle.

> **Note:** *The only drawback of reusing a rig is that joints driven by IKs might get values in their rotation attributes. The best solution to correct this is still to create an entire new skeleton by snapping it to a skeleton you have just finished.*

3   Revise the rig

You should now take some time to revise the entire rig and bring modifications as needed.

4   Delete custom attributes

If some nodes have custom attributes that are no longer required, you can easily delete them through the Channel Box.

- Select the *blendShapesManip*.

  Not all the blend shapes used for Leon are required for the squirrel.

- Highlight the custom attributes to delete in the Channel Box.

- **RMB** and select **Delete Attributes**.

5   Lock and hide attributes and nodes

- In the Hypergraph or the Outliner, go over each node and make sure you lock and hide them correctly.

Lesson 22: The Squirrel Rig

Tip: *Using a MEL script to do this could really speed up the task. For instance, the following script would lock and hide the translation attributes for all selected nodes:*

```
for($each in `ls -sl`)

{
        setAttr -k 0 ($each + ".tx");

        setAttr -k 0 ($each + ".ty");

        setAttr -k 0 ($each + ".tz");

        setAttr -l 1 ($each + ".tx");

        setAttr -l 1 ($each + ".ty");

        setAttr -l 1 ($each + ".tz");

}
```

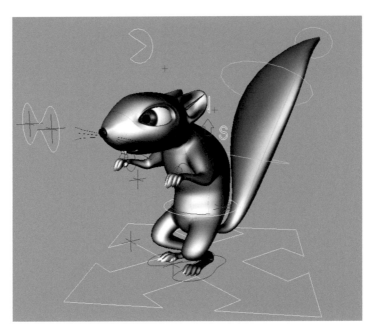

The finished rig

6   Save your work

- Save the scene as *22-squirrel rig 03.ma.*

Conclusion

In this lesson, you saved some valuable time by reusing Leon's rig for the squirrel. The goal of this lesson was not to create an entire rig, but to show that there are ways to reuse work already done. If the rig created here is not good enough for your needs, you can at least reuse bone placements to create a new skeleton, and also reuse most of the manipulators.

In the next lesson, you will bind the squirrel to the skeleton.

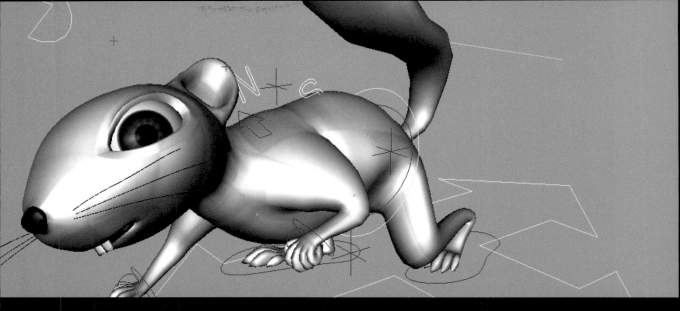

Lesson 23
Conversion and Skinning

In this lesson, you will bind the squirrel to its skeleton. In order to keep the lesson fast and simple, you will convert the NURBS patch model to polygons. You will then bind that new geometry to the skeleton.

In this lesson you will learn the following:

· How to convert the NURBS model to polygons and why;

· How to clean up the converted mesh;

· How to detach components if required;

· How to practice skinning a more complex character.

NURBS or polygons?

At this point, you have two choices concerning the binding of the squirrel. The first choice is to continue with the model entirely in NURBS, and bind using heavy tools that will maintain the stitching and tangency of the character together while being deformed. The second solution is to convert the model to polygons and bind it using the same tools that you used to bind Leon.

For this lesson, the choice is to convert the NURBS patch model to polygons and bind that new geometry to the skeleton. That way, the process of skinning the character will be much easier, since you will only need to weight a simple polygonal mesh rather than numerous individual NURBS patches.

Note: *You will have to create new texture reference objects when converting to polygons.*

Convert to polygons

1 Scene file

- Open the last scene from the previous lesson called *22-squirrel rig 03.ma*.

2 Hide the rig

- Set the *rigLayer*'s visibility to **Off**.
- Turn **Off** the referencing of the *geometryLayer*.

3 Convert to polygons

To create the polygonal mesh, you will only need to convert the NURBS patches that define the squirrel's body. You will not convert any accessories such as whiskers, eyes or teeth.

- Select all of the squirrel's skin surfaces.
- Select **Modify → Convert → NURBS to Polygons → ☐**.
- In the option window, set the following:

> **Type** to **Quads**;
>
> **Tessellation Method** to **General**;
>
> **U Type** to **Per Span # of Iso Params**;
>
> **Number U** to **3**;
>
> **V Type** to **Per Span # of Iso Params**;
>
> **Number V** to **3**;

- Click the **Tessellate** button.

  One polygonal surface is created for each NURBS patch.

- **Hide** the *geometryLayer*.

  You should now see only the polygonal surfaces.

The converted geometry

Note: *If you intend to smooth the meshes later in the process, you could convert sections of the squirrel geometry, such as the head, hands, and feet, with less density if needed.*

4 Combine the polygons

You now need to combine the polygonal meshes into a single mesh.

- Select all polygonal meshes.
- Select **Mesh → Combine**.
- Select **Edit Mesh → Merge** with a **Threshold** of **0.001**.
- Select **Display → Polygons → Border Edges**.

Lesson 23: Conversion and Skinning

5   Close borders

There are still borders on the model, especially where the number of spans from one patch to another was different, but any other border edges on the geometry should now be properly closed. You will now properly close the remaining borders by snapping vertices together.

- Select **Edit Mesh → Merge Edge Tool** to close borders that were not closed in the previous step.

Tip: *If vertices were merged in an inapropriate way, you can use **Edit Mesh → Detach Component** to split a vertex into one vertex per connected face.*

- **Split** polygonal faces where there are vertices missing in the neck, hands, and feet areas.

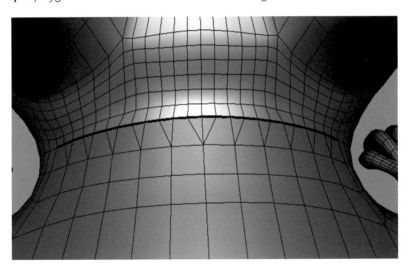

Splits to close the border edges

Tip: *You can delete half the model and mirror it if you don't want to repeat the previous steps for the other side.*

- Using **Snap to Point**, snap border edge vertices together.
- Select **Edit Mesh → Merge**.
- **Repeat** until all border edges other than the eye openings are closed.

> **Note:** *If some border edges are persistent, double-check if the normals are all pointing in the same direction. If not, use Normal → Conform.*

6 Finish the polygonal model

- Select the polygonal mesh and **rename** it *squirrel*.
- Select **Normals** → **Soften Edge** to make the geometry smooth looking.
- Select *squirrelLow;* then select **Edit** → **Delete By Type** → **History**.

> **Note:** *Do not use* **Delete** → **All by Type** → **History** *because the rig is using some history.*

7 Save your work

- Save the scene as *23-skinning 01.ma*.

Skinning

Now that you have proper polygonal geometry, you can bind it to the skeleton and paint its weights.

1 Bind to skeleton

- Display the *rigLayer*.
- Select all joints that you deem important for binding, and then **Shift-select** the *squirrel* geometry.
- Select **Skin** → **Bind Skin** → **Smooth Bind** → ❑.
- In the option window, make sure **Bind to** is set to **Selected Joints**.
- Click the **Bind Skin** button.

2 Paint weights

Using the same technique used to bind Leon, paint the weights of the *squirrel* geometry. The following outlines the steps to follow.

- Select the *squirrel* geometry.
- Select **Skin** → **Edit Smooth Skin** → **Paint Skin Weights Tool** → ❑.
- **Paint** the weights to a value of **1** to clearly define which influence goes where.

> **Tip:** *You only need to paint the left side of the body since you will mirror the joint influences.*

- Select **Skin → Edit Smooth Skin → Mirror Skin Weights**.
- **Refine** the binding by smoothing out the influences.
- Select **Skin → Edit Smooth Skin → Prune Small Weights**.
- Select **Skin → Edit Smooth Skin → Mirror Skin Weights**.

The refined binding

3 Save your work

- Save the scene as *23-skinning 02.ma*.

Other skinning

Now that the body is bound, you can bind the remaining squirrel objects.

1 Delete unused surfaces

- **Delete** all skin NURBS patches that were converted earlier.

2 Bind the eyes

- **Smooth bind** the eyes to the *Eye* joints.

3 Bind the whiskers

- **Rigid bind** the whiskers to the *Head* joint.

4 Bind the teeth

- **Rigid bind** the teeth to the *Head* joint.

Final touches

1 Delete the old texture reference objects

Delete the texture reference objects created in Project Two since they are no longer used.
You should then create new ones for the new polygonal geometry.

- Under the *txtGroup*, **delete** all the texture reference objects.
- Select the squirrel body, and then select **Texturing → Create Texture Reference Object.**
- **Repeat** for the *teethGroup***.**
- **Parent the new reference objects to the** *txtGroup***.**

> **Note:** *You might have to tweak the shaders and texture placements in order to suit the new squirrel scale.*

2 Make sure everything is parented and well named

3 Optimize the scene size

4 Test the squirrel's binding

- Try to pose the squirrel to see if everything deforms well.
- Make any required changes.

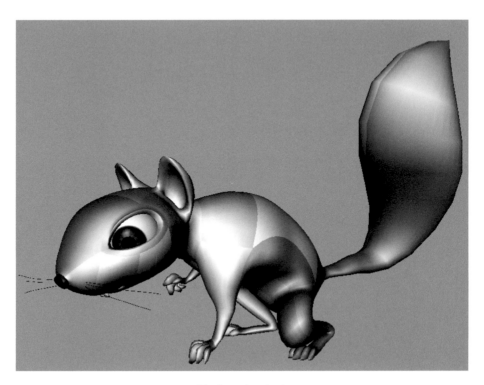

The bound squirrel

> **Note:** *It is normal that the viewport display of 3D textures is not exactly like the rendered look.*

5 Save your work

- Save the scene as *23-skinning 03.ma.*

Project 06

Conclusion

In this lesson, you converted a NURBS model to polygons for simplicity reasons, but feel free to experiment and try another workflow. You also gained added experience in skinning a more complex character.

In the next lesson, you will model blend shapes for the squirrel.

Final Touches

In order to finalize the squirrel's setup, you will create blend shapes by using the original NURBS patch model. You will then use the wrap deformer to transfer blend shapes from the NURBS model to the polygonal model. Once that is done, you will add secondary animation to give life to your animations. Finally, you will generate a low-resolution setup for animation.

In this lesson you will learn the following:

- How to sculpt NURBS patches;
- How to create blend shapes with multiple surfaces;
- How to use a wrap deformer;
- How to create blend shapes extracted from a wrap deformer;
- How to use jiggle on a spline IK;
- How to use a non-linear deformer;
- How to create a low-resolution model from the NURBS patch model.

NURBS or polygons?

You can create blend shapes using either NURBS or polygon geometry. You used the sculpt deformer on polygons to create Leon's blend shapes, so in this lesson you will sculpt NURBS and use a wrap deformer to create the squirrel's blend shapes.

If you don't feel comfortable creating the blend shape on NURBS patches, you can simply redo Lesson 21 using the squirrel's polygon skin.

Note: *This lesson explores another workflow, which could be useful in some situations.*

Sculpt target shapes

In this exercise, you will sculpt the squirrel NURBS model to create blend shapes.

1   Open an existing scene file

- Open the scene called *23-skinning 01.ma*.

   You will use this scene because the squirrel in it has proper scaling and is made of NURBS patches.

2   Delete unused nodes

- **Delete** the *rig* group and *txtGroup*.

- **Delete** the polygonal squirrel body.

- **Delete** all surfaces that are not intended to be part of the blend shapes.

Tip: *Keep any surfaces that are likely to help with the deformations, such as the eyes, teeth and whiskers.*

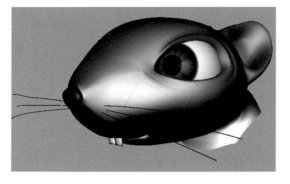

The head to be used for blend shapes

3   Save the scene

- Save the scene right away as *24-blendshapes 01.ma*.

4   Duplicate

You can now duplicate the head to sculpt the squirrel's facial expressions.

- **Rename** the *geometry* group to *original*.

- **Duplicate** the *original* group.

- **Rename** the new group to *leftBlink* and **move** it aside.

5   Sculpt

Since you will be using a wrap deformer to transfer the blend shapes to the polygonal mesh, you only need to carefully sculpt one side of the face. You will then mirror half of the head to create the other side of the blend shapes.

- Sculpt the skin surfaces by manipulating CVs, using wire deformers or by using the **Edit NURBS → Sculpt Geometry Tool**.

- Sculpt the following target shapes at your discretion:

     leftBlink, leftBlinkMid, leftWideOpen, leftLowerLidUp;

     jawDown;

     leftBrowUp.

> **Tip:** *One of the easiest ways to create blend shapes on NURBS surfaces is by duplicating a surface curve and using that curve as a wire deformer.*

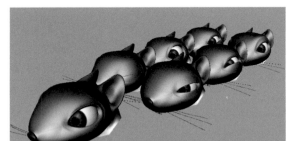

The squirrel's blend shapes

6   Save your work

- Save the scene as *24-blendshapes 01.ma*.

Blend shape deformer

Now that all the blend shapes have been modeled, you can create the blend shape deformer for all the face surfaces. Just like for Leon, you will create an in-between shape first, and then add the rest of the targets.

1 In-between shapes

- From the Outliner, select the *leftBlinkMid* group and then the *leftBlink* group.
- Add the *original* group to the selection.
- Select **Create Deformers → Blend Shape → ▢**.
- In the option window, turn **On** the **In-Between** checkbox.
- Click the **Create** button.

   You now have a proper blinking blend shape with an in-between shape to prevent the surface from interpenetrating the eye.

2 Rest of the shapes

- From the Outliner, select all the remaining target groups.
- Add the *original* group to the selection.
- Select **Edit Deformers → Blend Shape → Add → ▢**.
- In the option window, turn **On** the **Specify Node** checkbox.
- Click the **Apply and Close** button.

   All the target shapes are now part of the blend shape deformer on the base shape.

3 Test the shapes

- Test the blend shape deformer and make any changes required to the target shapes.

4 Delete the targets

- It is now safe to **delete** all the target groups.

5 Delete obsolete nodes

- **Delete** the whiskers, eyes, and upper teeth.

   You must keep the lower teeth since they are part of the jawDown shape.

6 Split the head

Since the blend shapes will be mirrored, you need to have only half of the head with the blend shapes. The head will then be duplicated and mirrored on the other side.

- **RMB** on the central surfaces and select **Isoparm**.

- Select all the central isoparms; then **detach** the surfaces.

  You should now have the entire head split in half.

- **Parent** all the new surfaces to the *original* group.

- **Group** the right surfaces and **rename** the group *notUsed*.

- **Hide** the *notUsed* group.

Note: *You must hide the surfaces because if you delete them, the blend shape deformer will no longer work correctly.*

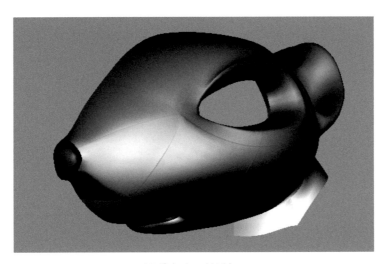

Half the head hidden

7   Mirror the head

- Select the *original*, and then select **Edit → Duplicate Special → ☐**.

- Turn **On** the **Duplicate Input Graph** checkbox.

- Click the **Duplicate Special** button.

  Doing so will duplicate the entire head, along with its blend shape deformer.

- Set the **Scale X** attribute of the new *original* to **–1**.

  You should now have the entire head again, but with a blend shape deformer to control each half.

- **Group** *original* and *original1* together and **rename** the new group *warpObjects*.

  It is important that all the properly deforming surfaces used in the wrap deformer be grouped together.

8 Save your work

- Save the scene as *24-blendshapes 02.ma*.

Wrap deformer

You will now open the bound squirrel scene file, and import the scene created in the previous exercise. You will then create wrap deformers between the base shape and the polygonal squirrel geometry.

1 Open an existing scene file

- Open the scene called *23-skinning 03.ma*.

2 Import the blend shapes

- Select **File → Import** and select the scene called *24-blendshapes 02.ma*.

  You now have the bound squirrel along with the blend shapes in your scene.

3 Prepare the model

- **Hide** the *rigLayer*.

- Select the *squirrel* polygonal geometry.

- In the Channel Box, under the **Inputs** section, highlight the *skinCluster* node.

- Set the **Envelope** attribute to **0.0**.

  Setting this attribute to zero disables a skinning deformer. By disabling this, you are temporarily turning off the skinning of the squirrel, which will ensure that it is in default position. It is important for the skin to be in its default position for the blend shapes to work correctly.

4 Separate teeth

For simplicity, and because you don't want the teeth to affect the squirrel geometry, you will have to take them out of the *wrapObjects* group.

- Select both *teethGroups* and **unparent** them.

- **Hide** the *teethGroup*s.

5 Wrap deformer

- Select the *squirrel* polygonal geometry, and then **Shift-select** the *wrapObjects* group.

- Select **Create Deformers → Wrap → ❑**.

- In the options, set the following:

    Weight threshold to **1.0**;

> **Max distance** to **0.1**;
>
> **Influence type** to **Points**.

- Click the **Create** button.

  After a few seconds, the wrap deformer will be created.

6   Teeth wrap deformers

- **Repeat** the previous step for each tooth.

7   Test the wrap deformer

- **Hide** the *wrapObjects* group.

- Through the Outliner, select one of the surfaces in the *wrapObjects* group.

- In the Channel Box, under the **Inputs** section, highlight the *blendShape* node.

- **Test** the blend shapes and see how the squirrel's polygonal geometry deforms.

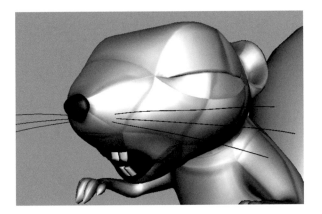

The wrap deformer affecting the polygonal geometry

Note: *In order to have the blend shapes affecting both sides of the head, you must edit the values of both blend shape deformers.*

8   Duplicate the polygonal geometry for each shape

- Turn **On** the *leftBlink* blend shape.

- Select the *squirrel* geometry.

- Select **Edit → Duplicate**.

- **Move** the duplicated geometry aside and **rename** it *leftBlink*.

- **Hide** the *leftBlink* geometry.
- Continue to extract each polygonal target shape:

  leftBlink, leftBlinkMid, leftWideOpen, leftLowerLidUp;
  rightBlink, rightBlinkMid, rightWideOpen, rightLowerLidUp;
  jawDown;
  leftBrowUp, rightBrowUp.

Tip: *The weight of the blink mid in-between target is* **0.5**.

9 Teeth blend shapes

- **Repeat** the previous step and **duplicate** both lower teeth while in the *jawDown* position.

10 Remove the wrap deformer

- **Delete** all the wrap objects that were previously imported.

  The wrap will automatically be deleted.

11 Group the targets

- **Group** all the target shapes that you have created.

12 Create the blend shape deformer

- **Create** all the target shapes (beside *blinkMid*), for the *squirrel* geometry.

Tip: *Make sure when you create the blend shape deformer that you set the* **Deformation Order** *option to* **Front Of Chain***. That way, the deformer will go before the skinning, which is what you want.*

- **Add** the in-between shapes for *leftBlinkMid* and *rightBlinkMid* to the squirrel's blend shape node.

Note: *Set the* **In-Between Weight** *to* **0.5**.

13 Lower teeth blend shape

- **Create** individual blend shape deformers for the lower teeth.
- **Connect** the main *jawDown* attribute on the *squirrel* blend shape deformer to the *jawDown* blend shape deformer of the teeth.

14 Test the blend shapes

- **Hide** the blend shape targets.

- **Test** the blend shapes and bring any changes to the target shapes, if needed.

15 Deformer set

Just as you did for Leon, you will now remove unaffected vertices from the blend shape deformer set. Doing so will greatly speed up the blend shape deformer.

- Select the *squirrel* geometry, and go to Component mode.

- Select all the vertices that will not be deformed by the blend shapes.

Vertices that can be removed from the blend shape deformer set

- Select **Window → Relationship Editors → Deformer Sets**.

- In the left column, highlight the *blendShape1Set*.

- In the left column menu, select **Edit → Remove Selected Items**.

The selected vertices will be removed from the blend shape deformer set.

16 Double check the deformer set members

- **Deselect** all the vertices.

- In the Relationship Editor, **RMB** on the *blendShape1Set* and select **Select Set Members**.

Only the head vertices should be selected.

17 Delete the targets

- **Delete** the target shapes.

Lesson 24: Final Touches

18 Enable the skin cluster

- Select the *squirrel* geometry.

- In the Channel Box, under the **Inputs** section, highlight the *skinCluster* node.

- Set the **Envelope** attribute to **1.0**.

19 Optimize Scene Size

20 Connect blendShapesManip

- Show the *rigLayer*.

- **Add** all the blend shapes attributes to the *blendshapesManip* just as you did for Leon.

- Select **Window → General Editors → Connection Editor**.

- **Load** the *blendShapesManip* on the left side.

- **Load** the *blendShape1* node on the right side.

- **Connect** the attributes of the *blendShapesManip* to the *blendShape1* node.

21 Test the rig

Pose using blend shapes

22 Save your work

- Save the scene as *24-blendshapes 03.ma*.

Jiggle deformers

Jiggle deformers will add dynamic secondary animation to the squirrel's whiskers.

1 Whiskers

- **Hide** the *rigLayer*.
- Select all the whiskers; then go to Component mode.
- Select all the CVs except the ones close to the head.

2 Jiggle

- With the CVs still selected, select **Create Deformer → Jiggle Deformer → □**.
- In the option window, set the following:

    Stiffness to **0.2**;

    Damping to **0.2**;

    Weight to **0.9**.

- Click the **Create** button.

  A jiggle deformer is created for each surface.

3 Jiggle weights

- Go back to Object mode.
- Select **Edit Deformers → Paint Jiggle Weights Tool → □**.
- In the tool options, set the **Paint Operation** to **Smooth**.
- Click the **Flood** button one or twice.

4 Preferences

- Select **Window → Settings/Preferences → Preferences**.
- In the **Timeline** category, make sure **Playback Speed** is set to **Play every frame**.

> **Tip:** *Always make sure to play every frame before playing dynamic animation.*

- Click the **Save** button.

5 Test the jiggle

- Go to frame **1**.
- Select the *Head* joint, and press **s** to set a keyframe.

- **Move** the *Head* joint, and press **s** to set a keyframe at frames **10**, **20** and **30**.
- **Playback** the scene to see the behavior of the jiggle deformer.

Note: *Don't forget to delete the animation when you are done.*

6 Tweak the jiggle attributes

Since there are multiple jiggle deformers, you will now change them all at once.

- Type *jiggle** in the **Input Line** to select all the jiggle nodes in the scene.
- In the Channel Box, highlight the *jiggle* node.
- **Tweak** the attributes of the deformer and **playback** the scene to see its effect.

7 Tail jiggle

You can add jiggle on the spline of a spline IK. This is possible because the jiggle deformer is evaluated after the spline has been animated.

- **Unhide** the *tailSpline*.
- Select the CVs controlling the tail, without the ones closer to the tail base.
- **Repeat** the previous steps to create a jiggle deformer with the following values:

    Stiffness to **0.1**;

    Damping to **0.05**;

    Weight to **0.9**.

Tip: *It is a good idea to add custom attributes on the rig in order to control and scale the effect of the jiggle deformers.*

Non-linear deformer

In this exercise, you will add a non-linear sine deformer, which will simulate subtle wind movement in the tail. A sine non-linear deformer will move the affected vertices in a sinusoidal way, according to the placement of the deformer handle. The deformer will be inserted in front of the deformation order, so it will affect the tail before it is deformed by the rig.

1 Sine deformer

- Select the tail vertices to be deformed by the sine deformer.
- Select **Create Deformers → Nonlinear → Sine**.

    The sine deformer is created and selected.

2   **Tweak the sine deformer**

- In the **Inputs** section of the Channel Box, select the *sine1* node.
- Set the following:

   Amplitude to **0.02**;

   Wavelength to **2.0**;

   Dropoff to **-1.0**;

   Low Bound to **0.0**;

   High Bound to **3.0**;

- **Rotate** the sine deformer so it follows the angle of the tail and **move** it so its bottom end is located at the base of the tail.

   By placing the deformer like this, you ensure that there will be no deformation at the base of the tail and more deformation toward the tip.

The sine deformer placement

3   **Test the sine deformer**

- **Highlight** the **Offset** attribute in the Channel Box, and then **MMB+drag** in the viewport to see the effect of the sine deformer on the tail.
- **Tweak** the sine deformer as needed.

Note: *The orientation and placement of the deformer handle will change the way the deformer affects the geometry.*

Lesson 24: Final Touches

4 **Deformation order**

- **RMB** on the *squirrel* geometry and select **Inputs → All Inputs**.
- **MMB+drag** *Non Linear(sine1)* on *Blend Shape(blendShape1)*.

  Doing so will change the deformation order so the sine deformer will affect the geometry before any other deformers.

- Click the **Close** button.

5 **Parent the sine deformer**

- **Parent** the *sine1Handle* node to the *rig* group.

  Since the deformer affects the geometry at its default position, it must remain at the center of the world in order to deform the tail correctly. Because you might want to move it to deform the tail in different ways, no lock will be required.

Tip: *Remember to animate the **Offset** attribute of the sine1 node to activate the wind on the tail.*

6 **Save your work**

- Save the scene as *24-squirrel hires.ma*.

Low resolution model

Before calling the rig final, you will need to generate a low-resolution model for real-time animation. The low-resolution model will be created starting from the NURBS patch model.

1 **Scene file**

- Open the scene called *22-squirrel rig 03.ma*.

Note: *This scene contains the NURBS patch squirrel model.*

2 **Clean up**

- **Delete** the *rig* group.

3 **Convert**

- Select all the body NURBS patches.
- Select **Modify → Convert → NURBS to Polygons → ❒**.
- In the option window, set the following:

> **Type** to **Quads**;
>
> **Tessellation Method** to **General**;
>
> **Number U** and **V** to **1**.

• Click the **Tessellate** button.

There is now a low-resolution polygonal squirrel body.

> **Note:** *If the resulting geometry is too dense to be low resolution, you can use* **Edit NURBS** → **Rebuild Surfaces** → □ *to rebuild all the NURBS patches to a lower resolution.*

4   Tweak the conversion

There might be some surfaces that need a higher resolution in order to be good enough for the low-resolution model. For instance, the tail could use more resolution.

• **Hide** the *squirrelLayer*.

• Select the tail and then highlight the *nurbsTessellate* node in the Channel Box.

• Tweak the **U** and **V Number** settings to add some resolution to the model.

• **Repeat** the previous step for any other surfaces that require more resolution.

5   Combine and merge

• **Combine** the low-resolution surfaces.

• **Merge** vertices and **split** edges in order to finalize the low-resolution geometry.

> **Tip:**   *You can choose to tweak half the model, and then mirror and combine them together.*

• Set the normals of the geometry to be soft.

6   Shading

• **Assign** a simple brown *lambert* shader to the squirrel skin.

7   Delete all history

8   Optimize scene size

The low resolution squirrel

9 **Save the low resolution model**

• Save the scene as *24-squirrel lores.ma*.

10 **Open the final squirrel and merge the low-resolution model**

• Open the scene called *24-squirrel hires.ma*.

• **Import** the scene called *24-squirrel lores.ma*.

11 **Skinning**

• Select the original *squirrel* geometry.

• Execute the following MEL script:

```
select `skinCluster -q -inf`;
```

The above MEL command will select all the influences affecting the squirrel geometry.

• **Shift-select** the low-resolution *squirrel* geometry.

• Select **Skin → Bind Skin → Smooth Bind**.

12 **Copy skinning**

• Select the original *squirrel* geometry, and then **Shift-select** the low-resolution geometry.

• Select **Skin → Edit Skin → Copy Skin Weights**.

13 **Bind the rest of the low-resolution model**

14 **Blend shapes**

Use what you have learned in this project to transfer the blend shapes from the high-resolution model to the low-resolution model using a wrap deformer.

Project 06

The low-resolution squirrel rigged

15 Clean the scene

Clean up the scene by deleting the high-resolution models. Then make sure everything is named appropriately and optimize the scene size.

16 Save your work

- Save the scene as *24-squirrel lores.ma*.

Conclusion

In this lesson, you saw how to model blend shape targets starting from a NURBS patch model. And using both the wire deformer and wrap deformer was a good way to learn different methods of deforming geometry. By utilizing mirroring, you only had to create half the blend shapes, thus saving you some valuable time.

You have also managed to add secondary animation to the squirrel's setup using various deformers. Finally, you created and rigged the low-resolution model, which will come in handy when you will start animating.

In the next project, you will animate Leon, the squirrel, and the starry catfish together

Lesson 24: Final Touches

Project 07

In Project Seven, you will animate scenes with Leon, the squirrel, and the starry catfish. You will first experience keyframing by animating a simple walk with Leon. Once that is done, you will learn about references and set up a simple scene.

While building the scene, you will set up some constraints on Leon and the squirrel so that he can keep his pet in his shirt pocket. You will then block out an animation where Leon points out at the catfish that is swimming among the stars.

Lastly, you will do some experimentations with lip-synch and full body IK.

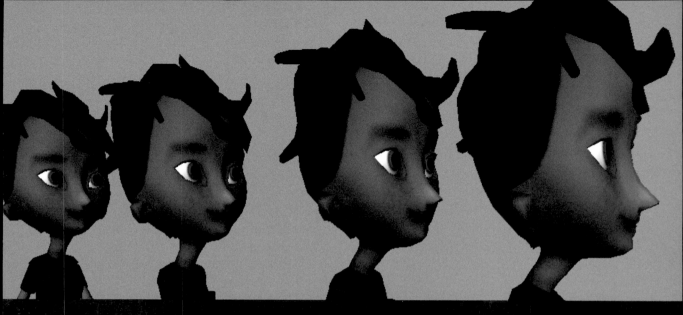

Lesson 25
A Simple Walk

Now that you have finished creating the character rigs, it is time to animate them. You will start by animating Leon walking forward. This is where you put the controls you worked on over the last few lessons to the test.

In this lesson you will learn the following:

Workflow

There are several approaches to animating a character. This lesson is by no means meant to be an exhaustive examination of character animation, but it will go through a basic animation workflow that can easily be adapted to your own workflow requirements.

Character sets

Before you start, you will create character sets to simplify the selection and keyframing process. A character set is a collection of attributes organized in a central place from the same or separate objects that are intended to be animated together. Character sets don't have to be actual physical characters like Leon; specifically, they are a collection of attributes that you want to animate all together.

The benefit of working with character sets is that you don't have to keyframe each individual attribute in the set. Once the character set is active, simply pose your selections and when you set a key, each attribute in the character set gets keyframed.

You created the Leon rig to be easily controlled by only a few control objects. Now you are going to organize those objects into a central collection, further simplifying the animation process.

> **Note:** *The attributes of a character set are aliased to the original attributes, which means they are intermediate attributes that are directly connected to the ones you are animating.*

You can select character sets from either the Outliner or Hypergraph, or you can use the menu **Character → Select Character Set Nodes**.

You can set the current character set from the menu **Character → Set Current Character Set**, or from the pull-down menu in the lower-right corner of the Timeline.

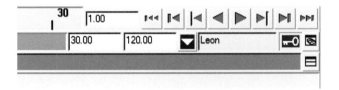

The Character menu

Create a character set

1 Open an existing scene

 • Open the scene file called *25-simple walk 01.ma*.

 This scene contains the Leon setup created in Project 5.

2 Select the appropriate objects

The first step to creating a character set is selecting all of the objects that are going to be included in that set.

 • Select all of the manipulators, locators, and animatable joints.

> **Note:** *Do not include non-animated objects because their attributes might end up with animation curves, which could increase the scene file size as well as slow down loading time and playback speed.*

3 Create the character set

 • Select **Character → Create Character Set → ▢**.

 • In the option window, select **Edit → Reset Settings**.

 • Set the following:

   Name to *Leon*;

   Include to **All keyable**.

 • Press the **Create Character Set** button.

 The attributes in the Channel Box should now appear yellow, which means they are connected and included in the character set.

4 Editing the character set

When you created Leon's rig, you restricted unnecessary attributes by locking them and making them non-keyable. Because of this, Leon's character set does not contain any superfluous attributes.

Although you have taken care to prevent unwanted attributes in the character set, it is a good idea to check the attributes of the character set in the Relationship Editor to make sure there is nothing missing or unessential.

 • Select **Window → Relationship Editors → Character Sets...**

 • Click on the **+** beside the *Leon* character set in the left column.

 All of the attributes in this character set will be listed.

- Check to make sure that the Leon character set has no unwanted attributes.

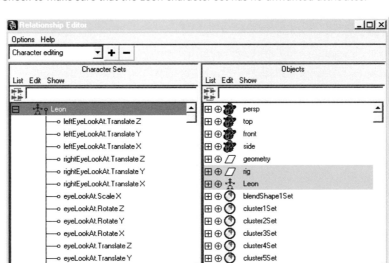

The Relationship Editor

5 Edit attributes in the character set

- If you find attributes that don't belong to the character set, highlight them and select **Edit → Remove Highlighted Attributes** from the left side of the Relationship Editor.

- If you find attributes missing from the character set, highlight them in the right column of the Relationship Editor.

Note: *You can also add and remove attributes from the selected character set by using* **Character → Add to Character Set** *and* **Character → Remove from Character Set.**

Keyframing preparation

Before you begin to set keys for the walk cycle, it is a good idea to change the **Move Tool** and **Rotate Tool** settings.

1 Transformation modes

- Select **Modify → Transformation Tools → Move Tool → □**.

- In the option window, set **Mode** to **Local**.

Using the **Move Tool** *in the* **Local** *option will allow you to move objects according to their local space, rather than world space, which is generally preferable when animating a character.*

- Select **Modify** → **Transformation Tools** → **Rotate Tool** → ❑.
- In the option window, set **Rotate Mode** to **Local**.

2 Key options

- Click on the **Animation Preferences** button at the right of the Timeline.
- In the **Categories** column, select **Settings** → **Animation**.
- In the **Tangents** section of the Animation Key Preferences, set **Weighted Tangents** to **On**.

  Weighted tangents provide more control over the shape of a curve between keys in the Graph Editor.

- Set the **Default In Tangent** and **Default Out Tangent** to **Clamped**.

  Clamped keys are a good starting point for character animation because they prevent values from overshooting between keys of similar value, while providing spline smoothness between keys of different values.

- Click the **Save** button.

3 Animation range

- Set the **Start Time** to **1** and the **End Time** to **120**.
- Set the **Playback Start Time** to **1**, and the **Playback End Time** to **30**.

  *Setting the start/end times and playback start/end times differently will allow you to focus on the animated cycle, which will go from **1** to **30**. The rest of the animation will then be cycled from frames **30** to **120**.*

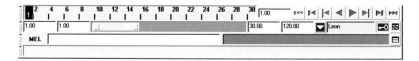

Time slider

4 Save your work

- Save the scene as *25-simple walk 02.ma*.

Animating the walk

Artistically, a good walk cycle should not only get the character from point A to point B, but also express the character's personality. Technically, a good walk cycle should start with a generic walking pose that can easily be modified to reflect the character's mood.

Creating a walk cycle involves animating a character in several key positions. You want to start with both feet on the ground, and then animate one leg lifting as it shifts forward. The first part of this process is the animation of the feet sliding on the ground. The lifting of the feet will be added later.

1   Go to frame 1

2   Set Leon's arms to FK

While Leon's arms could be animated with IK, FK is generally more appropriate for the type of action made here.

- Select the *leftHandManip and rightHandManip*.

- Set the **Ik Fk Blend** attributes to **0**.

3   Current character set

- Make sure that the name *Leon* is displayed in the **Current Character Set** field at the right of the Timeline.

- If *Leon* is not the current character set, click on the **down arrow** button next to the character set field and select *Leon*.

Now when you set a key, a keyframe will be set on all Leon attributes.

4   Pose Leon

The first step in animating Leon's walk cycle is posing him.

- Select *leftFootManip* and **move** it to **−5** on the **Z-axis**.

> **Note:** *At this point, Leon's feet will lift away from the manipulator. You will correct this later by animating Leon's foot attributes.*

- Select *rightFootManip* and **move** it to **2** on the **Z-axis**.
- Select *rightPoleVector* and also **move** it forward by **5** units.
- Select *hipsManip* and **move** it to **−1** on the **Y-axis**.

Leon posed at frame 1

For a cycled walk to behave properly, it is important to have a constant stride length for the feet and hips. If you calculate the distance between the feet (from the values set above), you will see that a stride will be equal to **7** units and a full step will be equal to **14** units.

5   **Set a key**

   • Press **s** to set a key.

   Because the current character is set to Leon, a keyframe is set on all of Leon.

6   **Advance to frame 15**

7   **Move the left leg forward**

   • Select the *leftFootManip* and **move** it forward by **14** units relative to the current value in the Channel Box, ending up at **9** units.

   • Select the *leftPoleVector* and also **move** it forward by **14** units.

8   **Move Leon forward**

   • Select the *hipsManip* and **move** it forward by **7** units.

9   **Set a key**

10 Test the animation

- **Click+drag** between frames **1** and **15** in the Time slider to test the animation.

11 Advance to frame 30

12 Move the right leg and hips forward

- Select the *rightFootManip* and **move** it forward by **14** units.
- Select the *rightPoleVector* and **move** it forward by **14** units.
- Select the *hipsManip* and **move** it forward by **7** units.

> **Tip:** *You can change values in the Channel Box using mathematical expressions. For instance, if you need to add 14 units to the current value of 2, you can type +=14 in the Channel Box and then press Enter, which will change the value to 16 units.*

13 Set another key

14 Test the animation

- **Playback** the animation.

15 Save your work

- Save the scene as *25-simple walk 03.ma*.

Cycle the animation

Now that the first step has been animated, you will cycle the curves to keep Leon walking beyond the current frame range.

1 Open the Graph Editor

- Select **Window → Animation Editors → Graph Editor**.
- Select the *Leon* character set in the left column of the Graph Editor.

> **Note:** *If you don't see it, make sure the Leon character set is currently selected at the bottom of the main interface.*

- Select **View → Frame All** to display all *Leon* character set animation curves.

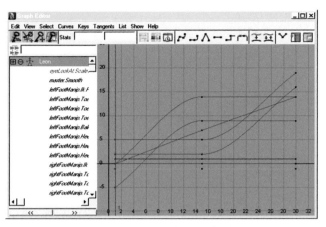

Animation curves in the Graph Editor

2 Select the animation curves

- **Click+drag** a selection box over all of the curves.

- To display the values of the animation curves outside the recorded keyframe range, select **View → Infinity**.

3 Cycle the curves

- Select **Curves → Pre Infinity → Cycle**.

  Cycling before the keys is not essential, but it can be helpful once you start editing animation curves.

- Select **Curves → Post Infinity → Cycle**.

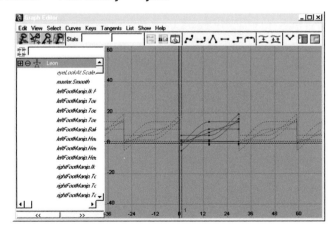

Cycled animation curves

Lesson 25: A Simple Walk

Project 07

4 Increase the playback range

- **Click+drag** on the box at the end of the current Range Slider and drag it until the playback range is from **1** to **120**.

 Tip: *You can double-click on the Range Slider to maximize to the entire animation range or to minimize it to the partial animation range.*

5 Play the animation

Instead of moving forward, Leon keeps covering the same ground every **30** frames. This is because the **Cycle** option was used. For Leon to move forward in the cycle, the **Cycle With Offset** option must be used.

6 Cycle the curves with offset

- With the curves still selected in the Graph Editor, select **Curves** → **Post Infinity** → **Cycle With Offset**.
- Select **Curves** → **Pre Infinity** → **Cycle With Offset**.

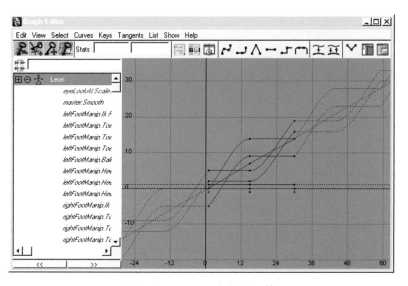

Animation curves cycled with offset

7 Play the animation

Leon should now continue to move forward as he walks.

8 Turn off the character set

For the time being, the *Leon* character set should be turned off so that individual attributes can be edited.

- Select **None** in the **Current Character Set** menu.

9 Curve tangencies

As you watch the animation, you will notice that Leon seems to be limping. This is because the tangencies of the animation curves are broken between the cycles.

- Select both foot manipulators.

  Since there are no active character sets, you can see the animation curves in the Graph Editor.

- Select **Translate Z** in the left column for each manipulator.

  Selecting attributes displays only those animation curves. You can see there is a clear break in tangency of those curves between cycles.

- Select both animation curves.

- Select **Tangents → Flat**.

- **Playback** the animation.

  The motion of the legs is now correct.

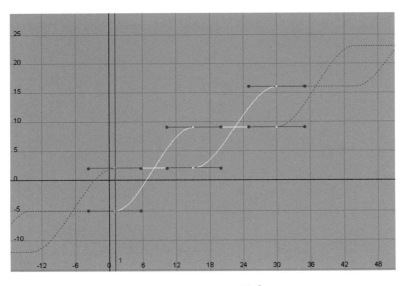

Translation Z animation curves with flat tangency

Note: *It is important when working with cycled animation that the curves interpolate appropriately from the last frame in the cycle to the first frame in the cycle.*

10 **Save your work**

- Save the scene as *25-simple walk 04.ma*.

Raising the feet

Currently, Leon's feet drag on the ground as he walks. Now you will animate the raising of his feet using *breakdown keys*. Breakdown keys are different from standard keys in that they maintain their relative position between regular keyframes. This is useful for actions that, by their nature, tend to have relative timing. In the case of Leon's walk, the timing of the foot raise is relative to the foot hitting the ground, so it is beneficial for the timing of the raise to adjust according to changes made in the timing of the fall.

1 **Go back to frame 1**

- Go back to frame **1** and set the playback range to go from **1** to **30**.

2 **Lift the left foot**

- Select the *leftFootManip*.

- Switch to the side view and **click+drag** in the Time slider until the left foot lines up with the right foot.

- **Translate** the *leftFootManip* **2** unit on the **Y-axis**.

- **Rotate** it **25** degrees on the **X-axis**.

Left foot raised and rotated

3 Set a breakdown key

- With the *leftFootManip* still selected, select **Animate** → **Set Breakdown**.

  A light green tick mark will appear in the timeline, denoting a breakdown key.

4 Repeat for the right foot

- Advance to the frame where the right foot lines up with the left foot; in this case, it's frame **23**.

Note: *You may find that the feet don't perfectly line up as they pass each other. Select the frame where they are the closest.*

- **Move** and **rotate** the *rightFootManip* as you did for the left foot.

5 Set another breakdown key

6 Set the playback range from 1 to 120

7 Playback the animation

8 Change the tangency of the curves

- In the Graph Editor, display the **Translate Y** animation curve for the *leftFootManip*.

- Select the key at frame **15**.

- Select **Tangent** → **In Tangent** → **Linear**.

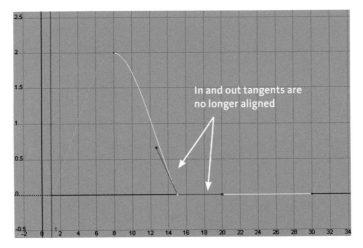

In and out tangents are no longer aligned

Frame 15 with in tangent set to linear

Before changing the in tangent of this key, the curve decelerated as it interpolated into the key, causing the foot to decelerate as it approached the ground. Now, the curve interpolates into the key at a more constant speed, causing the foot to hit the ground at a constant speed.

Note: *You don't need to change the tangent on the right foot since its animation is already broken by the animation cycle.*

9   Play the animation

Animate the rolling heel action

Now you will animate the motion of Leon's heels as they hit and peel off the ground.

1   Right foot's heel rotation

- Go to frame **1**.
- Set *rightFootManip*'s **Heel Rot Z** attribute to **−10**.
- Highlight the attribute; then **RMB** and select **Key Selected**.
- Go to frame **4**.
- Set **Heel Rot Z** to **0**.
- Set a key.
- Go to frame **30**.
- Set **Heel Rot Z** to **−10**.
- Set a key.

2   Left foot's heel rotation

- Go to frame **15**.
- Set *leftFootManip*'s **Heel Rot Z** attribute to **−10**.
- Set a key.
- Go to frame **18**.
- Set **Heel Rot Z** to **0**.
- Set a key.

3   Heel tangencies

The heel action is good, but the animation curves can be improved.

- Display the curves for the *left* and *rightFootManip* in the Graph Editor.
- Select both **Heel Rot Z** animation curves and change their tangency to **Flat**.

4   Break tangents

- Select the **Heel Rot Z** attribute for the *rightFootManip*.
- Select the key at frame **4**.
- Select **Keys** → **Break Tangents** in the Graph Editor.

  With its tangency broken, the in and out tangent handles on the key can be independently edited.

- Select the tangent handle on the left side of the key and invoke the **Move Tool**.
- **MMB+drag** so that the tangent handle points toward the key at frame **1**.

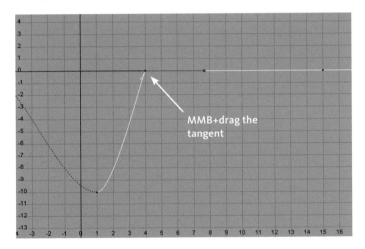

Key at frame 4 with edited broken tangency

5   Weight tangents

- Select the key at frame **23**.
- Select **Keys** → **Free Tangent weights** in the Graph Editor.

> **Note:** *When animation curves are non-weighted and you wish to make them weighted, simply select* **Curves** → **Weighted Tangents**. *Doing so specifies that the tangents on the currently selected animation curves can be weighted.*

- Select the tangent handle on the right side of the key.
- Hold down the **Shift** key, and then **MMB+drag** to adjust the shape of the curve.

  Changing the tangent weight adjusts the timing of the curve. In this case, the timing out of the key is made slower.

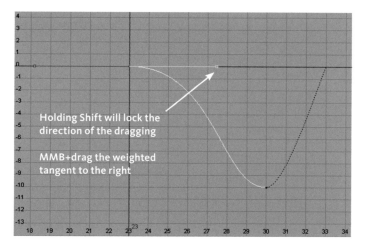

Key at frame 22 with tangent weight adjusted

6 Adjust the left foot

- Select the key at frame **18**, break its tangency, and point the left tangent handle at the key at frame **15**.
- Select the key at frame **8**, free its tangent weight, and adjust the shape.

  Make sure the animation curves for both feet have basically the same shape. If necessary, adjust the curves so they match each other.

7 Save your work

- Save the scene as *25-simple walk 05.ma*.

Animating the foot peeling off the ground

Now that you have animated the heel action, you will animate the foot peeling off the ground.

1 Left foot's ball rotation

- Go to frame **1**.
- Set *leftFootManip*'s **Ball Rot** value to **40**.

Note: *If you have set limits on your custom attributes that are inadequate, you must revise your setup to give proper animation ranges.*

- Set a key.
- **MMB+drag** the current time in the Time slider to frame **30**.

  MMB+dragging *in the Time slider will cause the time to change, but not the animation. You can then keyframe an attribute with the exact same value.*

- Set another key only for the *leftFootManip*'s **Ball Rot** attribute.
- Go to frame **25**.
- Set *leftFootManip*'s **Ball Rot** value to **0**.
- Set a key.

2   Right foot's ball rotation

- Go to frame **15**.
- Set *rightFootManip*'s **Ball Rot** value to **40**.
- Set a key.
- Go to frame **10**.
- Set *rightFootManip*'s **Ball Rot** value to **0**.
- Set a key.

3   Playback the animation

4   Flat animation curves

- Flatten the tangents of the **Ball Rot** animation curve for both feet.

5   Save your work

- Save the scene as *25-simple walk 06.ma*.

Hips motion

Now that Leon's basic forward motion has been established, you will animate the up and down motion as he walks.

1   **Enable Auto Key**

-   Turn **On** the **Auto Key** button located on the right side of the Time slider.

    The Auto Key option will set a keyframe automatically as soon as you change the values of keyed attributes.

Note: *There must be at least one keyframe on the changing attribute in order for Auto Key to set a keyframe.*

2   **Hips moving down keyframes**

-   Select *hipsManip* and **key** its **Translate Y** attribute at **–1** at frames **1, 15,** and **30.**

3   **Animate the hips moving up**

-   Advance to the frame where the left foot passed the right foot, at frame **8.**

-   **Move** *hipsManip* up on the **Y-axis** by **0.5** units.

    A key is automatically set on this attribute.

-   **MMB+drag** to frame **23** in the Time slider.

Note: *Since you didn't change the attribute's value in this step, Auto Key did not keyframe the attribute for you. Thus, you need to set a keyframe manually.*

-   Set a key on the *hipsManip*'s **Y-axis** attribute in the Channel Box.

4   **Weight shift**

Now you will animate Leon's side-to-side motion so that it looks like he's shifting his weight on the grounded foot.

-   Go to frame **8.**

-   Select *hipsManip* and set its **Translate X** to **–1.**

-   Select *hipsOverrideManip* and set its **Rotate Z** to **–5.**

Weight shift at frame 8

5   **Advance to the weight shift frame**

- Go to frame **23**.

- Select *hipsManip* and set its **Translate X** to **1**.

- Select *hipsOverrideManip* and set its **Rotate Z** to **5.**

6   **Play the animation**

- Increase the **playback range** to **1** to **120** and playback the animation.

7   **Save your work**

- Save the scene as *25-simple walk 07.ma*.

Compensating for Leon's center of gravity

Now that you have animated Leon's side-to-side action, it's a good time to adjust the movement of his feet and body to compensate for his shifting center of gravity. First you will adjust his feet.

1   Lifted left foot

- Select *leftFootManip* and go to frame **8**.

- Set its **Translate X** value to **−0.25**.

- Set its **Y-Rotation** attribute so the foot points a little bit outward.

- Set a breakdown key for these attributes by highlighting them in the Channel Box; then **RMB** and select **Breakdown Selected**.

Note: *You are using a breakdown key because the other keys you set for this object at frame 8 were breakdown keys.*

2   Lifted right foot

- Select *rightFootManip* and advance to frame **23**.

- Set its **Translate X** value to **0.25**.

- Set its **Rotation** attribute so the foot points a little bit outward.

- Set a breakdown key for these attributes.

3   Spine side-to-side motion

- Select *spineManip*.

- Go to frame **8**.

- Set *spineManip*'s **Translate Z** to **−0.2**.

- Advance to frame **23**.

- Set *spineManip*'s **Translate Z** to **0.2**.

  This step will compensate inversely for the hips motion.

4   Adjust the head

- Select *neckManip*.

- Go to frame **8**.

- Set *neckManip*'s **Rotate Y** to **5**.

- Advance to frame **23**.

- Set *neckManip*'s **Rotate Y** to **−5**.

  This step will compensate inversely for the spine motion.

5   **Play the animation**

6   **Adjust the curves as necessary**

7   **Save your work**
- Save the scene as *25-simple walk 08.ma*.

Put one foot in front of the other

As you watch Leon's animation, you will notice that he walks strangely, not putting one foot in front of the other. You will now correct that.

1   **Left foot motion**
- Select *leftFootManip*.
- In the Graph Editor, highlight its **Translate X** animation curve.
- Select the keys that have zero values at frames **1**, **15**, and **30**.
- In the **Value Field** at the top of the Graph Editor, enter **−0.5** and press **Enter**.

2   **Right foot motion**
- Select *rightFootManip*.
- In the Graph Editor, highlight its **Translate X** animation curve.
- Select the keys that have zero values at frames **1**, **15**, and **30**.
- In the **Selected Key's Value** field at the top of the Graph Editor, enter **0.5** and press **Enter**.

3   **Play the animation**

4   **Adjust the curves as necessary**

Offset the hips timing

Leon's basic body motion is complete. Now is a good time to refine it a little by offsetting the timing of some of his actions.

1   **Offset animation curves**
- Select *hipsManip*.
- In the Graph Editor, select all of the animation curves.
- In the **Selected Key's Time** field, type **+=1**.

Lesson 25: A Simple Walk

Mathematical expressions such as += are very useful for adjusting the values of a curve as a whole. In this case, typing +=1 will push each key in the selected curves forward one frame in time. This function also works with subtraction, multiplication, and division.

2   Play the animation

3   Save your work

- Save the scene as *25-simple walk 09.ma*.

Animating Leon's arms

Leon's arms now need to swing at his side, and you will use FK rather than IK. Since Leon's arm joints weren't included in the *Leon* character set when it was created, they should be added before they are animated.

1   Go to frame 1

2   Select the elbow and shoulder joints for both arms

- Select the *Left* and *Right Arm* and *ForeArm* joints.

3   Add the arm joints to the Leon character set

- Select **Windows → Relationship Editors → Character Sets...**

- Select the *Leon* character set in the left column.

- Select **Edit → Add Objects To Character Set**.

  The rotation attributes of the arm joints are now part of the Leon character set.

4   Rotate the arms down

- Select the *LeftArm* and *RightArm* joints.

- If their **rotation** values are not zero, set them to be **0**.

- Set their **Rotate Z** attributes to **–75** degrees.

- Set their **Rotate X** attributes to **20** degrees.

5   Balance the arms back and forth

- Set the **Rotate Y** attribute of the *LeftArm* to **–30** degrees.

- Set the **Rotate Y** attribute of the *RightArm* joint to **30** degrees.

- **Key** the rotation for both joints by pressing **Shift+e**.

- **MMB+drag** to frame **30**.

- Press **Shift+e** again.

- Go to frame **15**.
- Set the **Rotate Y** attribute of the *LeftArm* joint to **30** degrees.
- Set the **Rotate Y** attribute of the *RightArm* joint to **–30** degrees.
- **Key** the rotation of both joints.

6 Balance the elbows

- Go to frame **1**.
- Set the **Rotate Y** for *LeftForeArm* to **–20** degrees.
- **Key** that attribute.
- **MMB+drag** to frame **30**.
- **Key Rotate Y** again.
- Go to frame **15**.
- Set a key for **Rotate Y** at **0** degrees.
- Go to frame **1**.
- Set **Rotate Y** for *RightForeArm* to **0** degrees and set a **key**.
- **MMB+drag** to frame **30**.
- Set a **key** for **Rotate Y** again.
- Go to frame **15**.
- Set a key for **Rotate Y** at **–20** degrees.

7 Cycle the animation

- Select the *Left* and *Right Arm* and *ForeArm* joints.
- **Cycle** their animation curves in the Graph Editor and correct the tangency as needed.

8 Offset the animation

- Select both *Arm* joints and offset their timing by using +=1.
- Select both *ForeArm* joints and offset their animation using +=3.

  Doing so will create a nice balancing effect on the arms, where the forearm moves slightly after its parent.

9 Playback the scene

Lesson 25: A Simple Walk

Leon's animated arms

10 Save your work

- Save the scene as *25-simple walk 10.ma*.

Buffer curves

When animating, you will often find it helpful to compare the results of a change made to an animation curve with the original curve. *Buffer curves* allow you to easily switch back and forth between two versions of the same attribute.

1 Create buffer curve snapshots

- Select both *ForeArm* joints

- Open the Graph Editor.

- Select all the animation curves.

- Select **Curves → Buffer Curve Snapshot**.

   Duplicates of the rotation curves have been saved into memory.

- Select **View → Show Buffer Curves**.

   You will not see a change at the moment as the buffer curves are in exactly the same position as the original curves.

2 Scale the curves

- Select **Edit → Scale → ☐**.

- **Reset** the **Scale Keys** options.

Project 07

- Set the **Value Scale/Pivot values** to **2.0** and **0.0**.

  *This will scale the values of the keys by a factor of **2.0**, using **0.0** as the scale pivot.*

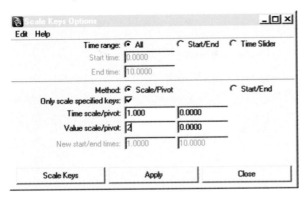

The Scale Keys window

- Click the **Scale Keys** button.

  The values of the curves have now been doubled, and the buffer curves show the original values.

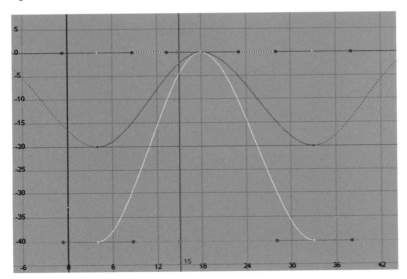

The animation curves and the buffer curves

3   Play the animation

4   Swap the buffer curves

The motion of the forearms is different, but it's hard to say whether it's better. You will now swap these curves with the buffer curves, which currently store the original rotation values.

- In the Graph Editor, select **Curves → Swap Buffer Curves**.

   The Graph Editor now uses curves with the original rotation values.

5   Play the animation

Decide which curve you prefer and set it as the current curve.

6   Save your work

- Save the scene as *25-simple walk 11.ma*.

Leon's overall animation

The principle advantage of this approach to animating a walk cycle is that once it is set up, it is easy to edit and modify the walk. You will now make adjustments to the curves to change how Leon walks.

1   Scale the hips and feet to create a faster and longer walk

- Select *hipsManip*, both *footManips* and both legs' poleVectors.
- Select the **Translate Z** animation curves for all these nodes in the Graph Editor.
- Select **Edit → Scale**.
- **Reset** the **Scale Keys** options.
- Set the **Value Scale/Pivot** values to **1.25** and **1.0**.

   *This will scale the values of the keys by a factor of **1.25**, using frame **1** as the scale pivot.*

- Click the **Scale Keys** button.

2   Play the animation

Leon now covers twenty-five percent more ground each strides in the same time.

3   Adjust Leon's vertical motion

Since Leon's knees now snap due to over extending, you will need to compensate with an up and down hips motion.

- Select *hipsManip*'s **Translate Y** curve in the Graph Editor.
- Select all the keys.

- Invoke the **Move Tool**.
- Hold down **Shift** and **click+drag** the keys down.
- Stop when Leon's knees no longer snap throughout the animation.

4   Scale keys manipulator

- Select *hipsOverrideManip*'s **Rotate Z** curve in the Graph Editor.
- From the main interface, select **Modify** → **Transformation Tools** → **Scale Tool** → ◻.
- Click on the Graph Editor's title bar.

  A new set of options will appear in the Scale Tool's option window.

- Select **Manipulator**.
- A box will appear around the selected curve.

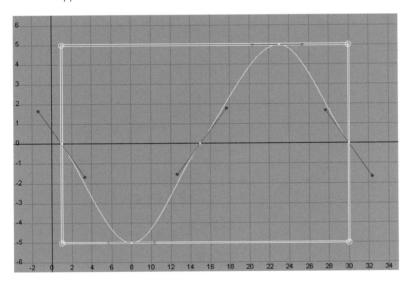

The scale keys manipulator

- **Playback** the animation and **scale** the curve by adjusting the manipulator.

  Be careful to scale the keys only up or down and not side to side, or the timing will be thrown off.

- Experiment with the scale values while the animation plays until you are happy with the motion.

5 Continue animating

Continue animating Leon until you are satisfied with his animation. Animate secondary animation on the eyes, clavicles, and fingers.

Refined Leon animation

Cleaning up

Although Leon was set up carefully, his character set contains unnecessary animation, called *static channels* (animation curves that represent no change in value). Any attribute that is included in the character set but has not been manipulated thus far will have static channels.

Now that Leon's walk is basically done, it's a good time to delete these channels. Deleting the channels will have no effect on Leon's walk, but it will reduce the size of the scene file.

1 Delete the static channels

- Select **Edit → Delete All By Type → Static Channels**.

All the static animation curves in the scene are now deleted.

2 Save your work

- Save the scene as *25-simple walk 12.ma*.

Conclusion

Animation is a key part of character rigging because a rig must be tested and verified as it is being put together.

You will want to have a high degree of confidence in a rig before you go too far down the path of skinning and building higher orders of control. Understanding the animator's needs is also an important function of the character rigger.

In this lesson, you learned how to animate a simple walk cycle. Animation here was done in a rudimentary fashion using low resolution geometry, but it is a good method for streamlining the performance. You also learned about character sets, the best friend of any animator.

In the next lesson, you will learn about file referencing.

Lesson 26
References

File referencing

File referencing allows users to assemble multiple objects, shading materials, and animation into a scene without importing the files into the scene. That is, the contents that appear in the scene are read or referenced from pre-existing files that remain separate and unopened. File referencing makes possible collaborative production in situations where multiple users need to work concurrently and share various assets in complex scenes.

For instance, in a production context you might have several scenes for accessories, background, and character (ABCs). Those scenes are usually assembled into shots, scenes, or sequences. Without using references, all the ABCs would need to be duplicated, and depending on how many shots you have in the project, it could result in lots of wasted disk space and a lot of work in order to replace or update one of the ABCs.

A scene file that references other files lower in the hierarchy is known as a *parent scene*. A parent scene reads or references other files that make up a scene from where they reside on disk (or on a network). These files are known as referenced *child scenes*.

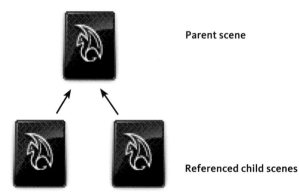

Parent scene

Referenced child scenes

Logic of file referencing

Even though the referenced child scenes appear within the currently open parent scene, they remain separate from the currently open parent scene at all times. When the currently open parent scene file is saved, all the connections to the child scene are saved, but any referenced scene data is not saved within it.

> **Note:** *In the case of a parent scene referencing a character that was animated, only the animation data is saved with the parent scene. That way, the parent scene size remains very small.*

Create references

In the following exercise, you will prepare the animation scene file to be used all along this project. To do so, you will reference the required ABCs.

1 Scene file

- Create a new scene.

2 Create a reference

- Select **File** → **Create Reference** → ☐.

- In the option window, set the following:

    Use Namespaces to **On;**

    Resolve all nodes with this string: *leon.*

- Click the **Reference** button.

    A browse dialog will appear, letting you choose the file to reference.

- Select the scene named *leon lores.ma* which can be found in Project 7 of the *support_files.*

- Click the **Reference** button.

    Leon is loaded into memory and displayed in the current scene.

3 Outliner

- Open the Outliner.

    Notice that the Leon nodes were prefixed with leon: (that namespace was defined in the previous step).

- Select a Leon node in the Outliner and press the **Delete** key.

    An error message will be displayed specifying that objects from a reference file are read-only and thus cannot be deleted.

Note: *In the Outliner, the small blue diamond shape on the object icon tells you that this node is part of a reference. In the Hypergraph, the name of the node is red when it is part of a reference.*

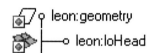

The diamond icon in the Outliner

4 Create a deferred reference

- Select **File** → **Create Reference** → ❑.
- In the option window, set the following:

    Deferred to **On**;

    Resolve all nodes with this string: *squirrel.*

- **Browse** for the scene called *squirrel lores.ma.*

    The reference is added to the scene but is not loaded.

5 Reference Editor

- Select **File** → **Reference Editor.**

    The Reference Editor is the place where you can see all references in the current scene.

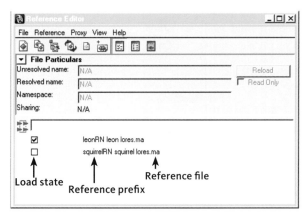

The Reference Editor

- **Load** the *squirrel* reference by turning **On** its checkbox.

    The squirrel is loaded in the current scene.

> **Note:** *By checking* **On** *and* **Off** *the checkboxes, you can load and unload references.*

6 Fish reference

- Select **File** → **Create Reference** → ❑.
- In the option window, set the following:

    Deferred to **Off**;

    Resolve all nodes with this string: *fish.*

- **Browse** for the scene called *catfish lores.ma*.

  The starry catfish is now loaded in the scene.

7   Background reference

- Select **File** → **Create Reference** → ☐.
- In the option window, set **Resolve all nodes with this string**: *background*.
- **Browse** for the scene called *background.ma*.

8   Save your work

- Save the scene as *26-references 01.ma*.

Temporary references

You will now create a temporary reference file with only a simple cube in it. Doing so will let you create a scene with all the references needed, but with stand-ins for objects that are not yet modeled.

1   Scene file

- Create a new scene.

2   Stand-in

- **Create** a primitive cube.
- **Rename** the cube as *boat*.

  Later in this exercise, you will come back and model Leon's boat.

3   Save the scene

- Save the scene as *boat.ma*.

4   Open the parent scene file

- Open the scene called *26-references 01.ma*.

  Notice that each child reference is being loaded at this time.

5   Boat reference

- Select **File** → **Create Reference** → ☐.
- In the option window, set **Resolve all nodes with this string**: *boat*.
- **Browse** for the scene called *boat.ma* you have just created.

6 Select the reference's contents

- Select **File → Reference Editor...**
- Highlight the *boat* reference.
- In the Reference Editor, select **File → Select File Contents**.

  The reference objects created earlier are now selected.

7 Place the objects

- **Move** the *fish*'s master node up in the sky.
- **Move** the *boat* cube back in the water.
- **Move** *Leon* 's master node next to the boat.
- **Move** the *squirrel*'s master node next to Leon's pocket.

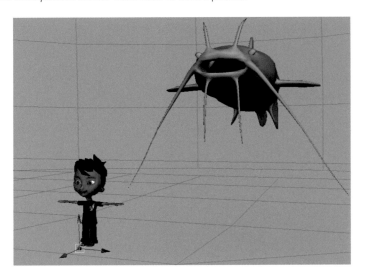

The scene is taking shape

8 Save your work

- Save the scene as *26-references 02.ma*.

Update a reference

You have placed the various ABCs in the parent scene, but it would be nice to have the boat modeled. Here, you can either take some time to model a small fishing boat, or you can use a saved scene. After this exercise, the next time you will open the parent scene, the boat will be loaded.

1   Scene file

- Open the scene called *boat.ma*.

    This contains a primitive cube standing in for the boat.

2   Model the boat

- Take some time to model a small fishing boat from the cube.

OR

- **Import** the file *boatFinal.ma* in your scene.

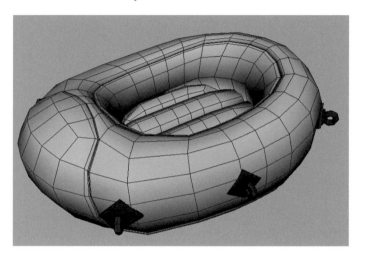

The boat model

3   Clean up

- Select **Edit → Delete All by Type → History**.

- Open the Outliner and delete obsolete nodes, such as the original stand-in cube.

4   Boat hierarchy

When you created the stand-in file, you named the temporary cube *boat*. Since you moved the cube in the parent scene, if you want the new boat to be moved to the same location, you must call the group *boat*.

- **Rename** the mesh to *boat*.

OR

- **Rename** the group which contains all the geometry to *boat*.

> **Note:** *It is important to understand that a parent scene saves only the names and attribute connections. When you update a reference, it is important to keep t he names and attributes of the reference identical. If Maya doesn't find certain nodes or attributes, it will not be able to connect their related data and you might end up losing information.*

5 Layer

It would be nice to have the boat on a layer so that you can set its visibility in the parent scene.

- **Create** a new layer and rename it *geometryLayer*.

- **Add** the *boat* geometry to the new layer.

6 Save your work

- Save the scene and overwrite *boat.ma*.

7 Open the parent scene

Now that the reference has been modified, the next time the parent scene referencing that scene is loaded, the new objects will be updated correctly.

- Open the scene called *26-references 02.ma*.

  The boat is in the same position as the stand-in cube because it has the same name and attributes.

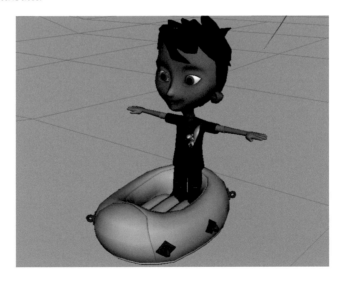

The boat is now updated in the parent scene

Note: *If the parent scene is already open, you can also reload the reference through the Reference Editor.*

Replace references

When you created the setups for Leon and the squirrel, you created low-resolution and high-resolution files. Later in this project, when you have animated the characters, you will want to see the animation on the high-resolution models. Since the high- and low-resolution files have the same rig names and attributes, you will be able to switch the references seamlessly.

The following example will show you how to replace a reference.

1 Reference Editor

- Still in the parent scene, select **File → Reference Editor.**

- Highlight the *squirrel* reference.

- Select **Reference → Replace Reference**.

  A file browser is now displayed, where you can specify the file to replace the current squirrel reference.

- Select the file *squirrel hires.ma.*

- Click on the **Reference** button.

  The high-resolution squirrel is now loaded and correctly placed in the scene. Also notice that the squirrel reference scene has changed to squirrel hires.ma in the Reference Editor.

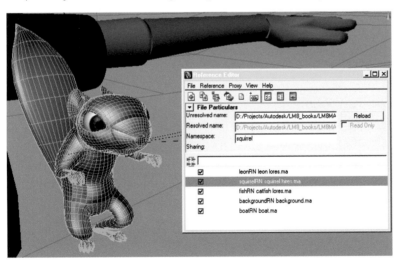

The high-resolution squirrel reference

2 Save your work

- Save the scene as *26-references 03.ma*.

Switch references in a text editor

It is nice that you can switch references within Maya, but sometimes it can be a long and tedious job. For instance, you would have to open the parent scene (and load all of its references), replace the reference (which loads the new reference), and then save the parent scene.

By using the Maya ASCII format, which saves the scene in plain text, you can replace a reference file by editing the parent scene in any text editor.

The following example shows how to replace the current squirrel with its low-resolution scene, without even opening Maya.

1 Scene file in a Text Editor

- **Open** the scene called *26-references 03.ma* in a text editor.

2 Locate the reference lines

- At the top of the file content, **locate** the following lines:

```
file -rdi 1 -ns "squirrel" -rfn "squirrelRN" "./scenes/squirrel
hires.ma";

file -r -ns "squirrel" -dr 1 -rfn "squirrelRN" "./scenes/squirrel
hires.ma";
```

Note: *The path to the squirrel file might be different, so that it points at the file on your computer or network.*

3 Replace the reference lines

- **Replace** the scene name from *squirrel hires.ma* to *squirrel lores.ma* as follows:

```
file -rdi 1 -ns "squirrel" -rfn "squirrelRN" "./scenes/squirrel
lores.ma";

file -r -ns "squirrel" -dr 1 -rfn "squirrelRN" "./scenes/squirrel
lores.ma";
```

4 Save your changes

5 Open the scene in Maya

- **open** the scene called *26-references 03.ma*.

> **Tip:** *If you have the scene already open in Maya, reopen it but do not save. That would overwrite the edits made in the text editor.*

Selective preload

Sometimes it is important to be able to open a scene file without all of its references. In order to load only chosen references, you must enable an option before opening a scene.

1   File open options

- Select **File → Open Scene → ❑**.

- In the option window, set to **On** the **Selective preload** option.

  Next time you will open a scene file with references, the following window will appear and ask you which references should be loaded.

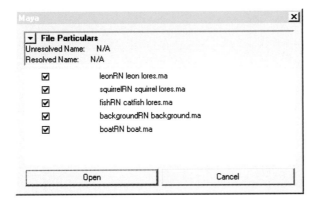

The selective preload option window

Conclusion

Using references in a production environment or even to build a simple scene is a great workflow that can save you quite a lot of time. In this lesson, you learned the different ways of using file references and you now understand their purpose and usage.

In the next lesson, you will set up some constraints between the boat, Leon, and the squirrel.

Constrain	
Point	▢
Aim	▢
Orient	▢
Scale	▢
Parent	▢
Geometry	▢
Normal	▢
Tangent	▢
Pole Vector	▢
Remove Target	▢
Set Rest Position	
Modify Constrained Axis	

Lesson 27
Constraints

In this lesson, you will use constraints to have one object follow another. Constraints are used
often in animation, and a user must understand their purpose and setup in order to control

Constraint types

The numerous constraint types are outlined here:

Point constraint

A point constraint causes an object to move to and follow the position of an object, or the average position of several objects. This is useful for having an object match the motion of other objects.

Aim constraint

An aim constraint keeps an object aimed toward another object.

Orient constraint

An orient constraint matches the orientation of one object to one or more other objects. Orient constraints are useful for keeping objects aligned.

Scale constraint

A scale constraint matches the scale of one object to one or more other objects. Scale constraints are useful for keeping objects the same size.

Parent constraint

A parent constraint relates the position (translation and rotation) of one object to another object, so that they behave as if part of a parent-child relationship.

Geometry constraint

A geometry constraint restricts an object's pivot to a NURBS surface, NURBS curve, subdivision surface, or polygonal surface.

Normal constraint

A normal constraint keeps an object's orientation so that it aligns with the normal vectors of a NURBS or polygonal surface.

Tangent constraint

A tangent constraint keeps an object moving along, and oriented to, a curve. The curve provides the path of the object's motion, and the object orients itself to point along the curve.

Pole vector constraint

A pole vector constraint causes the end of a pole vector to move to and follow the position of an object, or the average position of several objects.

Note: *Most of these constraints were already used in the rigging lessons, but were not intended for animation.*

Constrain Leon to the boat

You will now constrain Leon to the boat so you can animate it floating around.

1   Scene file

- Open the scene from the last lesson called *26-references 03.ma*.

2   Create a point constraint

- Select the *boat:boat*, then **Shift-select** *leon:master*.

Tip: *The object you want to be constrained must always be selected last.*

- Select **Constrain → Point Constraint → ❏**.
- **Reset** the options, and then click on the **Add** button.

  Leon will move to fit his pivot to that of the boat.

3   Test the constraint

- **Move** the *boat* around.

  You will notice that Leon is obeying the position of the boat, but not its rotations.

A point constraint

4 Undo the constraint

- **Undo** until Leon goes back to his original position.

5 Create a parent constraint using Maintain Offset

In the previous steps, you could clearly see that you would need to constrain Leon both in position and rotation. Instead of creating two constraints, one for translations and one for rotations, you will use the parent constraint, which simulates a parent-child relationship. You will also use the Maintain Offset option, which will prevent Leon's pivot from snapping to the pivot of the boat.

- **Move** and **rotate** Leon's *master* so it is correctly placed in the boat.

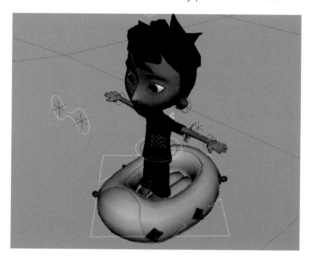

Correct position of Leon in the boat

- Select the *boat:boat*; then **Shift-select** *leon:master*.
- Select **Constrain → Parent Constraint → ❑**.
- **Reset** the options, and make sure **Maintain Offset** is set to **On**.
- Click the **Add** button.

Leon now maintains his offset to the boat and is properly constrained.

6 Save your work

- Save the scene as *27-constraints 01.ma*.

Constrain the squirrel to Leon's pocket

As another constraint setup, you will now constrain the squirrel in Leon's pocket. Using the following setup, you will be able to move the pet as needed within the pocket.

1 **Create a locator**

- **Create** a locator and rename it *pocketControl*.

- **Move** the *pocketControl* inside Leon's pocket.

- **Parent** the *pocketControl* to the top central pocket manipulator.

- **Freeze** the *pocketControl* attributes.

2 **Move the squirrel into position**

- **Move** and **rotate** the squirrel *master* so it is correctly placed in Leon's pocket.

- **Pose** the squirrel appropriately.

- **Move** the pocket manipulators to fix any interpenetration.

3 **Parent constraint**

- Select the *pocketControl*, and then **Shift-select** the squirrel *master*.

- Select **Constrain → Parent Constraint**.

  The squirrel is now constrained to the pocketControl, which is in turn parented to the pocket setup.

4 **Test the constraint**

- **Pose** Leon to see if the squirrel follows correctly.

- **Move** the top central pocket manipulator to see if the squirrel follows along.

The squirrel follows Leon's motion

Constraint weight

Every constraint has at least one weight attribute. There can be multiple weight attributes if you define multiple targets on a single constrained object. These attributes determine the percentage of weight coming from a target object.

When the weight is set to **0**, that specific object target is said to be disabled. When the weight is set to **1**, that specific object target is said to be fully enabled.

To see a constraint's weight attribute, select the constrained object, then highlight the constraint node in the **Inputs** section of the Channel Box. The weight attribute is usually labeled with the name of the target object, followed by the weight index (**W0** for instance).

In this exercise, you will add the boat as a target object to the parent constraint on the squirrel. Doing so will allow you to blend the squirrel position from holding the pocket to standing on the boat.

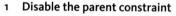

> **Note:** *Constraints' weights are to be used to blend between target objects and not between constraint and animation. You will be blending constraints and animation in the next lesson.*

1 Disable the parent constraint

- Select the squirrel's *master*.
- In the Channel Box, under the **Inputs** section, highlight the *parentConstraint* node.
- Set the **Pocket Control W0** attribute to **0.0**.

  Doing so turns **Off** the constraint on the pocketControl object and places the master back at its position before creating the constraint.

2 Position the hand

- **Move** and **rotate** the squirrel *master* so it holds on the front of the boat.

3 Parent constraint

- Select the *boat*, then **Shift-select** the squirrel's *master*.
- Select **Constrain → Parent Constraint**.

  In the Channel Box, you can now see a second target weight on the parentConstraint node called **Boat W1**.

4 Tweak the weights' attributes

- Set the **Pocket Control W0** attribute to **1.0** and the **Boat W1** attribute to **0.0**.

  The squirrel is now in the pocket.

- Set the **Pocket Control W0** attribute to **0.0** and the **Boat W1** attribute to **1.0**.

  The squirrel is now on the front of the boat.

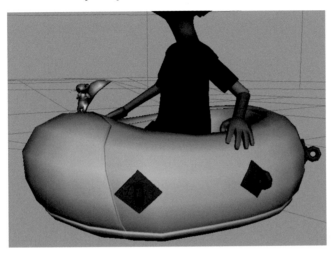

The squirrel can now be either in the pocket or on the boat

5   **Constraint interpolation type**

Blending between targets can sometimes be tricky because the constraint node might interpolate the rotations of the constrained object in an inappropriate way (flipping). If you notice this while changing the weight attributes, the following should help solve the problem:

- **Repeat** the last step, but set keyframes on the weight attributes at frame 1 and 10.
- **Scrub** in the Timeline to see the interpolation between the two targets.

  The squirrel's rotations might be twisted up as it transit between the targets.

- In the Channel Box with the constraint highlighted, change the **Interp Type** attribute to one of its possible options, such as **Average**, **Shortest**, **Longest**, or **No Flip**.

6   **Save your work**

- Save the scene as *27-constraints 02.ma*.

Conclusion

In this lesson, you experimented with a few constraints that will be used throughout this project. Key concepts such as the constraint types, the Maintain Offset option, and the weight attributes were covered.

In the next lesson, you will animate a complete scene.

Lesson 28
Character Animation

In this lesson, you will animate Leon and the squirrel in a boat, looking at the stars. This exercise will give you experience with common tasks in character animation such as blocking animation, interaction with an object, anticipation, and follow-through.

In this lesson you will learn the following:

- About the animation workflow;
- How to study motion as a guideline for the animation;
- How to block your animation;
- How to switch and animate constrained objects;
- How to playblast your animation;
- How to optimize playback refresh.

Animation workflow

This lesson is an outline of a suggested animation workflow that you can follow— or you can take this any direction you choose. Whichever workflow you use, there are several helpful animation tools and techniques that you might want to keep in mind.

Storyboarding

The storyboard is where you hope to find as many problem areas and special requirements as possible. Here is where you note and plan for timing issues that may occur.

For the particular animation created here, following is a short text description of the motion you will attempt to achieve:

> Leon is hopping into his boat, where his squirrel awaits him. As they float away, a huge starry fish approaches in the sky. The squirrel sees the fish and jumps into Leon's pocket. Leon turns his head to figure out why his squirrel is scared. The huge fish passes over them, causing a strong wind to blow. Leon, unbalanced in his boat, stares at the sky with his eyes wide open. The squirrel slowly pops out of the pocket, completely stunned.

Motion study

Once you have completed the storyboard to assess the basic timing and actions of the character, you need to evaluate how the characters need to move.

"When in doubt, go to the motion study," is a refrain of professionals at leading production companies. There is no substitute for learning character animation from real live examples. To do this, there is no better example than your own body.

Throughout this lesson, try to stand up and move the way you would like your character to. As you are moving and repeating the movement, concentrate on the different parts of your body and the timing of your motion.

You can also use digitized video of a performance as flipbooks and bring them into Maya as image planes. Fcheck serves as a great method for quickly viewing the reference motion. While not as fast, image planes work very well as a frame-by-frame placement guide.

Blocking

Before setting keys for the detailed motion, you will block the shot. Blocking a shot consists of setting key poses every 5–10 frames to rough out the animation. Working with character sets is a good way to set general keyframes on all attributes of your characters.

For scenes where the motion is not repetitive, it is important to study the extreme positions the character gets into. These are the poses that really define the feel of the animation.

After blocking, you will review the motion, asking the following questions:

- Do the motion and timing work in this scene?
- Is the motion too fast/slow?
- Is there continuity with other shots?

Don't worry about the motion details until you are comfortable with the generalized motion.

In-betweens and breakdowns

Once you have finalized the blocked motion, it's time to start rounding out the motions. The in-between is responsible for creating the interpolations from one blocked key to the next. It shapes the motion away from the linear point-to-point motion you have established.

In-betweens can occur every 3 to 5 frames, or as needed. When your character is moving very fast, the in-betweens could occur on every frame. At this stage, you are not concerned with perfect motion. The resulting motion will look better than the blocked motion, but it will still need some fine-tuning. Study your own movement or a reference video; you may be surprised where and when these keys occur.

Consider using breakdown keys for your in-between keyframes. Breakdown keys are designed to be placed between blocked poses so they can later be moved in the Timeline to maintain the relationship between the standard keyframes. Although adjusting overall timing may not be used as much if you are working straight from a motion test, it is still a good idea to get in the habit of using breakdown keys. It will also be useful if you decide to change the timing of your animation later on.

Also, consider using sub-characters for your in-between poses so you don't key all of the attributes in the entire character set. A main character set can be created to block out the animation, while sub-characters can be used to key specific parts of the character. For example, the legs and hips can be their own sub-character that controls all of the lower body motion.

When in-betweening, try to avoid keying all of the attributes on an object as you did when you blocked out the motion for the animation. In some places, you may still want to set a key on all the keyable attributes. However, in more focused places, you will want to key only the selected object. Use the **RMB** in the Channel Box to key individual attributes by selecting **Key Selected** or **Breakdown Selected**. This will result in liner curves in the Graph Editor. The fewer keys you set in this phase, the easier it is to make major changes later.

After you have completed a cursory in-between, save this file as your rough in-between. If you need to make major changes to the animation, this is where you will most likely start.

The motion study is the chief guide for adding in-betweens. Some of the main movements that may escape the casual observer have been pointed out. This is a largely self-guided exercise based on motion study and your creative interpretation. Decide for yourself whether to use standard keyframes or breakdown keys.

Lesson 28: Character Animation

After the in-betweens are finished, you will go back through and address the rough edges and start working on the details that make the animation interesting.

Working with the characters

Once you have animation ideas and a basic storyboard done, it is time to start working with the characters in 3D. Following are some guidelines for your animation:

- Frame 1: Everyone is in position with Leon having one foot in the boat.
- Frame 15: Leon pushes and hops into the boat; the squirrel is looking at him.
- Frame 30: Leon sits in the boat. The starry fish is getting closer.
- Frame 45: The squirrel points at the fish in the sky behind Leon.
- Frame 55: The squirrel anticipates jumping. Leon anticipates turning his head.
- Frame 65: The squirrel jumps into Leon's pocket. Leon turns his head.
- Frame 75: The huge fish plunges over them. The boat starts rocking.
- Frame 85: Leon is pushed by the wind and the squirrel sticks his head out of the pocket.
- Frame 105: The fish goes out of the frame. Both Leon and the squirrel are stunned.

 Note: *This is only a guide to where the extreme poses could be. If you want, set up a list of the poses you wish to block.*

1 Scene file

- Open the scene file from the previous lesson called *27-constraints 02.ma*.

2 Create character set

As you can see if you are using the support files, the character sets have already been created for you in a way similar to what you did in Lesson 25. If you require any other character or sub-character sets, feel free to implement them.

3 First frame

Leon is getting ready to push and hop into the boat. The squirrel is posed on the tip of the boat.

- Go to frame **1**.
- Set the squirrel's parent constraint to be on the boat.
- **Pose** all characters appropriately using the different nodes and manipulators.
- Set a **key** for all characters by making their character sets active and hitting the **s** key.

Frame 1

Tip: *Don't bother at this point with too much detail. Parts such as fingers, tail, eyes, etc. are subject to change as you continue animating the scene and should be done last.*

4   At large

Leon has just pushed the boat and now stands in it on one leg. The squirrel is looking around.

- Go to frame **15**.

- Pose all characters appropriately.

- Set a **key** for all character sets.

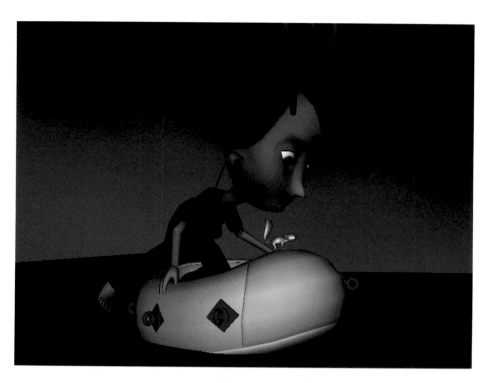

Frame 15

5   Sitting in the boat

Leon should now get down on his knees in the boat. As the boat turns, the squirrel must anticipate the pointing at the fish. It should do so by actually moving slightly in the opposite way of pointing. The fish should be slowly swimming closer.

- Go to frame **30**.

- Pose all characters appropriately.

- Set a **key** for all character sets.

Frame 30

6   Squirrel points at star fish

The squirrel will now jump up and stretch, pointing at the starry fish. Leon should be
surprised by his pet's movements. The boat keeps on moving in a steady drifting way.

- Go to frame **45**.

- Pose all characters appropriately.

- Set a **key** for all character sets.

Lesson 28: Character Animation

Frame 45

7 Anticipation

The squirrel should now anticipate jumping into Leon's pocket. At the same time, Leon should be anticipating turning his head. Remember that anticipation is most likely to be in the opposite direction from the motion, like a spring being compressed before its release.

- Go to frame **55**.
- Pose all characters appropriately.
- Set a **key** for all character sets.

Frame 55

8   Jump in the pocket

The squirrel jumps in mid-air, aiming for the pocket. At the same time, Leon starts turning his head toward the fish.

This step will require some constraint animation because the squirrel should move from the boat to the pocket.

- Go to frame **65**.

- Pose all characters appropriately except the squirrel, and set a keyframe.

- Select the squirrel *master*, which is constrained to the boat and the pocket.

- Go to frame **55**.

- Set a keyframe on the *master* in **translation** and **rotation**.

   This is the last good position of the squirrel on the boat.

- Go to frame **65**.

- **Move** the squirrel's *master* up in the air and set a keyframe in **translation** and **rotation**.

The squirrel has now been animated to fly off between frames **55** *and* **65**, *but the constraint seems to be off prior to frame* **55**. *This is because Maya has created a special setup to let you use both constraints and animation on the squirrel.*

- Locate the **Blend Squirrel:squirrel** attribute on the squirrel *master*.

  This attribute specifies blending between the animation and constraint. When this attribute is at **0**, *the animation will prevail; when it's at* **1**, *the constraint takes over.*

- Go to frame **55**.

- Set a keyframe on the **Blend** attribute to **1**.

- Go to frame **65**.

- Set a keyframe on the **Blend** attribute to **0**.

  The animation on the master is now correct up to frame **65**.

- **Pose** the squirrel, which should look like it's flying to the pocket. Try not to move the squirrel away from his master node too much.

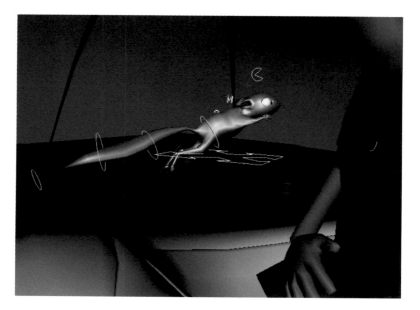

The squirrel at frame 65

9   Squirrel gets in the pocket

The squirrel should now plunge into the pocket. You should not worry here about any interpenetration. In fact, it is recommended to hide the squirrel into Leon's chest in order to place it appropriately for when it will pop back out head first. You can also place Leon's hand over the pocket to hide the way the squirrel gets into the pocket.

- Go to frame **75**.
- **Key** the squirrel's master closer to the pocket.
- **Pose** all characters appropriately.
- Set a **key** for all character sets.

Frame 75

10   The fish passes by

The fish should now be right over Leon. You should have Leon looking above, and the boat should be at quite an angle because of the wind. You should hide the squirrel completely in Leon's chest and get it ready to take its head out of the pocket.

- Go to frame **85**.
- **Pose** all characters appropriately.
- Set a **key** for all character sets.

You also need to switch the constraint from the boat to the pocket for the squirrel's master. The following will do this.

- Set a key at frame **85** on the **Pocket Control W0** weight to **1** and **Boat W1** weight to **0**.
- Set a key at frame **84** on the **Pocket Control W0** weight to **0** and **Boat W1** weight to **1**.

  Doing so switches the weight of the constraint in a single frame. You must now blend the squirrel's animation from the animation back to the constraint.

• Set a keyframe on the **Blend** attribute to **0** at frame **84**.

• Set a keyframe on the **Blend** attribute to **1** at frame **85**.

*The squirrel's constraint now blends back to its active constraint state for frame **85**.*

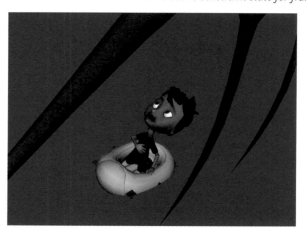

Frame 85

11 Squirrel pops out

As the final blocking pose, you shall take the squirrel's head out, looking at the fish. The fish should also go out of frame.

• Go to frame **105**.

• Pose both characters appropriately.

• Set a **key** for both character sets.

Frame 105

1 Save your work

- Save your scene as *28-animation 01.ma*.

Playblast

A *playblast* is a way to view and evaluate your animation quickly. It is a very fast screen grab that captures the animation of the current camera as it is currently displayed. Thus, you can see your animation in Wireframe mode, Shaded mode, or Shaded-with-Texture mode (which may take a little longer to calculate). The purpose of this tool is to get real-time playback by using a compressed movie file.

At each stage of creating the animation, you should playblast your animation to create motion tests and to evaluate your work in real time.

The following steps will create a playblast of your scene.

1 Playblast the animation

- Position the view to an advantageous position to see all the action.
- Set the playback range to go from frame **1** to frame **105**.
- Display the model as you would like, with textures for instance.
- Select **Window** → **Playblast** → **□**.

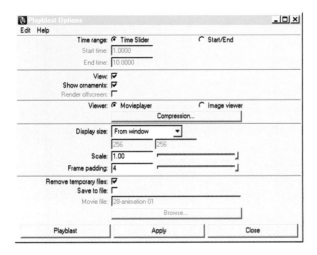

Playblast options

- Click the Playblast button.
- Wait for the playblast to be complete.

  Once the playblast is over, the movie it created will be played for you.

Tip: *Be careful to not put other windows in front of the Maya interface. Since the playblast is a screen capture, that would stop the playblast of your scene.*

- View the playblast, scrub through, and note areas that need work.

Fine-tune the motion

Once you are comfortable with the in-betweens, you can start to fine-tune the motion. This is the stage that never ends. This is where you can find yourself tweaking and adding keys on every frame. You want to avoid doing that as much as possible. Here are some things to keep in mind that will hopefully keep you on target.

Working in layers of refinements

Work on major keys and in-betweens first, and then secondary and tertiary keys next, working in layers of refinement.

Keep your keyframes organized

Get your main keyframes looking as good as possible first; then break down into the next layer of in-betweens. Once this layer looks good, go to the next layer. You will find you have intimate knowledge of these milestone keys, instead of having random keys scattered all over the timeline.

Adjust the animation curves in the Graph Editor

In the Graph Editor, you can get a lot of mileage out of a key by working with the tangency or method of interpolation. Keeping keys on whole frames makes for much cleaner curve management and editing.

Remove superfluous keys

Remove keys that don't seem to be contributing or were made ineffective. This is best done in the Graph Editor, where you can see the direct result on the curve by removing the key. If you make a mistake, simply undo the removal.

Testing

Test in the work area and in playblasts. It is often a good idea to take a break while you build a movie. Come back to the computer a little fresher to view the movie and plan the changes you will make.

Add subtle motions to major and minor joints and control points

You will often find that after the basic in-betweens are completed, it is time to look at parts of the character you have not keyed at all. The hands and head are very important, as are the shoulders and hip joints that will contribute to the motion of the attached joints. Rotations and translations in all dimensions are what create the subtleties of realistic movement.

Offset the motion of joints to achieve secondary motion

Offsetting is the act of delaying a joint's motion in relation to the surrounding joints. This is often seen as a breaking movement. When an arm, for example, moves toward an object that it wants to pick up, it does not move in unison at once toward its target. Rather, it will break at the main joint (elbow) first, then at the wrist, and finally the fingers.

Consider another example— the hand. When you make a fist, all of your fingers do not close at once. Some fingers may begin to close ahead of others while some may start late but finish first. These subtle movements and accelerations are at the heart of realistic motion.

High-resolution models

When your animation is quite refined, you might want to look at the high-resolution characters in order to track final modifications to be done.

Utilizing what you learned in Lesson 27, use the Reference Editor to replace the low-resolution characters with the high-resolution characters. You can then playblast your animation and see if there are places on the characters that behave differently than the low-resolution models.

Once that is done, you can call the animation final and try rendering the scene to see the final results.

A final render

Optimization

There are several options for optimizing feedback when setting up the animation of a character.

Display optimization

NURBS and subD geometry can be viewed at many levels of accuracy. By selecting the geometry and then pressing **1**, **2**, or **3** on the keyboard, you can select between coarse, medium, and fine display accuracy. This will not affect how the geometry is rendered, only how it will display. There are several options under the Display menu that affect the performance of Maya's display.

NURBS and subDs smoothness

Under the **Display** menu you will find a sub-menu for **NURBS** and **Subdiv Surfaces** smoothness. These options control how these surfaces are displayed.

- **Hull** displays the selected geometry in the crudest form. From the option box you can adjust the coarseness of the hull display.

- **Rough**, **Medium**, and **Fine** are as you would expect and are selected by pressing the **1**, **2**, or **3** key on the keyboard. The option box for each of these allows you to decide whether you want this mode to affect the selected object or all objects.

- **Custom Smoothness** is a user defined setting for NURBS display smoothness only. There are many customizable settings in the option box allowing for almost infinite combinations to suit your needs.

Fast interaction

Display → **Object Display** → **Fast Interaction** enables the user to interact with the scene more quickly by temporarily changing the resolution of the geometry while the scene is being manipulated, and then switching back to the higher resolution after the scene has settled. This setting will also improve playback of animation in the timeline, but be prepared for some degraded-looking geometry.

Animation preferences

In **Window** → **Settings/Preferences** → **Preferences**, the **Timeline** section has a few settings that will influence the way Maya plays your animation. In the **Playback** section you have options to change the following:

Update View

Update the **Active** panel or **All** panels.

Looping

Determines the **Looping** method.

Playback Speed

Play every frame: Maya will play every frame regardless of frame rate settings.

Real-time: This setting forces Maya to play back at the frame rate that is set in **Time** in the **Settings** section. The video frame rate is 30fps and film is 24fps.

Half /Twice: Maya plays back at half or twice the specified frame rate.

Other: Maya will playback at a user defined percentage of the specified frame rate.

In the **Settings** section you also have options to change:

Time: Maya can playback at a wide range of frame rates.

Performance settings

Under **Window → Settings/Preferences → Performance Settings**, there are several other options that you can set to improve playback speed.

Conclusion

In this lesson, you animated characters interacting. Understanding the animation process and the animation toolset is a must for every animator. The animation process usually will involve a blocking course and then cycles of refinement until the performance is as good as the schedule permits.

Your characters also used character sets to aid keyframing their attributes. A typical fully articulated character can contain hundreds of attributes that will need to be keyed.

Optimization is also important for maintaining an animatable environment. Work to keep the interface light so there is not too much waiting time for the application to refresh.

The next lesson will be a quick overview about importing audio into your scene.

Lesson 28: Character Animation

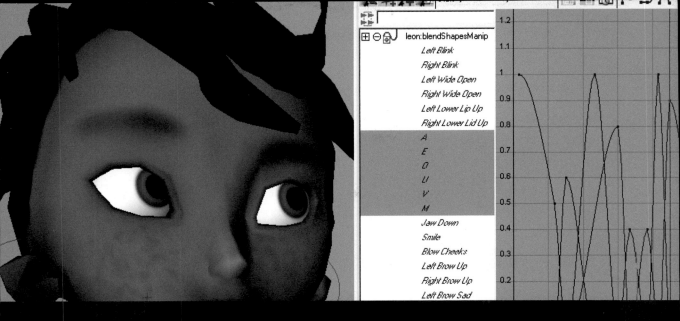

Lesson 29
Lip-synch

In this lesson, you will import an audio file and have Leon lip-synch to it. Even though this lesson is quite short, there is a lot of experience to gain in lip-synching.

Project 07

Animating Leon

You will now use Leon's blend shapes to lip-synch over a simple recorded audio file. Work through the following steps to create the lip-synch animation, but keep in mind that experimentation is the key to good lip-synching.

1 Scene file

- Create a new scene.
- **Reference** the file *leon lores.ma*.

2 Import an audio file

In the *sound* directory of the current project's support files, you will find a simple audio track of Leon talking.

- Select **File → Import**.
- Select *audio.wav* from the *sound* directory.

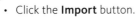

Note: *Make sure the file type is set to* **Best Guess (*.*)**.

- Click the **Import** button.

The sound file is imported in the scene but is not currently active.

- **Load** the sound file by pressing **RMB** in the timeline and selecting **Sound → audio.**

The waveform will appear in the Timeline. To hear it in playback, you must set the **Playback Speed** *to* **Real Time** *in your animation preferences. You can also scrub in the Timeline to hear the audio.*

Note: *Interactive performance is critical when doing lip-synching. If the computer is sluggish while you scrub through the Time slider, it will be difficult to judge the timing of the sound.*

3 Timeline option

In order to better see the waveforms in the Timeline, you will now change its height.

- Select **Window → Settings/Preferences → Preferences**.
- Highlight the **Timeline** category.
- Set the **Timeline Height** to **4x**.

Doing so will change the Timeline height in the main interface.

- Click the **Save** button.

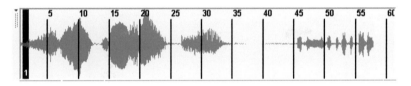

Audio in the Time slider

- Set the Time slider to go from frame **0** to frame **60**.

4   Keyframe a blink

When doing lip-synch animation, it is generally a good idea to do the actual lip movement last. Animating the eyes and head movement first helps to set the context for the lip movement, which reduces the likelihood of over-animated, or *chattery*, mouth action.

- Select the Leon's *blendShapesManip* node.
- Go to frame **1**.
- Keyframe the **Left** and **Right Blink** attributes.

> **Tip:**   *It is better to set keyframes directly on the affected attributes in order to prevent the creation of static channels.*

- Go to frame **3**.
- Set the **Left** and **Right Blink** to **1.0** and set a key.
- Go to frame **5**.
- Set the **Left** and **Right Blink** to **0.0** and set a key.

You have just keyframed a full blink over 5 frames.

5   Dragging keys

When settings keys, you might want to offset certain keyframes in the Time slider without having to go into the Graph Editor. It is possible to drag keyframes directly in the Time slider.

- Hold down **Shift**, then **click+drag** from frame **1** to **5** in the Time slider.

  A red manipulator should be displayed.

- **Click+drag** in the middle of the manipulator to offset the keyframes.
- **Click+drag** the arrows of the manipulator to scale the keyframes.

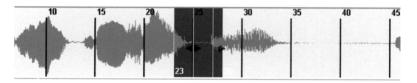

Dragging keys in the Time slider

6   Duplicate blinks

The red manipulator in the Time slider can also be used to copy keyframes.

* With the manipulator still active over the blink keyframes, **RMB** in the Time slider and select **Copy**.

* **Move** the current time to another location, then **RMB**, and select **Paste** → **Paste**.

  A new eye blink has been pasted at the current time.

7   Head animation

Take some time to animate the head and eyes moving along with the audio.

Tip: *Base your animation on the waveform to know where a certain word is spoken.*

8   Preview your animation

Tip: *If the playback is not quite realtime, it might be a better idea to playblast the sequence. To do so, RMB in the Time slider and select **Playblast**.*

9   General facial expression

* Select Leon's *blendShapesManip* node.
* Go to frame **1**.
* Set **Left Brow Up** to **1**.
* Set **M** to **1**.
* Set a keyframe on those two attributes.
* **Keyframe** the other facial blend shapes based on your own ideas.

10   Save your work

* Save your scene as *29-lipsynch 01.ma*.

Phonemes

It is now time to keyframe the phonemes of the audio track onto Leon. Just like other types of animation, you want to first block the animation, then refine the in-betweens, and finish by fine-tuning the overall lip-synch.

1 Blocking

Following is a breakdown of Leon's phonemes to use for this specific audio file. It should give you an idea about the timing and which phonemes to use, but you should experiment with different values to shape the mouth properly.

Frame 1: **M**;

Frame 7: **M**;

Frame 9: **A, Jaw Down**;

Frame 14: **M**;

Frame 18: **E**;

Frame 20: **M**;

Frame 23: **A, O**;

Frame 25: **M, Blow Cheeks**;

Frame 27: **O**;

Frame 32: **O, M**;

Frame 36: **M**;

Frame 30: **E**;

Frame 38: **M**;

Tip: *Mix multiple shapes to achieve more precise mouth shapes.*

2 Playblast the animation

3 Save your work

• Save your scene as *29-lipsynch 02.ma.*

Refinement

At this point, you might want to double-check the animation tangents to make sure that the shapes blend well together. You might also want to start refining the overall animation.

You should consider switching Leon's reference to playblast the high-resolution model.

High resolution animated Leon

Continue experimenting with the curves in the Graph Editor and playblasting the animation. As you work with the character, it is advisable to make playblasts frequently and early on. This feedback is necessary to anticipate how the flow of the motion is occurring. Avoid the temptation to apply keys on every frame in an effort to pronounce every little nuance and syllable. A good rule in facial animation is *less is more*. Try to animate with as few keys as possible.

Conclusion

In this lesson, you experienced a lip-synching workflow. You also learned a couple of tricks with keyframes in the Time slider. The key to good lip-synching is to practice a lot to get your brain used to timing and motion. You should now have the confidence to finalize Leon and the squirrel in the scene from the previous lesson.

The next and final lesson will take you through an overview of the full body IK feature.

Lesson 30
Full Body IK

In this lesson, you will learn how to create a full body IK (FBIK) setup. You will start by changing Leon's setup to a simple FK skeleton. Then you will add joint labels so you can easily assign the full body IK to the skeleton. You will then learn about the general behavior of the full body IK.

In this lesson you will learn the following:

FK rig

The full body IK works well with biped or quadruped characters using only FK skeletons. This means that if you want to use Leon's rig with a full body IK, you will need to either convert it to work only with FK, or attempt to convert the entire rig and make it compatible with the full body IK. For this lesson, you will simply convert Leon to use a FK skeleton.

1   Scene file

- Open the scene file called leon lores.ma.

  This scene is the same setup you used in the previous lessons, which is Leon bound with blend shapes.

2   Strip the rig to simple FK

- Select all manipulators, except the *lookAt*, the *blendshapes*, the *ears* and the *master* manipulators.

- **Delete** the selected manipulators.

- Select **Edit → Delete All by Type → IK Handles**.

- **Delete** the curves coming from the spline IKs.

- **Delete** the aim constraints from the eyes.

- In the Outliner, set **Display → DAG Objects Only** to **Off**.

- Scroll down and **Delete** the *multiplyDivide1* utility node controlling both forearm roll bones.

  You should now have a simple FK skeleton with its geometry.

- **Hide** any selection handles.

3   Make the attributes unlocked and keyable

- Select **Edit → Select All by Type → Joints**.

- Through the Channel Control window, make all the **rotation** and **visibility** attributes **unlocked** and **keyable**.

- Set all the joints to be visible.

- Make sure the *Hips* joint has its **translation** attributes unlocked.

4   Preferred angle

- Select the *Hips* joint, **RMB**, and select **Assume Preferred Angle**.

  Doing so will reset the skeleton into its original position.

5 Save your work

- Save the scene as *30-fullbodyIK 01.ma*.

Naming convention

Since the beginning of this book, you have been giving specific names to your nodes. Your process for naming the joints that are part of Leon's skeleton is very important since the full body IK can automate some tasks when using those specific names.

Note: *The following name convention can be somewhat confusing. Remember, the names represent the limb and not the articulations.*

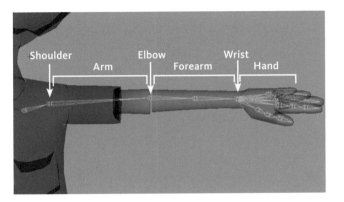

Naming convention

1 Naming convention

- Following is a list of base nodes that are required to properly create a full body IK. Make sure your joint names follow this list:

	Head
LeftArm	*RightArm*
LeftForeArm	*RightForeArm*
LeftHand	*RightHand*
	Spine
	Hips
LeftUpLeg	*RightUpLeg*
LeftLeg	*RightLeg*
LeftFoot	*RightFoot*

- Following is a list of auxiliary nodes that can be used if needed. Make sure your joint names follow this list:

	Neck
LeftShoulder	*RightShoulder*
LeftFingerBase	*RightFingerBase*
LeftToeBase	*RightToeBase*

- Any other spine joints should be named as follows:

  Spine1

  Spine2

  ...

  Spine9

- Any other neck joints should be named as follows:

  Neck1

  Neck2

  ...

  Neck9

- Any roll joints should be named as follows:

LeftUpLegRoll	*RightUpLegRoll*
LeftLegRoll	*RightLegRoll*
LeftArmRoll	*RightArmRoll*
LeftForeArmRoll	*RightForeArmRoll*

- Any finger and toe joints should start with the following:

LeftHand	*RightHand*
LeftFoot	*RightFoot*

  and end with the following:

  Thumb1, 2, 3, 4

  Index1, 2, 3, 4

  Middle1, 2, 3, 4

  Ring1, 2, 3, 4

  Pinky1, 2, 3, 4

  ExtraFinger1, 2, 3, 4

> **Note:** *Other nodes can be named any other way.*

Joint labelling

Alternatively, if you used different names, you can use joint labels. Joint labels tag your character's joints for full body IK so that when you create your FBIK effectors, all the labeled joints are then included in the full body IK solution. When using the joint labelling and naming method, you can label only your character's base joints, or you can label all your character's base, roll, and many of the auxiliary joints.

The following shows you how to display joint labels and how to modify them.

1   Automatic labelling

- Select the *Hips* joint.

- Select **Skeleton** → **Joint Labelling** → **Show All Labels.**

  Doing so will display the labels of each joints in the viewport.

- Click on **Skeleton** → **Joint Labelling** → **Label Based on Joint Names.**

  Notice that several joint labels were automatically found. You now need to correct them and add the missing ones.

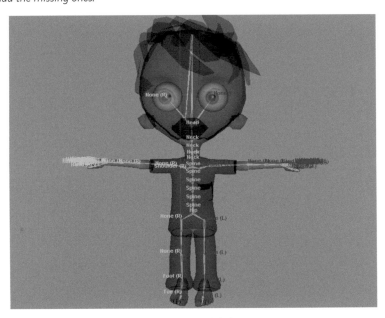

The automatic labeling

Tip: *You can turn off the joint labels by selecting Skeleton → Joint Labelling → Hide All Labels.*

2 Joint labelling

- Tear off the menu **Skeleton → Joint Labelling → Add FBIK Labels.**
- **Select the** *LeftArm* **joint.**
- Click on Label Left and then click on Label Arm from the Add FBIK Labels menu.
- **Select the** *LeftShoulder* **joint.**
- **Click on Label Collar.**
- Repeat the previous steps to label all the joints correctly based on the naming convention from the previous exercise.

Full body IK

You can now use the joint labels or joint names to create the full body IK.

Note: *For the full body IK setup, you don't want any connections on any joints of the skeleton. If you have input connections on some joints, you will need to delete them.*

1 Create the full body IK

- Select the *Hips* joint.
- Select **Skeleton → Full Body IK → Add Full Body IK → ▢.**
- In the option window, set **Identify joints** to **By name**.
- Click the **Add** button.

  The full body IK should be created.

Tip: *If the full body IK was not created, look in the Script Editor for details.*

2 Size up the FBIK nodes

- In the **Input Line**, select the **Select by name** option and type *Eff.

  Doing so will select all the FBIK effectors.

- Invoke the **Scale Tool** and **scale** up the effectors to your liking.

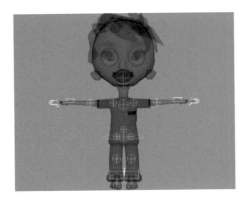

The created FBIK rig

The rig tries to reach the effectors

3   Tweak the rig

Now that the full body IK setup is created, you can put back any setups you would like on Leon's skeleton. For instance, you can add the aim constraints for the eyes.

4   Test the FBIK

Take some time to translate and rotate the different FBIK effectors to see how they behave. Notice that if you pull an effector too far, the rest of the body should stretch out, attempting to reach it.

- When you are done experimenting, select **Skeleton → Full Body IK → Go to Stance Pose.**

Leon should now be back in his default position.

5   Save your work

- Save the scene as *30-fullbodyIK 02.ma.*

Floor contact

A nice FBIK feature is the ability to define floor contacts. In this exercise, you will define floor contact for the feet. This guarantees that Leon will not be able to move his feet or toes below the floor. When calculating the feet/floor contact, note that if the toes go through the floor but the heel does not, the toes will bend automatically.

1   Create floor planes

- Select both foot effectors.

- Select **Skeleton → Full Body IK → Add Floor Contact Plane**.

One plane for each foot was created. Those planes can be animated just like any other object.

Lesson 30: Full Body IK

Tip: *Animate floor contact planes to mimic a staircase.*

2   **Adjusting the floor contact markers**

When you added floor planes to the feet, floor contact markers were also created and displayed in the viewport.

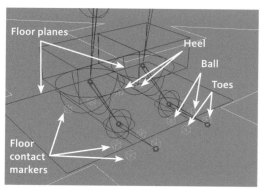

Feet floor contact markers

Note: *Hand floor contacts can also be created, but you will not use them in this project.*

- Select any foot floor contact marker.
- In the Channel Box, highlight the *hikFloorContactMarker1* from the Shapes section.
- At the bottom of the Channel Box, tweak the foot floor contact attributes to best define the geometry of Leon's feet.

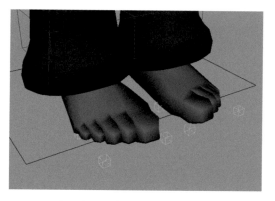

The adjusted floor contact markers

- Try rotating the foot effectors on their X-axis to see how the floor affects them.

  You should see that the heel will go up and the toes will bend to suit your rotation and the floor.

The effect of the floor contacts on the foot animation

Pinning

Pinning defines how a limb reacts as you move the FBIK effectors. Pinning an effector in translation will prevent it from moving if any other body part is moved. Pinning a marker in rotation will keep its rotation if any other body part is moved.

If a marker does not have pinning, it will move with the rest of the body. If it is pinned both in translation and rotation, it will be locked in space.

1   Changing the pinning
- Select the *LeftHandEff.*
- In the Channel Box, change the **Pinning** attribute to **unpinned**.
- Select the *RightHandEff* and **move** it away from the body.

  Notice how the left arm moves with the spine just as if it was in FK.

- Change the **Pinning** of the LeftHandEff to **pinTranslate**.
- Select the *RightHandEff* and **move** it.

  Notice how the left arm tries to stay in its position by freely rotating to follow the rest of the body.

- Change the **Pinning** of the *LeftHandEff* to **pinRotate**.
- Select the *RightHandEff* and **move** it.

Lesson 30: Full Body IK

Notice how the left arm tries to keep its rotation while the right arm will move freely.

- Change the **Pinning** of the LeftHandEff to **pinAll**.
- Select the *RightHandEff* and **move** it.

Notice how the left arm tries to keep its position as long as you don't stretch the body too far.

Note: *The shape of the effectors changes depending on the pinning type.*

2 Save your work

- Save the scene as *30-fullbodyIK 03.ma*.

Posing Leon

You have now set up the FBIK rig in a way that will make it easy to pose and animate Leon. In this exercise you will pose and set keyframes on Leon.

1 IK manipulations

- Try to pose Leon using the FBIK effectors.

Notice how fast Leon moves into a certain pose.

2 FK manipulations

- Try to pose Leon using your original skeleton.

The FBIK works like a combined FK/IK rig, where you can use the IK effectors for placement or the FK joints for rotation.

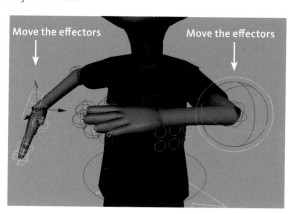

The IK/FK capabilities of the FBIK rig

3   Keyframes

When you press the **s** hotkey to keyframe Leon's FBIK rig, you will notice that lots of keyframes are being generated. This is because Maya needs to keyframe both the IK and FK rig in order to keep them synchronized. Note that you can also keyframe Leon's original skeleton, and Maya will also keyframe the FBIK rig.

4   Keyframe body parts

One excellent feature of the FBIK rig is that you can keyframe the entire FBIK rig or only your chosen body part. The following will show you how to keyframe only the wanted nodes.

- Select the *LeftHandEff*.

  Notice in the lower right corner of the interface, in the current character field, that the _leftArm sub-character is selected. This means that keyframes will be generated only on that body part.

> **Note:** *If you want to turn Off this automatic behavior, you can set it by selecting* **Skeleton → Full Body IK → Body Part Autoload**.

- Click on the **Current Character** field to select another body part or the entire *fbikCharacter*.

> **Note:** *You can also set special keyframes using* **Animate → Set Full Body IK Keys** *or by pressing the* **Ctr+f** *hotkey.*

Conclusion

You have now been introduced to the basics of the full body IK workflow. You were taught how to set up floor contact and how to use pinning. Lastly, you experimented with keyframing the character's effectors, body parts and skeleton. This is a lot of information to start working with, but being able to use the power of the full body IK will greatly speed up any animation tasks.

Index

Index

Index

Notes

Notes

NOTES

THE MAGAZINE FOR 3D ARTISTS

If you're serious about 3D, you need 3D World. Each issue of this high-quality magazine comes packed with news, inspiration and practical advice for leading software packages, including 3ds Max, Maya, LightWave 3D, Cinema 4D and XSI

View the latest subscription offers online at:
www.myfavouritemagazines.co.uk

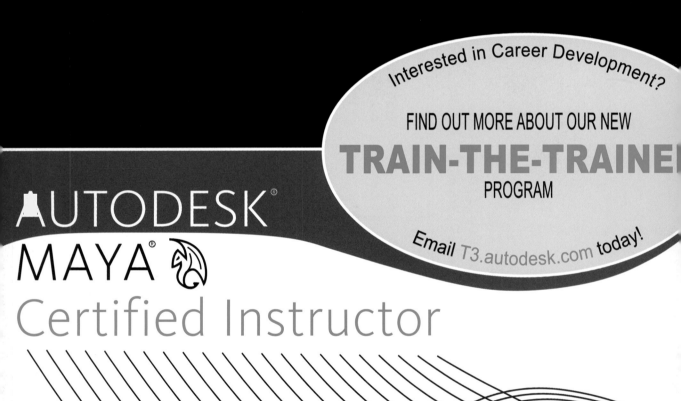

Revolutionary Visual Computing Solutions
The definition of performance. The standard for quality.

As a DCC professional, your workflow demands graphics solutions that keep up with your abilities. With NVIDIA Quadro® graphics solutions at your side, you can accelerate your projects all the way through the end of production.

For more information on NVIDIA solutions, please visit **www.nvidia.com**